Nikon D600: From Snapshots to Great Shots

Rob Sylvan

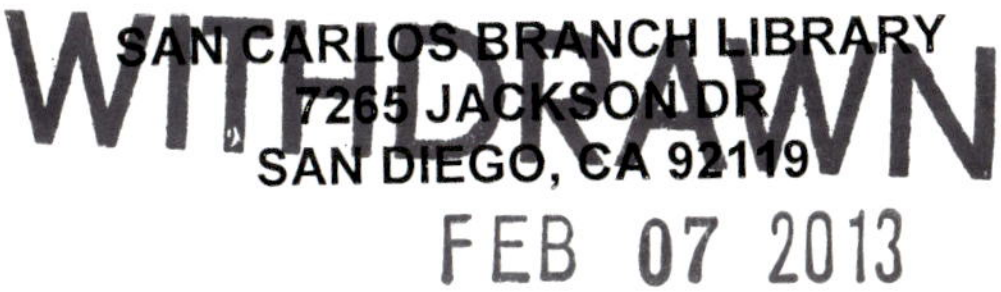

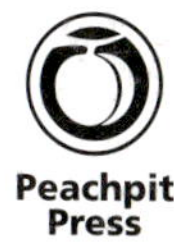
Peachpit Press

Nikon D600: From Snapshots to Great Shots
Rob Sylvan

Peachpit Press
www.peachpit.com

To report errors, please send a note to errata@peachpit.com
Peachpit Press is a division of Pearson Education.

Project Editor: Valerie Witte
Production Editor: Lisa Brazieal
Copyeditor: Scout Festa
Proofreader: Patricia J. Pane
Composition: WolfsonDesign
Indexer: Valerie Haynes Perry
Cover Image: Rob Sylvan
Cover Design: Aren Straiger
Interior Design: Riezebos Holzbaur Design Group
Back Cover Author Photo: Rob Sylvan

ISBN-13: 978-0-321-90495-9
ISBN–10: 0-321-90495-8

9 8 7 6 5 4 3 2 1

Printed and bound in the United States of America

DEDICATION

For my brother, Dan; his partner, Charlie; and my six nieces and nephews, Raymond, Maggie, Kayla, Justin, Jayda, and Nekos. I love you guys.

ACKNOWLEDGMENTS

My deepest thanks go to Jeff Revell, the author of a number of books in the From Snapshots to Great Shots series. Jeff is a tremendous photographer and gifted teacher. Thank you for providing such a sound foundation upon which to build.

Any book that has reached the final stage of being published is actually the work of many hands (eyes, brains, and hearts too) behind the scenes. I owe everyone at Peachpit a great deal of gratitude, but specifically Ted Waitt, Valerie Witte, Lisa Brazieal, Scout Festa, Patricia J. Pane, WolfsonDesign, Aren Straiger, Sara Jane Todd, Scott Cowlin, and Nancy Aldrich-Ruenzel, who were instrumental in getting this book finished, looking so darn fantastic, and out into the world. Thank you all.

A special thanks to David Brommer and B&H Photo Video for help in securing the D600 I used to write this book.

I am grateful for all that I have learned from my friends at the National Association of Photoshop Professionals and at the Digital Photo Workshops, from the fantastic instructors at Photoshop World, and from countless numbers of fellow photographers. You all have taught and inspired me over the years.

I also want to thank my wife, Paloma, for being the love of my life and my number one supporter during this project; my son, Quinn, for assisting me on many shoots and being the model in many more; and my family, friends, and neighbors—Ea, Avery, William, Adrienne, Emma, Julia, Paige, Ella, John, Kris, Gabby, Ed, Jaylin, Alden, Hayden, Alex, Charlie, Dan, Raymond, Maggie, Kayla, Justin, Jayda, Nekos—for being a part of the book in large and small ways.

Contents

CHAPTER 6: PERFECT PORTRAITS 129

CHAPTER 7: LANDSCAPE PHOTOGRAPHY 157

Introduction

The D600 is a wonderful bit of camera technology and a very capable tool for creating photographs that you will be proud to show others. The intention of this book is not to be a rehash of the owner's manual that came with the camera, but rather to be a resource for learning how to improve your photography while specifically using your D600. I am very excited and honored to help you in that process, and to that end I have put together a short Q&A to help you get a better understanding of just what it is that you can expect from this book.

Q: IS EVERY CAMERA FEATURE GOING TO BE COVERED?

A: Nope, just the ones I felt you need to know about in order to start taking great photos. Believe it or not, you already own a great resource that covers every feature of your camera: the owner's manual. Writing a book that just repeats this information would have been a waste of my time and your money. What I did want to write about was how to harness certain camera features to the benefit of your photography. As you read the book, you will also see callouts pointing you to specific pages in your owner's manual that are related to the topic being discussed. For example, I discuss the use of Live View, but there is more information available on this feature in the manual. I cover the function as it applies to our specific needs, but I also give you the page numbers in the manual so you can explore it even further.

Q: SO IF I ALREADY OWN THE MANUAL, WHY DO I NEED THIS BOOK?

A: The manual does a pretty good job of telling you how to use a feature or turn it on in the menus, but it doesn't necessarily tell you why and when you should use it. If you really want to improve your photography, you need to know the whys and whens to put all of those great camera features to use at the right time. To that extent, the manual just isn't going to cut it. It is, however, a great resource on the camera's features, and for that reason I treat it like a companion to this book. You already own it, so why not get something of value from it?

Q: WHAT CAN I EXPECT TO LEARN FROM THIS BOOK?

A: Hopefully, you will learn how to take great photographs. My goal, and the reason the book is laid out the way it is, is to guide you through the basics of photography as they relate to different situations and scenarios. By using the features of your D600 and this book, you will learn about aperture, shutter speed, ISO, lens selection, depth of field, and many other photographic concepts. You will also find plenty of full-page photos that include captions, shooting data, and callouts so you can see how all of the photography fundamentals come together to make great images. All the while, you will be learning how your camera works and how to apply its functions and features to your photography.

Q: WHAT ARE THE ASSIGNMENTS ALL ABOUT?

A: At the end of most of the chapters, you will find shooting assignments, where I give you some suggestions as to how you can apply the lessons of the chapter to help reinforce everything you just learned. Let's face it—using the camera is much more fun than reading about it, so the assignments are a way of taking a little break after each chapter and having some fun.

Q: SHOULD I READ THE BOOK STRAIGHT THROUGH, OR CAN I SKIP AROUND FROM CHAPTER TO CHAPTER?

A: Here's the easy answer: yes and no. No, because the first four chapters give you the basic information that you need to know about your camera. These are the building blocks of using the D600. After that, yes, you can move around the book as you see fit, because the following chapters are written to stand on their own as guides to specific types of photography or shooting situations. So you can bounce from portraits to landscapes and then maybe to a little action photography. It's all about your needs and how you want to address them. Or, you can read the book straight through. The choice is up to you.

Q: IS THERE ANYTHING ELSE I SHOULD KNOW BEFORE GETTING STARTED?

A: In order to keep the book short and focused, I had to be selective about what I included in each chapter. The problem is that there is a little more information that might come in handy after you've gone through all the chapters. So as an added value for you, I have written a bonus chapter: Chapter 12, "Creative Compositions." It will lead you through some photography tips and techniques that will make your photographs even better. To access the bonus chapter, just log in to or join Peachpit.com (it's free), then enter the book's ISBN on this page: www.peachpit.com/store/register.aspx. After you register the book, a link to the bonus chapter will be listed on your Account page under Registered Products. Note: If you purchased an electronic version of this book, you're set—Chapter 12 is already included in it.

Q: IS THAT IT?

A: One last thought before you dive into the first chapter. My goal in writing this book has been to give you a resource that you can turn to for creating great photographs with your Nikon D600. Take some time to learn the basics and then put them to use. Photography, like most things, takes time to master and requires practice. I have been a photographer for many years and I'm still learning. Always remember, it's not the camera that makes beautiful photographs—it's the person using it. Have fun, make mistakes, and then learn from them. In no time, I'm sure you will transition from a person who takes snapshots to a photographer who makes great shots.

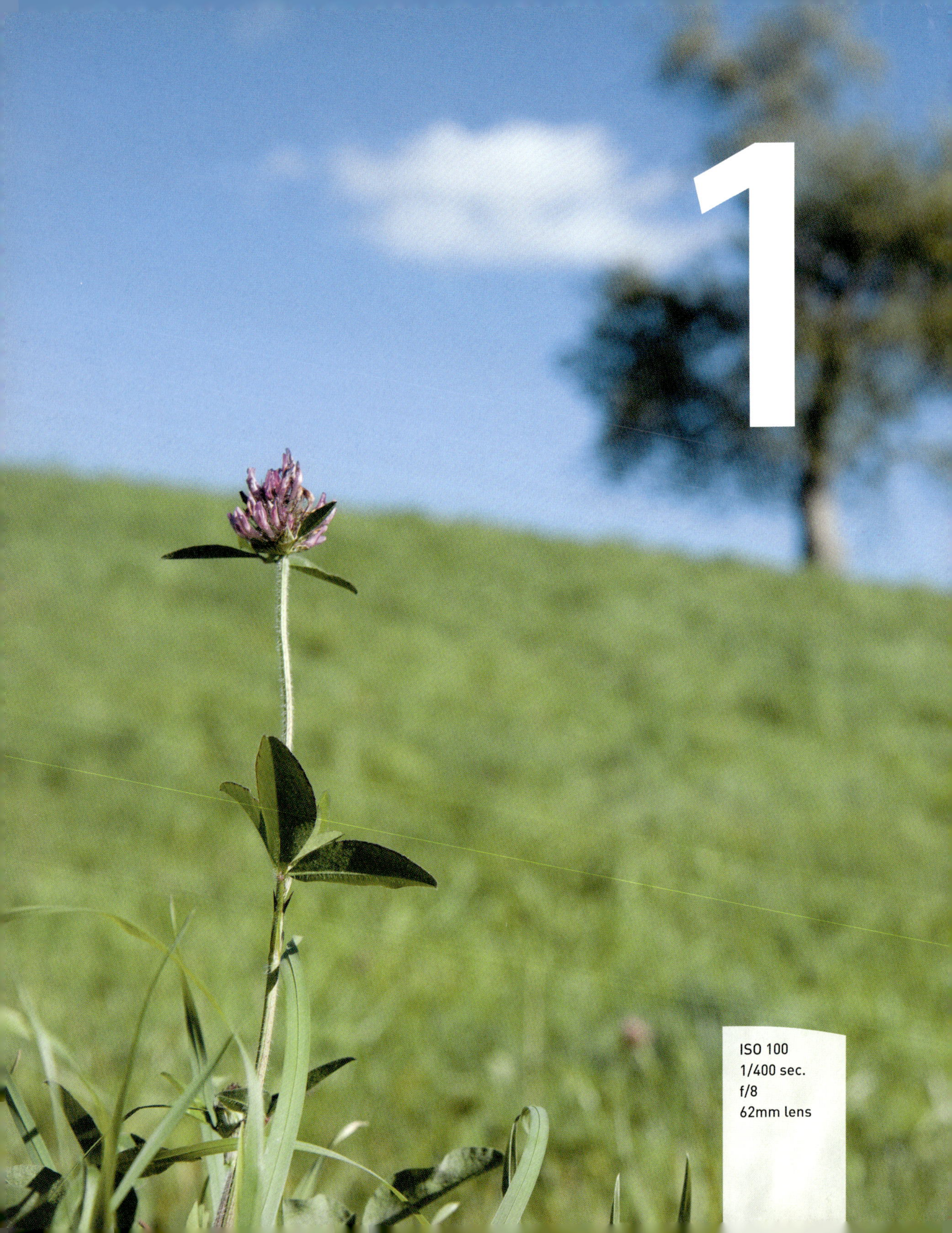

1

ISO 100
1/400 sec.
f/8
62mm lens

The D600 Top Ten List

TEN TIPS TO MAKE YOUR SHOOTING MORE PRODUCTIVE RIGHT OUT OF THE BOX

Whenever I get a new camera, I am always eager to jump right in and start cranking off exposures. What I really should be doing is sitting down with my instruction manual to learn how to use all of the camera features, but what fun is that? After all, we all know that instruction manuals are for propping up that short leg on the family room table, right?

Of course, this behavior always leads me to frustration in the end—there are always issues that would have been easily addressed had I known about them before I started shooting. Maybe if I had a Top Ten list of things to know, I could be more productive without having to spend countless hours with the manual. So this is where we begin.

The following list will get you up and running without suffering many of the "gotchas" that come from not being at least somewhat familiar with your new camera. So let's take a look at the top ten things you should know before you start taking pictures with your Nikon D600.

PORING OVER THE CAMERA

CAMERA FRONT

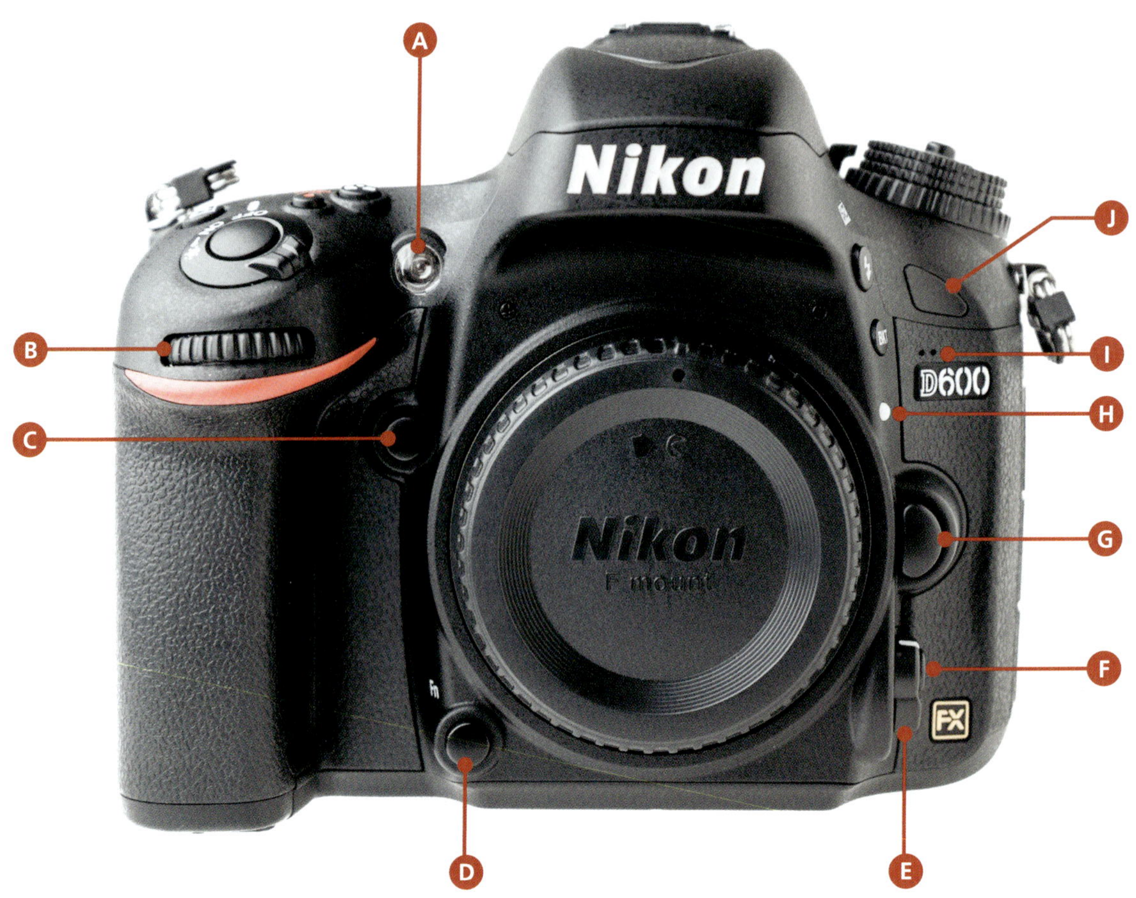

A Red-eye reduction/AF-assist illuminator
B Sub-command dial
C Depth of field preview button
D Fn (Function) button
E Focus-mode selector
F AF-mode button
G Lens release button
H Lens mounting mark
I Microphone
J Infrared receiver

CAMERA BACK

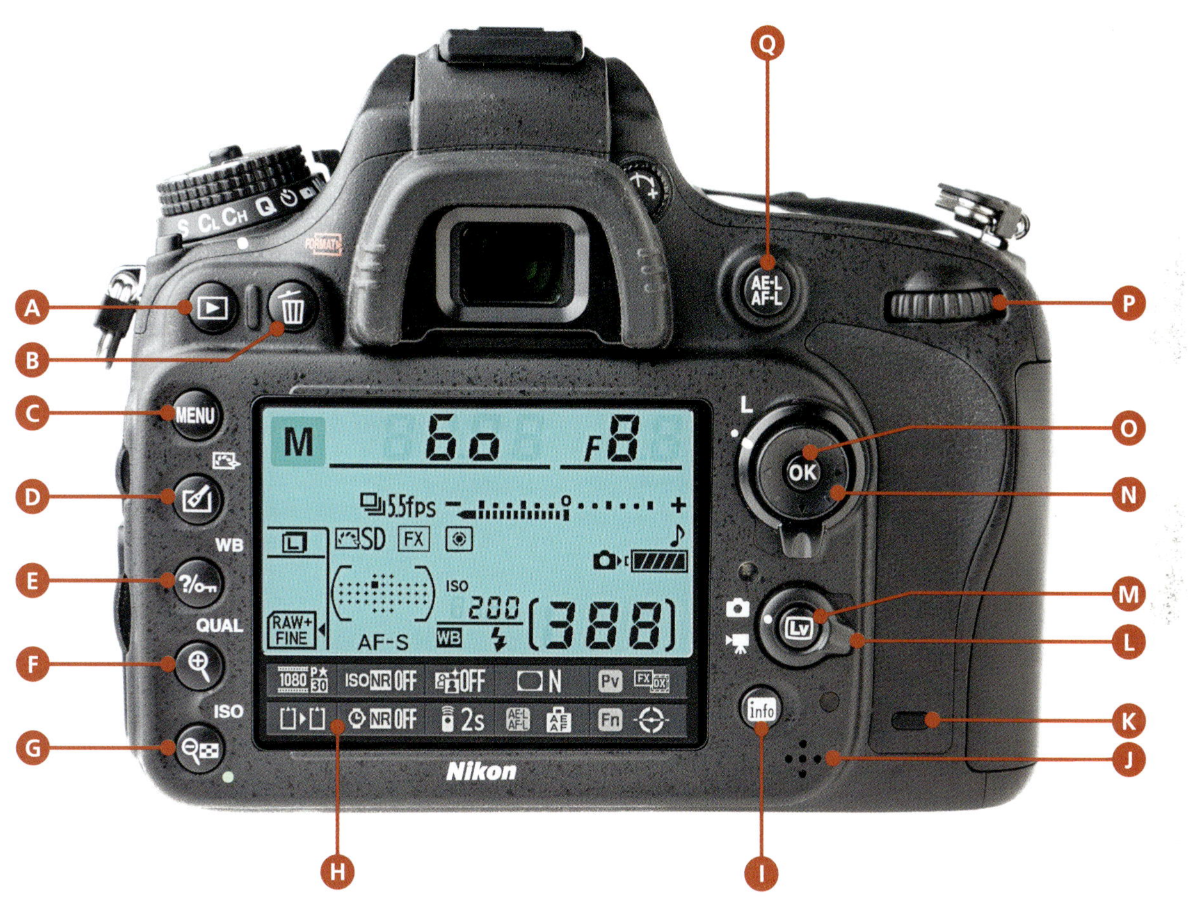

- A Playback button
- B Delete Image button
- C Menu button
- D Retouch/Picture Control button
- E Help/Protect/White Balance button
- F Playback zoom in/ Image Quality button
- G Playback zoom out/ISO button
- H LCD monitor/information screen
- I Info button
- J Speaker
- K Infrared receiver
- L Live View selector
- M Live View button
- N Multi-selector
- O OK button
- P Main Command dial
- Q AutoExposure/ AutoFocus lock button

PORING OVER THE CAMERA

CAMERA TOP

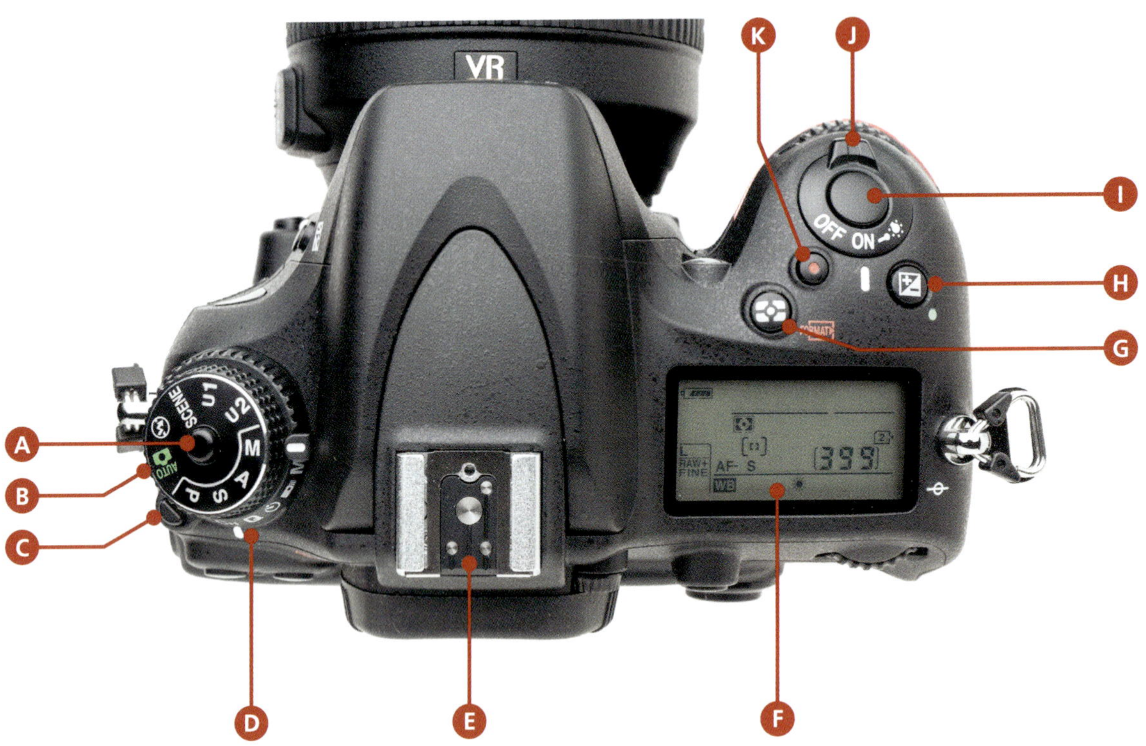

- A Mode dial lock release
- B Mode dial
- C Release mode dial lock release
- D Release mode dial
- E Accessory shoe
- F Control panel
- G Metering button
- H Exposure compensation
- I Shutter release button
- J Power switch
- K Movie-record button

1. CHARGE YOUR BATTERY

I know that this will be one of the hardest things for you to do because you really want to start shooting, but a little patience will pay off later.

When you first open your camera and slide the battery into the battery slot, you will be pleased to find that there is probably juice in the battery and you can start shooting right away. What you should really be doing is getting out the battery charger and giving that power cell a full charge. Not only will this give you more time to shoot, it will start the battery off on the right foot. No matter what claims the manufacturers make about battery life and charging memory, I always find I get better life and performance when I charge my batteries fully and then use them right down to the point where they have nothing left to give. To check your battery level, put the battery in the camera, turn the camera on, and look for the battery indicator in the upper-left section of the top LCD screen. You can also see the battery level by pressing the Info button on the back of the camera and then locating the battery meter on the rear preview screen to the right side of the display (**Figure 1.1**).

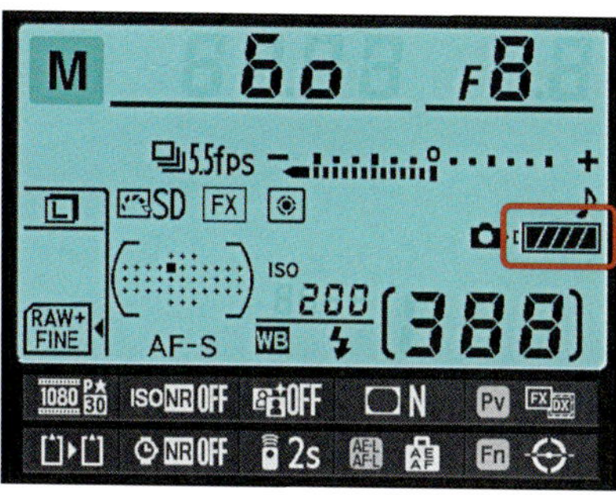

FIGURE 1.1
The LCD shows how much charge is left on your battery.

KEEPING A BACKUP BATTERY

If I were to suggest just one accessory that you should buy for your camera, it would probably be a second battery. Nothing is worse than being out in the field and having your camera die. Keeping a fully charged battery in your bag will give you the confidence that you can keep on shooting without fail. Not only is this a great strategy to extend your shooting time, but alternating between batteries will help lengthen their lives. No matter what the manufacturers say, batteries do have a life, and using them half as much will only lengthen their usefulness.

2. SET YOUR JPEG IMAGE QUALITY

Your new D600 has a number of image-quality settings to choose from, and you can adjust them according to your needs. Most people start shooting with the JPEG option because it allows them to capture a large number of photos on their memory cards and not have to deal with as much software processing later. The problem is that unless you understand what JPEG is, you might be degrading the quality of your images without realizing it.

The JPEG (Joint Photographic Experts Group) format has been around since about 1994 and was developed as a method of reducing large file sizes while retaining the original image information. (Technically, JPEG isn't even a file format—it's a mathematical equation for reducing image file sizes—but to keep things simple, we'll just refer to it as a file format.) The problem with JPEG is that, in order to reduce file size, it has to throw away some of the information. This is referred to as "lossy compression." This is important to understand, because while you can fit more images on your memory card by choosing a lower-quality JPEG setting, you will also be reducing the quality of your image. This effect becomes more apparent as you enlarge your pictures.

The JPEG file format also has one other characteristic: to apply the compression to the image before final storage on your memory card, the camera first applies all of the image processing. Image processing involves such factors as sharpening, color adjustment, contrast adjustment, noise reduction, and so on. Many photographers now prefer to use the RAW file format to get greater control over the image processing. We will take a closer look at this in Chapter 2, but for now, let's just make sure that we are using the best-quality JPEG possible.

The D600 has nine settings for the JPEG format. There are three settings each for the Large, Medium, and Small image-size settings. The three settings (Basic, Normal, and Fine) represent more or less image compression based on your choice. The Large, Medium, and Small settings determine the actual physical size of your image in pixels. Let's work with the highest-quality setting possible. After all, our goal is to make big, beautiful photographs, so why start the process with a lower-quality image?

SETTING THE IMAGE QUALITY

1. Press the Info button on the back of the camera to display all of the settings.
2. Press and hold the QUAL button on back of the camera to activate the image-quality settings on the information screen.
3. Use the Main Command dial to select the Fine quality setting (**A**).
4. To adjust the image size, rotate the Sub-command dial (**B**).

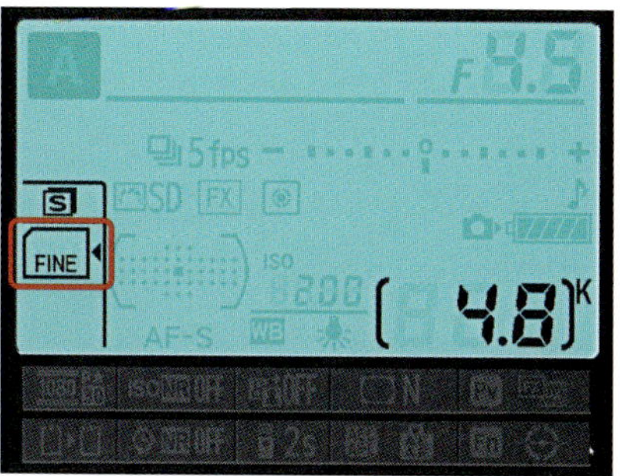

A

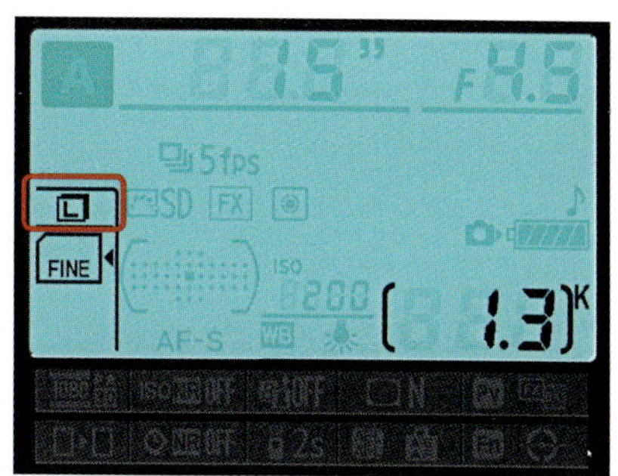

B

As you will see when scrolling through the quality settings, the higher the quality, the fewer pictures you will be able to fit on your card. If you have an 8 GB memory card, the quality setting we have selected will allow you to shoot about 506 photographs before you fill up your card. Always try to choose quality over quantity. Your pictures will be the better for it.

Manual Callout

For a chart that shows the image-quality settings with the number of possible shots for each setting, turn to page 334 in your user manual. Note that the settings we chose are for the FX (full frame) format.

3. SET THE CORRECT WHITE BALANCE

White balance correction is the process of rendering accurate colors in your final image. Most people don't even notice that light has different color characteristics, because the human eye automatically adjusts to changes in color temperature—so quickly in fact that everything looks correct in a matter of milliseconds.

When color film ruled the world, photographers would select which film to use depending on what their light source was going to be. The most common film was balanced for daylight, but you could also buy film that was color balanced for tungsten light sources. Most other lighting situations had to be handled by using color filters over the lens. This process was necessary for the photographer's final image to show the correct color balance of a scene.

Your camera has the ability to perform this same process automatically, but you can also choose to override it and set it manually. Guess which method we are going to use? That's right, once again your photography should be all about maintaining control over everything that influences your final image.

Luckily, you don't need to have a deep understanding of color temperatures to control your camera's white balance. The choices are given to you in terms that are easy to relate to and that will make things pretty simple. Your white balance choices are:

- **Auto:** The camera determines the best white balance setting and adjusts accordingly. Very useful in mixed lighting situations.
- **Incandescent:** Used for any occasion where you are using regular household-type bulbs for your light source. Tungsten is a very warm light source and will result in a yellow/orange cast if you don't correct for it.
- **Fluorescent:** Used to get rid of the green/blue cast that can result from using fluorescent lights as your dominant light source.
- **Direct sunlight:** Most often used for general daylight/sunlit shooting.
- **Flash:** Used whenever you're using the built-in flash or a flash on the hot shoe. You should select this white balance to adjust for the slightly cooler light that comes from using a flash. (The hot shoe is the small bracket that rests just above the eyepiece on the top of your camera. This bracket is used for attaching a more powerful flash to the camera; see Chapter 8 for more information.)
- **Cloudy:** The choice for overcast or very cloudy days. This and the Shade setting will eliminate the blue color cast from your images.
- **Shade:** Used when working in shaded areas that are still using sunlight as the dominant light source.

- **Kelvin:** This setting works well when you know the actual Kelvin temperature (color) of the lights that you are working with.
- **Pre:** Indicates that you are using a customized white balance that is adjusted for a particular light source. This option can be adjusted using an existing photo you have taken or by taking a picture of something white or gray in the scene.

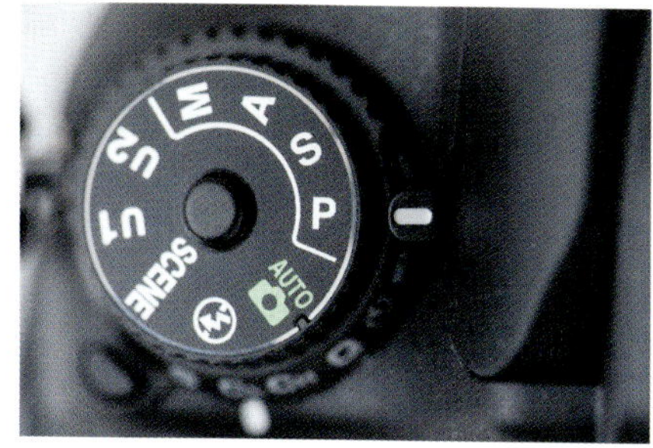

FIGURE 1.2
The camera's shooting modes are divided into the automatic scene modes and the professional modes (M, A, S, P, U1, and U2).

Your camera has two different "zones" of shooting modes to choose from. These are located on the Mode dial, which separates your choices into automatic scene modes and what I refer to as the professional modes. None of the automatic modes, which are chosen by turning the Mode dial to Auto, Flash Off, or Scene, allow for much customization, and that includes white balance. The professional modes, defined by the letter symbols M, A, S, P, U1, and U2, allow for much more control by the photographer (**Figure 1.2**).

SETTING THE WHITE BALANCE

1. After turning on or waking the camera, select one of the professional shooting modes, such as P (you can't select the white balance when using any of the automatic modes).
2. Press and hold the WB button (located on the back of the camera) to activate white balance, visible on the top control panel; or you can press the Info button and view the info screen on the rear LCD.
3. Rotate the Main Command dial to change the white balance mode.
4. If you want to use the Kelvin setting, rotate the Main Command dial to set the white balance to Kelvin and then use the Sub-command dial to set the desired temperature setting.

WHITE BALANCE AND THE TEMPERATURE OF COLOR

When you select white balances in your camera, you will notice that underneath several of the choices is a number—e.g., 5200K, 7000K, or 3200K. These numbers refer to the Kelvin temperature of the colors in the visible spectrum. The visible spectrum is the range of light that the human eye can see (think of a rainbow or the color bands that come out of a spectrum). The visible spectrum of light has been placed into a scale called the Kelvin temperature scale, which identifies the thermodynamic temperature of a given color of light. Put simply, reds and yellows are "warm," and greens and blues are "cool." Even more confusing can be the actual temperature ratings. Warm temperatures are typically lower on the Kelvin scale, ranging from 3000 degrees to 5000 degrees, while cool temperatures run from 5500 degrees to around 10000 degrees. Take a look at this list for an example of Kelvin temperature properties.

KELVIN TEMPERATURE PROPERTIES

Flames	1700K–1900K	**Daylight**	5000K
Incandescent bulb	2800K–3300K	**Camera flash**	5500K
White fluorescent	4000K	**Overcast sky**	6000K
Moonlight	4000K	**Open shade**	7000K

The most important thing to remember here is how the color temperature of light affects the look of your images. If something is "warm," it will look reddish-yellow, and if something is "cool," it will have a bluish cast.

4. SET YOUR COLOR SPACE

The color space deals with how your images will ultimately be used. It is basically a set of instructions that tells your camera how to define the colors in your image and then output them to the device of your choice, be it your monitor or a printer. Your camera has a choice of two color spaces: sRGB and Adobe RGB.

The first choice, sRGB, was developed by Hewlett-Packard and Microsoft as a way of defining colors for the Internet. This space was created to deal with the way that computer monitors actually display images using red, green, and blue (RGB) colors. Because there are no black pixels in your monitor, the color space uses a combination of these three colors to display all of the colors in your image.

In 1998, Adobe Systems developed a new color space, Adobe RGB, which was intended to encompass a wider range of colors than was obtainable using traditional cyan, magenta, yellow, and black colors (called CMYK) but doing so using the primary red, green, and blue colors. It uses a more widely defined palette of colors than the sRGB space and, therefore, looks better when printed.

A LITTLE COLOR THEORY

The visible spectrum of light is based on a principle called *additive color* and is based on three primary colors: red, green, and blue. When you add these colors together in equal parts, you get white light. By combining different amounts of them, you can achieve all the colors of the visible spectrum. This is a completely different process than printing, where cyan, magenta, and yellow colors are combined to create various colors. This method is called *subtractive color* and has to do with the reflective properties of pigments or inks as they are combined.

The choice you need to make when selecting your color space is based on whether you intend to use your photographs for prints or for online applications. The thing about selecting a color space is that it does not directly affect the color information of your images. It simply embeds the color space profile into the image file as instructions for your computer so that your output device (monitor or printer) can correctly interpret the colors.

SETTING THE COLOR SPACE

1. With the camera turned on, press the Menu button.
2. Using the Multi-selector, select the Shooting menu and then highlight the Color space option. Press the OK button (**A**).
3. Highlight your desired color space, and press the OK button once again (**B**).
4. Press the Menu button or the shutter release button to return to shooting mode.

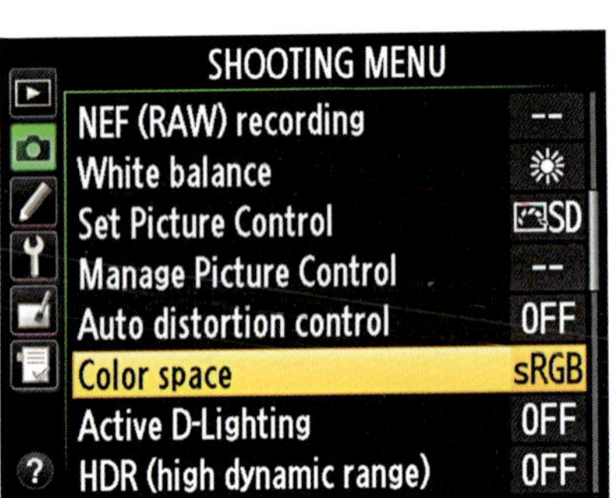

A

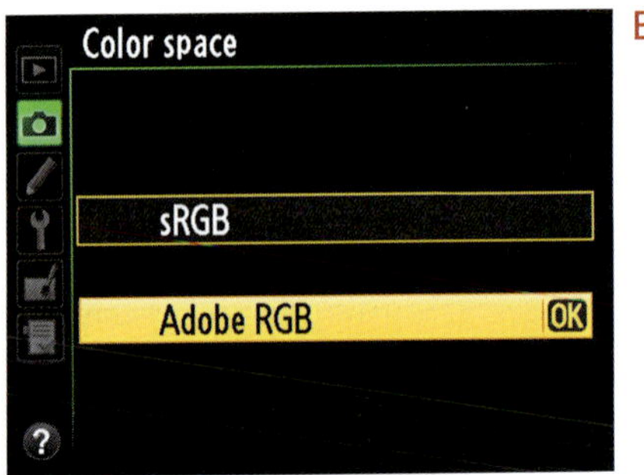

B

There will be no future indication of which space you have selected when you are looking at your pictures on the camera, so it's important to set this early and make changes if your output intentions change. If you forget which space you are currently using, press the Info button on the back of the camera and look for the color space in the bottom of the screen.

I typically use the Adobe RGB space when shooting because I like to print a lot of my images. If I decide to use them online, I use my image software application to change them to the sRGB color space. It is always better to go from a larger color space to a smaller one.

CHANGING SPACES

If you aren't sure about how you are going to be using your images, don't worry too much. Since the color space setting does not really affect the color of the image, it can always be changed later by using a photo-processing program.

5. CHOOSE YOUR ISO SETTING

The ISO setting in your camera allows you to choose the level of sensitivity of the camera sensor to light. The ability to change this sensitivity is one of the biggest advantages to using a digital camera. In the days of film cameras, you had to choose the ISO by film type. This meant that if you wanted to shoot in lower light, you had to replace the film in the camera with one that had a higher ISO. So not only did you have to carry different types of film, but you also had to remove one roll from the camera to replace it with another, even if you hadn't used up the current roll. Now all you have to do is go to your information screen and select the appropriate ISO.

Having this flexibility is powerful, but just as with the quality setting, the ISO setting has a direct bearing on the quality of the final image. The higher the ISO, the more digital noise the image will contain. Since our goal is to produce high-quality photographs, it is important to get control over all of the camera settings and bend them to our will. When you turn your camera on for the first time, the ISO will be set to Auto. This means that the camera is determining how much light is available and will choose what it believes is the correct ISO setting. Since you want to use the lowest ISO possible, you will need to turn this setting off and manually select the appropriate ISO.

Which ISO you choose depends on your level of available or ambient light. For sunny days or very bright scenes, use a low ISO such as 100. As the level of light is reduced, raise the ISO level. Cloudy days or indoor scenes might require you to use ISO 400 (**Figure 1.3**). Low-light scenes, such as when you are shooting at night, will mean you need to bump up that ISO to as high as 1600. The thing to remember is to shoot with the lowest setting possible for maximum quality.

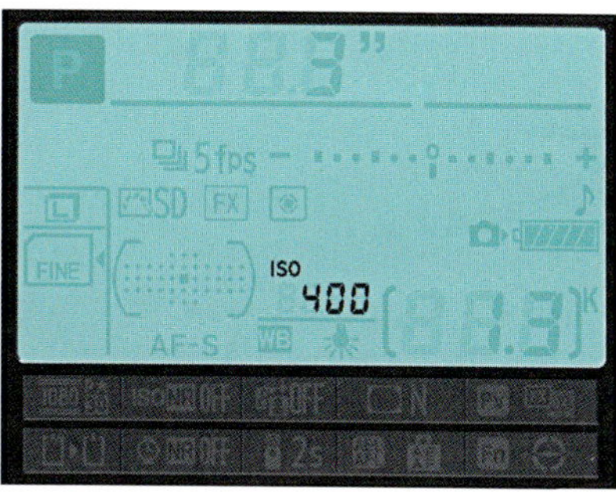

FIGURE 1.3
Press the Info button to see the selected ISO on the back LCD.

SETTING THE ISO

Press and hold the ISO button on the back of the camera while rotating the Main Command dial to select an ISO setting based on the available light. Release the button when you have made your selection. You can see the ISO change in the top control panel, inside the viewfinder, or, after pressing the Info button, on the back LCD.

The Auto ISO option is enabled by default only when you're using one of the automatic scene modes. When you're using one of the professional modes (M, A, S, and P; we'll discuss these in Chapter 4), the Auto ISO feature is automatically turned off. If you wish to use Auto ISO in one of these modes, you must activate it and set the auto parameters in the Shooting menu. If you're shooting in Auto mode, you cannot turn off the Auto ISO option at all.

NOISE

Noise is the enemy of digital photography, but it has nothing to do with the loudness of your camera operation. It is a term that refers to the electronic artifacts that appear as speckles in your image. Back in the days of film, we would have simply called the image "grainy." Digital noise appears in darker shadow areas and is a result of the camera trying to amplify the signal to produce visible information. The more the image needs to be amplified —by raising the sensitivity through higher ISO—the more noise there will be. To avoid digital noise, try to use a low ISO whenever possible.

6. SET YOUR FOCUS POINT AND MODE

The Nikon focusing system is well known for its speed and accuracy. The automatic focus modes will give you a ton of flexibility in your shooting. There is, however, one small problem inherent in any focusing system. No matter how intelligent it is, the camera is looking at all of the subjects in the scene and noting which is closest to the camera. It then uses this information to determine where the proper focus point should be. It has no way of knowing what your main emphasis is, so it is using a "best guess" system. To eliminate this factor, you should set the camera to single-point focusing so that you can ensure that you are focusing on the most important feature in the scene.

The camera has 39 separate focus points to choose from. They are arranged in a grid, but I always like to start by selecting the focus point in the center. Once you have become more familiar with the focus system, you can experiment with the other points, as well as the automatic point selection.

You should also change the focus mode to AF-S so that you can focus on your subject and then recompose your shot while holding that point of focus.

SETTING THE FOCUS POINT AND FOCUS MODE

1. To choose a single point of focus, wake the camera (if necessary) by lightly pressing the shutter release button.
2. Press and hold the AF-mode button on the front of the camera near the lens. Now rotate the Main Command dial to select AF-S (Single-servo AF) mode. This mode is used for photographing stationary objects but can be used in some motion shots as well.

The camera is now ready for single focusing. You will know if your subject is in focus by pressing the shutter button halfway while watching for the in-focus indicator to appear in the viewfinder. (Please review page 38 of your manual for a visual.) To focus on your subject and then recompose your shot, just place the focus point in the viewfinder on your subject, depress the shutter release button halfway until the in-focus indicator appears, and without letting up on the shutter button, recompose your shot and then press the shutter button all the way down to make your exposure (**Figure 1.4**).

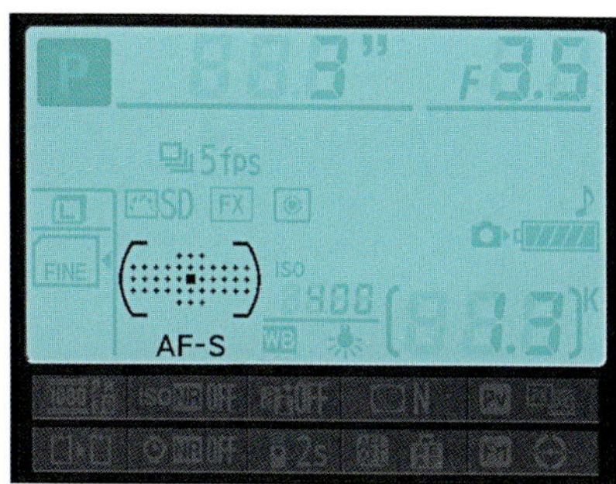

FIGURE 1.4
Using the center single focus point in AF-S mode allows you to focus on your subject and then recompose your photograph.

7. KNOW HOW TO OVERRIDE AUTOFOCUS

As good as the Nikon autofocus system is, there will be times when it just isn't doing the job for you. Many times this has to do with how you would like to compose a scene and where the actual point of focus should be. This can be especially true when you are using the camera on a tripod, where you can't pre-focus and then recompose before shooting. To take care of this problem, you will need to manually focus the lens. There are a multitude of lenses available for the D600, and they are not all the same when it comes to manual or autofocus control, so be sure to check the accompanying instruction manual for the lens.

Some lenses have a switch on the side for controlling the focus setting. You simply need to slide the switch at the base of the lens (located on the lens barrel near the body of the camera) from the M/A setting to the M setting (**Figure 1.5**). You can now turn the focus ring of the lens to set your focus, and the autofocus will not engage when you press the shutter release button. If your lens does not have a manual focus switch, you can use the focus mode selector switch located on the front of the camera just beneath the lens release button. Turn the switch from AF to M, and your lens will be all set for manual focusing.

I cover more manual focus situations in greater detail in future chapters.

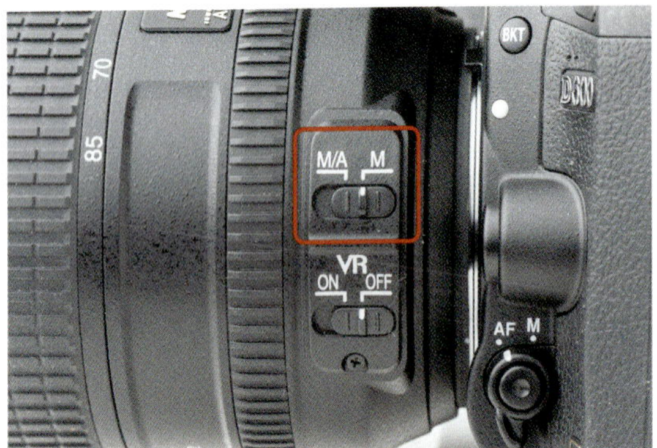

FIGURE 1.5
To manually focus, slide the focus switch on the lens to the M position.

8. DISABLE THE SLOT EMPTY RELEASE LOCK

This is one of the features that you may never pay attention to. That is, until it bites you right in the fanny. The short of it is that the camera is set up to take a picture even if there is no memory card in the slot. Why would anyone want this feature? Well, if you have the camera on display because you are trying to sell it, it's nice to have it actually take pictures and show them on the rear LCD screen just as if there were a card in it—that way, you don't have to worry about anyone taking off with the card.

The problem for the rest of us is that if we don't turn this feature off and we forget to check, we might assume that there is a card and start shooting. Of course, every image that is captured without a card will be thrown out with each new click of the shutter or when the camera is turned off. To their credit, Nikon does display a nice red Demo notation in the upper-left corner of the image, but believe me when I tell you that sooner or later this feature will come back to haunt you. The easiest way to safeguard yourself is to just lock the camera when there is no card in either of the two memory card slots.

TURNING ON THE DISABLE FUNCTION

1. Press the Menu button and locate the Custom Setting menu.
2. Highlight f Controls, and press OK (**A**).
3. Scroll down to f7 Slot empty release lock, and press OK (**B**).
4. Highlight LOCK Release locked, and press OK (**C**).

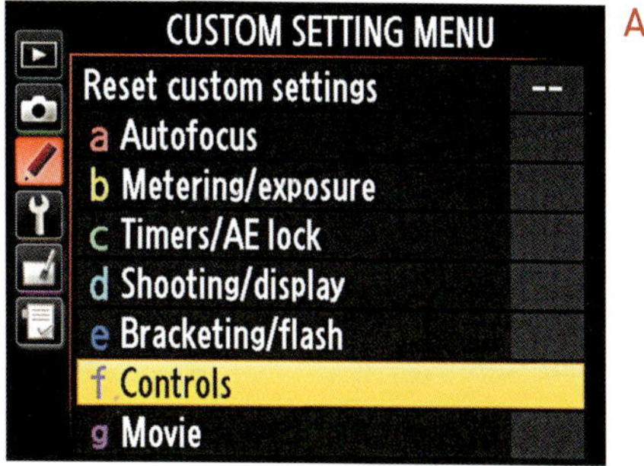

A

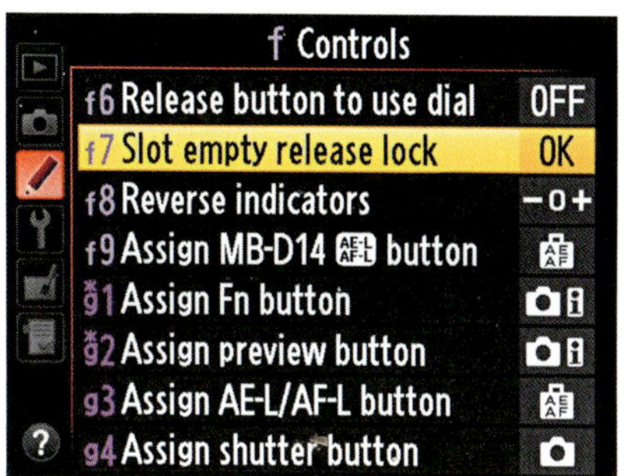

B

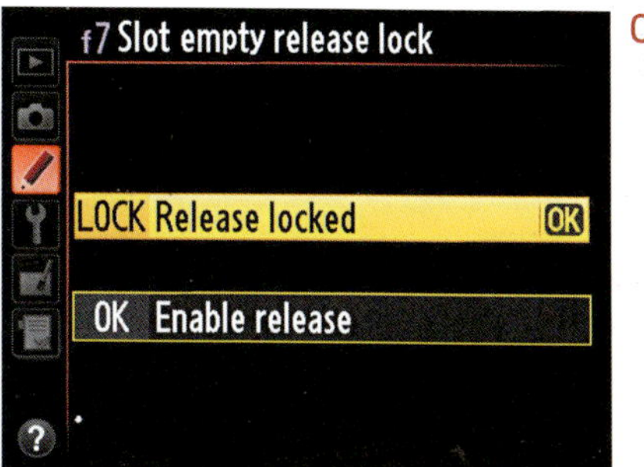

C

Now when you press the shutter release button without a card in the camera, you will find that the camera does nothing. This should be your cue to dig that memory card out of your camera bag.

9. TURN ON IMAGE REVIEW

One of the things that really surprised me when I first began shooting with the D600 was that the playback for reviewing images was turned off. I am used to seeing my images on the rear LCD screen after capturing a shot, so this is one of the first things that needed addressing. When turning the review on, I adjusted the default review time (the time that the monitor stays on after capturing a shot). It's also a good idea to check the auto-off durations for features like the menu screen. It can be very frustrating when you are trying to learn about the camera and its features and you have to keep pressing the Menu or Info button to bring the screen back to life. This is also the case when reviewing images on the screen after taking a picture. I don't know about you, but the default time of 4 seconds to review a shot seems very short. The answer to this problem is to increase the timer settings to longer durations. The D600 has five settings for the Monitor off delay function: Playback, Menus, Information display, Image review, and Live view. All of these can be found in the Custom Setting menu under item C4 in the Timers/AE Lock section. The image review feature can be turned on in the Playback menu. After turning on the image review, I like to set my image review to 20 seconds and the information display to 1 minute. I also change the Menus setting to 5 minutes. This might seem long, but I always end up turning it off before the end of the 5 minutes. It's just nice to have it on when I need it for a little longer.

TURNING ON IMAGE REVIEW

1. Press the Menu button and navigate to the Playback menu.
2. Select the Image review item and press OK (**A**).
3. Highlight On, and press OK to lock in your change (**B**).

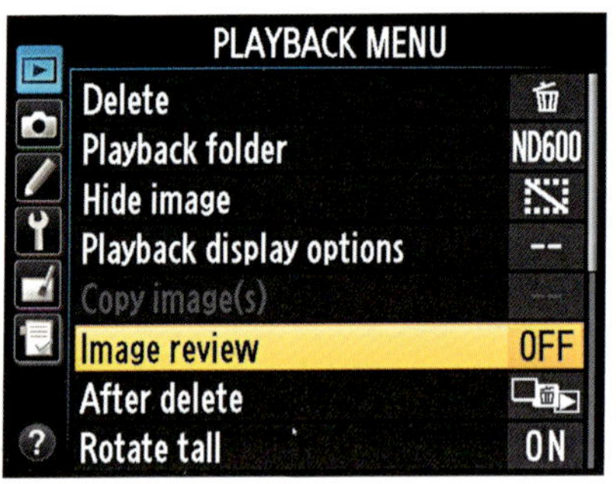

A

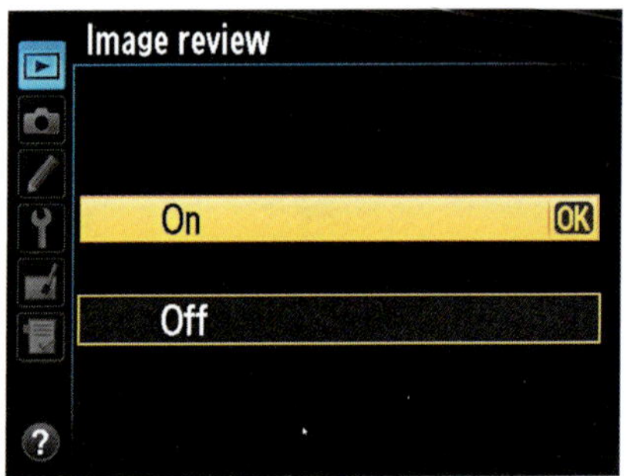

B

SETTING THE AUTO-OFF TIMERS

1. Press the Menu button and navigate to the Custom Setting menu (the pencil icon).
2. Select the item labeled c Timers/AE lock, and press OK (**A**).
3. Use the Multi-selector to scroll down to c4 Monitor off delay, and press OK (**B**).

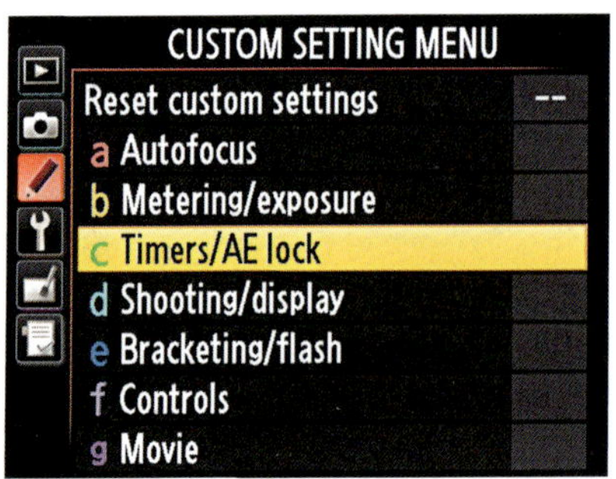

A

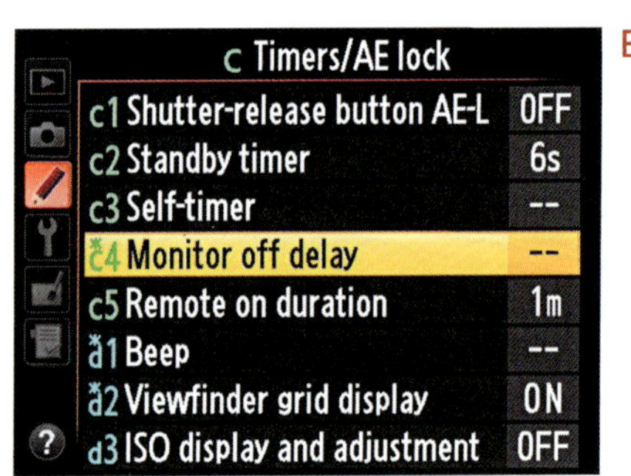

B

4. Select the items that need changing, such as Image review, and press OK (**C**).
5. Highlight the desired duration for the feature you want to adjust, and then press the OK button to lock in the change and return to the previous screen (**D**).

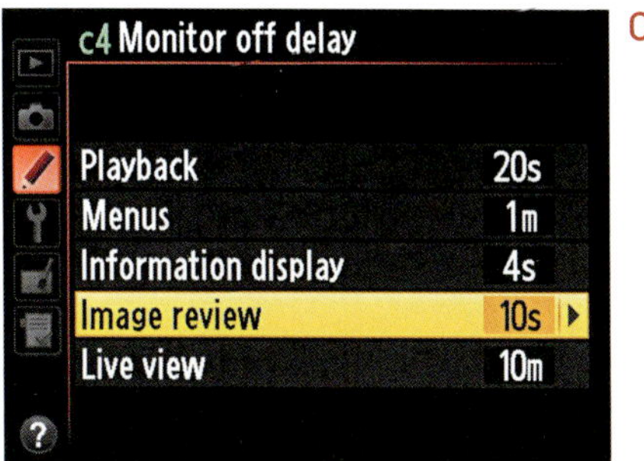

C

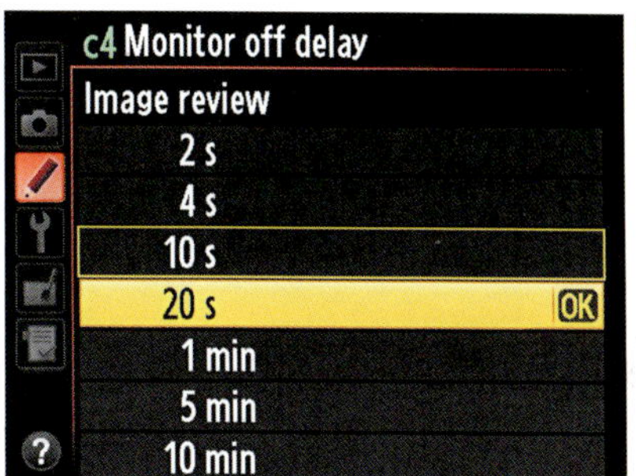

D

Once you have changed all of the settings, press the Menu button or shutter button to exit the menu screen and go back to shooting mode.

10. REVIEW YOUR SHOTS

One of the greatest features of digital cameras is their ability to give instant feedback. By reviewing your images on the camera's LCD screen, you can instantly tell if you got your shot. This visual feedback allows you to make corrections on the fly and make certain that all of your adjustments are correct before moving on.

When you first press the shutter release button, your camera quickly processes your shot and then displays the image on the rear LCD display. The default setting for that display is only 4 seconds, which is why we changed the review times (as discussed earlier).

Since we have already adjusted the auto-off timer, let's check out some of the other visual information that will really help you when shooting.

There are two display modes that give you different amounts of information while reviewing your photos. The default view (**Figure 1.6**) simply displays your image along with the image file name, date, time, and image-quality setting.

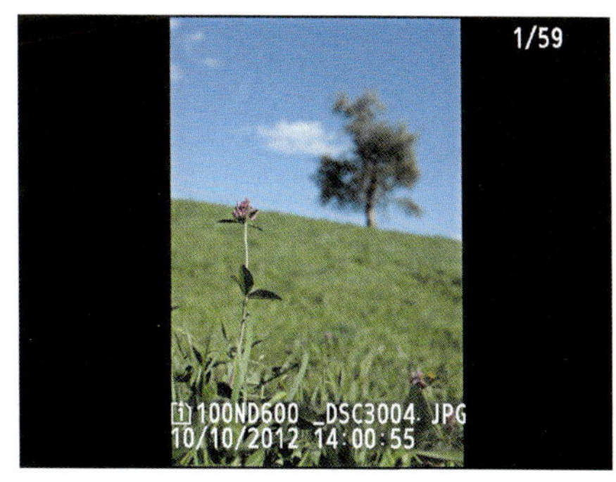

FIGURE 1.6
The default display mode on the D600.

To get more visual feedback, press the Multi-selector up to display the second display mode, called Overview (**Figure 1.7**). This view mode not only displays the same information as the default view, but it also includes camera settings such as aperture, shutter speed, lens length, white balance, exposure compensation, shooting mode, ISO, white balance setting, picture control, quality setting, any compensation settings, the active color space, and the picture control. The other noticeable item will be the histogram, which gives you important feedback on the luminance values in your image.

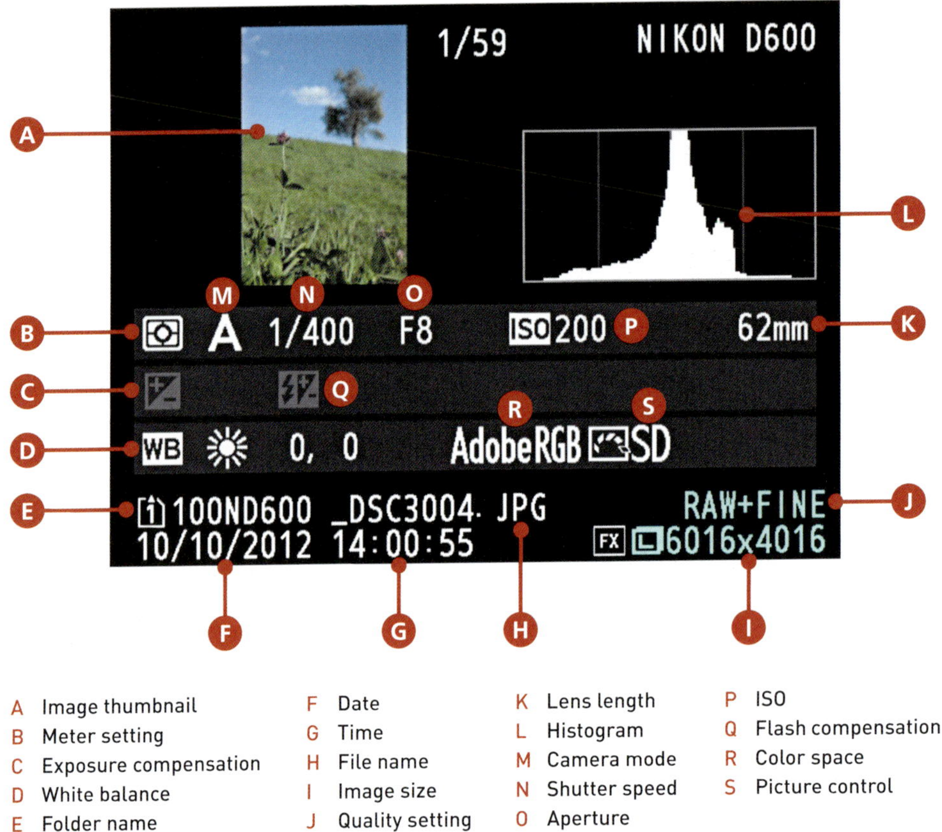

FIGURE 1.7
The Overview display mode gives you much more information.

A Image thumbnail
B Meter setting
C Exposure compensation
D White balance
E Folder name
F Date
G Time
H File name
I Image size
J Quality setting
K Lens length
L Histogram
M Camera mode
N Shutter speed
O Aperture
P ISO
Q Flash compensation
R Color space
S Picture control

Because the image thumbnail is so small, you probably won't want to use this display option as your default review setting, but if you are trying to figure out what settings you used or you want to review the histogram (see the sidebar "The Value of the Histogram"), you now have all of this great information available.

There are other display options available, but they must be turned on using the camera menu. These options can be found in the Playback menu under Playback display options (**Figure 1.8**). With this menu option, you can add display modes such as None (image only), Highlights, RGB Histogram (**Figure 1.9**), Shooting Data (**Figure 1.10**), and Focus Point. To add these items to your display, highlight them in the menu, add a checkmark by pressing right on the Multi-selector (**Figure 1.11**), and then go back to the Done option at the top and press the OK button (**Figure 1.12**). This last step is really important, because if you exit out before pressing OK on Done, your changes will not be locked in. Once you are done adding display options, you can review them by pressing the Playback button and continually pressing up on the Multi-selector to cycle through the views.

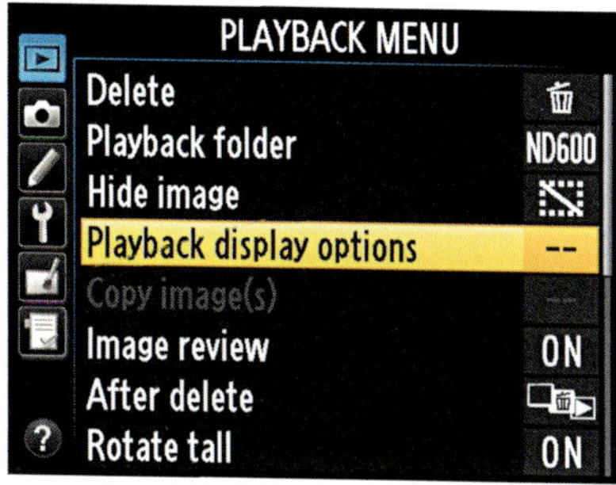

FIGURE 1.8
Select Playback display options.

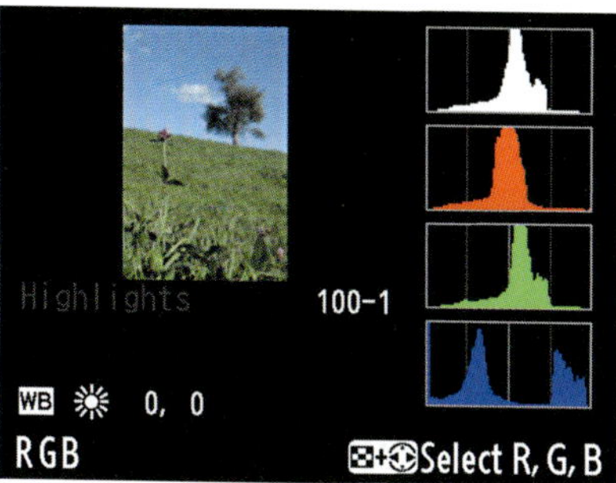

FIGURE 1.9
The RGB Histogram display mode.

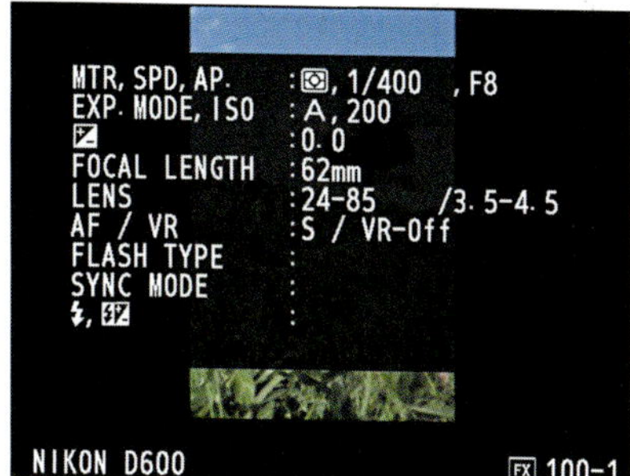

FIGURE 1.10
The Shooting Data display mode.

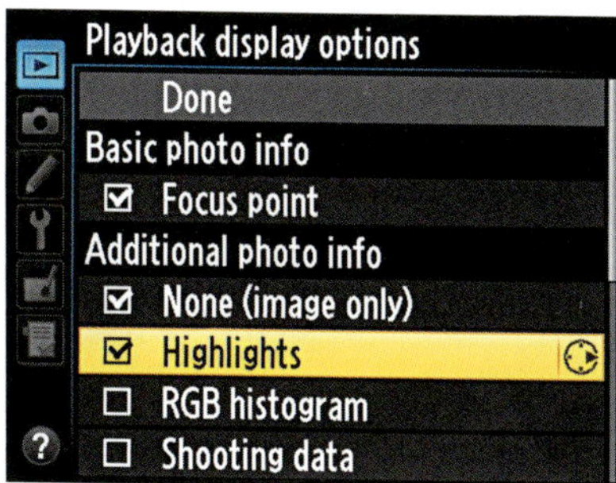

FIGURE 1.11
Add a checkmark to add an option to the display views.

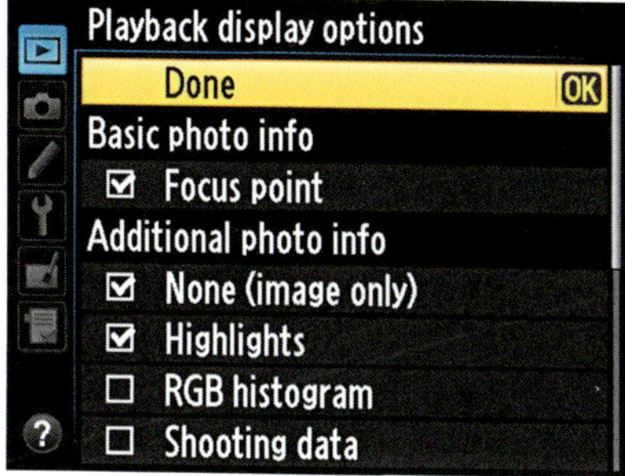

FIGURE 1.12
You must highlight the Done option and press OK to lock in the changes.

I don't use the RGB Histogram and Shooting Data settings, because they don't offer me any visual information that I find critical during a photo session. I do, however, always have the Highlights option turned on so that I can make sure I am not clipping any information from my image highlights. (Check out the "How I Shoot" section of Chapter 4 for more information about the Highlights display view and how to use it to improve your image quality.)

THE VALUE OF THE HISTOGRAM

Simply put, histograms are two-dimensional representations of your images in graph form. There are two histograms that you should be concerned with: luminance and color. Luminance is referred to in your manual as "brightness" and is most valuable when evaluating your exposures. In **Figure 1.13**, you see what looks like a mountain range. The graph represents the entire tonal range that your camera can capture, from the whitest whites to the blackest blacks. The left side represents black; the right side represents white. The heights of the peaks represent the number of pixels that contain those luminance levels (a tall peak in the middle means your image contains a large amount of medium-bright pixels). Looking at this figure, it is hard to determine where all of the ranges of light and dark areas are and how much of each I have. I can see that the largest peak of the graph is in the middle and trails off as it reaches the edges. In most cases, you would look for this type of histogram, indicating that you captured the entire range of tones, from dark to light, in your image. Knowing that is fine—but here is where the information really gets useful.

A histogram that has a spike or peak riding up the far left or right side of the graph means that you are clipping detail from your image. In essence, you are trying to record values that are either too dark or too light for your sensor to accurately record. This is usually an indication of over- or underexposure. It also means that you need to correct your exposure so that the important details will not record as solid black or white pixels (which is what happens when clipping occurs). There are times, however, when some clipping is acceptable. If you are photographing a scene where the sun will be in the frame, you can expect to get some clipping, because the sun is just too bright to hold any detail. Likewise, if you are shooting something that has true blacks in it—think coal in a mineshaft at midnight—there are most certainly going to be some true blacks with no detail in your shot.

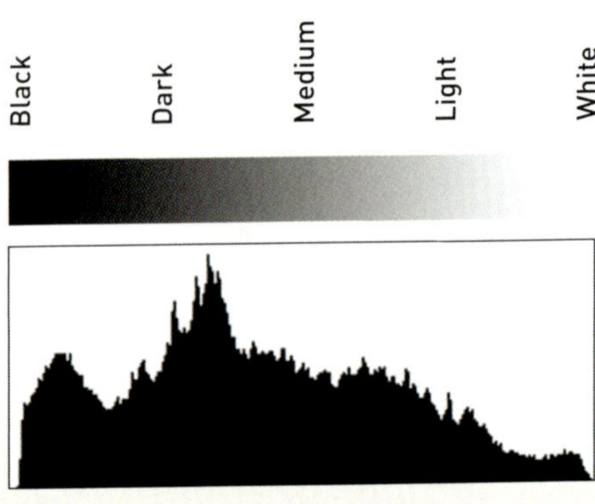

FIGURE 1.13

This is a typical histogram, where the dark to light tones run from left to right. The black to white gradient above the graph demonstrates where the tones lie on the graph and would not appear above your camera's histogram display.

The main goal is to ensure that you aren't clipping any "important" visual information, and that is achieved by keeping an eye on your histogram. Take a look at **Figure 1.14**. The histogram displayed on the image shows a heavy skew toward the left, with almost no part of the mountain touching the right side. This is a good example of what an underexposed image histogram looks like. Compare that to **Figure 1.15**, the histogram for the same image correctly exposed. Notice that even though there are two distinct peaks on the graph, there is an even distribution across the entire histogram.

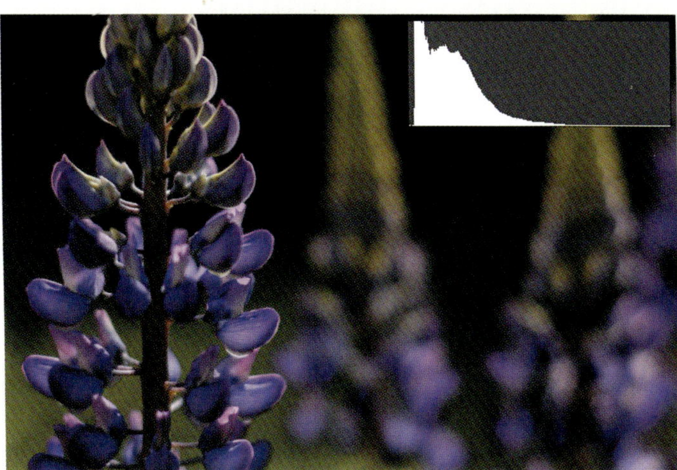

FIGURE 1.14 This image is about two stops underexposed. Notice that the histogram is skewed to the left.

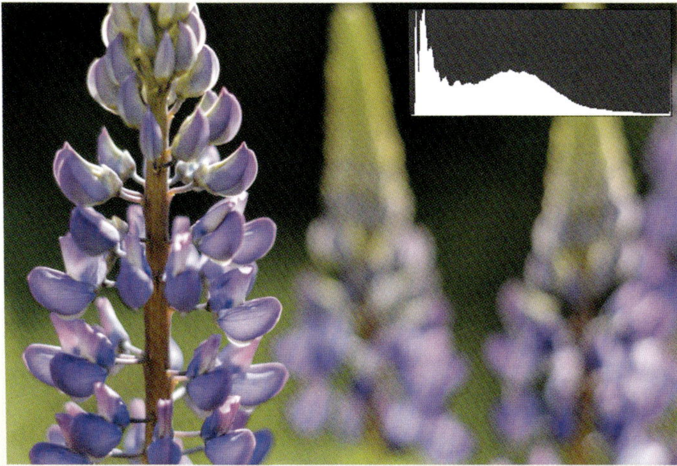

FIGURE 1.15 This histogram reflects a correctly exposed image.

DELETING IMAGES

Deleting or erasing images is a fairly simple process that is covered on pages 47 and 189 of your manual. To quickly get you on your way, simply press the Playback button and use the Multi-selector to find the picture that you want to delete. Then press the Delete (trash can) button located on the back of the camera to the right of the Playback button. When you see the confirmation screen, simply press the Delete button once again to complete the process.

Caution: Once you have deleted an image, it is gone for good. Make sure you don't want it anymore before you drop it in the trash.

Chapter 1 Assignments

Let's begin our shooting assignments by setting up and using all of the elements of the Top Ten list. Even though I have yet to cover the professional shooting modes, you should set your camera to the P (Program) mode. This will allow you to interact with the various settings and menus that have been covered thus far.

Basic camera setup

Charge your battery to 100% to get it started on a life of dependable service. Next, using your newfound knowledge, set up your camera to address the following: image quality, ISO, and color space.

Selecting the proper white balance

Take your camera outside into a daylight environment and photograph the same scene using different white balance settings. You can use the Program (P) mode right now, since we haven't covered any of the other modes. Pay close attention to how each WB setting affects the overall color cast of your images. Next, try moving inside and repeat the exercise while shooting in a tungsten lighting environment. Finally, find a fluorescent light source and repeat one more time.

Evaluating your pictures with the LCD display

Set up your image display properties and then review some of your previous assignment images using the different display modes. Review your shooting information for each image, and take a look at the histograms to see how the content of your photo affects the shape of the histograms.

Discovering the manual focus mode

Change your focus mode from autofocus to manual focus and practice a little manual focus photography. Get familiar with where the focus ring is and how to use it to achieve sharp images.

Share your results with the book's Flickr group!

www.flickr.com/groups/d600fromsnapshotstogreatshots

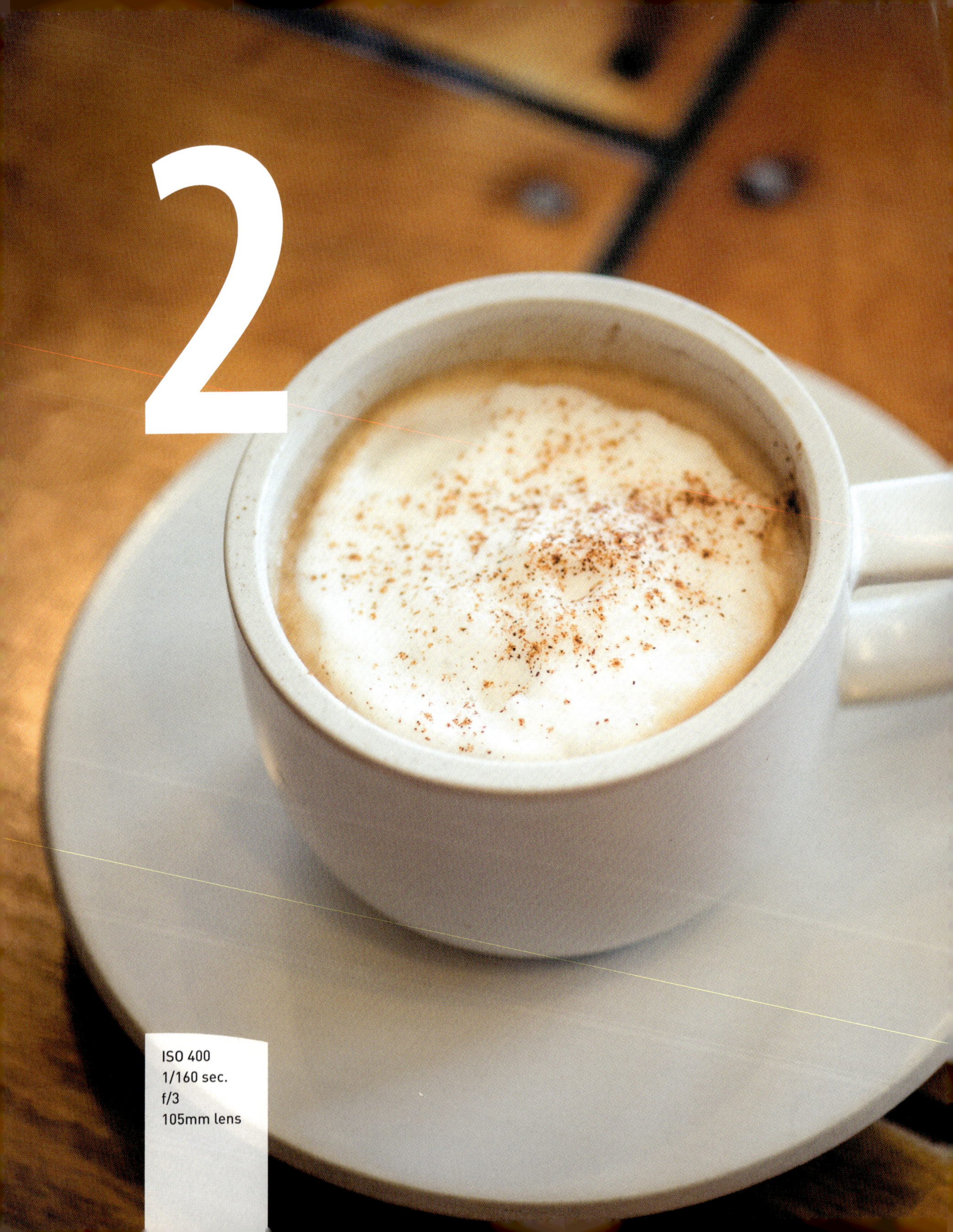

2

ISO 400
1/160 sec.
f/3
105mm lens

First Things First

A FEW THINGS TO KNOW AND DO BEFORE YOU BEGIN TAKING PICTURES

Now that we've covered the top ten tasks to get you up and shooting, we should probably take care of some other important details. You must become familiar with certain features of your camera before you can take full advantage of it. Additionally, we will take some steps to prepare the camera and memory card for use. So to get things moving, let's start off with something that you will definitely need before you can take a single picture: a memory card.

PORING OVER THE PICTURE

Every year, my little New England town has a harvest festival in the downtown area. Various vendors sell their wares, and craftspeople demonstrate their skills for the crowd. My son has been fascinated by the blacksmith for the last couple of years and was given a chance to operate the bellows on the forge. I wanted to create a photograph that told the story of him operating the bellows and that captured the intensity of the action, so I got down low and shot through the smoke and flames with a 70–200 mm lens.

The long lens helped me get tight on the action without getting too close to the fire.

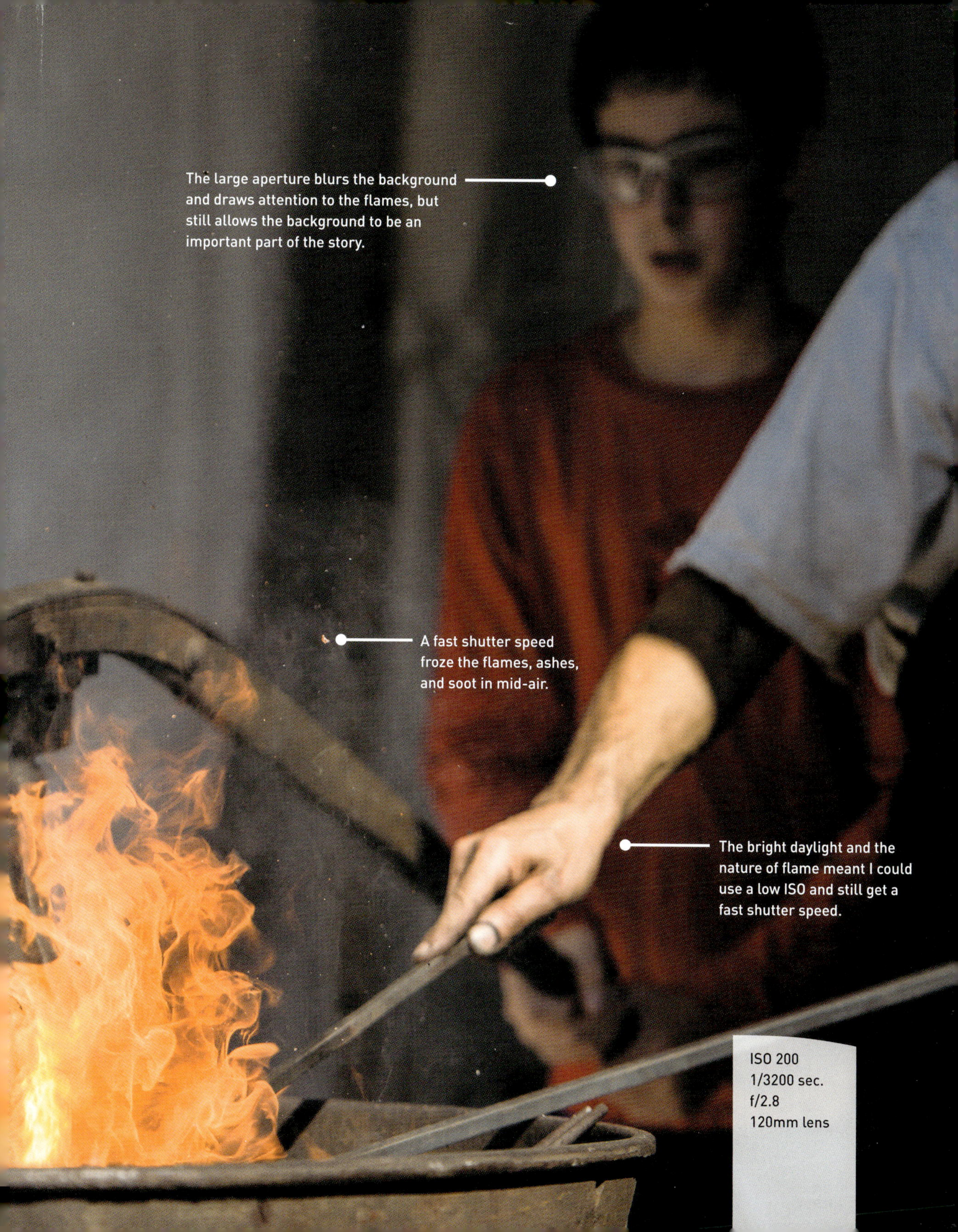

The large aperture blurs the background and draws attention to the flames, but still allows the background to be an important part of the story.

A fast shutter speed froze the flames, ashes, and soot in mid-air.

The bright daylight and the nature of flame meant I could use a low ISO and still get a fast shutter speed.

ISO 200
1/3200 sec.
f/2.8
120mm lens

CHOOSING THE RIGHT MEMORY CARD

Memory cards are the digital film that stores every shot you take until you move them to a computer. The cards come in all shapes and sizes, and they are critical for capturing all of your photos. It is important not to skimp when it comes to selecting your memory cards. The D600 has two memory slots, which accept Secure Digital (SD) memory cards (**Figure 2.1**).

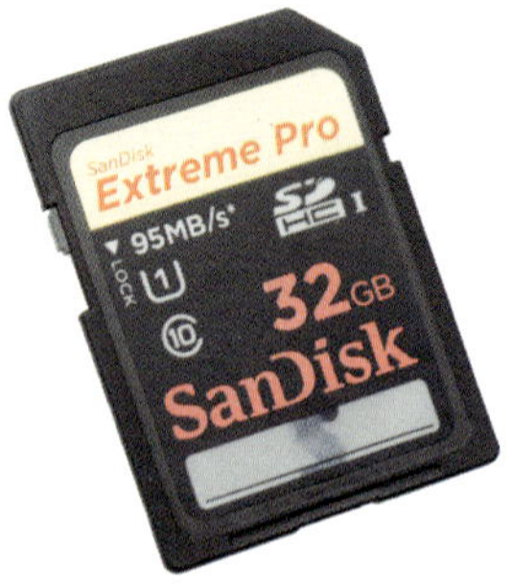

FIGURE 2.1
Make sure you select a card that has enough capacity to handle your photography needs.

If you have been using a point-and-shoot camera, chances are that you may already own an SD media card. Which brand of card you use is completely up to you, but here is some advice about choosing your memory card:

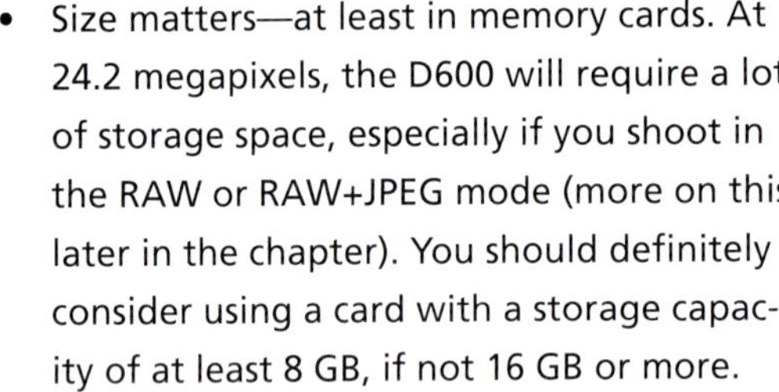

- Size matters—at least in memory cards. At 24.2 megapixels, the D600 will require a lot of storage space, especially if you shoot in the RAW or RAW+JPEG mode (more on this later in the chapter). You should definitely consider using a card with a storage capacity of at least 8 GB, if not 16 GB or more.
- Consider buying High Capacity (SDHC) cards. These cards are generally much faster, both when writing images to the card as well as when transferring them to your computer. If you are planning on shooting video, you can gain a boost in performance just by using an SDHC card with a class rating of at least 6. The higher the class rating of the SD card, the faster the write speed is.
- Buy more than one card. You can quickly ruin your day of shooting by filling your card and then having to either erase shots or choose a lower-quality image format so that you can keep on shooting. With the cost of memory cards what it is, keeping a spare just makes good sense.

Manual Callout

Nikon has a complete list of approved SD cards in the user's manual. Look at the chart on page 333 to see their recommendations.

FORMATTING YOUR MEMORY CARD

Now that you have your card, let's talk about formatting for a minute. When you purchase any new memory card, you can pop it into your camera and start shooting right away—and everything will probably work as it should. However, what you should do first is format the card in the camera. This process allows the camera to set up the card to record images from your camera. Just as a computer hard drive must be formatted, formatting your card ensures that it is properly initialized. The card may work in the camera without first being formatted, but chances of failure down the road are much higher.

As a general practice, I always format new cards or cards that have been used in different cameras. I also reformat cards after I have downloaded my images and want to start a new shooting session. Note that you should always format your card in the camera, not in your computer. Using the computer could render the card useless. You should also pay attention to the card manufacturer's recommendations with respect to moisture, humidity, and proper handling procedures. It sounds a little cliché, but when it comes to protecting your images, every little bit helps.

Most people make the mistake of thinking that the process of formatting the memory card is equivalent to erasing it. Not so. The truth is that when you format the card, all you are doing is changing the file management information on the card. Think of it as removing the table of contents from a book and replacing it with a blank page. All of the contents are still there, but you wouldn't know it by looking at the empty table of contents. The camera will see the card as completely empty, so you won't be losing any space, even if you had previously filled the card with images. Your camera will simply write the new image data over the previous data.

FORMATTING YOUR MEMORY CARD

1. Insert your memory card (or cards) into the camera (**A**).
2. Press the Menu button and navigate to the Setup Menu screen.

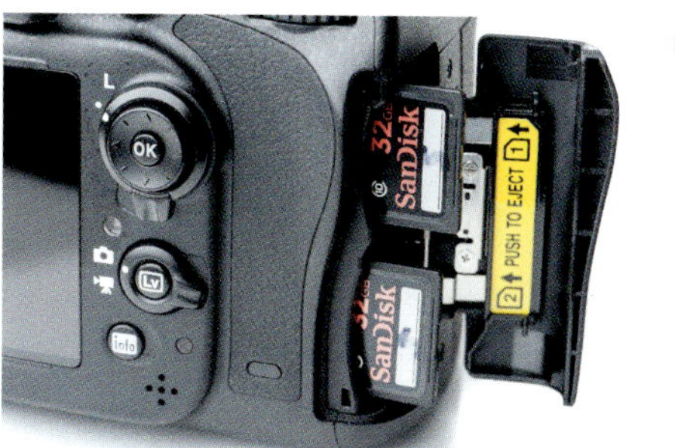

A

3. Use the Multi-selector on the back of the camera to highlight the Format memory card option, and press OK (**B**).
4. Select the memory slot that you want to format, 1 or 2 (**C**).
5. The next screen will show you a warning, letting you know that formatting the card will delete all images (**D**). Select Yes and press the OK button.
6. The card is now formatted and ready for use.

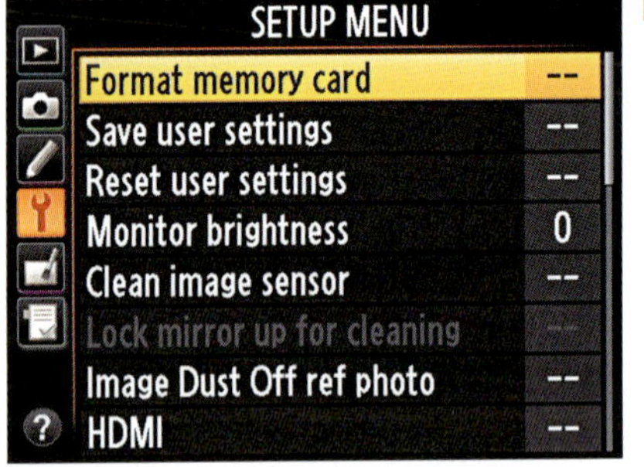

B

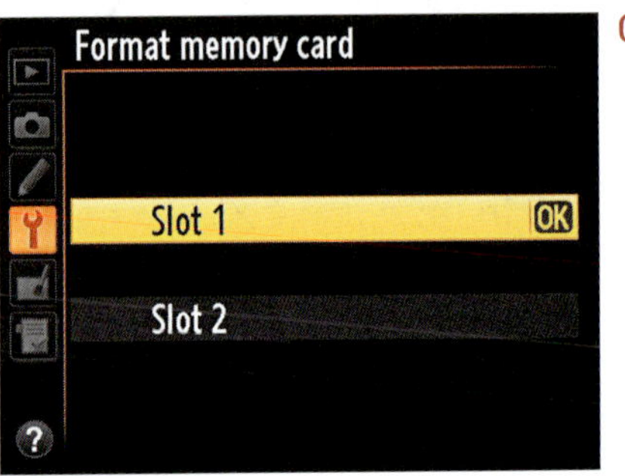

C

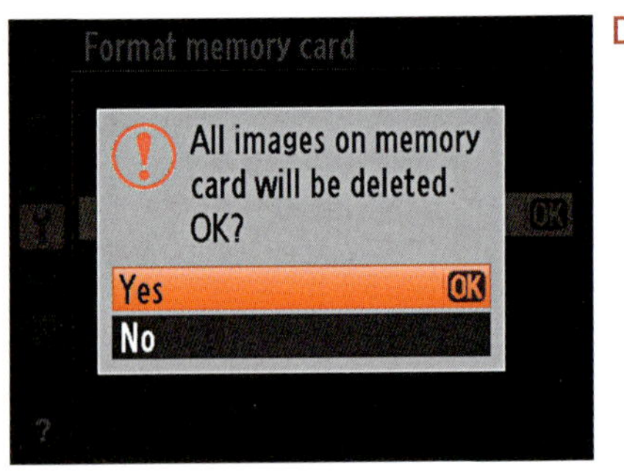

D

Manual Callout

There is also a quick format method that you can use to bypass the menus. Check out page 31 of the manual to see the steps.

UPDATING THE D600'S FIRMWARE

I know that you want to get shooting, but having the proper firmware can affect the way the camera operates. It can fix problems as well as improve operation, so you should probably check it sooner rather than later. Updating your camera's firmware is something that the manual completely omits, yet it can change the entire behavior of your camera's operating systems and functions. The firmware of your camera is the set of computer operating instructions that controls how your camera functions. Updating this firmware is a great way to not only fix little bugs but also gain access to new functionality. You will need to check out the information on the Nikon firmware update page (www.nikonusa.com/Service-And-Support/Download-Center.page) to see if a firmware update is available and how it will affect your camera, but it is always a good idea to be working with the most up-to-date firmware version available.

CHECKING THE CAMERA'S CURRENT FIRMWARE VERSION NUMBER

1. Press the Menu button and then navigate to the Setup menu.
2. Use the Multi-selector on the back of the camera to highlight the Firmware version option, and press OK (**A**).
3. Take note of the current version numbers (there are three of them), and then check the Nikon website to see if you are using the current versions (**B**).

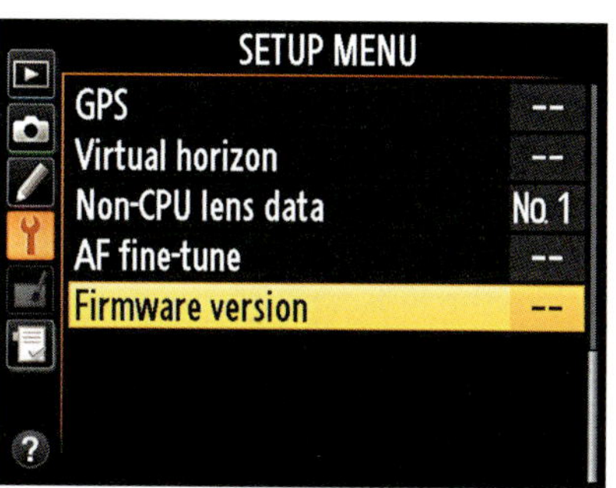

A

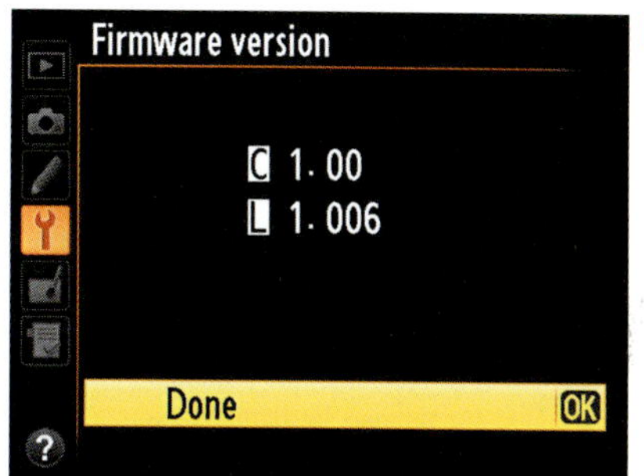

B

UPDATING THE FIRMWARE FROM YOUR MEMORY CARD

1. Download the firmware update file from the Nikon website. (You can find the file by going to the Download Center section of the Nikon camera site, clicking the Download Current Firmware link, and then locating the firmware update for your camera and computer operating system.)
2. Once you have downloaded the firmware to your computer and extracted it, you will need to transfer it to your memory card. The card must be formatted in your camera prior to loading the firmware to it.
3. With a freshly charged camera battery, insert the card into the camera and turn it on.
4. Follow the instructions listed previously for locating your firmware version, and you will now be able to update your firmware using the files located on the memory card.

As of the writing of this book, there are no firmware updates available for the D600. After you check your camera firmware version and the Nikon site for updates, continue to check back periodically to see if any updates become available.

CLEANING THE SENSOR

Cleaning camera sensors used to be a nerve-racking process that required leaving the sensor exposed to scratching and even more dust. Now cleaning the sensor is pretty much an automatic function. Every time you turn the camera on and off, you can instruct the sensor in the camera to vibrate to remove any dust particles that might have landed on it.

There are five choices for cleaning in the camera setup menu: Clean at startup, Clean at shutdown, Clean at startup and shutdown, Cleaning off, and Clean now. I'm kind of obsessive when it comes to cleaning my sensor, so I like to have it set to clean when I turn the camera on and off.

The one cleaning function that you will need to use via this menu is the Clean now feature. This should be done every time you remove the lens from the camera body. That's because removing or changing a lens will leave the camera body open and susceptible to dust sneaking in. If you never change lenses, you shouldn't have too many dust problems. But the more often you change lenses, the more chances you are giving dust to enter the body. It's for this reason that I have added the Clean now function to the custom My Menu list (see Chapter 11).

Every now and then, there will just be a dust spot that is impervious to the shaking of the Auto Cleaning feature. This will require manual cleaning of the sensor by raising the mirror and opening the camera shutter. When you activate this feature, it will move everything out of the way, giving you access to the sensor so that you can use a blower or other appropriate cleaning device to remove the stubborn dust speck. The camera will need to be turned off after cleaning to allow the mirror to reset.

If you choose to manually clean your sensor, use a device that has been made to clean sensors (not a cotton swab from your medicine cabinet). There are dozens of commercially available devices—such as brushes, swabs, and blowers—that will clean the sensor without damaging it. To keep the sensor clean, always store the camera with a body cap or lens attached.

The camera sensor is an electrically charged device. This means that when the camera is turned on, there is a current running through the sensor. This electric current can create static electricity, which will attract small dust particles to the sensor area. For this reason, it is always a good idea to turn off the camera prior to removing a lens. You should also consider having the lens mount facing down when changing lenses so that there is less opportunity for dust to fall into the inner workings of the camera.

USING THE CLEAN NOW FEATURE

1. Press the Menu button, then navigate to the Setup menu.
2. Use the Multi-selector on the back of the camera to highlight the Clean image sensor option and press OK (**A**).
3. Highlight the Clean now option and press the OK button (**B**). The camera will clean the sensor for about 2 seconds and then return to the menu.

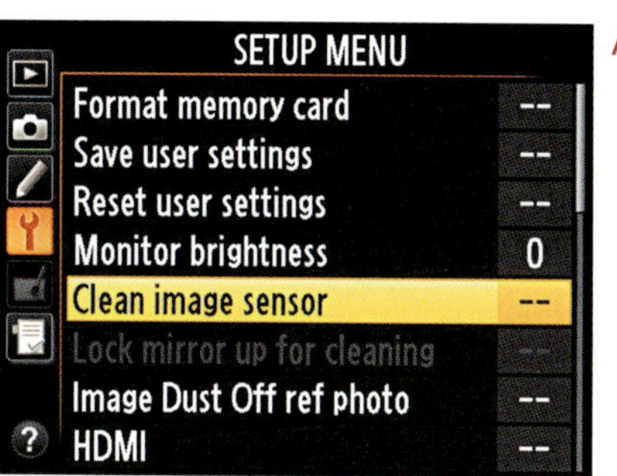

A

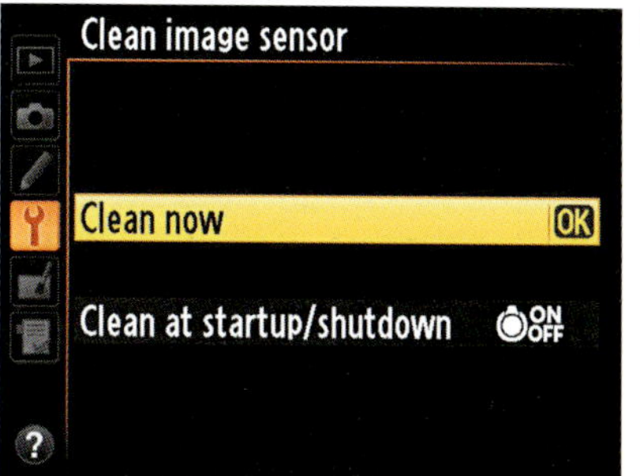

B

USING THE RIGHT FORMAT: RAW VS. JPEG

When shooting with your D600, you have a choice of image formats that your camera will use to store the pictures on the memory card. JPEG is probably the most familiar format to anyone who has been using a digital camera. I touched on this topic briefly in Chapter 1, so you already have a little background on what JPEG and RAW files are.

There is nothing wrong with JPEG if you are taking casual shots. JPEG files are ready to use right out of the camera. Why go through the process of adjusting RAW images of the kids opening presents when you are just going to email them to Grandma? Also, for journalists and sports photographers who are shooting the maximum frames per second and who need to transmit their images across the wire—again, JPEG is just fine. So what is wrong with JPEG? Absolutely nothing—unless you care about having complete creative control over all of your image data (as opposed to what a compression algorithm thinks is important).

As I mentioned in Chapter 1, JPEG is not actually an image format—it is a compression standard, and compression is where things go bad. When you have your camera set to JPEG—whether it is Fine, Normal, or Basic—you are telling the camera to process the image however it sees fit and then throw away enough image data to make it shrink into a smaller space. In doing so, you give up subtle image details that you will never get back in post-processing. That is an awfully simplified statement, but it's still fairly accurate.

SO WHAT DOES RAW HAVE TO OFFER?

First and foremost, RAW images are not compressed. Your camera does have a compressed RAW format, but it is lossless compression, which means there is no loss of actual image data. Note that RAW image files will require you to perform post-processing on your photographs. This is not only necessary—it is the reason that most photographers use it.

RAW images have a greater dynamic range than JPEG-processed images. This means that you can recover image detail in the highlights and shadows that just aren't available in JPEG-processed images.

There is more color information in a RAW image because it is a 12- or 14-bit image (depending on the camera and settings used), which means it contains more color information than a JPEG, which is always an 8-bit image. More color information means more to work with and smoother changes between tones—kind of like the difference between performing surgery with a scalpel as opposed to a butcher's knife. They'll both get the job done, but one will do less damage.

Regarding sharpening, a RAW image offers more control because *you* are the one who is applying the sharpening according to the effect you want to achieve. Once again, JPEG processing applies a standard amount of sharpening that you cannot change after the fact. Once it is done, it's done.

IMAGE RESOLUTION

When discussing digital cameras, image resolution is often used to describe pixel resolution or the number of pixels used to make an image. This can be displayed as a dimension, such as 6016 x 4016. This is the physical number of pixels in width and height of the image sensor. Resolution can also be referred to in megapixels (MP), such as 24.2 MP. This number represents the number of total pixels on the sensor and is commonly used to describe the amount of image data that a digital camera can capture.

Finally, and most importantly, a RAW file is your negative. No matter what you do to it, you won't change it unless you save your file in a different format. This means that you can come back to that RAW file later and try different processing settings to achieve differing results and never harm the original image. By comparison, if you make a change to your JPEG and accidentally save the file, guess what? You have a new original file, and you will never get back to that first image. That alone should make you sit up and take notice.

ADVICE FOR NEW RAW SHOOTERS

Don't give up on shooting RAW just because it means more work. Hey, if it takes up more space on your card, buy bigger cards or more small ones. Will it take more time to download? Yes, but good things come to those who wait. Don't worry about needing to purchase expensive software to work with your RAW files; you already own a program that will allow you to work with your RAW files. Nikon's ViewNX 2 software comes bundled in the box with your camera and gives you the ability to work directly on the RAW files and then output the enhanced results. That said, you will have more control if you use dedicated RAW processing software such as Nikon's CaptureNX 2, Apple's Aperture, or Adobe's Photoshop or Lightroom.

My recommendation is to shoot in JPEG mode while you are using this book. This will allow you to quickly review your images and study the effects of the lessons. Once you have become comfortable with all of the camera features, you should switch to shooting in RAW mode so you can start gaining more creative control over your image processing. After all, you took the photograph—shouldn't you be the one to decide how it looks in the end?

SHOOTING DUAL FORMATS

Your camera has the added benefit of being able to write two files for each picture you take, one in RAW and one in JPEG. If you have the RAW+JPEG setting selected, your camera will save your images in both formats on your card.

I think shooting RAW+JPEG is actually a good way to transition to shooting RAW. You get the ease and safety of the familiar JPEG, and the ability to compare the JPEG against your RAW processing experiences. This will obviously take up more space on your memory card and hard drive, but think of it as a stepping-stone on the path to shooting only RAW in the future. It took me a little while to make the transition, and looking back there are some shots I took in JPEG mode that I now wish I had a RAW version of that I could try to improve. Live and learn.

SHOOTING IN RAW+JPEG

1. Press and hold the QUAL button.
2. Use the Main Command dial to change the file type to RAW+JPEG (**A**).
3. Select one of the three RAW+JPEG settings: Fine, Normal, or Basic.
4. Use the Sub-command dial to change the size of the JPEG file (Large, Medium, or Small) (**B**).

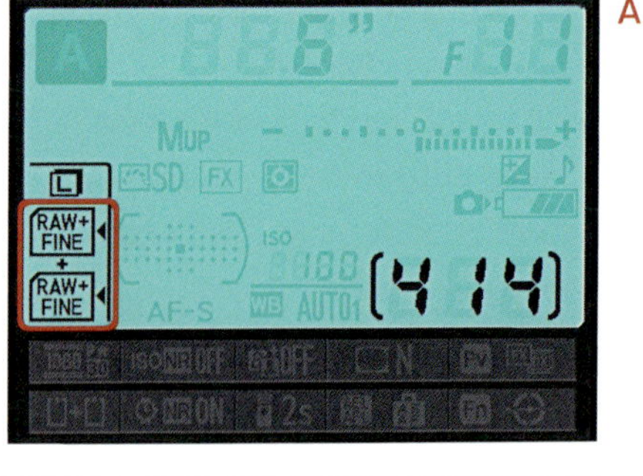
A

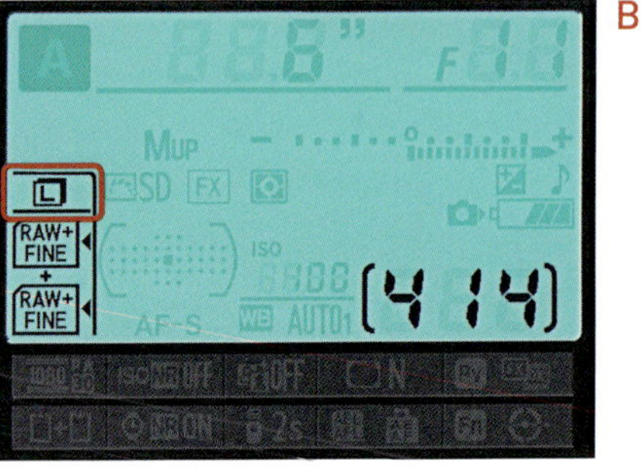
B

As you change the settings, you should see a change in the number of total images that you can capture before your card is full.

Having two memory card slots is handy because you can configure the role of the second card based on your needs. You have three options: Overflow, Backup, and RAW Slot 1 – JPEG Slot 2. For mission-critical work, I always choose Backup for the peace of mind of having all photos on two cards simultaneously. For more casual shooting, I use Overflow. And if you ever need to shoot RAW+JPEG and want to keep the JPEGs on their own card, it is nice to have that option, too.

CONFIGURE THE ROLE OF THE SECOND CARD

1. Press the Menu button, then navigate to the Setup menu.
2. Use the Multi-selector on the back of the camera to highlight the Role played by card in Slot 2 option, and press OK (**A**).
3. Highlight the option you can want to use and press OK (**B**).

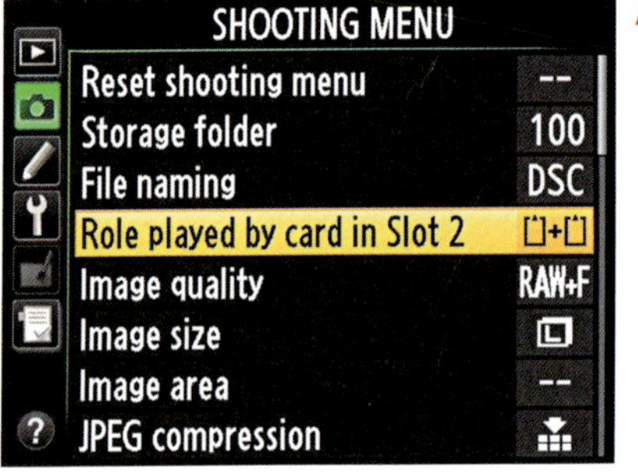

A

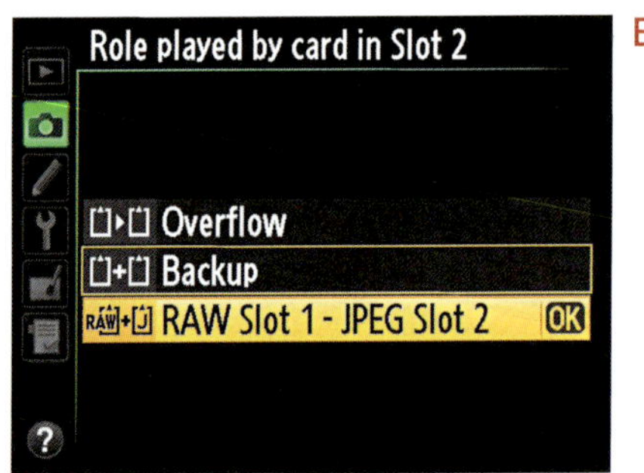

B

LENSES AND FOCAL LENGTHS

If you ask most professional photographers what they believe to be their most critical piece of photographic equipment, they would undoubtedly tell you that it is their lens. The technology and engineering that goes into your camera is a marvel, but it isn't worth a darn if it can't get the light from the outside onto the sensor. The D600, as a digital single lens reflex (DSLR) camera, uses the lens for a multitude of tasks, from focusing on a subject to metering a scene to delivering and focusing the light onto the camera sensor. The lens is also responsible for the amount of the scene that will be captured (the frame). With all of this riding on the lens, let's take a more in-depth look at the camera's eye on the world.

Lenses are composed of optical glass that is both concave and convex in shape. The alignment of the glass elements is designed to focus the light coming in from the front of the lens onto the camera sensor. The amount of light that enters the camera is controlled by the lens, the size of the glass elements, and the aperture mechanism within the lens housing. The quality of the glass used in the lens will also have a direct effect on how well the lens can resolve details and on the contrast of the image (the ability to deliver great highlights and shadows). Most lenses now routinely include things like the autofocus motor and, in some cases, a vibration reduction mechanism.

There is one other aspect of the camera lens that is often the first consideration of the photographer: lens length. Lenses are typically divided into three or four groups, based on the field of view they deliver.

Wide-angle lenses cover a field of view from around 110 degrees to about 60 degrees (**Figure 2.2**). There is also a tendency to get some distortion in your image when using extremely wide-angle lenses. This will be apparent toward the outer edges of the frame. As for which lenses would be considered wide angle, anything smaller than 50mm could be considered wide.

Wide-angle lenses can display a large depth of field, which allows you to keep the foreground and background in sharp focus. This makes them very useful for landscape photography. They also work well in tight spaces, such as indoors, where there isn't much elbow room available (**Figure 2.3**). They can also be handy for large group shots but, due to the amount of distortion, not so great for close-up portrait work.

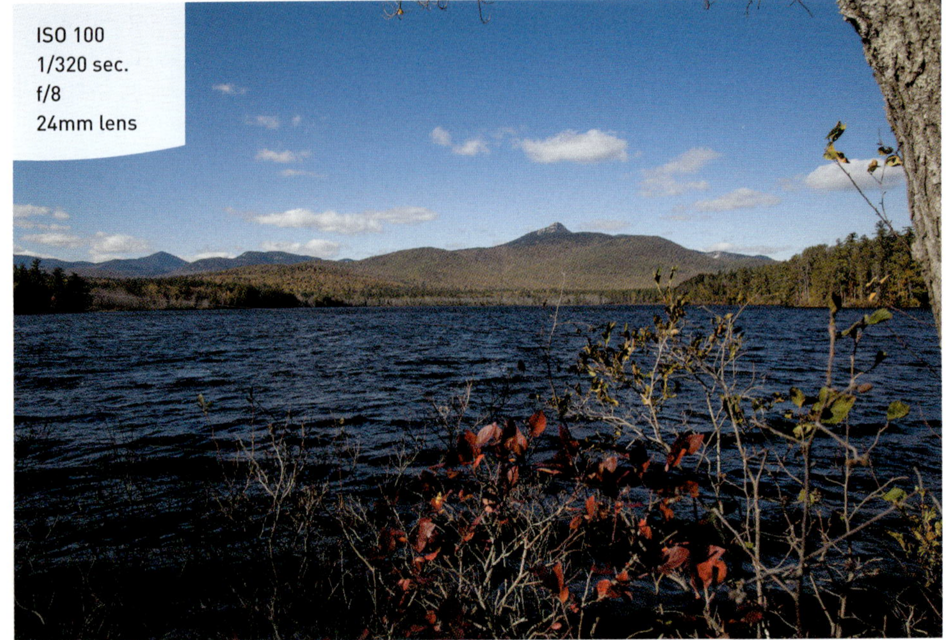

FIGURE 2.2
The 24mm lens setting provides a wide view of the scene but little detail of distant objects.

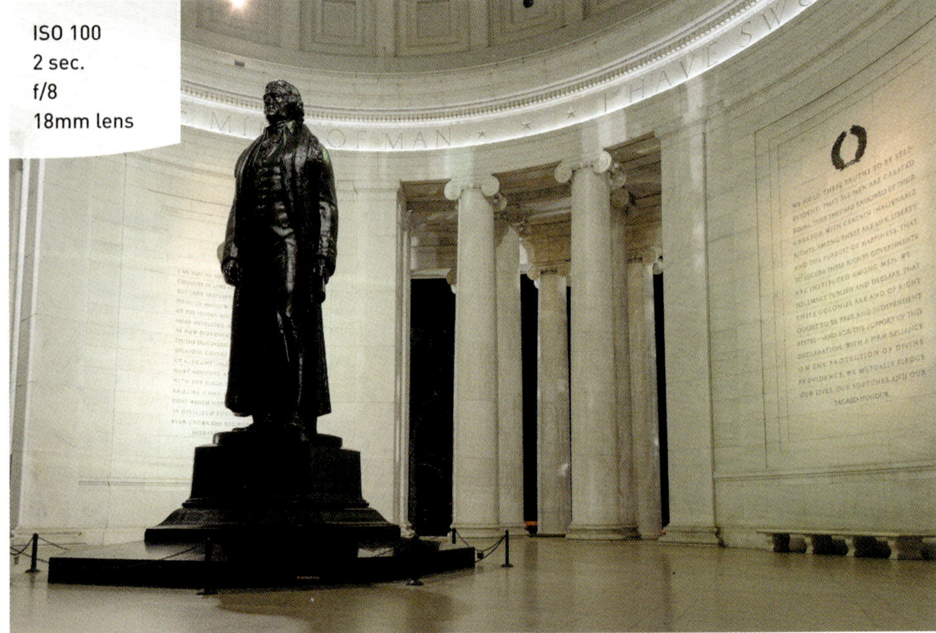

FIGURE 2.3
When shooting in tight spaces, such as indoors, a wide-angle lens helps capture more of the scene.

A *normal* lens has a field of view that is about 45 degrees and delivers approximately the same view as the human eye. The perspective is very natural, and there is little distortion in objects. The normal lens for full-frame digital cameras is the 50mm lens (**Figure 2.4**).

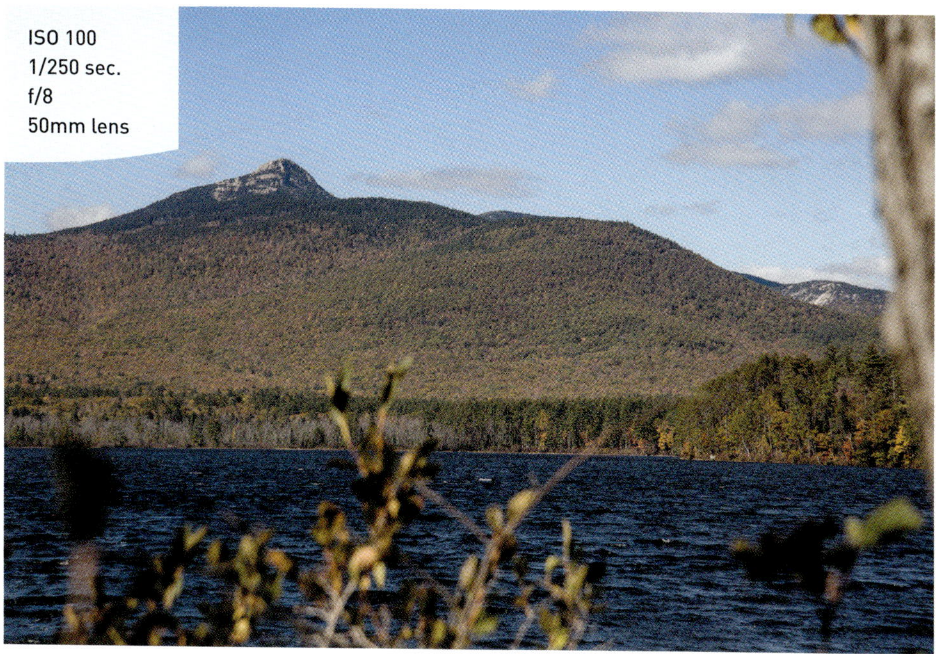

ISO 100
1/250 sec.
f/8
50mm lens

FIGURE 2.4
Long considered the "normal" lens for 35mm photography, the 50mm does not offer the same angle as the human eye, but objects seem about the same size in relation to each other.

Normal focal length lenses are useful for photographing people, architecture, and most other general photographic needs. They have very little distortion and offer a moderate range of depth of field (**Figure 2.5**).

Most longer focal length lenses are referred to as *telephoto* lenses. They can range in length from 135mm up to 800mm or longer and have a field of view that is about 35 degrees or smaller. These lenses have the ability to greatly magnify the scene, allowing you to capture details of distant objects, but the angle of view is greatly reduced (**Figure 2.6**). You will also find that you can achieve a much narrower depth of field. They also suffer from something called distance compression, which means they make objects at different distances appear to be much closer together than they really are.

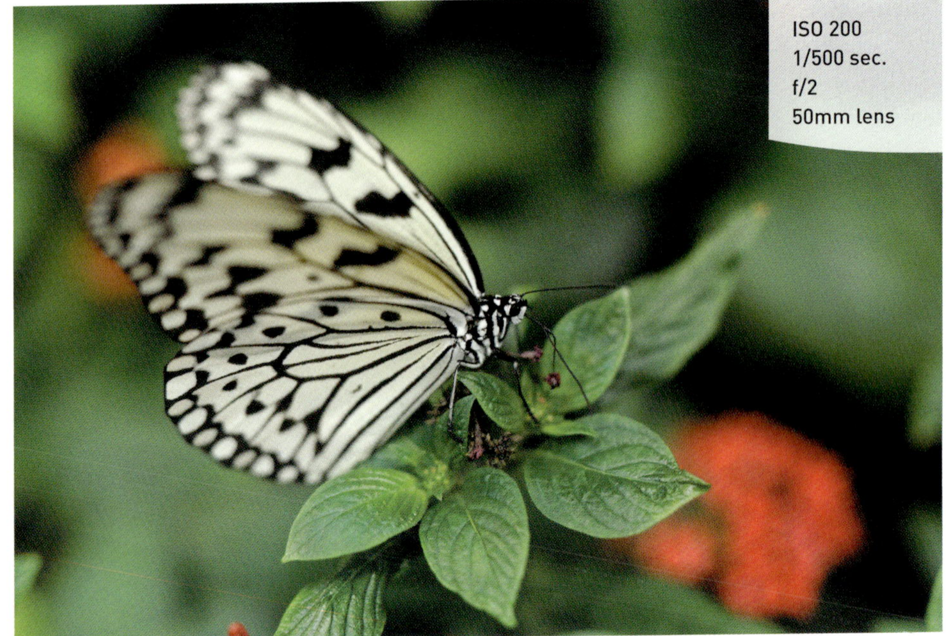

FIGURE 2.5
The normal lens worked well for this image, which I captured as I walked around a butterfly garden.

ISO 200
1/500 sec.
f/2
50mm lens

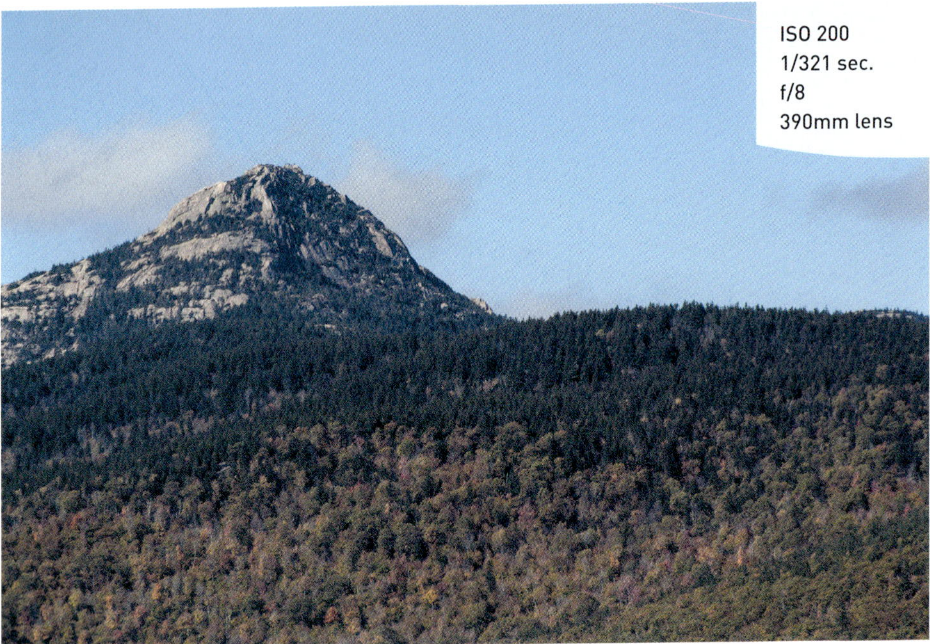

FIGURE 2.6
The telephoto lens allowed me to capture close-up detail of the distant peak without having to get physically closer.

ISO 200
1/321 sec.
f/8
390mm lens

Telephoto lenses are most useful for sports photography or any application where you just need to get closer to your subject. They can have a compressing effect—making objects look closer together than they actually are (**Figure 2.7**)—and a very narrow depth of field when shot at their widest apertures.

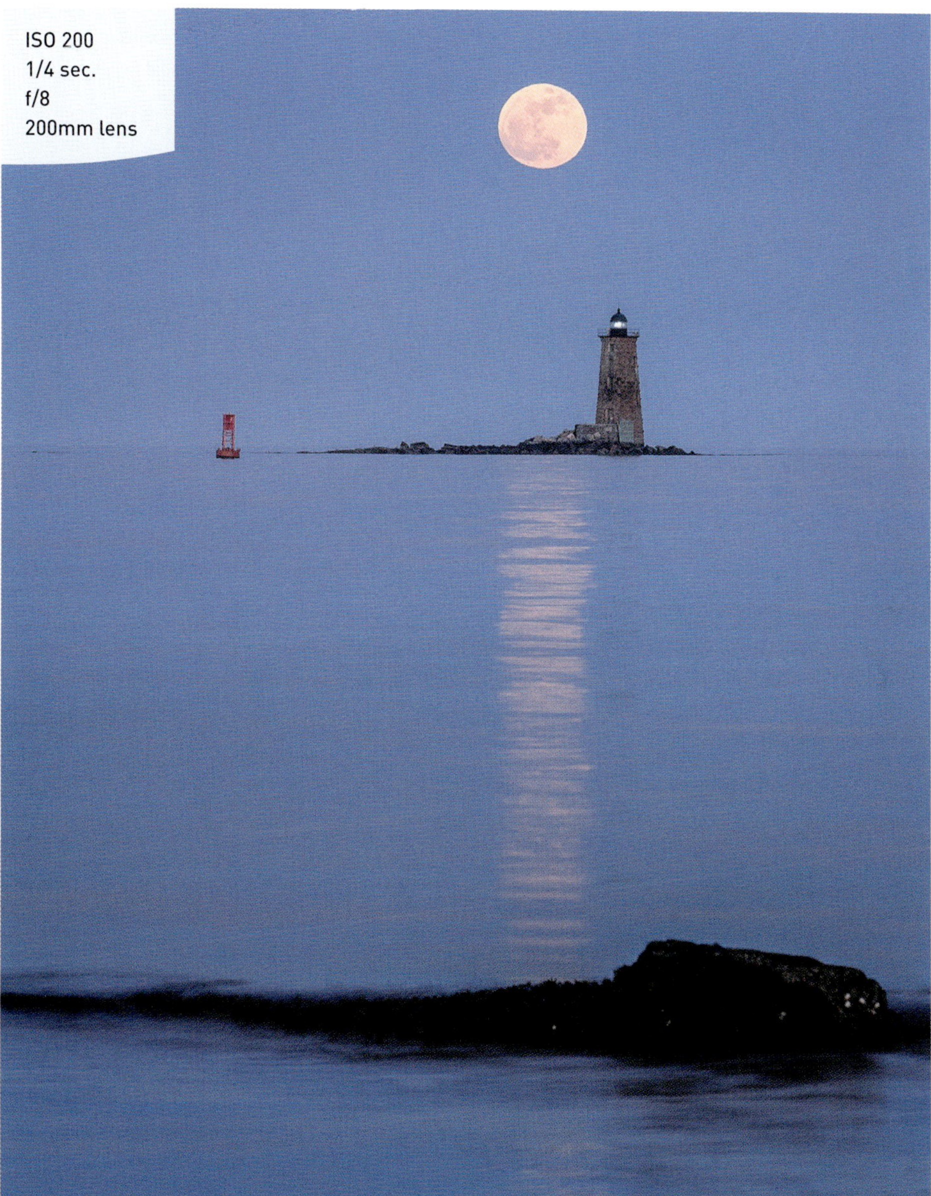

FIGURE 2.7
The compressing effect of the long telephoto lens makes the foreground rock, lighthouse, and moon look a lot closer together than they really are.

A *zoom* lens is a great compromise to carrying a bunch of single-focal-length lenses (also referred to as "prime" lenses). They can cover a wide range of focal lengths because of the configuration of their optics. However, because it takes more optical elements to capture a scene at different focal lengths, the light must pass through more glass on its way to the image sensor. The more glass, the lower the quality of the image sharpness. The other sacrifice that is made is in aperture. Zoom lenses typically have smaller maximum apertures than prime lenses, which means they cannot achieve a narrow depth of field or work in lower light levels without the assistance of vibration reduction, a tripod, or higher ISO settings. (We'll discuss all this in more detail in later chapters.)

Throughout the book, I occasionally make reference to lenses that are wider or more telephoto than the lenses that you may own, because I have a multitude of lenses that I use for my photography. This doesn't mean that you have to run out and purchase more lenses. It just means that if you do this long enough, you are sure to accumulate additional lenses, which will expand your ability to be even more creative with your photography.

WHAT IS EXPOSURE?

In order for you to get the most out of this book, I need to briefly discuss the principles of exposure. Without this basic knowledge, it will be difficult for you to move forward in improving your photography. Granted, I could write an entire book on exposure and the photographic process—and many people have—but for our purposes I will just cover some of the basics. This will give you the essential tools to make educated decisions in determining how best to photograph a subject.

Exposure is the process whereby the light reflecting off a subject reflects through an opening in the camera lens for a defined period of time onto the camera sensor. The combination of the lens opening, shutter speed, and sensor sensitivity is used to achieve a proper exposure value (EV) for the scene. The EV is the sum of the components necessary to properly expose a scene. The relationship that exists between these factors is sometimes referred to as the "exposure triangle."

At each point of the triangle lies one of the factors of exposure:

- **ISO:** Determines the sensitivity of the camera sensor. ISO stands for the International Organization for Standardization, but the acronym is used as a term to describe the sensitivity of the camera sensor to light. The higher the sensitivity, the less light is required for a good exposure. These values are a carryover from the days of traditional color and black and white films.
- **Aperture:** Also referred to as the f-stop, this determines how much light passes through the lens at once.
- **Shutter Speed:** Controls the length of time that light is allowed to hit the sensor.

Here's how it works. The camera sensor has a level of sensitivity that is determined by the ISO setting. To get a proper exposure—not too much, not too little—the lens needs to adjust the aperture diaphragm (the size of the lens opening) to control the volume of light entering the camera. Then the shutter is opened for a relatively short period of time to allow the light to hit the sensor long enough for it to record on the sensor.

ISO numbers for the D600 start at 100 and then double in sensitivity as you double the number. So 400 is twice as sensitive as 200. The camera can be set to use 1/2- or 1/3-stop increments, but for ISO just remember that the base numbers double: 200, 400, 800, and so on. There are also a wide variety of shutter speeds that you can use. The speeds on the D600 range from as long as 30 seconds to as short as 1/4000 of a second. Typically, you will be working with a shutter speed range from around 1/30 of a second to about 1/2000, but these numbers will change depending on your circumstances and the effect that you are trying to achieve. The lens apertures will vary slightly depending on which lens you are using. This is because different lenses have different maximum apertures. The typical apertures that are at your disposal are f/4, f/5.6, f/8, f/11, f/16, and f/22.

When it comes to exposure, a change to any one of these factors requires changing one or more of the other two. This is referred to as reciprocal change. If you let more light in the lens by choosing a larger aperture opening, you will need to shorten the amount of time the shutter is open. If the shutter is allowed to stay open for a longer period of time, the aperture needs to be smaller to restrict the amount of light coming in.

HOW IS EXPOSURE CALCULATED?

We now know about the exposure triangle—ISO, shutter speed, and aperture—so it's time to put all three together to see how they relate to one another and how you can change them as needed.

STOP

You will hear the term *stop* thrown around all the time in photography. It relates back to the f-stop, which is a term used to describe the aperture of your lens. When you need to give some additional exposure, you might say that you are going to "add a stop." This doesn't just equate to the aperture; it could also be used to describe the shutter speed or even the ISO. So when your image is too light or dark or you have too much movement in your subject, you will probably be changing things by a "stop" or two.

When you point your camera at a scene, the light reflecting off your subject enters the lens and is allowed to pass through to the sensor for a period of time dictated by the shutter speed. The amount and duration of the light needed for a proper exposure depends on how much light is being reflected and how sensitive the sensor is. To figure this out, your camera utilizes a built-in light meter that looks through the lens and measures the amount of light. That level is then calculated against the sensitivity of the ISO setting, and an exposure value is rendered. Here is the tricky part: there is no single way to achieve a perfect exposure, because the f-stop and shutter speed can be combined in different ways to allow the same amount of exposure. See, I told you it was tricky.

Here is a list of reciprocal settings that would all produce the same exposure result. Let's use the "sunny 16" rule, which states that when using f/16 on a sunny day, you can use a shutter speed that is roughly equal to the ISO setting to achieve a proper exposure. For simplification purposes, we will use an ISO of 100.

RECIPROCAL EXPOSURES: ISO 100

F-STOP	2.8	4	5.6	8	11	16	22
SHUTTER SPEED	1/4000	1/2000	1/1000	1/500	1/250	1/125	1/60

All of these combinations have the same result in terms of the exposure (i.e., how much light hits the camera's sensor). Also take note that every time we cut the f-stop in half, we reciprocated by doubling our shutter speed. For those of you wondering why f/8 is half of f/5.6, it's because those numbers are actually fractions based on the opening of the lens in relation to its focal length. This means that a lot of math goes into figuring out just what the total area of a lens opening is, so you just have to take it on faith that f/8 is half of f/5.6 but twice as much as f/11. A good way to remember which opening is larger is to think of your camera lens as a pipe that controls the flow of water. If you have one pipe that is 1/2" in diameter (f/2) and one that is 1/8" (f/8), which would allow more water to flow through? It would be the 1/2" pipe. The same idea works here with the camera f-stops; f/2 is a larger opening than f/4 or f/8 or f/16.

Now that we know this, we can start using this information to make intelligent choices in terms of shutter speed and f-stop. Let's bring the third element into this by changing our ISO by one stop, from 100 to 200.

RECIPROCAL EXPOSURES: ISO 200

F-STOP	2.8	4.0	5.6	8	11	16	22
SHUTTER SPEED	–	1/4000	1/2000	1/1000	1/500	1/250	1/125

Notice that, since we doubled the sensitivity of the sensor, we now require half as much exposure as before. We have also reduced our maximum aperture from f/2.8 to f/4 because the camera can't use a shutter speed that is faster than 1/4000 of a second.

So why not just use the exposure setting of f/16 at 1/250 of a second? Why bother with all of these reciprocal values when this one setting will give us a properly exposed image? The answer is that the f-stop and shutter speed also control two other important aspects of our image: motion and depth of field.

MOTION AND DEPTH OF FIELD

There are distinct characteristics that are related to changes in aperture and shutter speed. Shutter speed controls the length of time the light has to strike the sensor; consequently, it also controls the blurriness (or lack of blurriness) of the image. The less time light has to hit the sensor, the less time your subjects have to move around and become blurry. This can let you control things like freezing the motion of a fast-moving subject (**Figure 2.8**) or intentionally blurring subjects to give the feel of energy and motion (**Figure 2.9**).

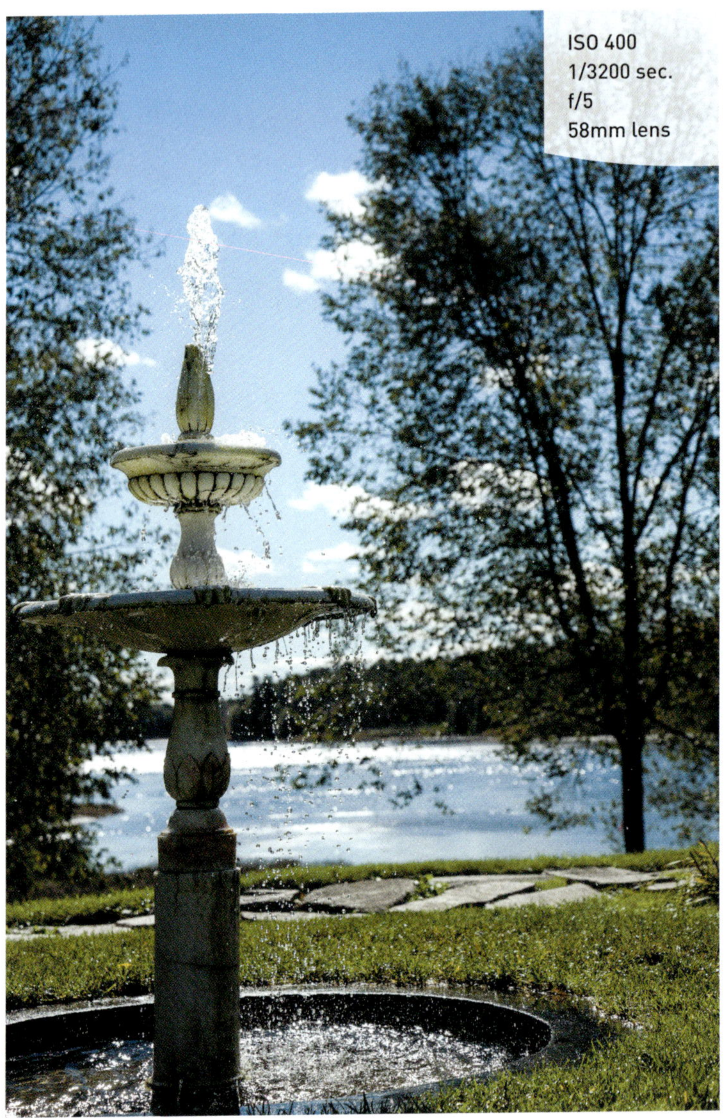

FIGURE 2.8
A fast shutter speed was used to freeze the water cascading out of this fountain.

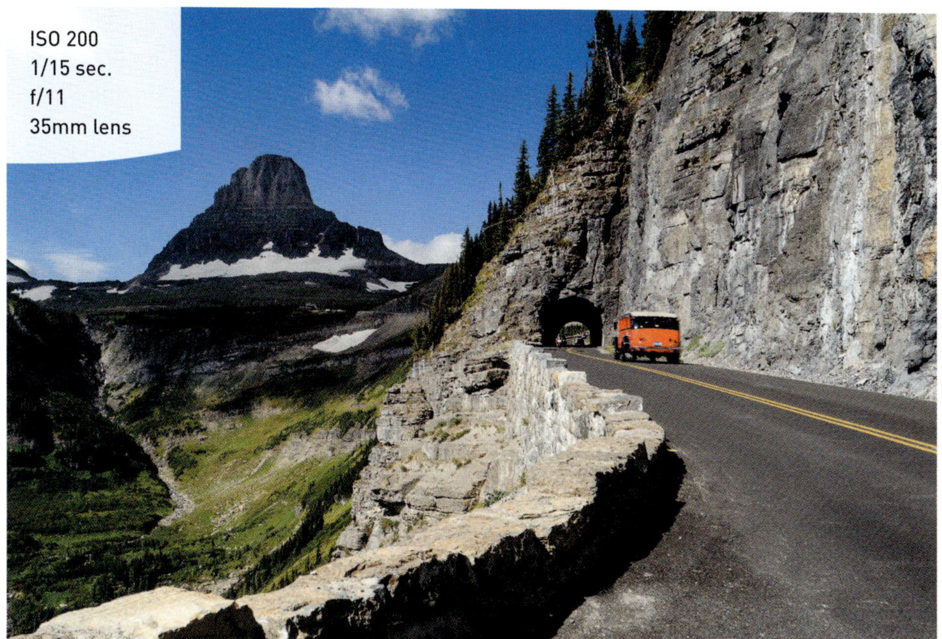

FIGURE 2.9
The slower shutter speed coupled with a neutral density filter shows the blurred motion of the bus moving up the road.

The aperture controls the amount of light that comes through the lens, but it also determines what areas of the image will be in focus. This is referred to as depth of field, and it is an extremely valuable creative tool. The smaller the opening (the larger the number, such as f/22), the greater the sharpness of objects from near to far (**Figure 2.10**). A large opening (or small number, like f/2.8) means more blurring of objects that are not at the same distance as the subject you are focusing on (**Figure 2.11**).

As we further explore the features of the camera, we will learn not only how to utilize the elements of exposure to capture properly exposed photographs, but also how we can make adjustments to emphasize our subject. It is the manipulation of these elements—motion and focus—that will take your images to the next level.

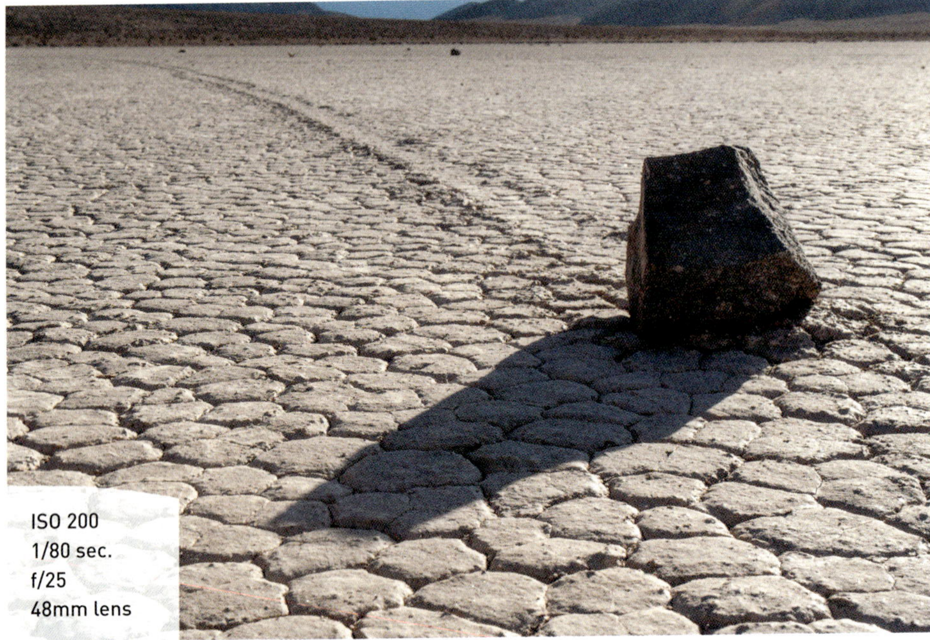

FIGURE 2.10 By using a small aperture, the area of sharp focus extends from a point that is near the camera all the way out to distant objects. In this photo, taken at "The Racetrack" in Death Valley, California, I wanted the rock closest to the camera to be in focus while maintaining good focus into the distance to show how far these mysterious rocks have traveled.

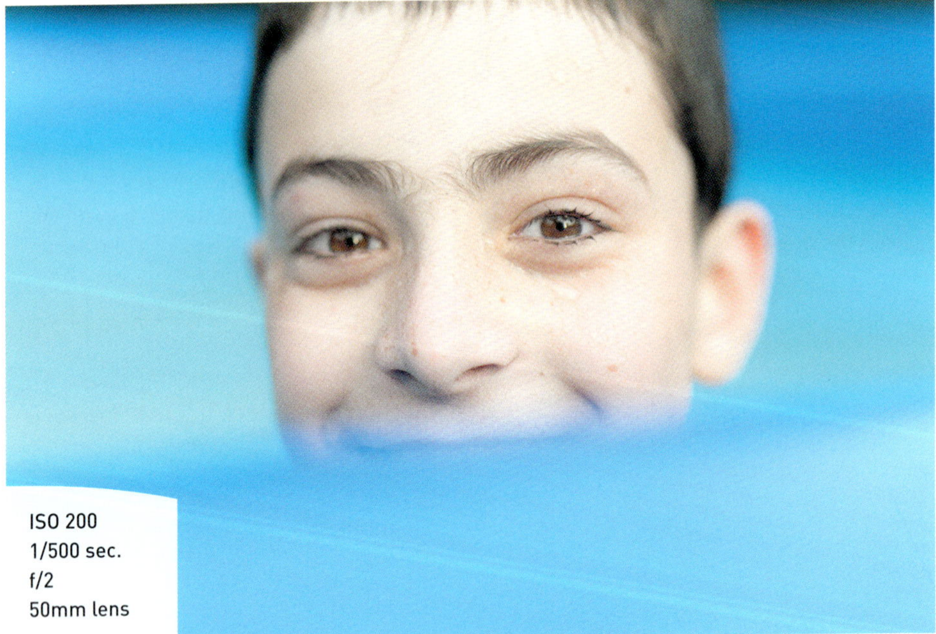

FIGURE 2.11 Isolating a subject is accomplished by using a large aperture, which produces a narrow area of sharp focus.

Chapter 2 Assignments

Formatting your card

Even if you have already begun using your camera, make sure you are familiar with formatting the Secure Digital card. If you haven't done so already, follow the directions given earlier in the chapter and format as prescribed (make sure you save any images that you may have already taken). Then perform the format function every time you have downloaded or saved your images or use a new card.

Checking your firmware version

Using the most up-to-date version of the camera firmware will ensure that your camera is functioning properly. Use the menu to find your current firmware version, and then update as necessary using the steps listed in this chapter.

Cleaning your sensor

You probably noticed the sensor-cleaning message the first time you turned your camera on. Make sure you are familiar with the "Clean now" command so you can perform this function every time you change a lens.

Exploring your image formats

I want you to become familiar with all of the camera features before using the RAW format, but take a little time to explore the format menu so you can see what options are available to you.

Exploring your lens

If you are using a zoom lens, spend a little time shooting with each focal length, from the widest to the longest. See just how much of an angle you can cover with your widest lens setting. How much magnification will you be able to get from the telephoto setting? Try shooting the same subject with a variety of focal lengths to note the differences in how the subject looks, as well as the relationship between the subject and the other elements in the photo.

Share your results with the book's Flickr group!

www.flickr.com/groups/d600fromsnapshotstogreatshots

3

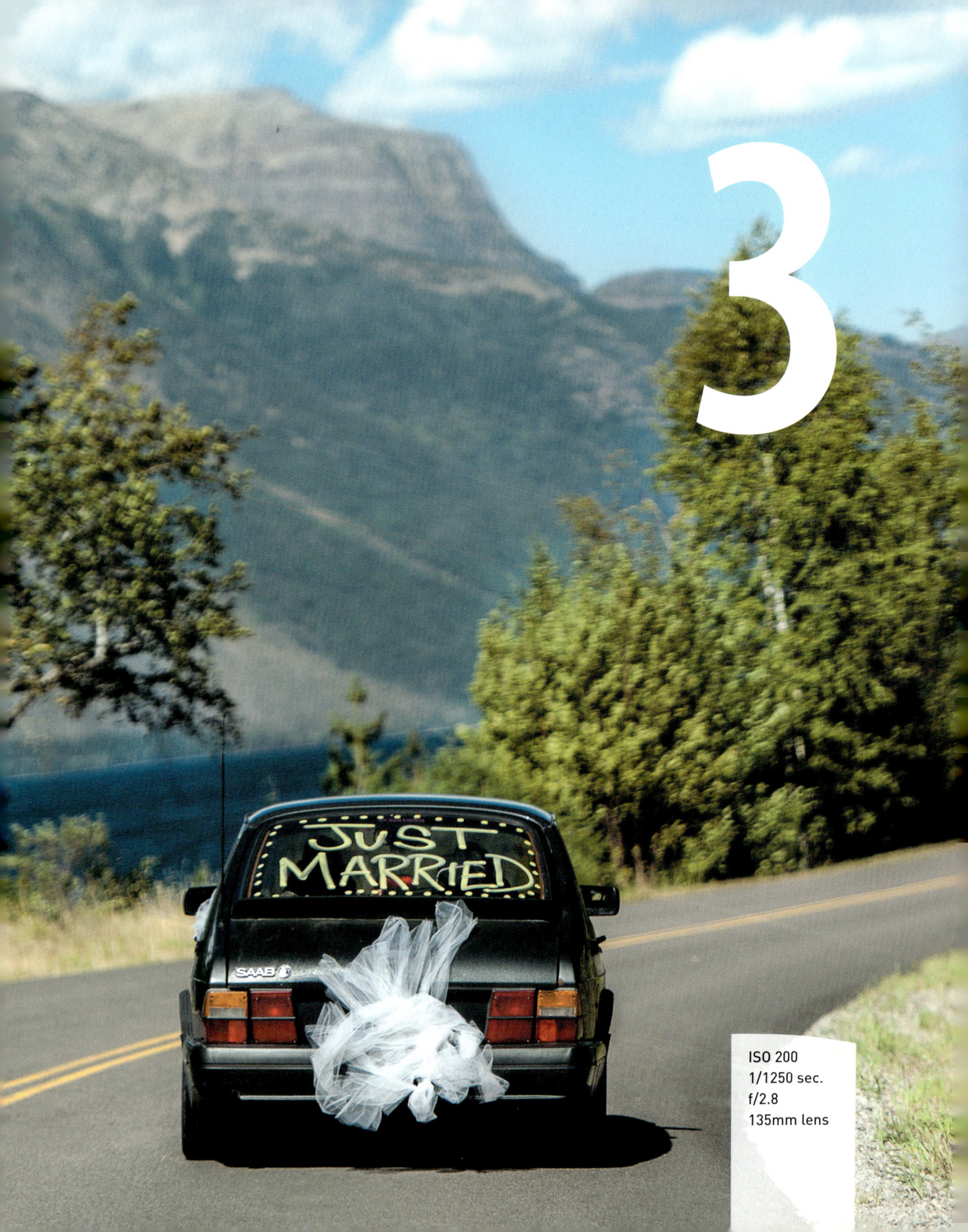

ISO 200
1/1250 sec.
f/2.8
135mm lens

The Auto Modes

GET SHOOTING WITH THE AUTOMATIC CAMERA MODES

Every digital photographer I know has taken photographs using what I call the green zone, or auto zone, and I'm not ashamed to admit that I still hang out there from time to time. The Nikon D600 has done an incredible job of simplifying some of the most complex camera settings and creating an excellent baseline for many shots. In this chapter, we're going to focus on how to use the built-in scene modes and on the advantages that even more experienced photographers can gain from using these presets. Let's take a look at the different modes and how and when to use them.

PORING OVER THE PICTURE

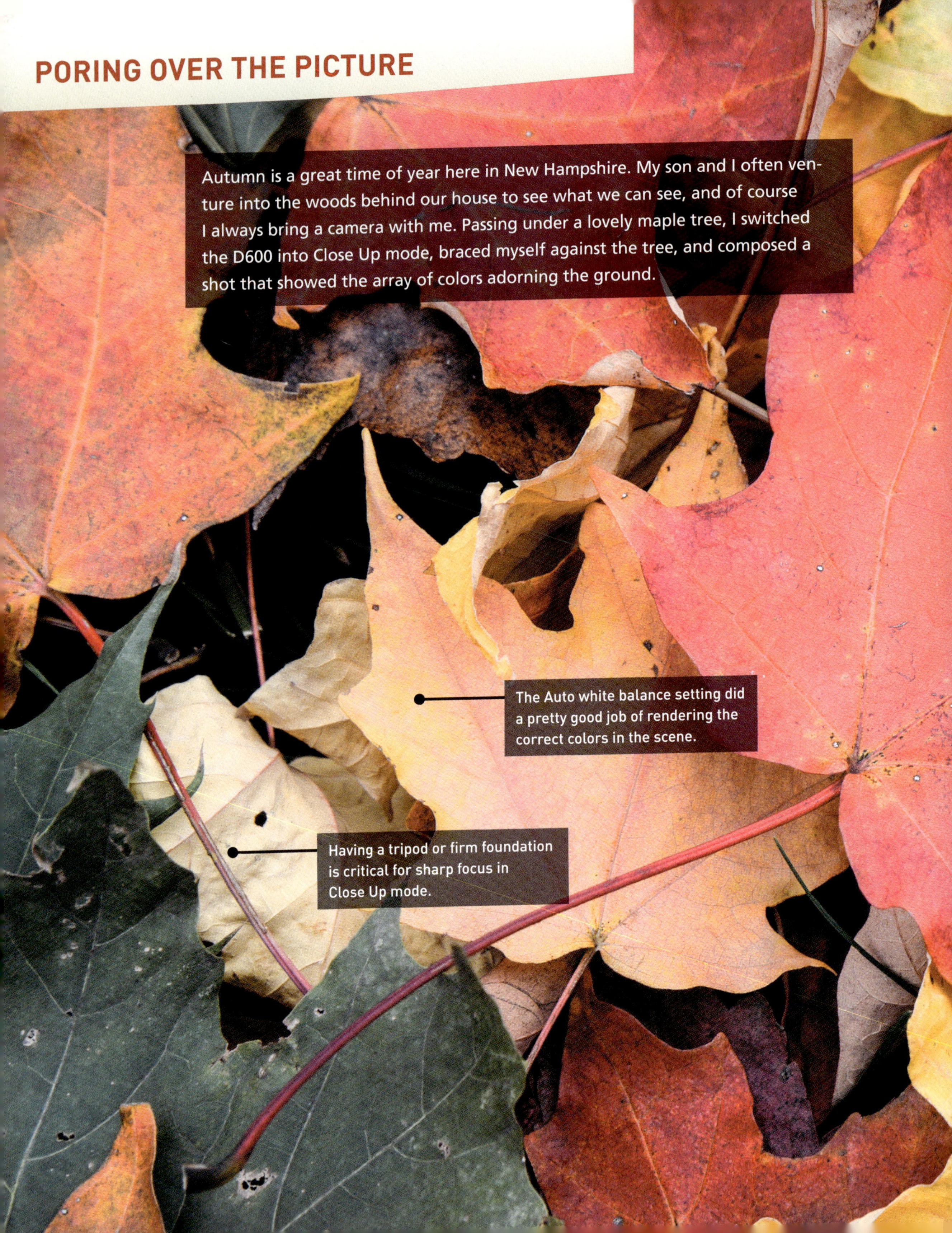

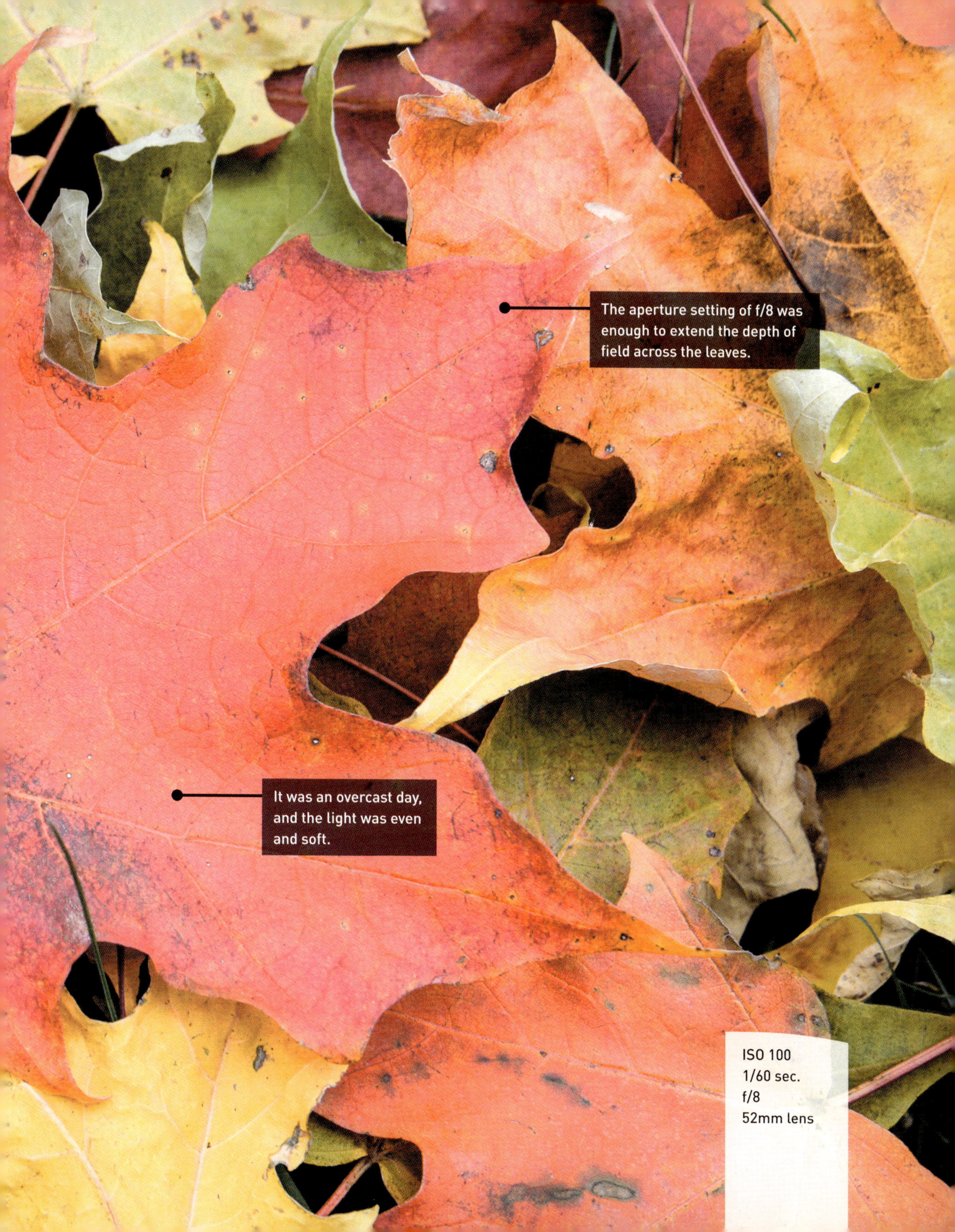
The aperture setting of f/8 was enough to extend the depth of field across the leaves.
It was an overcast day, and the light was even and soft.
ISO 100
1/60 sec.
f/8
52mm lens

AUTO MODE

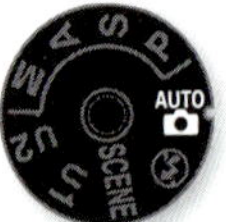

Auto mode is all about thought-free photography (**Figure 3.1**). There is little to nothing for you to do in this mode except point and shoot. Your biggest concern when using Auto mode is focusing. The camera will use the automatic focusing modes to achieve the best possible focus for your picture. Naturally, the camera is going to assume that the object that is closest to the camera is the one that you want in sharpest focus. Simply press the shutter button down halfway while looking through the viewfinder, and you should see one of the focus points light up over the subject. Of course, you know that putting your subject in the middle of the picture is not the best way to compose your shot. So wait for the chirp to confirm that the focus has been set, and then, while still holding down the button, recompose your shot. Now just press down the shutter button the rest of the way to take the photo. It's that easy. The camera will take care of all your exposure decisions, including when to use flash.

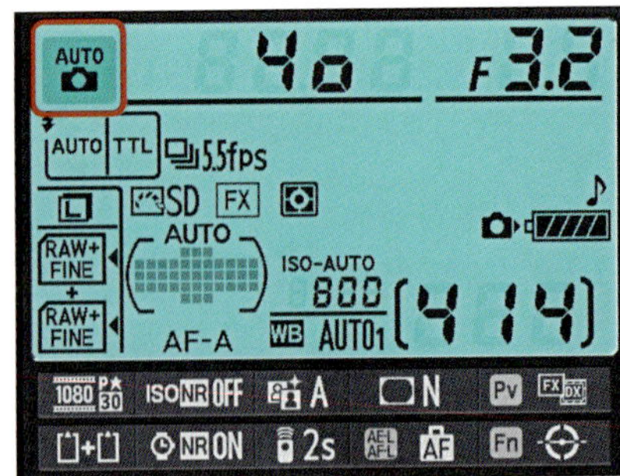

FIGURE 3.1
To shoot in Auto mode, all you need to do is move the Mode dial so that the green camera icon lines up with the white line. It's as simple as that!

If you're not sure of what setting to use—or if exposure, aperture, and speed are confusing—then start by using Auto mode. This mode can be an excellent learning tool. Take a photograph using Auto mode, and note the ISO, aperture, and speed the camera uses. This is a great way to become familiar with settings. Then as you become more familiar with the settings, you can begin to change them to better create your vision. I also find that Auto mode is useful when you want to hand your camera to someone else for a quick group shot (**Figure 3.2**) without having to fiddle with settings or talk them through how to use your camera.

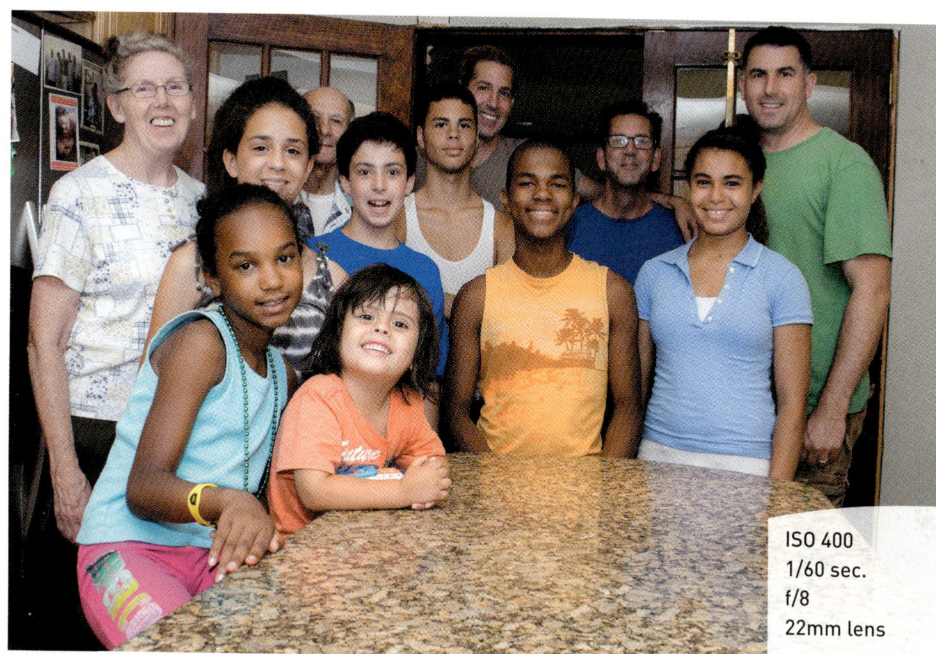

ISO 400
1/60 sec.
f/8
22mm lens

FIGURE 3.2
When you're trying to get an impromptu group photo together, there may not be time to set everything the way you want it, so just pop it in Auto and say "cheese."

FLASH OFF MODE

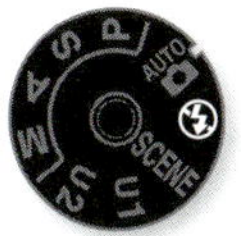

Sometimes you will be in a situation where the light levels are low but you don't want to use the flash. It could be that you are shooting in a place that restricts flash photography, such as a museum, or maybe you want to take advantage of the available light, as when shooting candles on a birthday cake. This is where Flash Off mode comes into play (**Figure 3.3**).

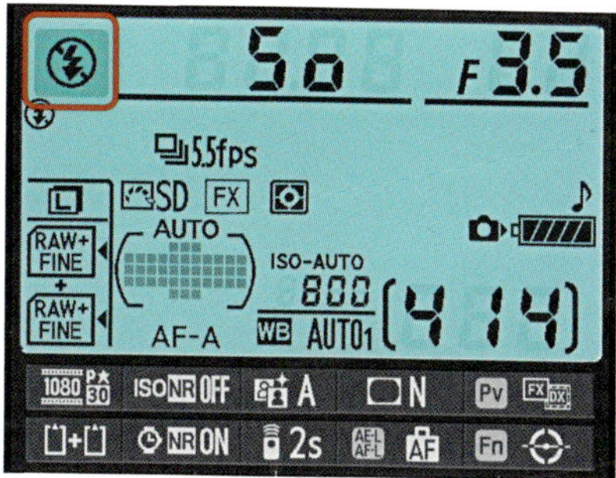

FIGURE 3.3
To shoot in Flash Off mode, turn the Mode dial to the Flash Off symbol. This will prevent your flash from firing.

By keeping the flash from firing, you will be able to use just the available ambient light while the camera automatically modifies the ISO setting to assist you in getting a good exposure (**Figure 3.4**). While most of the new Vibration Reduction (VR) lenses being sold today allow you to handhold the camera at much slower shutter speeds and still get good results, you'll want to keep an eye on the shutter speed and be prepared to use a tripod (or really brace yourself well) if the shutter speed drops below 1/60 of a second. The other downfalls to this mode are the Auto ISO setting (which will quickly take your ISO setting up high) and the possibility of getting blur from subject movement (due to slow shutter speeds).

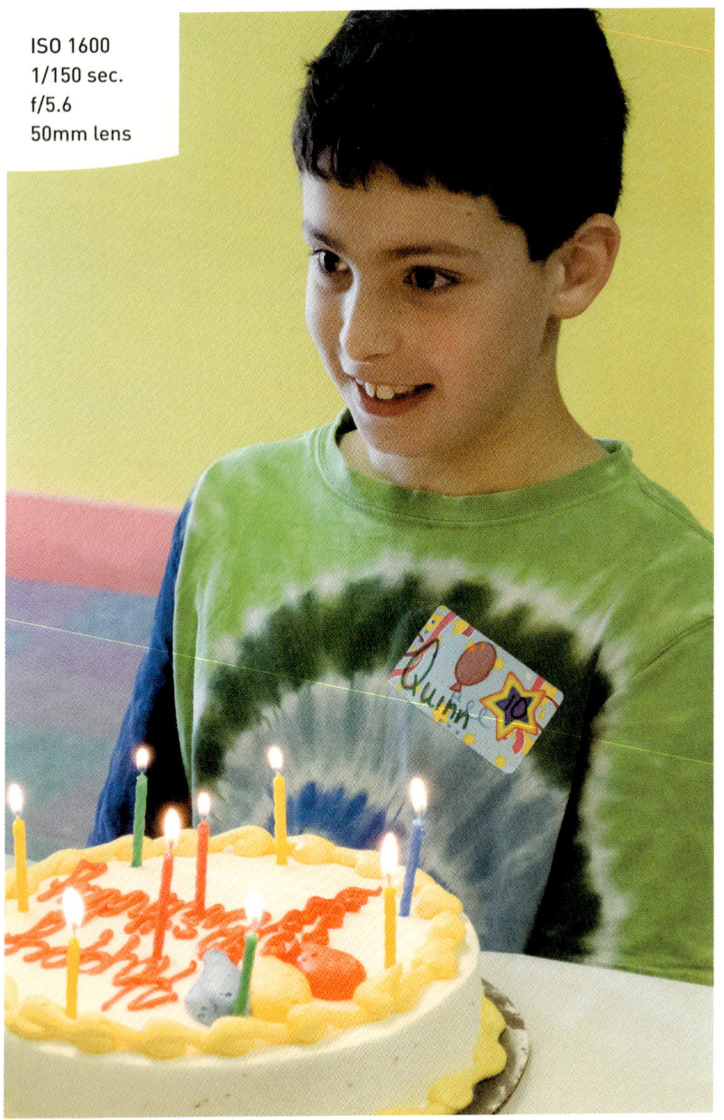

ISO 1600
1/150 sec.
f/5.6
50mm lens

FIGURE 3.4
I didn't want the flash to overpower the candles and what little light was coming in from the window on the side.

SCENE MODES

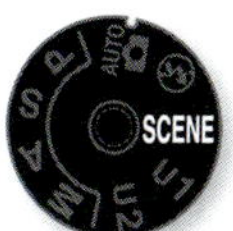

Most DSLR cameras have only seven or eight automatic modes at their disposal, but the D600 takes things to a whole new level, with 19 additional scene modes to choose from (**Figure 3.5**). Nikon has anticipated many of the typical shooting scenarios that you will encounter and created scene modes that are optimized for those situations. We're going to focus on a few of the most popular modes in detail, but first, here's how to find them.

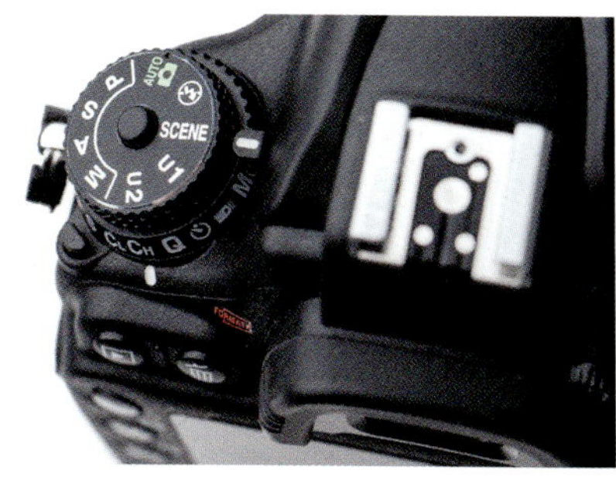

FIGURE 3.5
Remember that you have over 19 preset modes to choose from, so have fun and experiment a little.

USING THE SCENE MODES

1. Set the Mode dial to the Scene setting.
2. Press the Info button to turn on the information screen on the back of the camera.
3. Rotate the Command dial until the appropriate scene appears on the information screen.

PORTRAIT

Auto mode is accurate much of the time, but one of its problems is that it has no idea what type of subject you are photographing and therefore uses the same settings for each situation. Shooting portraits is a perfect example. When you take a photograph of someone, you typically want the emphasis to be on the person, not on the stuff going on in the background.

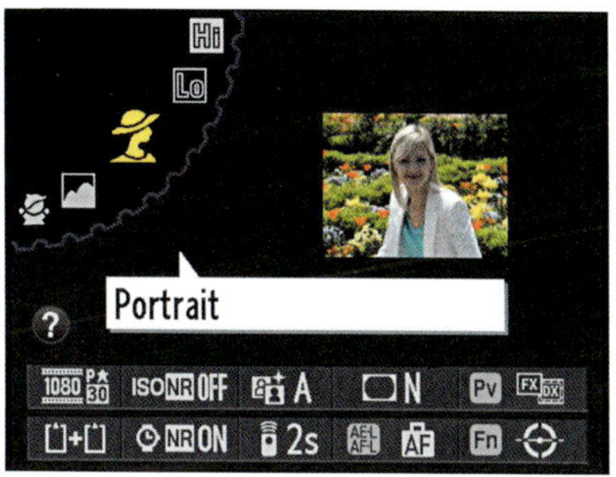

FIGURE 3.6
Portrait mode will create soft and natural-looking skin tones.

This is what Portrait mode is all about (**Figure 3.6**). When you set your camera to this mode, you are telling the camera to select a larger aperture so that the depth of field is much narrower and objects in the background are blurrier. This blurry background places the attention on your subject (**Figure 3.7**). The other feature of this mode is the automatic selection of the D600's built-in Portrait picture control (we'll go into more detail about picture controls in later chapters). This feature is optimized for skin tones and will also be a little softer to improve the look of skin.

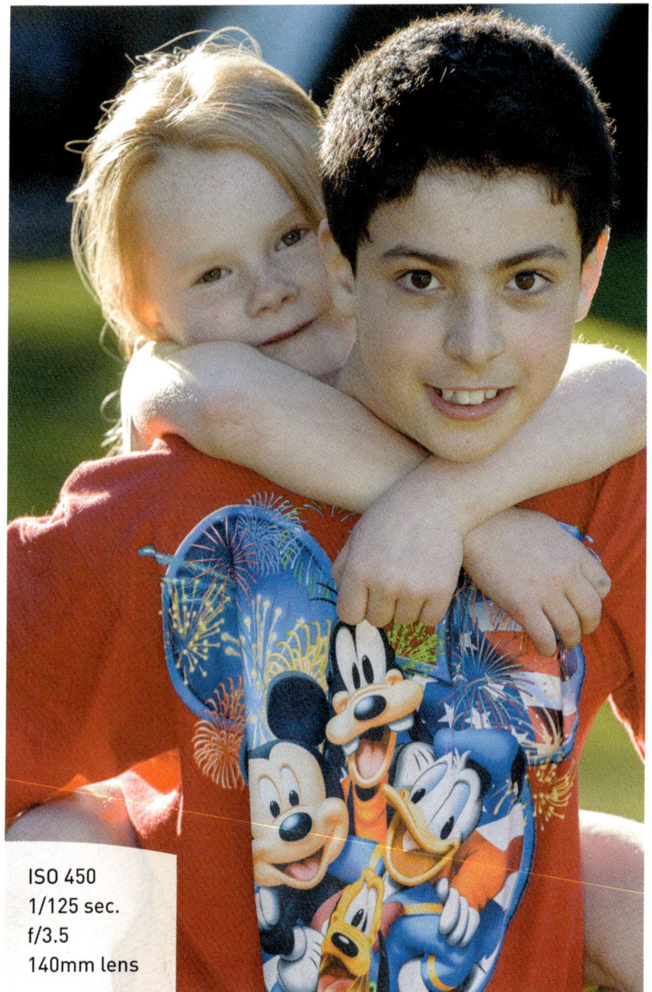

ISO 450
1/125 sec.
f/3.5
140mm lens

FIGURE 3.7
Portrait mode is a great choice for subjects like this. Not only does it pick a good aperture, but it also uses the picture control that works best for people.

USING THE BEST LENS FOR GREAT PORTRAITS

When you're using Portrait mode, use a lens that is 70mm or longer. The longer lens will give you a natural view of the subject, as well as aid in keeping the depth of field narrow.

LANDSCAPE

As you might have guessed, Landscape mode has been optimized for shooting landscape images (**Figure 3.8**). Particular emphasis is placed on the picture control, with the camera trying to boost the greens and blues in the image (**Figure 3.9**). This makes sense, since the typical landscape would be outdoors, where grass, trees, and skies should look more colorful. This picture control also boosts the sharpness that is applied during processing. The camera uses the lowest ISO settings possible in order to keep digital noise to a minimum.

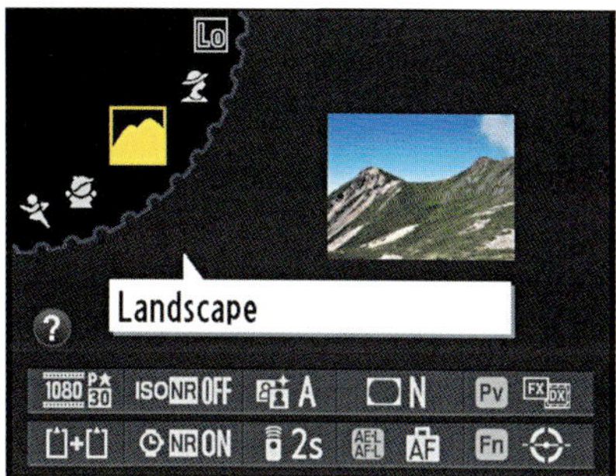

FIGURE 3.8
Landscape mode will increase color saturation and turn the AF-assist illuminator off.

The downfall to this setting is that, once again, there is less control over the camera settings; for example, exposure compensation is not allowed. However, you can change the Focus Mode, Image Quality, ISO, and AF-area mode settings. Note that the flash cannot be used in Landscape mode.

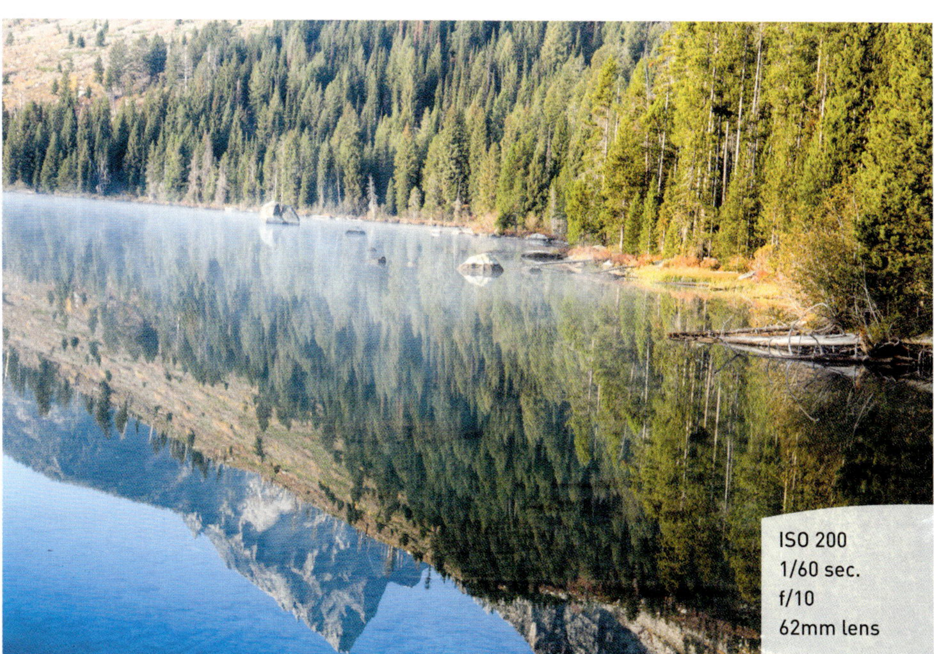

FIGURE 3.9
A low ISO was used to reduce digital noise, and the reflected blue skies and green trees benefited from the increased saturation.

CHILD

Photographing children can be tough. Those little stinkers are fast, and if you've ever tried to photograph a two-year-old, you know the challenge of getting him or her to sit still. Child mode tries to solve this problem by blending the Sports and Portrait modes (**Figures 3.10** and **3.11**). Since children are seldom still, the camera will try to use a slightly faster shutter speed to freeze any movement. The picture control has also been optimized to render the bright, vivid colors that one normally associates with pictures of children. It's a great mode to use for those kids on the go or to capture a very brief moment that you don't want to miss.

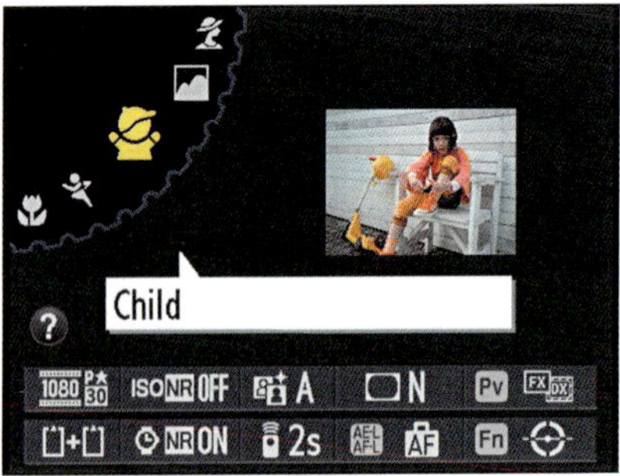

FIGURE 3.10
Child mode is best for snapshots of children on the go.

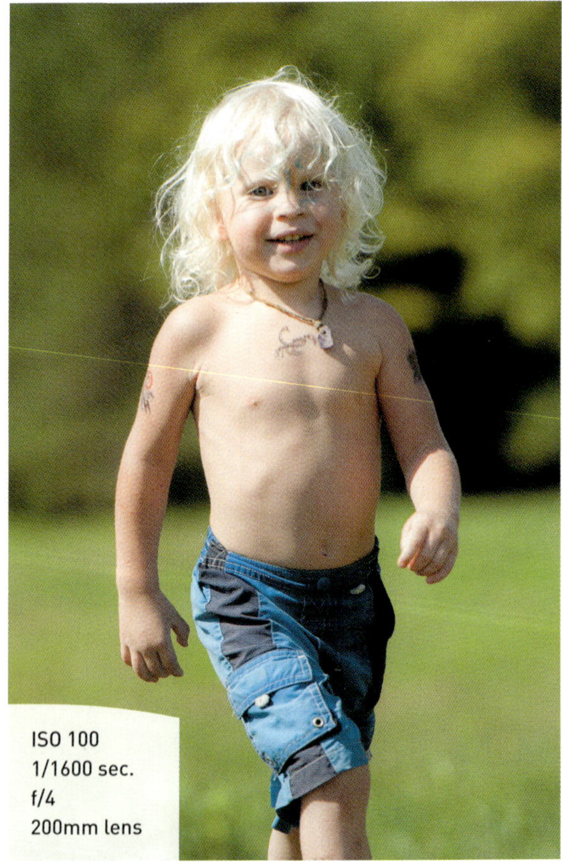

FIGURE 3.11
Child mode tries to use a fast shutter speed and make colors brighter and more vivid.

SPORTS

Although this is called Sports mode, you can use it for any moving subject (**Figure 3.12**). The mode is built on the principles of sports photography: continuous focusing, large apertures, and fast shutter speeds (**Figure 3.13**). To handle these requirements, the camera sets the focus mode to AF-A, the AF-Area mode to Dynamic, the aperture to a very large opening, and the ISO to Auto. Overall, these are sound settings that will capture most moving subjects well. We will take an in-depth look at all of these features, like Continuous drive mode, in Chapter 5.

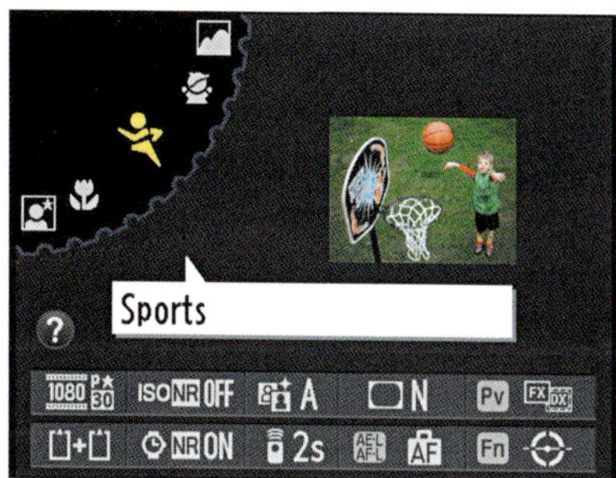

FIGURE 3.12
Sports mode is best used when you want to freeze motion. When the camera is in this mode, the built-in flash and AF-assist illuminator are turned off.

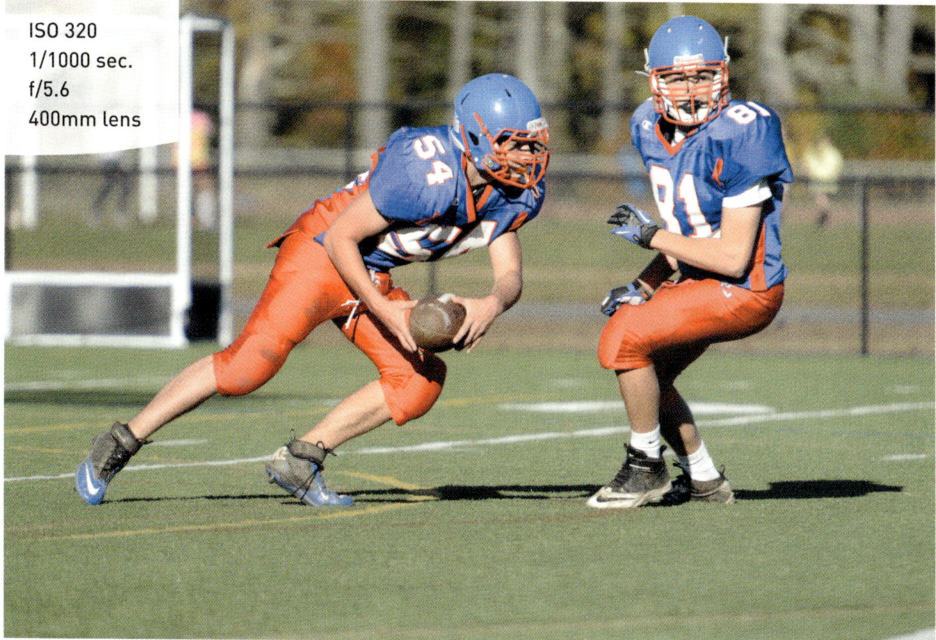

FIGURE 3.13
This is the type of shot that was made for Sports mode, where action-freezing shutter speeds and continuous focusing capture the moment.

You can, however, run the risk of too much digital noise in your picture if the camera decides that you need a very high ISO. This is why you have the ability to change some options within Sports mode, such as the ISO and the release mode (single and continuous). When using Sports mode, you can also change the focus mode to Manual, which is especially handy if you know when and where the action will take place and want to pre-focus the camera on a spot and wait for the right moment to take the photo.

CLOSE UP

Although most zoom lenses don't support true "macro" settings, that doesn't mean you can't shoot some great close-up photos. The key is to use your camera-to-subject distance to fill the frame and still achieve sharp focus. This means that you move yourself as close as possible to your subject while still being able to get a good, sharp focus. Often, your lens will be marked with the minimum focusing distance. On my 24-85mm zoom, it is about a foot with the lens set to 85mm. To help get the best focus in the picture, Close Up mode will use the smallest aperture it can while keeping the shutter speed fast enough to get a sharp shot (**Figures 3.14** and **3.15**). It does this by raising the ISO or turning on the built-in flash—or a combination of the two.

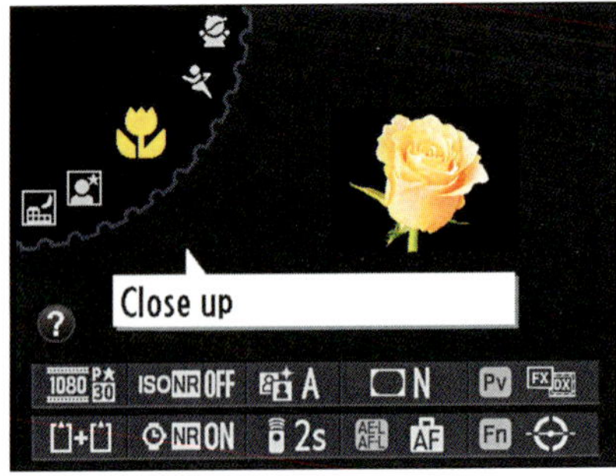

FIGURE 3.14
Close Up mode is best used for flowers, small objects, and insects. If you're into macro photography, then this is the mode to use.

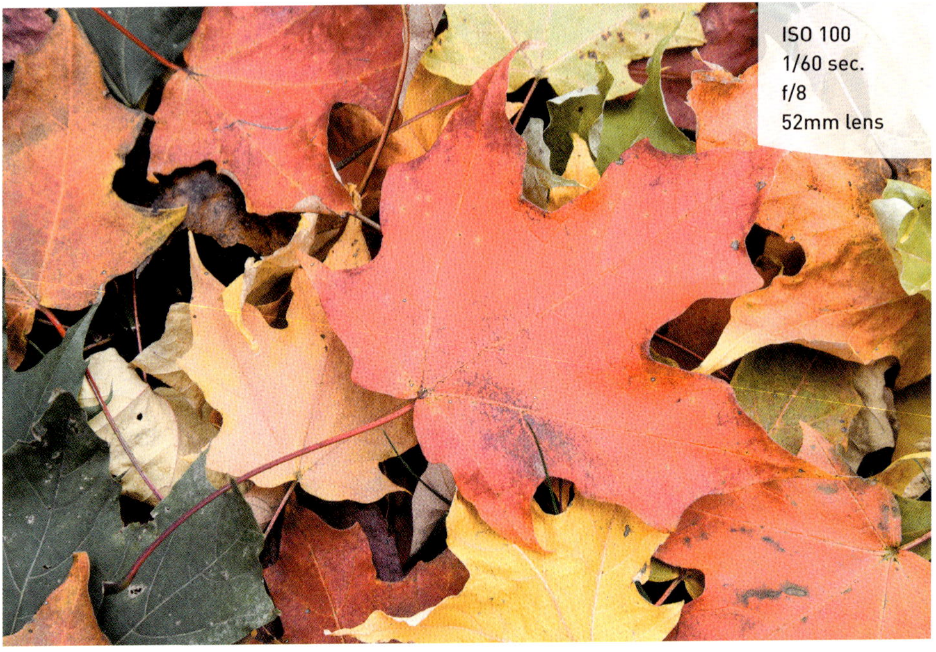

FIGURE 3.15
Close Up mode provided the proper exposure to capture the smallest of details.

Fortunately, there are several other settings that you can change in this mode. The flash will be set to Auto by default, but you can also change it to Auto-Redeye or Off, depending on your needs. The ISO can be changed from the Auto setting to one of your own choosing. This probably only needs to be done in low-light settings when Auto ISO starts to move up to maintain exposure values. Other settings that can be changed are image quality, release mode, focus mode, and AF-area mode.

NIGHT PORTRAIT

You're out on the town at night and you want to take a nice picture of someone, but you want to show some of the interesting scenery in the background as well. You could use Auto mode, which would probably turn on the flash and take the photo. The problem is that, while it would give you a decent exposure for your subject, the background would be completely dark. The solution is to use Night Portrait mode (**Figure 3.16**). When you set the dial to this mode, you are telling the camera that you want to use a slower-than-normal shutter speed so that the background is getting more time (and thus more light) to achieve a proper exposure.

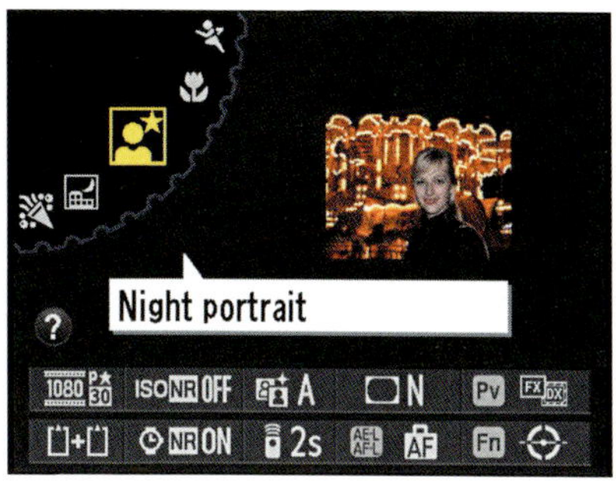

FIGURE 3.16
Night Portrait mode's info screen.

The typical shutter speed for using flash is about 1/60 of a second or faster (but not faster than 1/200 of a second). By leaving the shutter open longer, the camera allows more of the background to be exposed so that you get a much more balanced scene (**Figure 3.17**). This is also a great mode for taking portraits during sunset. Once again, the camera uses an automatic ISO setting by default, so you will want to keep an eye on it to make sure the setting isn't so high that the noise levels ruin your photo.

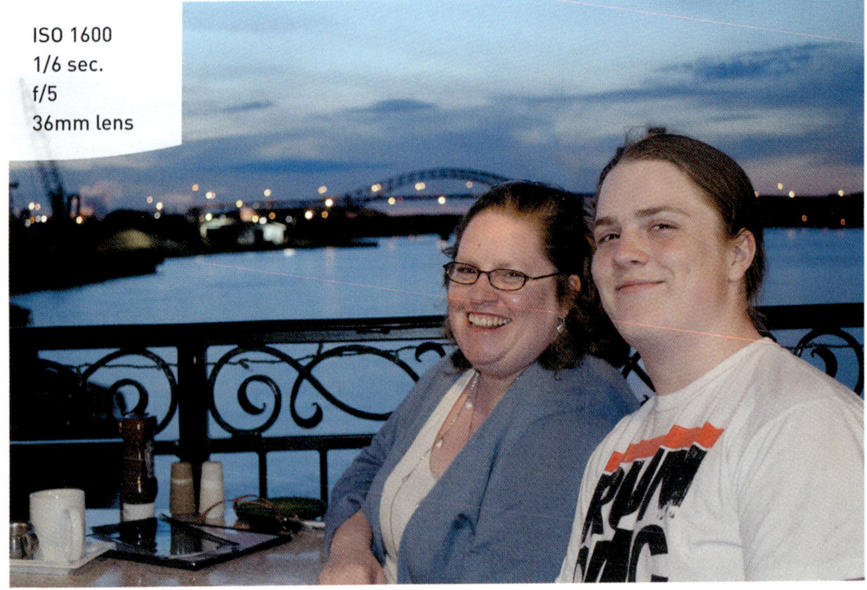

FIGURE 3.17
Night Portrait uses a slower shutter speed, higher ISO, and larger aperture to balance the background lights with the flash exposure.

OTHER SCENE MODES TO EXPLORE

While the scene modes in the previous section tend to be the ones used most, there are quite a few others you might want to investigate. Just keep rotating the Mode dial to switch between them.

NIGHT LANDSCAPE

A tripod or stable shooting surface is definitely recommended for Night Landscape mode (**Figure 3.18**). By using low ISOs, longer shutter speeds, and noise reduction, you can capture great cityscapes with more accurate colors. The flash and focus-assist functions are turned off for this mode, so focusing might be a little difficult. If so, try moving your focus point.

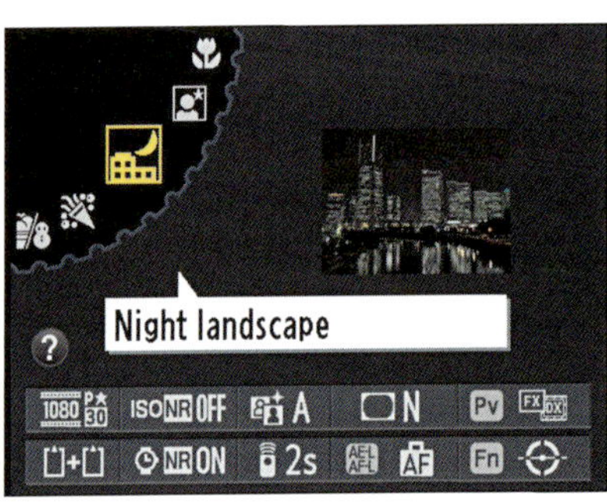

FIGURE 3.18
Night Landscape mode helps reduce noise and unnatural colors. This mode is great for capturing a city skyline at night. Because it uses slow shutter speeds, a tripod is recommended so that the lights don't get blurred.

PARTY/INDOOR

This mode is very much like Night Portrait mode except it is optimized for indoor use (**Figure 3.19**). The flash is automatically set to Auto-Redeye and will use the red-eye reduction lamp to help eliminate the red-eye that often occurs when using a flash indoors.

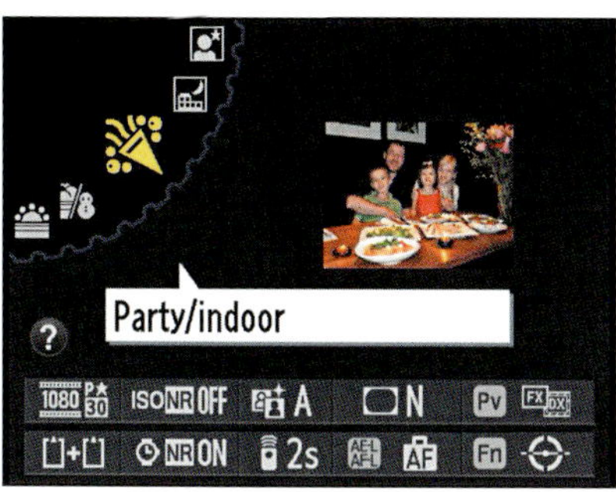

FIGURE 3.19
Party/Indoor mode is great when you want to capture a special moment at a birthday party or wedding.

BEACH/SNOW

Shooting in a bright environment like the beach or a ski resort can have a bad effect on your images. The problem is that beaches and snow often reflect a lot of light and can fool the camera's light meter into underexposing. This means that the snow would come out looking darker than it should. To solve this problem, you can use Beach/Snow mode (**Figure 3.20**), which will overexpose slightly, giving you much more accurate tones.

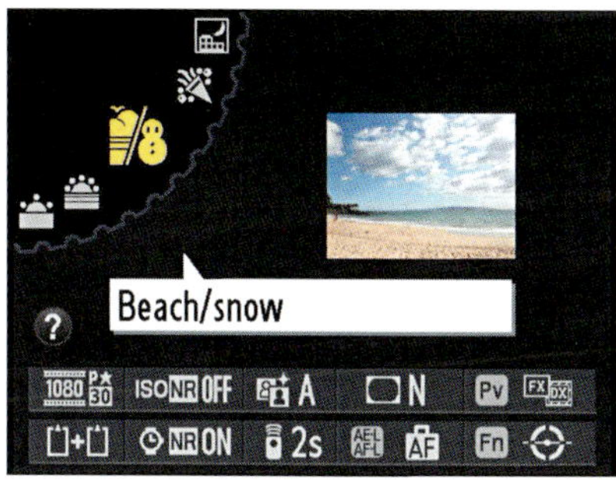

FIGURE 3.20
Beach/Snow mode helps you capture vacations by the water or in winter, when the brightness of the sand or snow would otherwise trick the camera into underexposing. The built-in flash and AF-assist illuminator are turned off in this mode.

SUNSET

Sunset mode is a great way to capture a beautiful scene at dusk. This setting will increase the saturation and optimize the colors in a sunset. What I love about this setting is that most sunsets are fairly predictable, so an automatic mode works great (**Figure 3.21**). If you are on vacation or just want to enjoy the moment, the last thing you need to worry about is fumbling around with camera settings. Just move the dial to Sunset mode, sit back, relax, and let your camera do the work. One word of advice—this mode will use a longer exposure, so to avoid blurry photos, use a tripod or steady your camera on a solid, level surface. You do have the option to change your ISO in this mode, so if you're unable to steady your camera on a tripod or solid surface, I recommend increasing your ISO so that your speed is equal to or greater than the focal length of your lens. By doing this, you reduce your chances of camera shake (blurry photos).

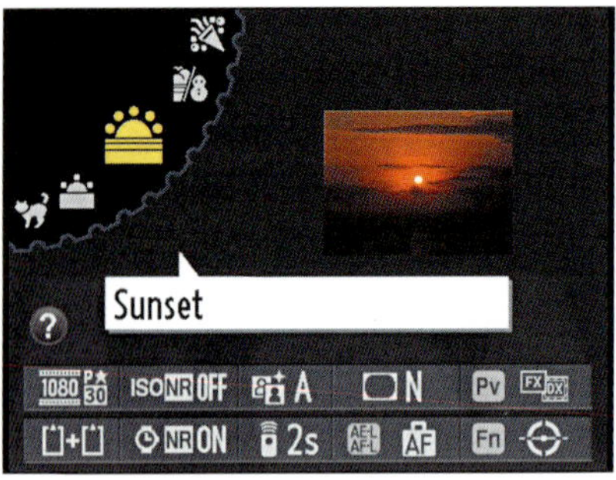

FIGURE 3.21
Sunset mode creates deeper hues during sunset and sunrise. A tripod is recommended with this mode.

DUSK/DAWN

There are some great photo opportunities that take place before the sun rises and after it sets. The only problem is that the typical camera settings don't truly capture the vibrancy of the colors. The Dusk/Dawn setting is optimized for low-light photography and helps boost colors and eliminate noise from longer exposures (**Figure 3.22**).

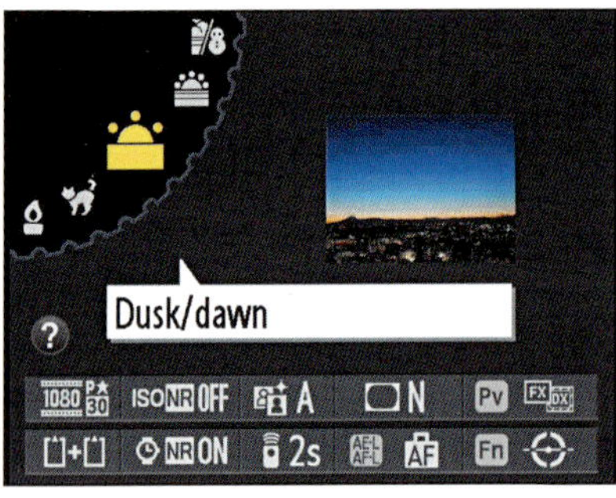

FIGURE 3.22
Dusk/Dawn mode maintains the muted colors of early morning and evening. The flash and AF-assist illuminator are off in this mode. A tripod is recommended with this mode because of its potentially longer shutter speeds.

PET PORTRAIT

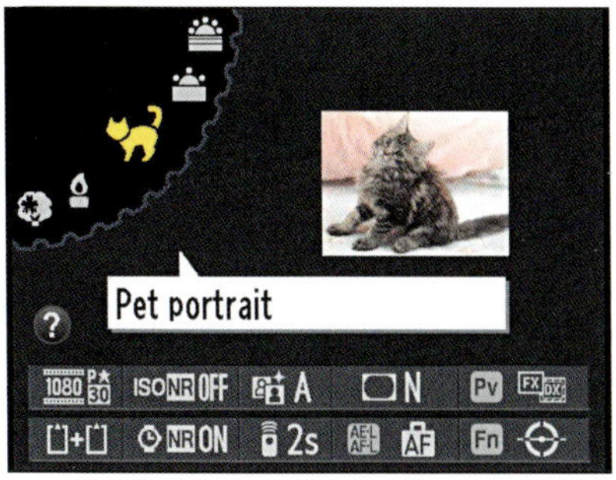

This mode is similar to the Portrait mode in that it uses larger apertures and faster shutter speeds (**Figure 3.23**). The difference is that Portrait mode is optimized for human skin, with adjustments to the hues and color values. Pets don't normally have any skin showing, so the sharpness and hues are adjusted accordingly.

FIGURE 3.23
Pet Portrait mode works well when you are photographing a pet and don't want to scare it off with the AF-assist illuminator.

CANDLELIGHT

Sometimes it's pretty easy to know when to use a particular mode. This mode is similar to Flash Off mode, but it is tweaked for the color of candlelight and will give you much more pleasing results (**Figure 3.24**). If you are photographing people in candlelight, try using a tripod and have them hold fairly still to reduce image blur.

BLOSSOM

This mode is very similar to the Landscape setting but with a few slight adjustments. The color settings for Blossom have been optimized for use outdoors where there are many flowers in full bloom (**Figure 3.25**).

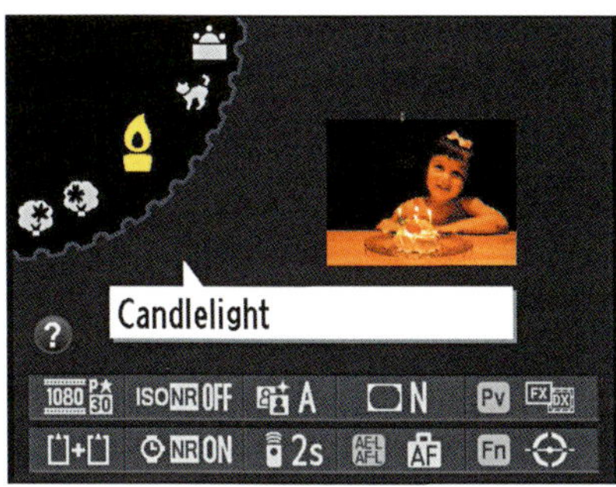

FIGURE 3.24
Candlelight mode helps in low-light conditions. The built-in flash is disabled, and a tripod is recommended.

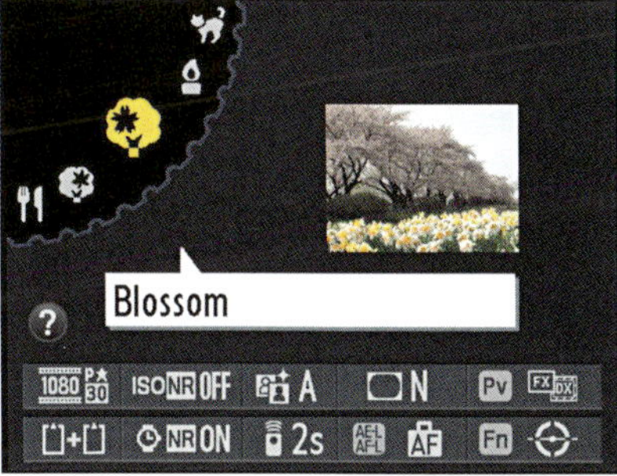

FIGURE 3.25
Blossom mode is best used when photographing a field of flowers. A tripod is recommended to avoid blur, and flash is unavailable.

AUTUMN COLORS

If you live in an area that has great fall color (like I do), you will want to give this mode a try (**Figure 3.26**). The big advantage to this scene mode is that it is optimized for the red and yellow hues that are present in autumn, and it really makes them pop. It also turns off the flash, since the light from a flash can wash out the color in the leaves. Try using this mode when the leaves have turned and the skies are overcast. You will get some amazing color in your images.

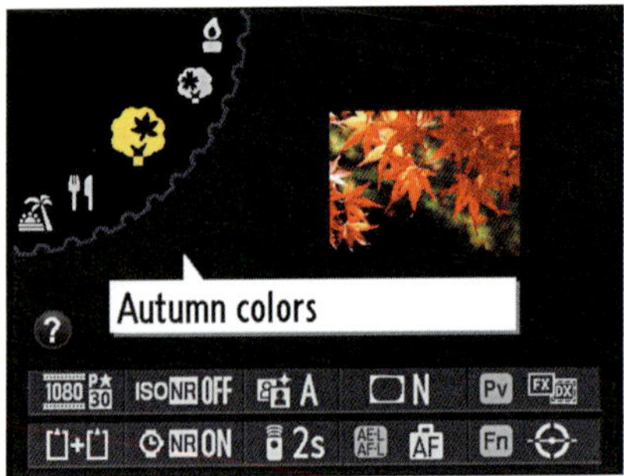

FIGURE 3.26
Autumn Colors mode creates bright yellows and reds in autumn leaves. A tripod is recommended; flash is unavailable in this mode.

FOOD

Food photography is very popular of late, and Nikon has provided you with a scene mode that is perfect for this type of work (**Figure 3.27**). When you select this mode, the camera will use large apertures for fairly narrow depth of field, slightly overexposed settings to keep things bright, and a picture control that makes colors slightly more vivid.

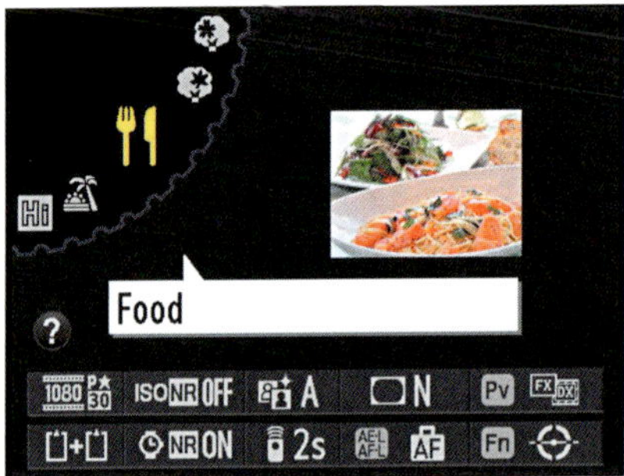

FIGURE 3.27
Food mode creates vivid colors. A tripod is advised with this mode; you will have use of the flash if needed.

SILHOUETTE

Silhouette mode (**Figure 3.28**) does things like adjust the exposure for the brightest area of the scene as well as turn off the Active D-Lighting feature (see Chapter 9 for more on Active D-Lighting). This is necessary, since Active D-Lighting tries to boost exposure in shadow areas, which is the opposite of the effect you want when trying to get a nice silhouette.

HIGH KEY

Images that are bright throughout can present a challenge, with the bright environment tending to fool the camera into making an image that is darker than desired. Using the High Key setting (**Figure 3.29**) forces the camera to overexpose a little and really lighten up those bright objects in your image.

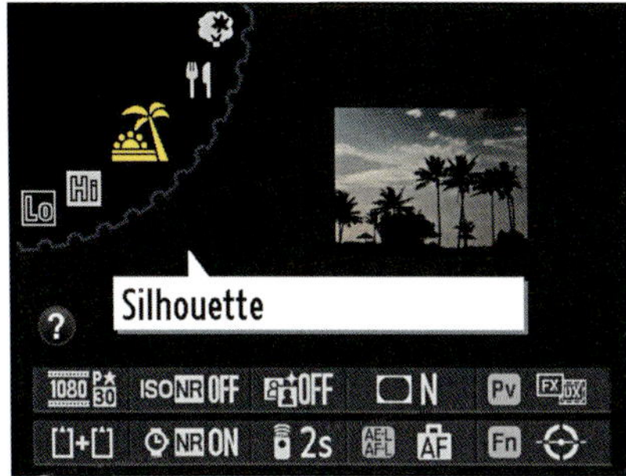

FIGURE 3.28
Silhouette mode creates a silhouette of the subject against brighter backgrounds. A tripod is recommended for this mode.

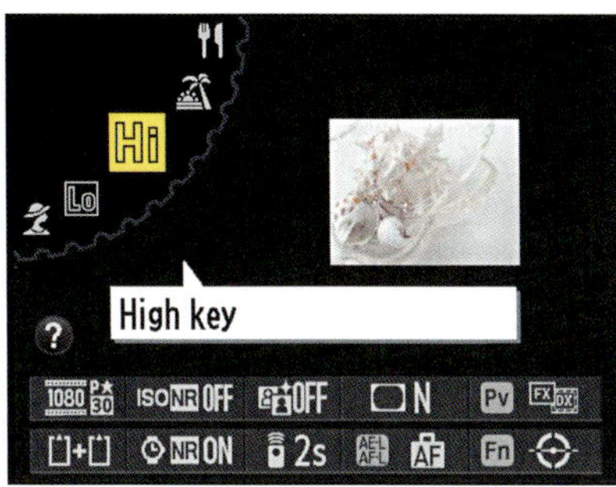

FIGURE 3.29
High Key mode creates very light and bright images; the flash is turned off in this mode.

LOW KEY

Low-key photos are typically meant to have an overall dark look. But when you're shooting a low-key scene, your camera's light meter will usually try to make everything brighter by adding some exposure (much like the beach/snow scenario in reverse). If you want to keep things on the dark side, use Low Key mode (**Figure 3.30**), which will keep the flash turned off and underexpose things just a little bit.

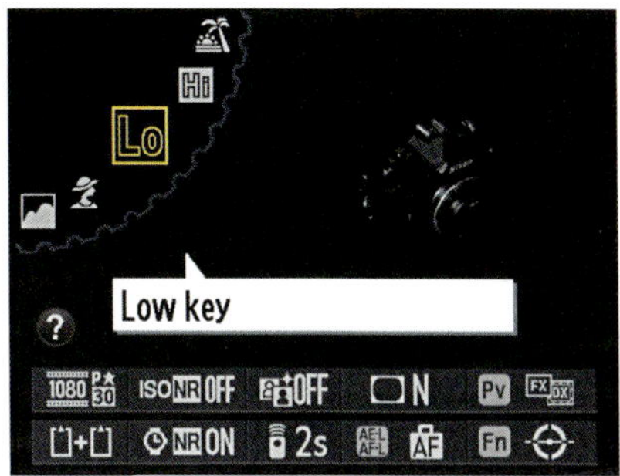

FIGURE 3.30
Low Key mode is best for times when you want to create a dark or subdued image. It will turn off the flash and is best used with a tripod.

WHEN YOU MIGHT NOT WANT TO USE AUTO MODE

With so many easy-to-use camera modes, why would anyone ever want to use anything else? Well, the first thing that comes to my mind is control. It is the number one benefit of using a DSLR camera. The ability to control every aspect of your photography will open up creative avenues that just aren't available in the automatic scene modes. Let's face it: there is a reason the Mode dial is split into two categories. Let's look at what we are giving up when we work in the scene modes.

- **White balance.** There is no choice available for white balance; you are simply stuck with the Auto setting. This isn't necessarily a bad thing, but your camera doesn't always get it right. And in the scene modes, there is just no way to change it.
- **Picture control.** All of the automatic modes have specifically tuned picture controls. Some of them use the control presets, such as Landscape or Vivid, but there is no way to change the characteristics of the controls while in the auto modes.
- **Metering.** All of the auto scene modes use the Matrix metering mode to establish the proper exposure. This is generally not a downside, but there are specific scenarios that would benefit from a center or spot metering solution, which we will cover in later chapters.
- **Exposure compensation.** You will notice that in each and every automatic scene mode, the ability to adjust the exposure through the use of the exposure compensation feature has been completely turned off. This makes it very difficult to make the slight adjustments to exposure that are often needed.
- **Active D-Lighting.** This is another feature that is unavailable for changing in the auto modes. There are default settings for this feature that change from scene to scene, but there is no way for you to override the effect.
- **Flash compensation.** Just like exposure compensation, there is no way to make any adjustments to the power output of the flash. This means that you are stuck with whatever the camera feels is correct, even if it is too weak or too strong for your particular subject.
- **Exposure bracketing.** One way to make sure that you have at least one good exposure is to use the bracketing feature of the camera, which takes images at varying exposures so you can get just the right look for your image. Unfortunately, this feature is unavailable when using the scene modes.

Another thing you will find when using any of the automatic scene modes is that there are fewer choices in the camera menus for you to adjust. Each scene mode presents its own set of restrictions for the available menu items. These aren't the only restrictions to using the automatic scene modes, but they should be enough to make you want to explore the options on the other side of the Mode dial, which I like to call the professional modes.

LIVE VIEW

Live View is the feature on your D600 that allows you to see a real-time view of what the camera is looking at via the rear LCD display. Using Live View can be helpful when you want to see or shoot from an angle that doesn't let you put your eye up to the viewfinder. It is also an excellent way of previewing any changes to the white balance or picture style, because their effects will be visible on the screen. You'll find more on Live View in Chapters 6 and 7.

FOCUS MODES ON THE NIKON D600

Three focus modes are available on the D600. You can easily select the mode that will be most beneficial for the type of photography you are doing. The standard mode is called AF-S, which allows you to focus on one spot and hold the focus until you take the picture or release the shutter button. The AF-C mode will constantly refocus the camera on your subject the entire time you are depressing the shutter release button; this is great for sports and action photography. The AF-A mode is a combination of both of the previous modes, using AF-S mode unless it senses that the subject is moving, when it will switch to AF-C mode.

Chapter 3 Assignments

These assignments have you shooting in the various automatic scene modes so that you can experience the advantages and disadvantages of using them in your daily photography.

Shooting in Auto mode

It's time to give up complete control and just concentrate on what you see in the viewfinder. Set your camera to Auto and practice shooting in a variety of conditions, both indoors and outside. Take notice of the camera settings when you are reviewing your pictures. Try using the AF-S focus point to pick a spot to focus on, and then recompose before taking the picture.

Checking out Portrait mode

Grab your favorite photogenic person and start shooting in Portrait mode. Try switching between Auto and Portrait mode while photographing the same person in the same setting. You should see a difference in the sharpness of the background and the skin tones. If you are using a zoom lens, set it to about 55mm if available.

Capturing the scenery with Landscape and Close Up modes

Take your camera outside for some landscape and macro work. First, find a nice scene, and then with your widest available lens, take some pictures using Landscape mode. Then switch back to Auto so you can compare the settings used for each image, as well as the changes to colors and sharpness. Now while you are still outside, find something in the foreground—a leaf or a flower—and switch the camera to Close Up mode. See how close you can get, and take note of the f-stop that the mode uses. Then switch to Auto and shoot the same subject.

Stopping the action with Sports mode

This assignment requires you to find a subject that is in motion. That could be the traffic in front of your home or your child at play; the only real requirement is that the subject be moving. This will be your opportunity to test out Sports mode. There isn't a lot to worry about here—just point and shoot. Try shooting a few frames one at a time, and then go ahead and hold down the shutter button and shoot a burst of five or six frames. It will help if your subject is in good available light to start with so that the camera won't be forced to use high ISOs.

Let your camera do the mentoring

How many times have you wondered what settings you should use for a particular shot? If you're in doubt, place your camera on the auto settings and take note of what your camera thinks is the best ISO, aperture, and speed. Your camera won't always be right, but it's going to give you a great baseline. Then adjust one element at a time and retake the shot to see what happens. This will help you understand how each setting affects the shot.

Share your results with the book's Flickr group!

www.flickr.com/groups/d600fromsnapshotstogreatshots

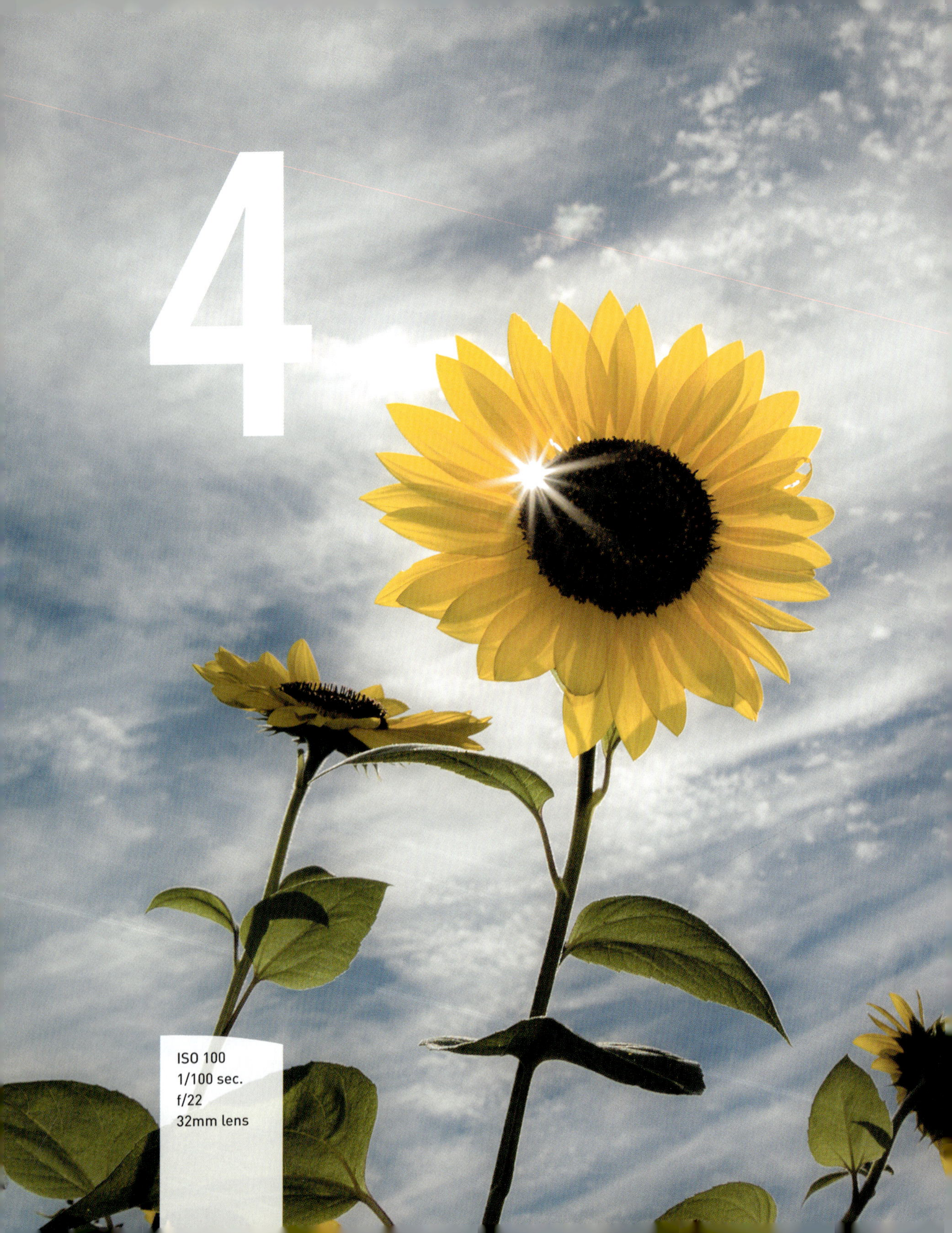

4

ISO 100
1/100 sec.
f/22
32mm lens

The Professional Modes

TAKING YOUR PHOTOGRAPHY TO THE NEXT LEVEL

Most professional photographers use a few select modes that offer the greatest control over their photography. Anyone who has been involved with photography for any period of time knows that these modes are the backbones of photography. They allow you to influence two of the most important factors in taking great photographs—namely, *aperture* and *shutter speed*. To access these modes, you simply hold the Mode button, turn the Main Command dial to one of the letter-designated modes, and begin shooting. But wouldn't it be nice to know exactly what those modes control and how to make them do our bidding? Well, if you really want to take that next step in controlling your photography, it is essential that you understand not only how to control these modes, but why you are controlling them. So let's switch over to the first of our professional modes: Program.

PORING OVER THE PICTURE

This photo—of one of the barns on Mormon Row in Grand Teton National Park—is the very last photo I took on a recent workshop with the Digital Photo Workshops before packing up the gear and heading home. The sun had set behind the mountains, but the full moon had risen and was shining bright. I used the Bulb setting to make this 2-minute exposure and was pleased to have the Big Dipper moving across the sky as an added bonus.

The long exposure created a daytime look with a nighttime sky.

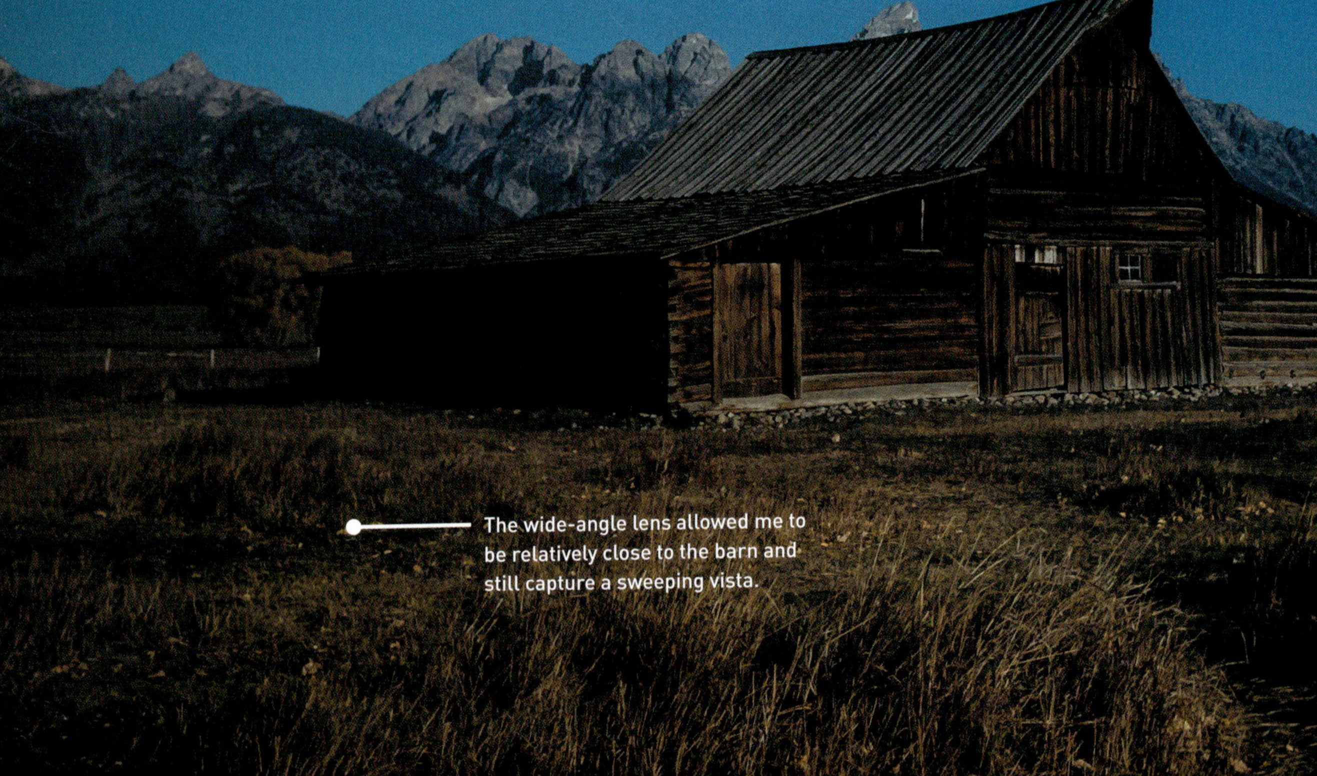

The wide-angle lens allowed me to be relatively close to the barn and still capture a sweeping vista.

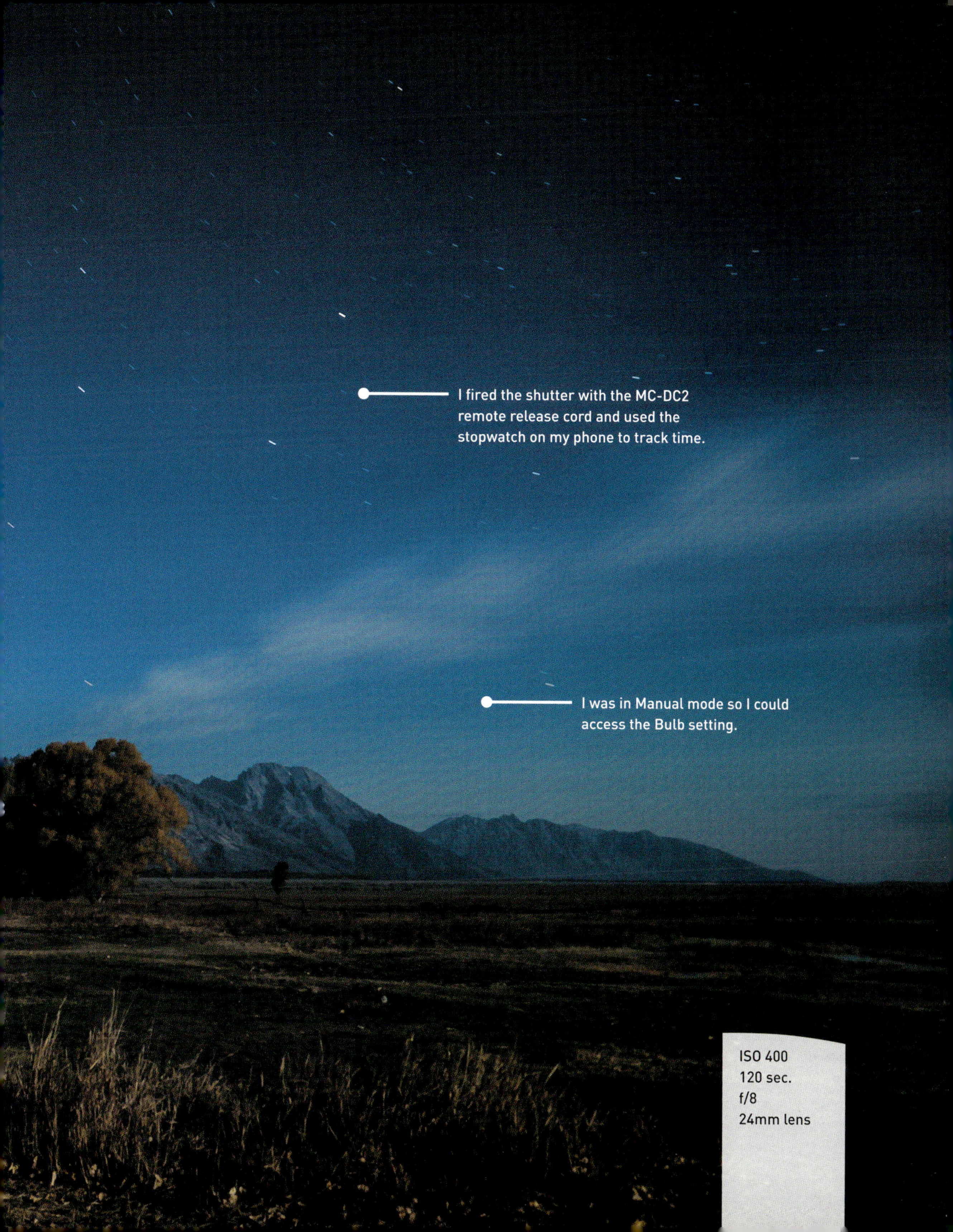

I fired the shutter with the MC-DC2 remote release cord and used the stopwatch on my phone to track time.

I was in Manual mode so I could access the Bulb setting.

ISO 400
120 sec.
f/8
24mm lens

P: PROGRAM MODE

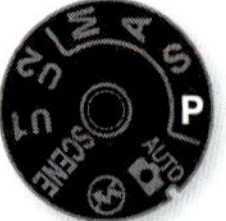

I think of Program mode as a good place to begin for those graduating from the automatic or scene modes. There is a reason that Program mode is only one click away from the automatic modes: With respect to aperture and shutter speed, the camera is doing most of the thinking for you. So if that is the case, why even bother with Program mode?

Manual Callout

To see available settings for each mode, check out the table on pages 309–311 of your owner's manual.

First, let me say that I rarely use Program mode, because it just doesn't give as much control over the image-making process as the other professional modes. There are occasions, however, when it comes in handy, like when I am shooting in widely changing lighting conditions and don't have the time to think through all of my options, or when I'm not very concerned with having ultimate control of the scene. Think of a picnic outdoors in a partial shade/sun environment. I want great-looking pictures, but I'm not looking for anything to hang in a museum. If that's the scenario, why choose Program over one of the scene modes? Because it gives me choices and control that none of the scene modes can deliver.

WHEN TO USE PROGRAM (P) MODE INSTEAD OF THE AUTOMATIC SCENE MODES

It's graduation time and you're ready to move on to a more advanced mode but not quite ready to jump in with both feet. When does Program mode come in handy?

- When shooting in a casual environment where quick adjustments are needed
- When you want more control over the ISO
- If you want to make corrections to the white balance
- When you want to change shutter speeds or the aperture to achieve a specific result

Let's go back to our picnic scenario. As I said, the light is moving from deep shadow to bright sunlight, which means that the camera is trying to balance our three photo factors (ISO, aperture, and shutter speed) to make a good exposure. From Chapter 1, we know that Auto ISO is generally not what we want except when shooting in Auto mode. Well, in Program mode, you can choose which ISO you would like the camera to base its exposure on. The lower the ISO number, the better the quality of the photograph but the less light sensitive the camera becomes. It's a balancing act, with the main goal always being to keep the ISO as low as possible—too low an ISO, and we will get camera shake in our images from a long shutter speed; too high an ISO, and we will have an unacceptable amount of digital noise. For now, let's go ahead and select ISO 400 so that we provide enough sensitivity for those shadows while allowing the camera to use shutter speeds that are fast enough to stop motion.

STARTING POINTS FOR ISO SELECTION

Many years ago, camera manufacturers were racing to create cameras with more megapixels. Today the digital race is more about higher ISO. Photographers want to be able to shoot in lower-light conditions without the risk of digital noise. There is a lot of discussion concerning ISO in this and other chapters, but it might be helpful for you to know where your starting points should be for your ISO settings. The first thing you should always do is use the lowest possible ISO setting. Your D600 has a working range of 100–6400. These are good starting points for your ISO settings:

- 100: Bright, sunny day
- 200: Hazy or outdoor shade on a sunny day
- 400: Indoor lighting at night or cloudy conditions outside
- 800: Late night, low-light conditions, or sports arenas at night
- 1600: Very low light; possibly candlelight or events where no flash is allowed
- 3200-6400: Extremely low light (some digital noise will be present; however, less than ever before)

These are just suggestions; you'll have to adjust as necessary. Your ISO selection will depend on a number of factors that are discussed later in the book.

With the ISO selected, we can now make use of the other controls built into Program mode. By rotating the Main Command dial, we have the ability to shift the program settings. Remember, your camera is using the internal meter to pick what it deems suitable exposure values, but sometimes it doesn't know what it's looking at and how you want those values applied (**Figures 4.1** and **4.2**).

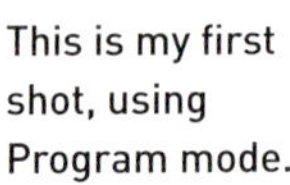

FIGURE 4.1
This is my first shot, using Program mode.

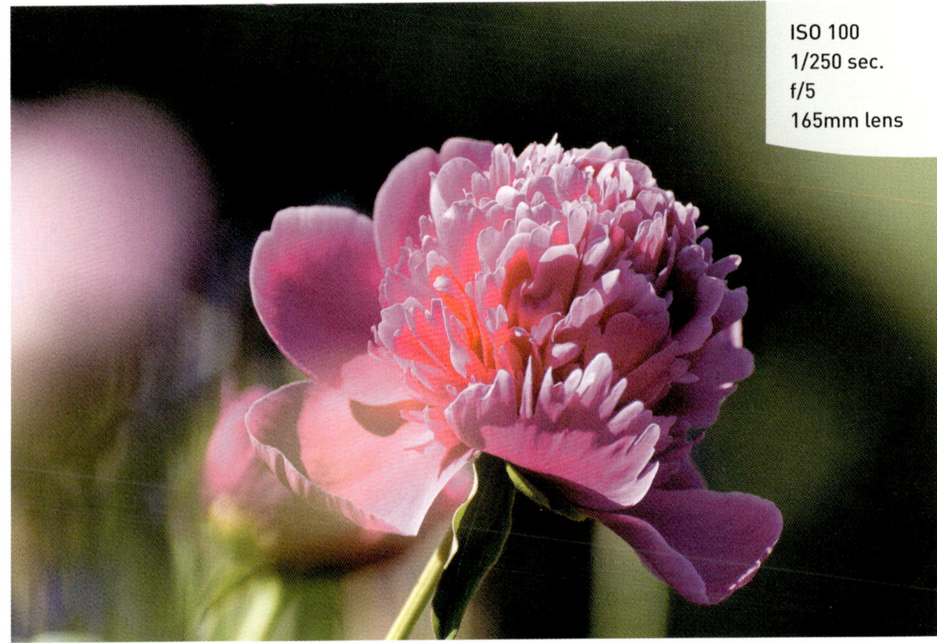

FIGURE 4.2
To get greater depth of field, I decreased the size of the aperture by rotating the Main Command dial to the left, and the shutter speed slowed down to maintain the same exposure value.

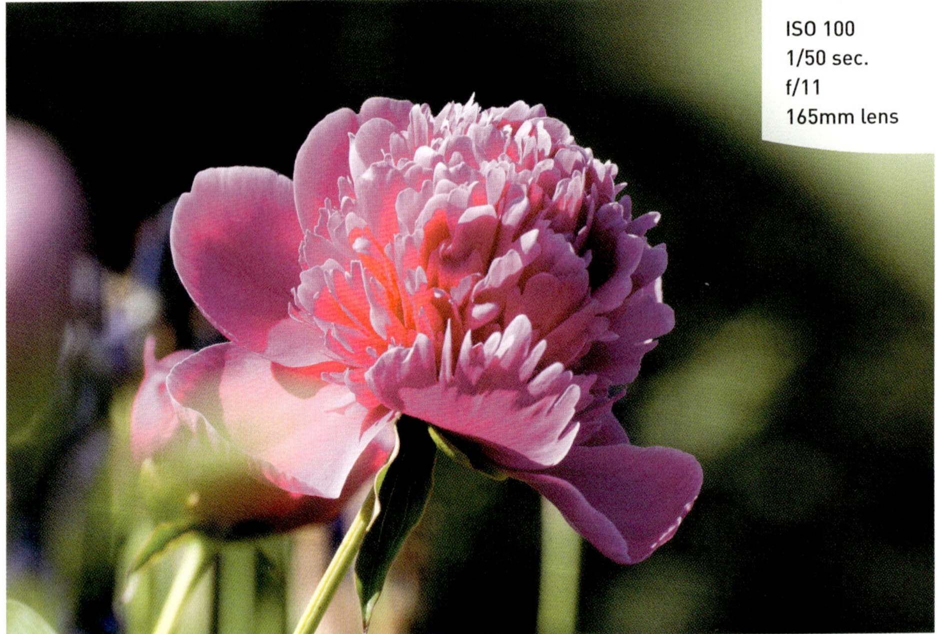

With the program shift, you can influence what the shot will look like. Do you need faster shutter speeds in order to stop the action? Just turn the Main Command dial to the right. Do you want a smaller aperture so you get greater depth of field? Turn the dial to the left until you get the desired aperture. The camera shifts the shutter speed or aperture accordingly to get a proper exposure.

When you rotate the Main Command dial, you will notice a small star appear above the letter P in the top control panel and the rear display. This star is an indication that you modified the exposure from the one the camera chose. To go back to the default Program exposure, simply turn the dial until the star goes away or switch to a different mode and then back to Program mode again.

Let's set up the camera for Program mode and see how we can make all of this come together.

SETTING UP AND SHOOTING IN PROGRAM MODE

1. Turn your camera on, press the Mode dial release lock, and turn the Mode dial to align the **P** with the indicator line.
2. Select your ISO by pressing and holding the ISO button (on the back left of the camera) while rotating the Main Command dial with your thumb.
3. The ISO will appear on the top display. Choose your desired ISO, and release the ISO button to lock in the change.
4. Point the camera at your subject, and then activate the camera meter by depressing the shutter button halfway.
5. View the exposure information in the bottom of the viewfinder or in the display panel on the back of the camera.
6. While the meter is activated, use your thumb to roll the Command dial left and right to see the changed exposure values.
7. Select the exposure that is right for you and start clicking. (Don't worry if you aren't yet sure what the right exposure is. We will work on making the right choices for those great shots beginning with the next chapter.)

S: SHUTTER PRIORITY MODE

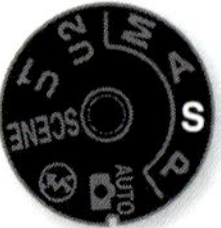

S mode is what photographers commonly refer to as Shutter Priority. Just as its name implies, it is the mode that prioritizes, or places major emphasis on, the shutter speed above all other camera settings.

Like Program mode, Shutter Priority mode gives us more freedom to control certain aspects of our photography. In this case, we are talking about shutter speed. The shutter speed determines how long your camera's sensor is exposed to light. The longer the shutter remains open, the more time your sensor has to gather light. The shutter speed also, to a large degree, determines how sharp your photographs are. This is different from the image being sharply in focus. One of the major influences on the sharpness of an image is the blurring that is caused by camera shake and the subject's movement. Because a slower shutter speed means that light from your subject is hitting the sensor for a longer period of time, any movement by you or your subject will show up in your photos as blur.

SHUTTER SPEEDS

A *slow* shutter speed refers to leaving the shutter open for a long period of time—like 1/30 of a second or longer. A *fast* shutter speed means that the shutter is open for a very short period of time—like 1/250 of a second or shorter.

WHEN TO USE SHUTTER PRIORITY MODE

- When working with fast-moving subjects where you want to freeze the action (**Figure 4.3**); much more on this in Chapter 5
- When you want to emphasize movement in your subject with motion blur (**Figure 4.4**)
- When you want to use a long exposure to gather light over a long period of time (**Figure 4.5**); more on this in Chapter 8
- When you want to create that silky-looking water in a waterfall (**Figure 4.6**)

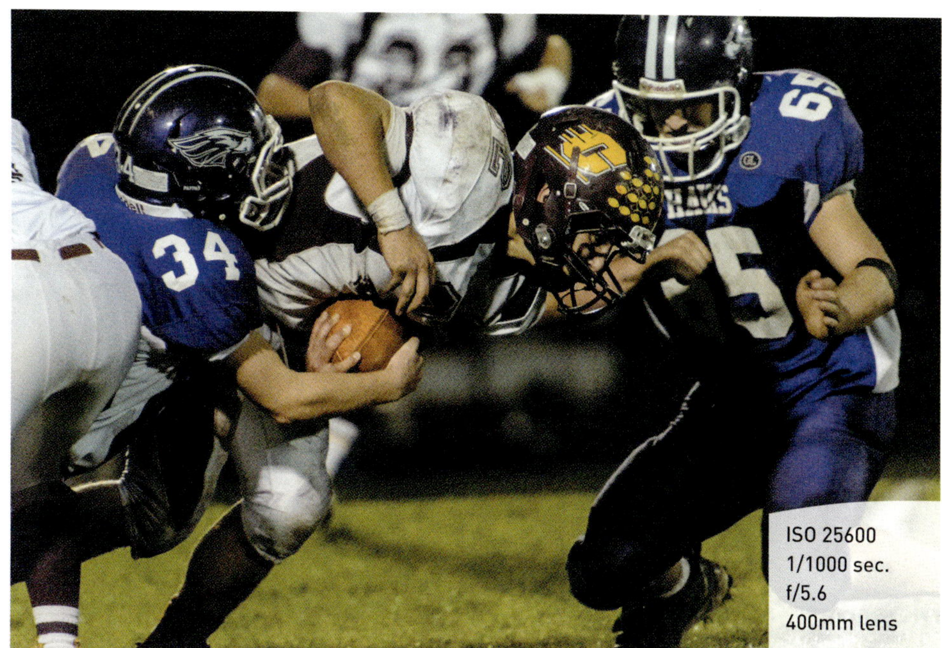

FIGURE 4.3
Even the fastest of subjects can be frozen with the right shutter speed.

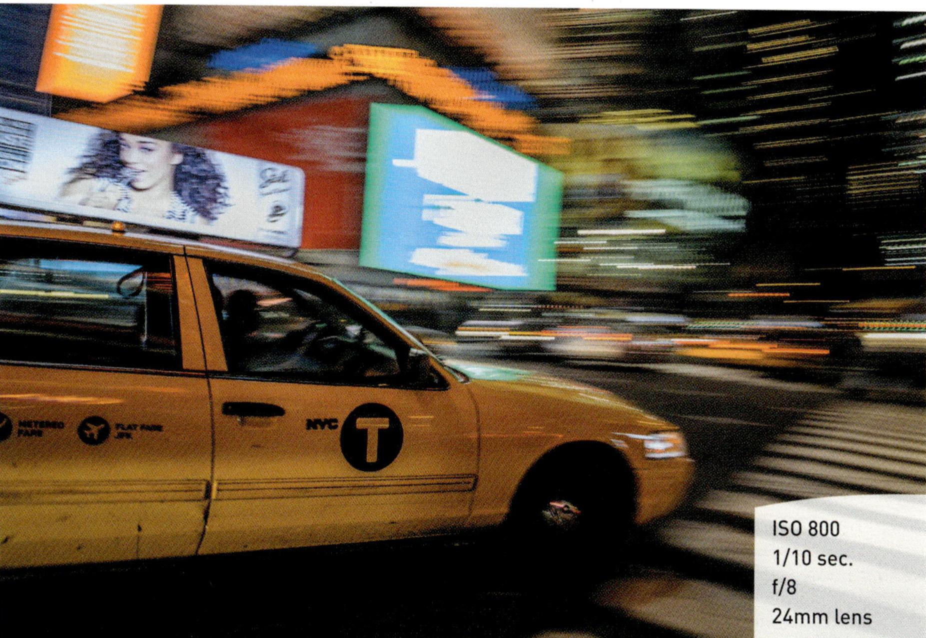

FIGURE 4.4
Slowing down the shutter speed and following the motion conveys a sense of movement in the shot.

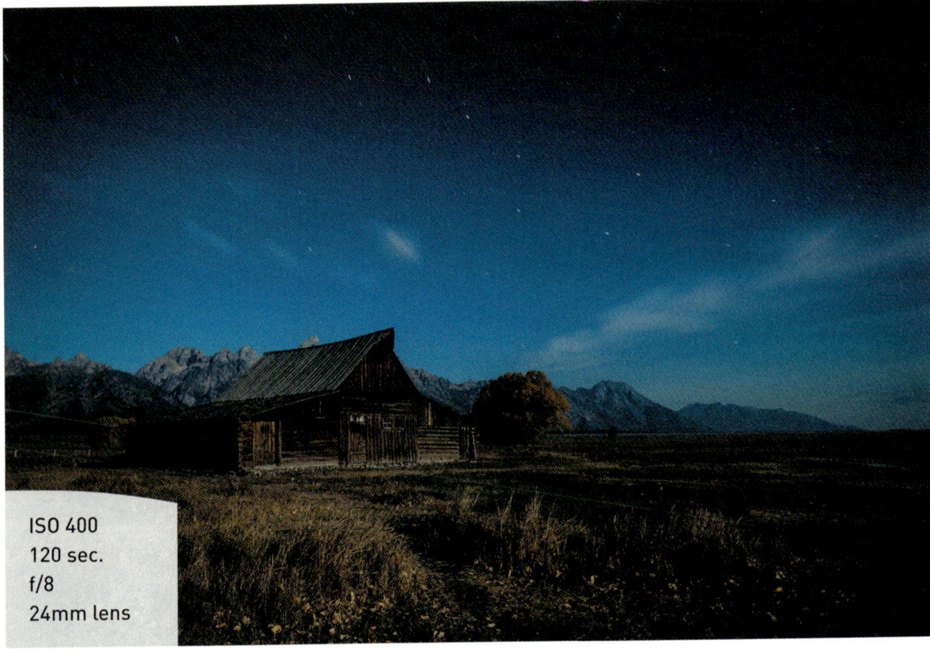

FIGURE 4.5
With a long enough exposure, moonlight can look like daylight.

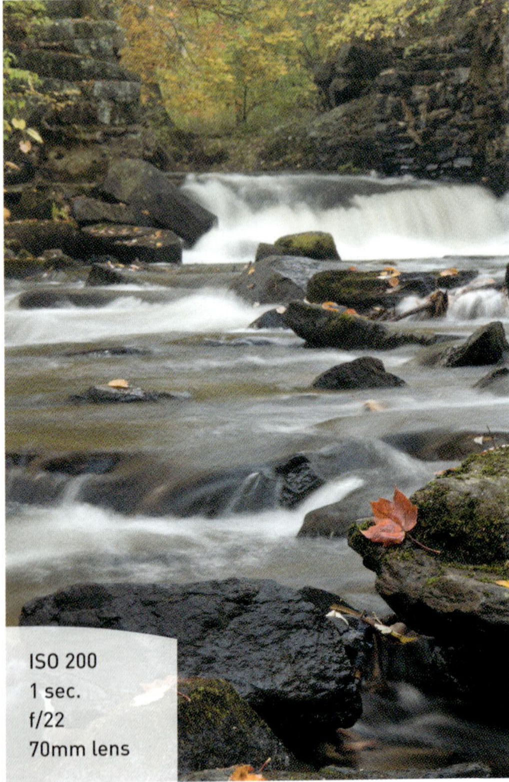

FIGURE 4.6
Increasing the length of the exposure gives moving water a misty look.

As you can see, the subject of your photo usually determines whether or not you will use Shutter Priority mode. It is important that you can visualize the result of using a particular shutter speed. The great thing about shooting with digital cameras is that you get instant feedback by viewing your shot on the rear LCD monitor. But what if your subject won't give you a do-over? Such is often the case when shooting sporting events. It's not like you can ask the quarterback to throw that touchdown pass again because your last shot was blurry from a slow shutter speed. This is why it's important to know what those speeds represent in terms of their ability to stop the action and deliver a blur-free shot.

First, let's examine just how much control you actually have over the shutter speeds. The D600 has a shutter speed range from 1/4000 of a second all the way down to 30 seconds. With that much latitude, you should have enough control to capture almost any subject. The other thing to think about is that Shutter Priority is considered a "semi-automatic" mode. This means that you are taking control over one aspect of the total exposure while the camera handles the other. In this instance, you are controlling the shutter speed and the camera is controlling the aperture. This is important, because there will be times that you want to use a particular shutter speed but your lens won't be able to accommodate your request.

For example, you might encounter this problem when shooting in low-light situations. If you are shooting a fast-moving subject that will blur at a shutter speed slower than 1/125 of a second and your lens's largest aperture is f/3.5, you might find that your aperture display in the viewfinder and the control panel will blink. This is your warning that there won't be enough light available for the shot—due to the limitations of the lens—so your picture will be underexposed. It does not, however, prevent you from taking the shot, so you need to be aware of the warning and the results.

Another case where you might run into this situation is when you are shooting moving water. To get that look of silky, flowing water, it's usually necessary to use a shutter speed of at least 1/15 of a second. If your waterfall is in full sunlight, you may see the aperture readout blink because the lens you are using only stops down to f/22 at its smallest opening. In this instance, your camera is warning you that you will be overexposing your image. There are workarounds for these problems, which we will discuss later (see Chapter 7 for all the details), but it is important to know that there can be limitations when using Shutter Priority mode.

SETTING UP AND SHOOTING IN SHUTTER PRIORITY MODE

1. Turn your camera on. Press the Mode dial release lock, and turn the Mode dial to align the **S** with the indicator line.
2. Set your ISO by pressing the ISO button; select the appropriate setting by looking at the ISO readout on the control panel or by pressing the Info button on the back of the camera and looking at the info display on the rear LCD monitor.
3. Once your ISO is set, point the camera at your subject, and then activate the camera meter by depressing the shutter button halfway.
4. View the exposure information in the bottom area of the viewfinder or in the control panel.
5. While the meter is activated, use your thumb to roll the Main Command dial left and right to see the changed exposure values. Roll the dial to the right for faster shutter speeds and to the left for slower speeds.

A: APERTURE PRIORITY MODE

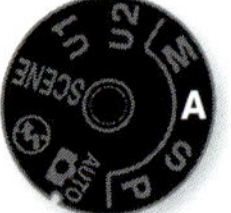

You wouldn't know it from its name, but Aperture Priority mode is one of the most useful and popular modes in DSLR photography. Aperture Priority is one of my favorite modes, and I believe that it will quickly become one of yours as well. Aperture Priority is deemed a semi-automatic mode because it allows you to once again control one factor of exposure while the camera adjusts for another.

Why, you may ask, is this one of my favorite modes? It's because the aperture of your lens dictates depth of field. Depth of field, along with composition, is a major element in how you direct attention to what is important in your image. It is the controlling factor when determining how much of your image is sharp. If you want to isolate a subject from the background, such as when shooting a portrait, you can use a large aperture to keep the focus on your subject and make both the foreground and background blurry. If your emphasis is on keeping the entire scene sharply focused, such as with a landscape scene, then using a small aperture will render the greatest depth of field possible.

WHEN TO USE APERTURE PRIORITY MODE

- When shooting portraits or wildlife (**Figure 4.7**)
- When shooting most landscape photography (**Figure 4.8**)
- When shooting macro, or close-up, photography (**Figure 4.9**)
- When shooting architectural photography, which often benefits from a large depth of field (**Figure 4.10**)

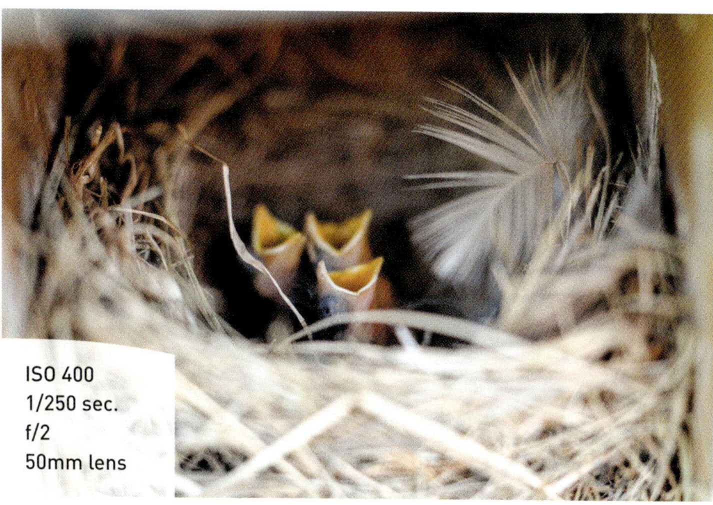

ISO 400
1/250 sec.
f/2
50mm lens

FIGURE 4.7
A large aperture created a very blurry background, so all the emphasis is on the subject.

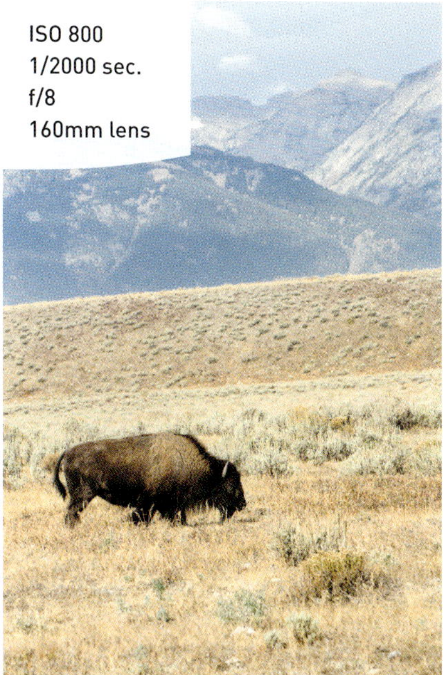

ISO 800
1/2000 sec.
f/8
160mm lens

FIGURE 4.8
The smaller aperture setting brings sharpness to near and far objects.

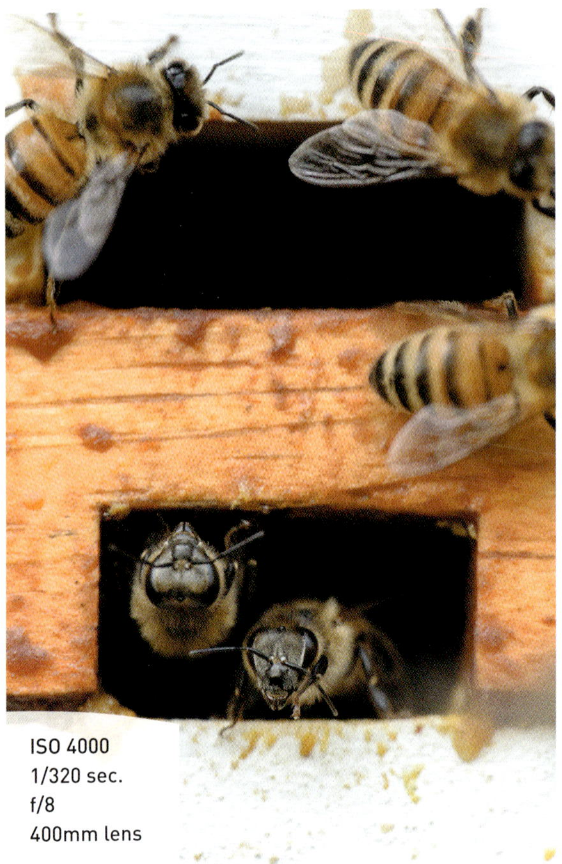

ISO 4000
1/320 sec.
f/8
400mm lens

FIGURE 4.9
A small aperture was used to capture the smiling faces of my bees as they emerged from the hive.

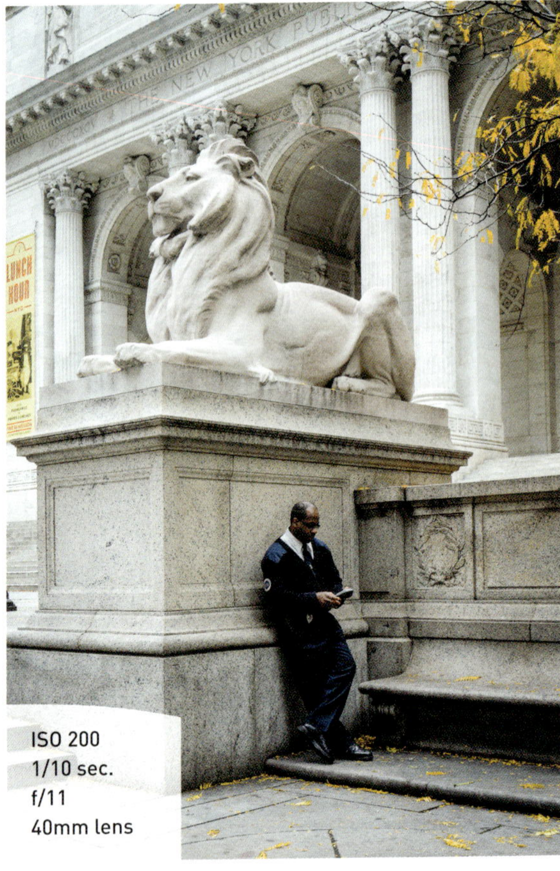

ISO 200
1/10 sec.
f/11
40mm lens

FIGURE 4.10
I like to use smaller apertures for architectural shots to keep everything in focus.

So we have established that Aperture Priority (A) mode is highly useful in controlling the depth of field in your image. But it's also pivotal in determining the limits of available light that you can shoot in. Different lenses have different maximum apertures. The larger the maximum aperture, or f-stop, the less light you need to achieve an acceptably sharp image. You will recall that in Shutter Priority mode, there is a limit at which you can handhold your camera without introducing movement or hand shake, which causes blurriness in the final picture. If your lens has a larger aperture, then you can let in more light all at once, which means that you can use faster shutter speeds. This is why lenses with large maximum apertures, such as f/1.4, are called "fast" lenses.

On the other hand, bright scenes require the use of a small aperture (such as f/16 or f/22), especially if you want to use a slower shutter speed (**Figure 4.11**). That small opening reduces the amount of incoming light, and this reduction of light requires that the shutter stay open longer.

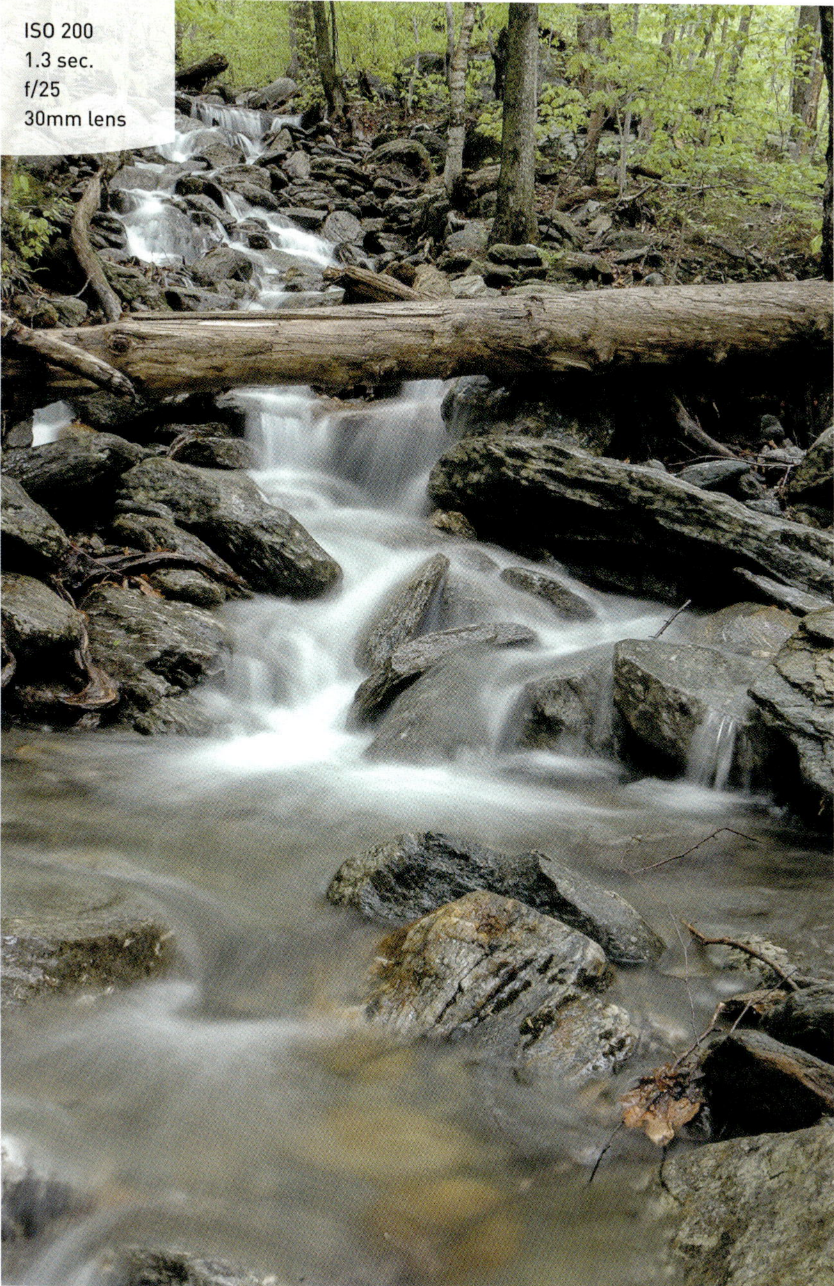

FIGURE 4.11
A wide-angle lens combined with a small aperture added to the depth of field. It also created the need for a long shutter speed, which helped add fluidity to the falling water.

SETTING UP AND SHOOTING IN APERTURE PRIORITY MODE

1. Turn your camera on. Press the Mode dial release lock, and turn the Mode dial to align the **A** with the indicator line.
2. Set your ISO by pressing the ISO button; select the appropriate setting by looking at the ISO readout on the control panel or by pressing the Info button on the back of the camera and looking at the info display on the rear LCD monitor.
3. Once your ISO is set, point the camera at your subject, and then activate the camera meter by depressing the shutter button halfway.
4. View the exposure information in the bottom area of the viewfinder or in the control panel.
5. While the meter is activated, use your index finger to roll the Sub-command dial left and right to see the changed exposure values. Roll the dial to the right for a smaller aperture (higher f-stop number) and to the left for a larger aperture (smaller f-stop number).

F-STOPS AND APERTURE

When referring to the numeric value of your lens aperture, you will find it described as an *f-stop*. F-stop is one of those old photography terms that, technically speaking, relates to the focal length of the lens (e.g., 200mm) divided by the effective aperture diameter. These measurements are defined as "stops" and work incrementally with your shutter speed to determine proper exposure. Older camera lenses used one-stop increments to assist in exposure adjustments, such as 1.4, 2, 2.8, 4, 5.6, 8, 11, 16, and 22. Each stop represents about half the amount of light entering the lens iris as the larger stop before it. Today, most lenses don't have f-stop markings, since all adjustments to this setting are performed via the camera's electronics. The stops are also now typically divided into 1/3-stop increments to allow much finer adjustments to exposures, as well as to match the incremental values of your camera's ISO settings, which are adjusted in 1/3-stop increments as well.

ZOOM LENSES AND MAXIMUM APERTURES

Some zoom lenses (like the 24–85mm kit lens) have a variable maximum aperture. This means that the largest opening will change depending on the zoom setting. In the example of the 24–85mm zoom, the lens has a maximum aperture of f/3.5 at 25mm and only f/4.5 when the lens is zoomed out to 85mm.

M: MANUAL MODE

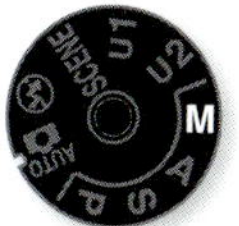

Once upon a time, long before digital cameras and program modes, there was manual mode. Only in those days it wasn't called "manual mode," because there were no other modes. It was just photography. In fact, many photographers cut their teeth on completely manual cameras. Let's face it—if you want to learn the effects of aperture and shutter speed on your photography, there is no better way to learn than by setting these adjustments yourself. But today, with the advancement of camera technology, many new photographers never give this mode a second thought. That's truly a shame, as it is not only an excellent way to learn your photography basics, it's also an essential tool to have in your photographic bag of tricks.

When you have your camera set to Manual (M) mode, the camera meter will give you a reading of the scene you are photographing, but it's your job to actually set both the f-stop (aperture) and the shutter speed to achieve a correct exposure. If you need a faster shutter speed, you will have to make the reciprocal change to your f-stop. Using any other mode, such as Shutter or Aperture Priority, would mean that you just have to worry about one of these changes, but Manual mode requires you to do it all yourself. This can be a little challenging at first, but after a while you will have a complete understanding of how each change affects your exposure, which will in turn improve the way that you use the other modes.

WHEN TO USE MANUAL MODE

- When learning how each exposure element interacts with the others (**Figure 4.12**)
- When your environment is fooling your light meter and you need to maintain a certain exposure setting (**Figure 4.13**)
- When shooting silhouetted subjects, which requires overriding the camera's meter readings (**Figure 4.14**)

FIGURE 4.12
The camera was set to Manual so I could expose properly for the bright lights while still using a slow-enough shutter to enhance the feeling of motion that exists in Times Square.

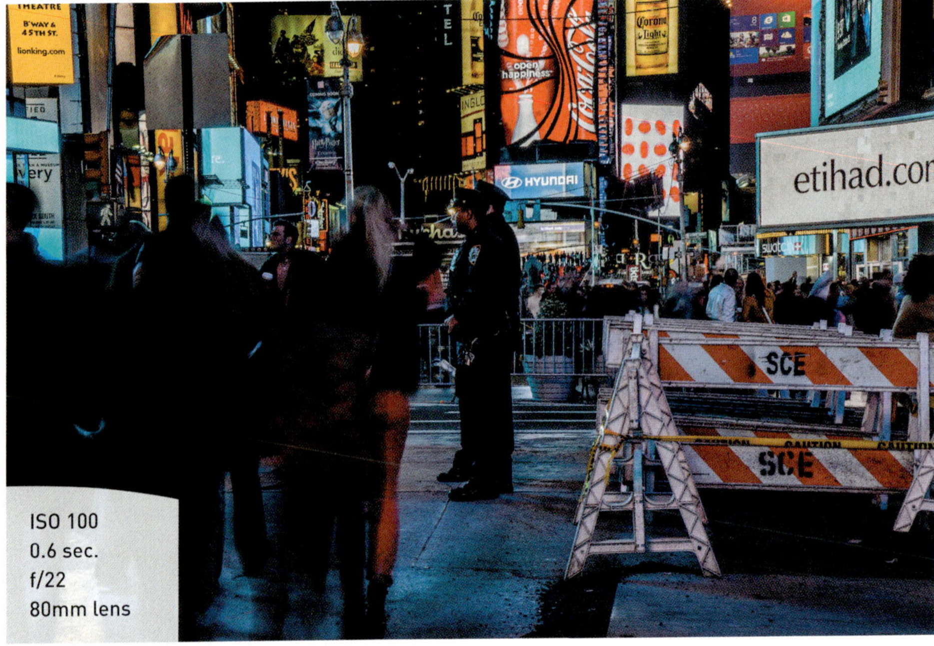

ISO 100
0.6 sec.
f/22
80mm lens

FIGURE 4.13
Beaches and snow are always a challenge for light meters. Add to that the desire to have exact control of depth of field and shutter speed, and you have a perfect scenario for Manual mode.

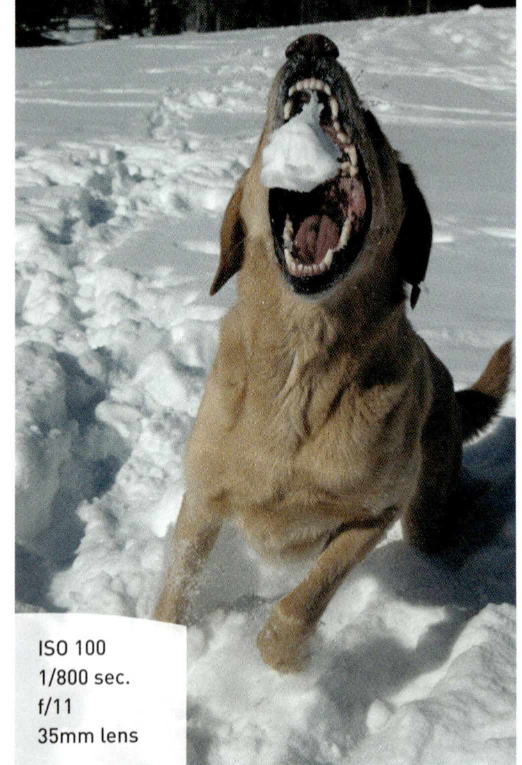

ISO 100
1/800 sec.
f/11
35mm lens

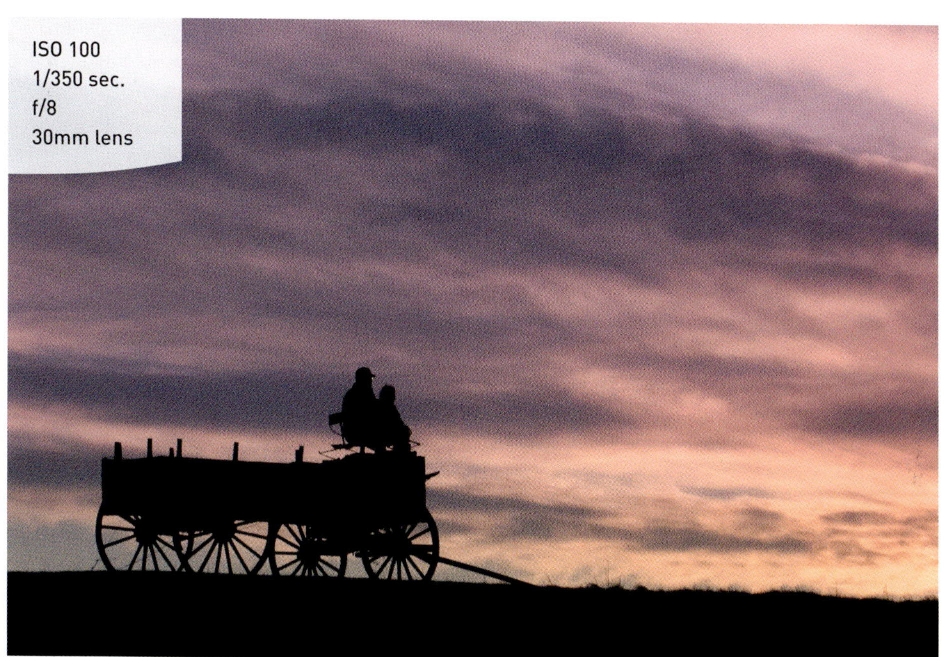

FIGURE 4.14 Although the meter was doing a pretty good job of exposing for the sky, I used Manual mode to push the foreground elements into complete silhouette and get richer color in the sunset.

SETTING UP AND SHOOTING IN MANUAL MODE

1. Turn your camera on. Press the Mode dial release lock, and turn the Mode dial to align the **M** with the indicator line.
2. Set your ISO by pressing the ISO button; select the appropriate setting by looking at the ISO readout on the control panel or by pressing the Info button on the back of the camera and looking at the info display on the rear LCD monitor.
3. Point the camera at your subject, and then activate the camera meter by depressing the shutter button halfway.
4. View the exposure information in the bottom area of the viewfinder or by pressing the Info button on the back of the camera and looking at the info display on the rear LCD monitor.
5. While the meter is activated, use your index finger to roll the Main Command dial left and right to change your shutter speed value until the exposure mark is lined up with the zero mark. The exposure information is displayed in the viewfinder (and on the rear LCD after pressing the Info button) (**Figure 4.15**) by a scale with marks that run from –2 to +2 stops. A proper exposure will line up with the

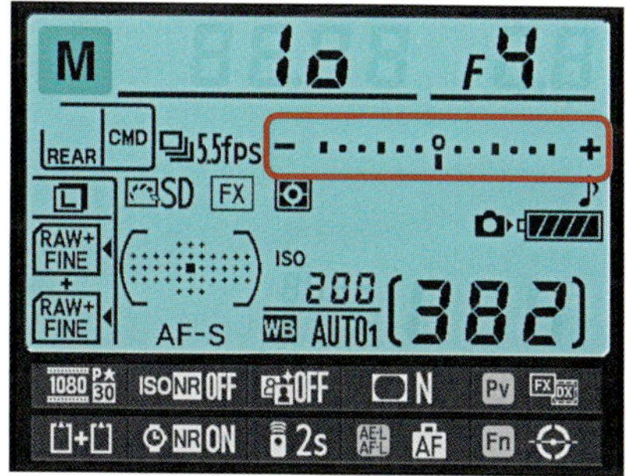

FIGURE 4.15 Use the over/under scale to find your exposure settings.

taller mark in the middle. As the indicator moves to the left, it is a sign that you will be underexposing (not enough light on the sensor to provide adequate exposure). Move the indicator to the right and you will be providing more exposure than the camera meter calls for; this is overexposure.

6. To set your exposure using the aperture, depress the shutter release button until the meter is activated. Then rotate the Sub-command dial to change the aperture. Rotate right for a smaller aperture (large f-stop number) and left for a larger aperture (small f-stop number).

USER SETTINGS MODE—SAVING YOUR FAVORITE SETTINGS TO THE MODE DIAL

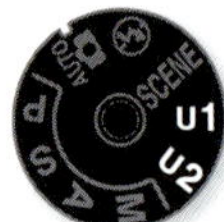

User Settings mode is a great feature if you'd like to access your favorite settings with the touch of a dial. These settings appear on the Mode dial as U1 and U2. If you have a favorite group of settings that you find you are using often and want to have them close at hand, then these modes are for you.

1. Under any of the semi-automatic modes or Manual mode, set the camera to your favorite settings, adjusting any or all of the following: aperture, shutter speed, ISO, flash, focus point, metering, and bracketing.
2. Go to the Setup menu, and select Save user settings (**A**).
3. Highlight Save to U1 or U2, then click OK to save your settings (**B**), (**C**).
4. When you want to use those settings again, just rotate the Mode dial to U1 or U2, and the camera will choose your saved settings so that you're ready to go.

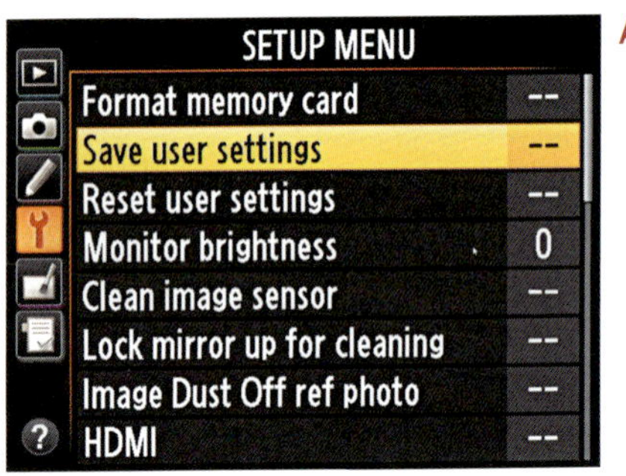

A

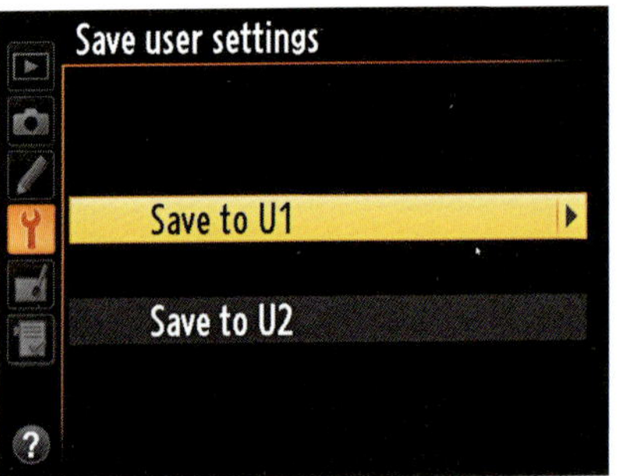

B

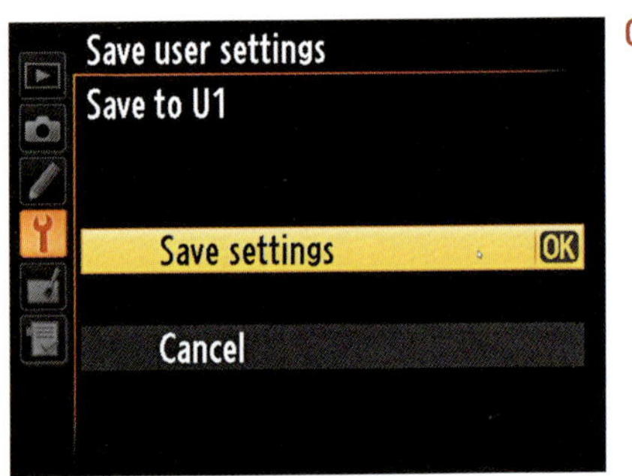

C

I find it useful to set up one user setting for Aperture Priority with bracketing turned on and ISO set to 100 for times when I want shoot that way (I find it too easy to forget that I have bracketing enabled). I have the other user setting configured for Shutter Priority with Auto ISO sensitivity enabled for times when freezing fast action is more important than ISO setting (and I also find it easy to forget that I have Auto ISO sensitivity enabled). This makes it simple for me to jump right to those settings, but also to jump out again.

HOW I SHOOT: A CLOSER LOOK AT THE CAMERA SETTINGS I USE

The great thing about working with a DSLR camera is that I can always feel confident that some things will remain unchanged from camera to camera. For me, these are the Aperture Priority (A) and Shutter Priority (S) shooting modes. Regardless of the subject I am shooting—from landscape to portrait to macro—I am almost always going to be concerned with my depth of field. Whether it's isolating my subject with a large aperture or trying to maximize the overall sharpness of a sweeping landscape, I always keep an eye on my aperture setting. If I do need to control the action (**Figure 4.16**), I use Shutter Priority. If I am trying to create a silky waterfall effect, I can depend on Shutter Priority mode to provide a long shutter speed and get the desired result. Or perhaps I am shooting a sporting event—I definitely need fast shutter speeds that will freeze the fast-moving action.

While the other camera modes have their place, I think you will find that, like myself and most other working pros, you will use the Aperture Priority and Shutter Priority modes for 90 percent of your shooting.

The other concern that I have when setting up my camera is just how low I can keep my ISO. This is always a priority for me, because a low ISO will always give the cleanest image. I raise the ISO only as a last resort, because each increase in sensitivity is an opportunity for more digital noise to enter my image. To that end, I always have the High ISO Noise Reduction feature turned on when shooting in JPEG mode (I use Adobe Photoshop Lightroom to deal with high ISO noise in the RAW format).

FIGURE 4.16
I got to join my aerial photographer buddy Dave Cleaveland on a helicopter flight over Maine during one of his recent jobs. A fast shutter speed was the most important factor in overcoming the vibration of the helicopter and keeping subjects sharp.

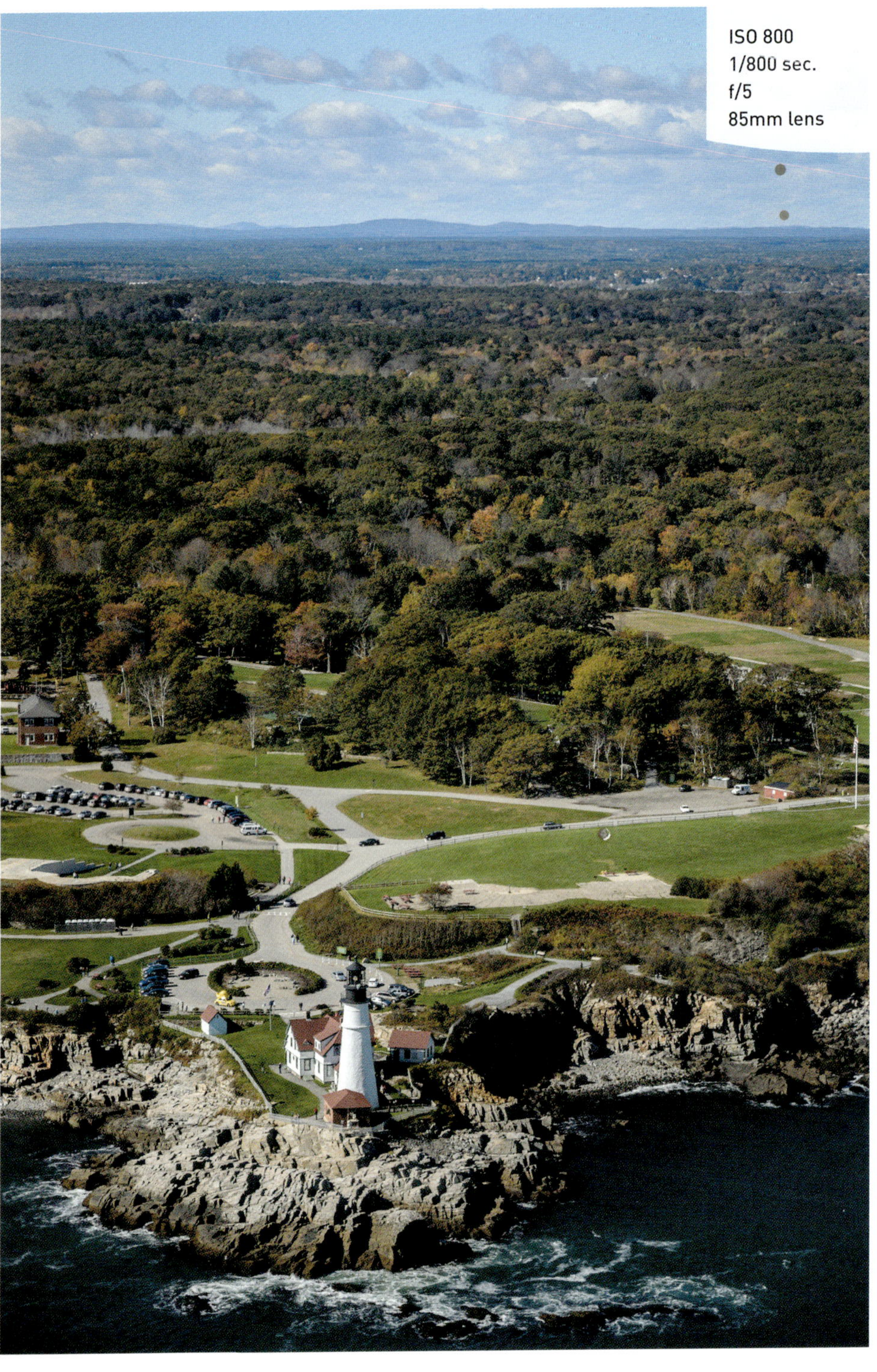

ISO 800
1/800 sec.
f/5
85mm lens

To make quick changes while I shoot, I often use exposure compensation so that I can make small over- and underexposure changes. This is different than changing the aperture or shutter because it is more like fooling the camera meter into thinking the scene is brighter or darker than it actually is. To get to this function quickly, I simply press the Exposure Compensation button and then dial in the desired amount of compensation. Truth be told, I usually have this set to –1/3 so that there is just a tiny bit of underexposure in my image. This usually leads to better color saturation.

One of the reasons I change my exposure is to make corrections when I see the blinkies in my rear LCD monitor. ("Blinkies" is not the real name for the highlight clipping warning, just the one that most photographers use.) Blinkies are the warning signal that part of my image has been overexposed to the point that I no longer have any detail in the highlights. When the Highlights feature is turned on, the display will flash between black and white whenever there is a potential of overexposing in the image. The black and white flashing will only appear in areas of the picture that are in danger of overexposure. To turn on this feature, go to the Playback menu and enable the feature as follows.

1. To set up the highlight warning for your camera, press the Menu button and then use the Multi-selector to access the Playback menu.
2. Once in the Playback menu, use the Multi-selector to choose Playback display options, and press OK (**A**).
3. Use the Multi-selector to move down to the Highlights option, and then press the OK button to add a checkmark (**B**).
4. Now move back up to the Done heading, and press the OK button again to lock in your change.

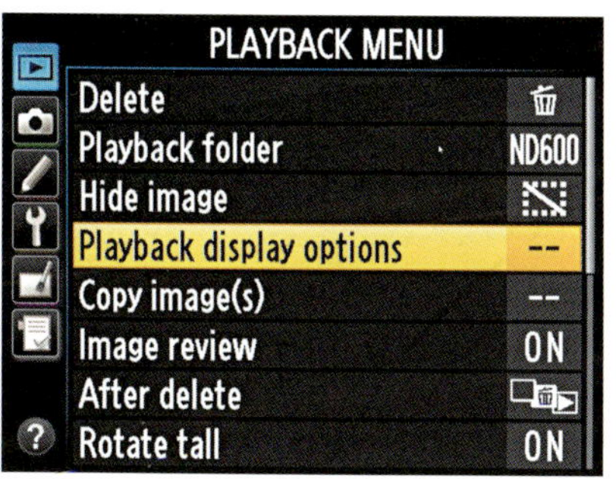

A

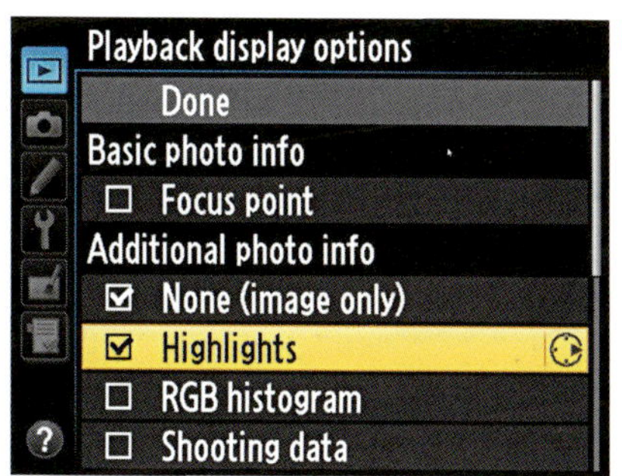

B

Once the highlight warning is turned on, I use it to check my images on the back of the LCD after taking a shot. If I see an area that is blinking (**Figure 4.17**), I will usually set the exposure compensation feature to an underexposed setting like –1/3 or –2/3 stops and take another photo, checking the result on the screen. I repeat this process until the warning is gone.

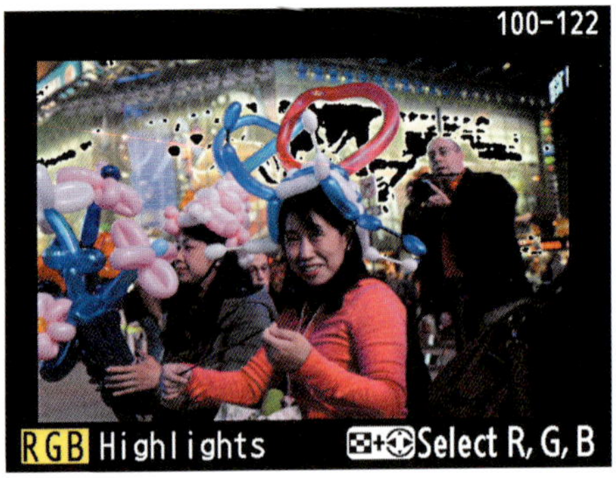

FIGURE 4.17
The blinking black and white areas (shown in this image as black) are a warning that part of the image is overexposed at the current camera settings.

Sometimes, such as when shooting into the sun, the warning will blink no matter how much you adjust the exposure, because there is just no detail in the highlights. Use your best judgment to determine if the warning is alerting you to an area where you want to retain highlight detail.

To see the highlight, or "blinkie," warning, you will need to change your display mode. To do this, press the Image Review button on the back of the camera and then press up or down on the Multi-selector until you see the word "Highlights" at the bottom of the display screen. This will now be your default display mode unless you change it or turn off the highlight warning.

As you work your way through the coming chapters, you will see other tips and tricks I use in my daily photography, but the most important tip I can give is that you should understand the features of your camera so you can leverage the technology in a knowledgeable way. This will result in better photographs.

Chapter 4 Assignments

This will be more of a mental challenge than anything else, but you should put a lot of work into these lesson assignments because the information covered in this chapter will define how you work with your camera from this point on. Granted, there may be times that you just want to grab some quick pictures and will resort to Program mode, but to get serious with your photography, you will want to learn the professional modes inside and out.

Moving Target

THE TRICKS TO SHOOTING SPORTS AND MORE

Now that you have learned about the professional modes, it's time to put your newfound knowledge to good use. Whether you are shooting a professional sporting event or a child on a merry-go-round, this chapter will teach you techniques that will help you bring out the best in your photography when your subject is in motion.

The number one thing to know when trying to capture a moving target is that speed is king! I'm not talking about how fast your subject is moving, but rather how fast your shutter is opening and closing. Shutter speed is the key to freezing the moment in time—but also to conveying movement. It's all in how you turn the dial. There are also some other considerations for taking your shot to the next level: composition, lens selection, and a few more items that we will explore in this chapter. So strap on your seatbelt and hit the gas, because here we go!

PORING OVER THE PICTURE

Shooting sports under the lights requires high ISO values.

I shot in the continuous drive mode using the Dynamic autofocus mode.

things always look brighter under the big lights. The reality is that the human eye adjusts rapidly to lower light levels, which can make you feel like there should be plenty of light. That was the case when I began shooting this football game. As it got later and later, I kept raising my ISO higher and higher so that I could maintain the fastest shutter speed possible. I set my focus point for the middle and then just tried to anticipate the action so I would be ready to catch photos—such as this interception, which was a pivotal moment in this high school game.

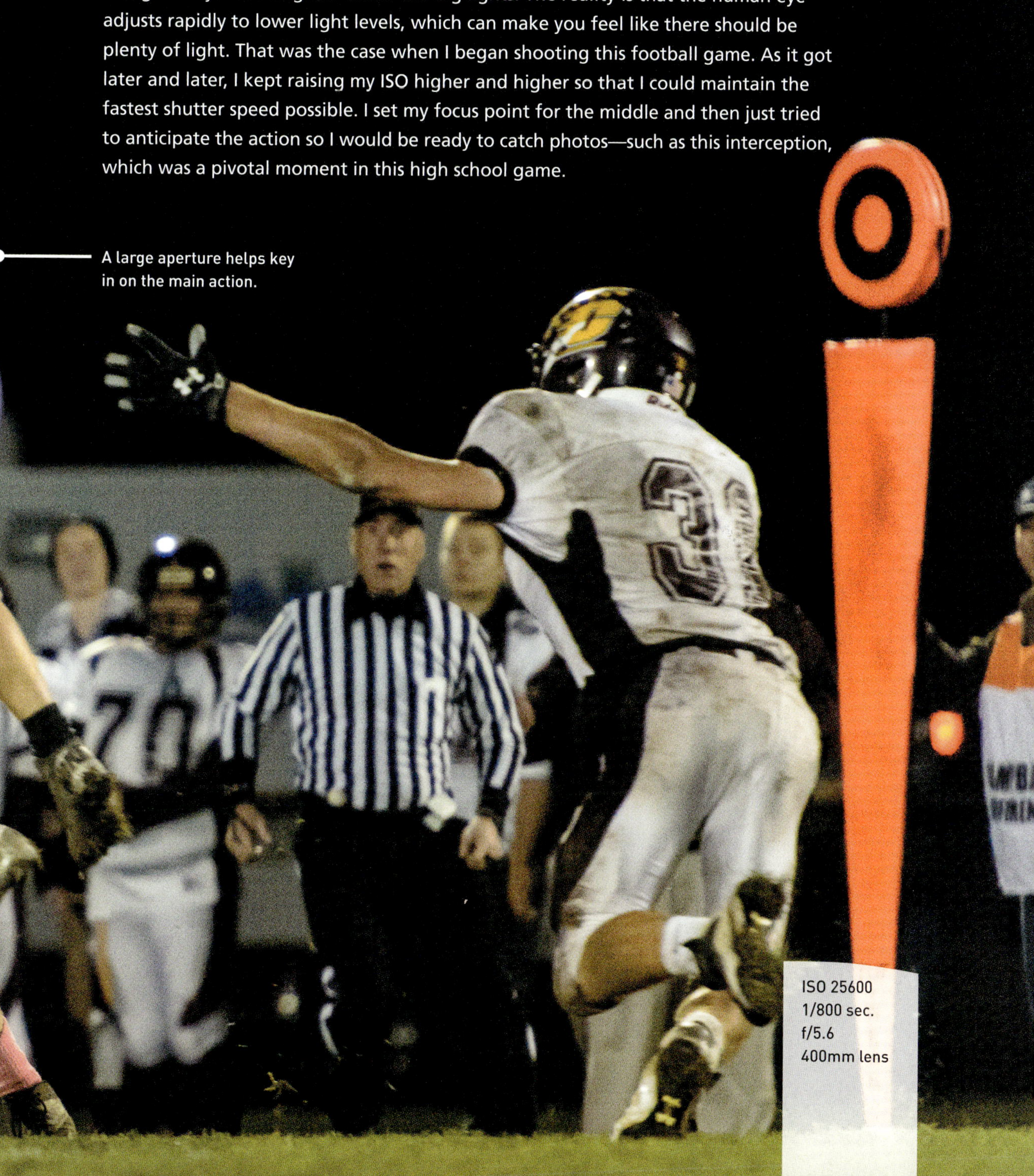

A large aperture helps key in on the main action.

ISO 25600
1/800 sec.
f/5.6
400mm lens

STOP RIGHT THERE!

Shutter speed is the main tool in the photographer's arsenal for capturing great action shots. The ability to freeze a moment in time often makes the difference between a good shot and a great one. To take advantage of this concept, you should have a good grasp of the relationship between shutter speed and movement. When you press the shutter release button, your camera goes into action by opening the shutter curtain and then closing it after a predetermined length of time. The longer you leave your shutter open, the more your subject will move within the frame, so common sense dictates that the first thing to consider is just how fast your subject is moving.

Typically, you will be working in fractions of a second. Just how long those fractions are depends on several factors. Subject movement, while simple in concept, is actually based on three factors. The first is the direction of travel. Is the subject moving across your field of view (left to right) or traveling toward or away from you? The second consideration is the actual speed at which the subject is moving. There is a big difference between a moving sports car and a child on a bicycle. Finally, the distance from you to the subject has a direct bearing on how fast the action seems to be taking place. Let's take a brief look at each of these factors to see how they might affect your shooting.

DIRECTION OF TRAVEL

Typically, the first thing that people think about when taking an action shot is how fast the subject is moving, but in reality the first consideration should be the direction of travel. Where you are positioned in relation to the subject's direction of travel is critically important in selecting the proper shutter speed. When you open your shutter, the lens gathers light from your subject and records it on the camera sensor. If the subject is moving across your viewfinder, you need a faster shutter speed to keep that lateral movement from being recorded as a streak across your image. Subjects that are moving toward or away from your shooting location do not move across your viewfinder and appear to be more stationary. This allows you to use a slightly slower shutter speed (**Figure 5.1**). A subject that is moving in a diagonal direction—both across the frame and toward or away from you—requires a shutter speed in between the two.

SUBJECT SPEED

Once the angle of motion has been determined, you can then assess the speed at which the subject is traveling. The faster your subject moves, the faster your shutter speed needs to be in order to "freeze" that subject (**Figure 5.2**). A person walking across your frame might only require a shutter speed of 1/60 of a second, whereas a cyclist traveling in the same direction would call for 1/500 of a second. That same cyclist traveling at the same rate of speed toward you, rather than across the frame, might only require a shutter speed of 1/125 of a second. You can start to see how the relationship of speed and direction comes into play in your decision-making process.

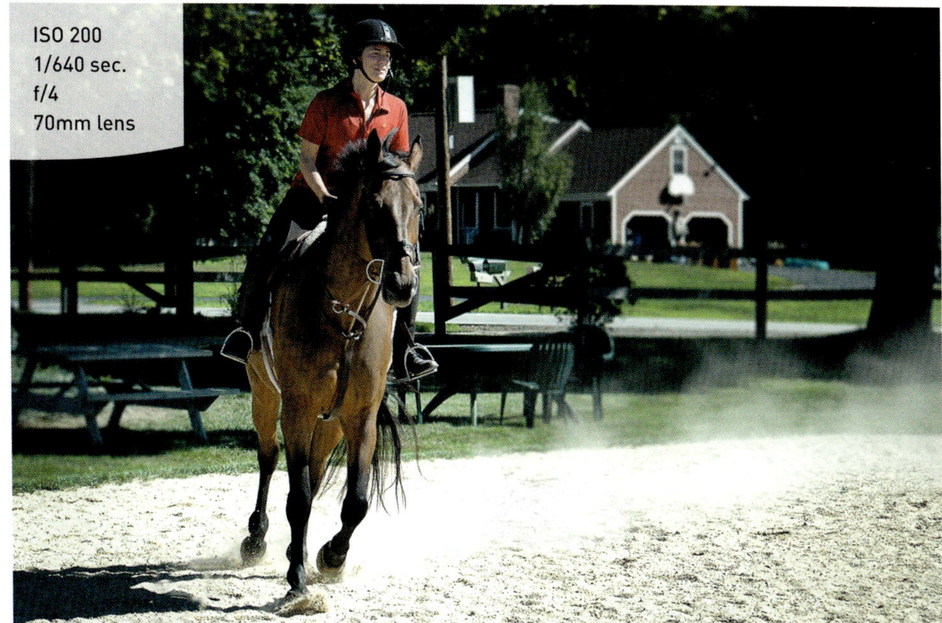

ISO 200
1/640 sec.
f/4
70mm lens

FIGURE 5.1 Action coming toward the camera at an angle can be captured with slower shutter speeds than one moving perpendicular to your position.

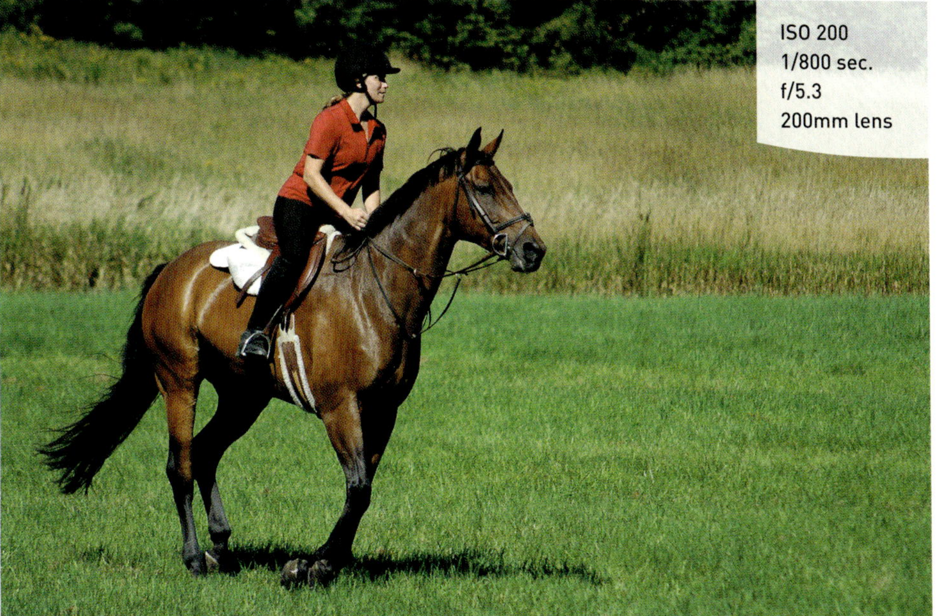

ISO 200
1/800 sec.
f/5.3
200mm lens

FIGURE 5.2 A fast-moving subject that is crossing your path will require a faster shutter speed.

SUBJECT-TO-CAMERA DISTANCE

So now we know both the direction and the speed of your subject. The final factor to address is the distance between you and the action. Picture yourself looking at a highway full of cars from up in a tall building a quarter of a mile from the road. As you stare down at the traffic moving along at 55 miles per hour, the cars and trucks seem to be moving slowly along the roadway. Now picture yourself standing in the median of that same road as the same traffic flies by at the same rate of speed.

Although the traffic is moving at the same speed, the shorter distance between you and the traffic makes the cars look like they are moving much faster. This is because your field of view is much narrower; therefore, the subjects are not going to present themselves within the frame for the same length of time. The concept of distance applies to the length of your lens as well (**Figure 5.3**). If you are using a wide-angle lens, you can probably get away with a slower shutter speed than if you are using a telephoto, which puts you in the heart of the action. It all has to do with your field of view. That telephoto gets you "closer" to the action—and the closer you are, the faster your subject will be moving across your viewfinder.

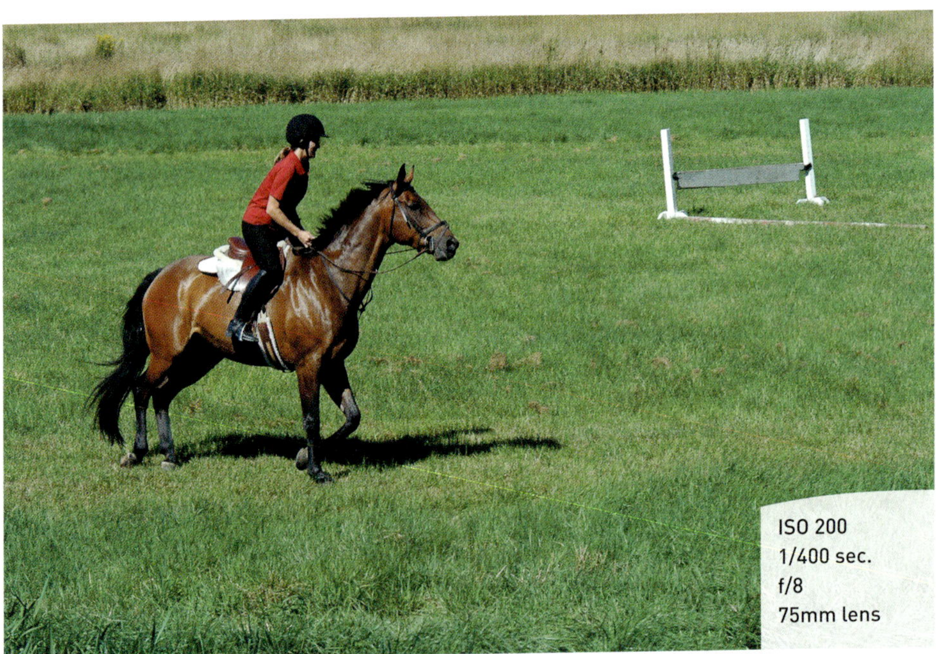

ISO 200
1/400 sec.
f/8
75mm lens

FIGURE 5.3
Because of the distance of the action from the camera, a slower shutter speed could be used.

USING SHUTTER PRIORITY (S) MODE TO STOP MOTION

In Chapter 4, you were introduced to the professional shooting modes. As discussed there, the mode that gives you ultimate control over shutter speed is Shutter Priority, or S, mode, where you are responsible for selecting the shutter speed while handing over the aperture selection to the camera. The ability to concentrate on just one exposure factor helps you quickly make changes on the fly while staying glued to your viewfinder and your subject.

There are a couple of things to consider when using Shutter Priority mode, both of which have to do with the amount of light that is available when shooting. Although you have control over which shutter speed you select in Shutter Priority mode, the range of shutter speeds that are available to you depends largely on how well your subject is lit.

ZOOM IN TO BE SURE

When you're reviewing your shots on the LCD, don't be fooled by the display. The smaller your image is, the sharper it will look. To ensure that you are getting sharp, blur-free images, make sure that you zoom in on your LCD display.

To zoom in on your images, press the Playback button located on the back of the camera and then press the Zoom In button (its icon is a magnifying glass with a plus sign on it) to zoom (**Figure 5.4**). Continue pressing the Zoom In button to increase the zoom ratio.

To zoom back out, simply press the Zoom Out button (the magnifying glass with the minus sign on it) or press the Playback button again.

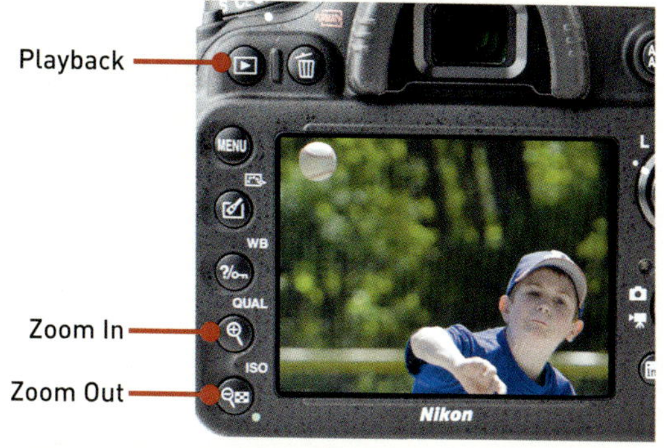

FIGURE 5.4
Zooming in on your image helps you confirm that the image is really sharp.

When shooting fast-paced action, you will typically be working with very fast shutter speeds. This means that your lens will probably be set to a large aperture. If the light is not sufficient for the selected shutter speed, you will need to do one of two things: select a lens that offers a larger working aperture, or raise the ISO of the camera.

Working off the assumption that you have only one lens available, let's concentrate on balancing your exposure using the ISO.

Let's say that you are shooting a football game at night, and you want to get some great action shots. You set your camera to Shutter Priority mode and, after testing out some shutter speeds, determine that you need to shoot at 1/800 of a second to freeze the action on the field. When you place the viewfinder to your eye and press the shutter button halfway, you notice that the f-stop is blinking. This is your camera's way of telling you that the lens has now reached its maximum aperture and you are going to be underexposed if you shoot your pictures at the currently selected shutter speed. You could slow your shutter speed down until the flashing stops, but then you would get images with too much motion blur.

The alternative is to raise your ISO to a level that is fast enough for a proper exposure. The key here is to always use the lowest ISO that you can get away with. That might mean ISO 100 in bright sunny conditions or ISO 6400 (or higher) for an indoor or night situation (**Figure 5.5**).

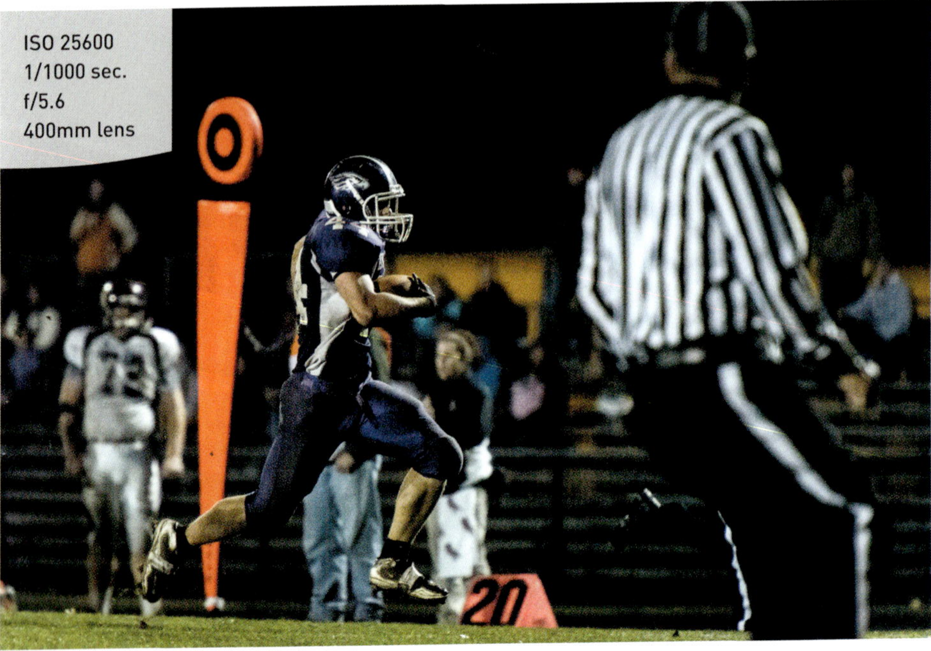

FIGURE 5.5 Sometimes the only way to stop action under the lights is to crank up your ISO.

Just remember that the higher the ISO, the greater the amount of noise in your image. This is the reason that you see professional sports photographers using those mammoth lenses perched atop a monopod: they could use a smaller lens, but to get those very large apertures, they need a huge piece of glass on the front of the lens. The larger the glass on the front of the lens, the more light it gathers, and the larger the aperture for shooting. For the working pro, the large aperture translates into low ISO (and thus low noise), fast shutter speeds, and razor-sharp action.

ADJUSTING YOUR ISO ON THE FLY

1. Look at the exposure values (the shutter speed and aperture settings) in the lower portion of your viewfinder or, after pressing the Info button, on the rear LCD.
2. If the aperture is flashing, then it's time to increase the ISO (**A**).
3. Select a higher ISO by observing the control panel while pressing and holding the ISO button on the back of the camera and rotating the Main Command dial to the right. Once the desired ISO is selected, simply release the ISO button (**B**).
4. If you now see that the aperture setting has stopped flashing in the display, shoot away. If you still see the aperture flashing, repeat step 3 until it is set correctly.

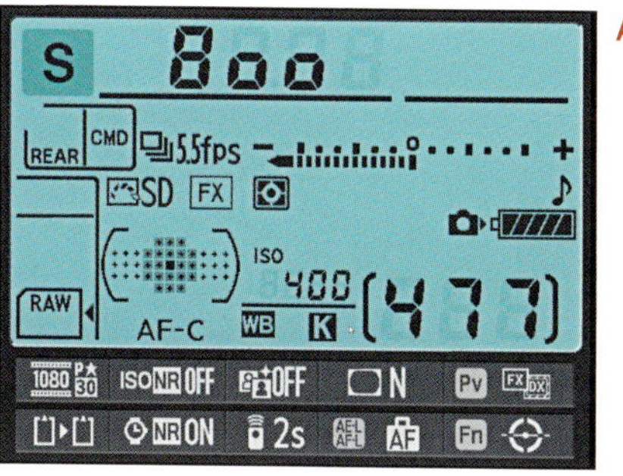

A

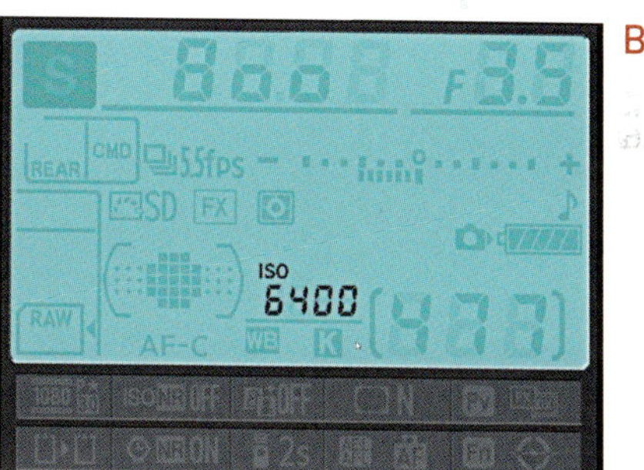

B

USING APERTURE PRIORITY (A) MODE TO ISOLATE YOUR SUBJECT

One of the benefits of working in Shutter Priority mode with fast shutter speeds is that, more often than not, you will be shooting with the largest aperture available on your lens. Shooting with a large aperture allows you to use faster shutter speeds, but it also narrows your depth of field.

To isolate your subject in order to focus your viewer's attention on it, a larger aperture is required. The larger aperture reduces the foreground and background sharpness: the larger the aperture, the more blurred they will be.

The reason that I bring this up here is that when you are shooting most sporting events, the idea is to isolate your main subject by having it in focus while the rest of the image has some amount of blur. This sharp focus draws your viewer right to the subject. Studies have shown that the eye is drawn to sharp areas before moving on to the blurry areas. Also, depending on what your subject matter is, there can be a tendency to get distracted by a busy background if everything in the photo is equally sharp. Without a narrow depth of field, it might be difficult for the viewer to establish exactly what the main subject is in your picture.

Let's look at how to use depth of field to bring focus to your subject. In the previous section, I told you that you should use Shutter Priority mode for getting those really fast shutter speeds to stop action. Generally speaking, Shutter Priority mode will be the mode you most often use for shooting sports and other action, but there will be times when you want to ensure that you are getting the narrowest depth of field possible in your image. The way to do this is by using Aperture Priority mode.

So how do you know when you should use Aperture Priority mode as opposed to Shutter Priority mode? It's not a simple answer, but your LCD screen can help you make this determination. The best scenario for using Aperture Priority mode is a brightly lit scene where maximum apertures will still give you plenty of shutter speed to stop the action.

Let's say that you are shooting a baseball game in the midday sun. If you have determined that you need something between 1/500 and 1/1250 of a second for stopping the action, you could just set your camera to a high shutter speed in Shutter Priority mode and start shooting. But you also want to be using an aperture of, say, f/2.8 to get that narrow depth of field. Here's the problem: if you set your camera to Shutter Priority mode and select 1/1000 of a second as a nice compromise, you might get that desired f/stop—but you might not. As the meter is trained on your moving subject, the light levels could rise or fall, which might actually change that desired f-stop to something higher like f/5.6 or even f/8. Now the depth of field is extended, and you will no longer get that nice isolation and separation that you wanted.

To rectify this, switch the camera to Aperture Priority mode and select f/2.8 as your aperture. Now, as you begin shooting, the camera holds that aperture and makes exposure adjustments with the shutter speed. As I said before, this works well when you have lots of light—enough light so that you can have a high-enough shutter speed without introducing motion blur (**Figure 5.6**).

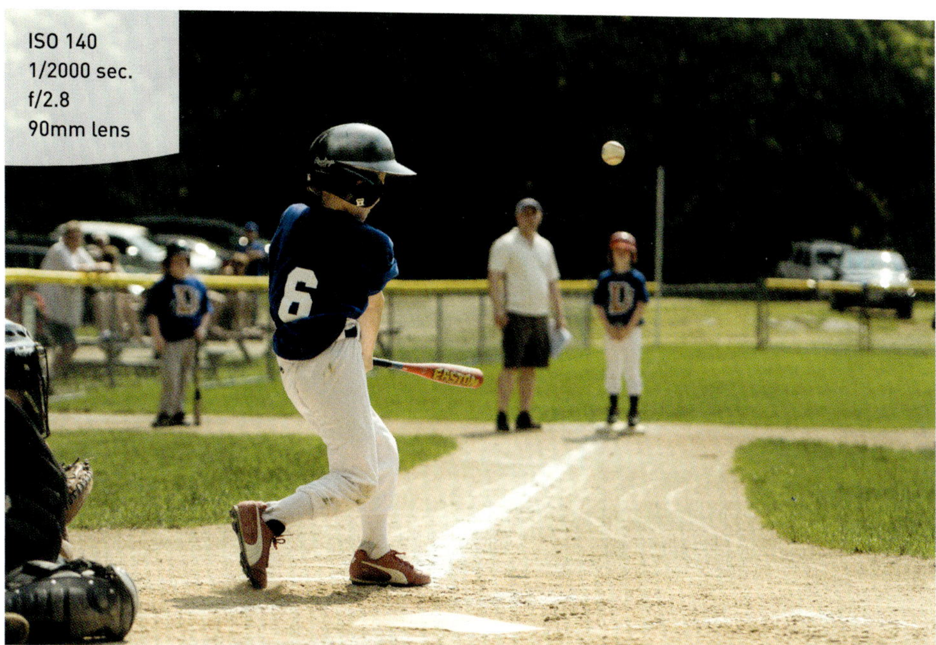

FIGURE 5.6
A sunny day means you can use Aperture Priority mode to lock in a large aperture while the camera sets a fast shutter speed.

THE AUTO ISO SENSITIVITY CONTROL TRICK

There is a very cool trick that can get you the best of both worlds and won't sacrifice your shutter speed or aperture. With the Auto ISO Sensitivity Control feature, you can set the camera to automatically select an ISO that keeps you at your preferred shutter speed, while using the largest aperture and lowest ISO possible. It will also put an upper limit on the ISO to keep you from getting too much noise in your images.

Here's the way it works. If I am shooting an activity that requires a shutter speed of 1/250 of a second, I set that as the minimum in the auto control settings. Then I decide that I can deal with the noise that is produced by an ISO up to 2000, so I set that as my maximum sensitivity. Since I would always like to use the lowest ISO, I set the low ISO sensitivity to 200. Once everything is set, the camera will adjust my ISO without any interaction from me, letting me shoot at my desired shutter speed at the lowest possible ISO and with the possible largest aperture setting. How you determine the acceptable noise level is entirely up to you and your particular output needs. In some cases, just getting the shot is paramount and a noisy shot of the peak moment is not a problem at all. In other cases, you might care more about the noise level, which will force you into slower shutter speeds or investing in a faster lens to get a wider aperture. We are always making these sorts of tradeoffs, and there is no one-size-fits-all answer.

SETTING UP THE AUTO ISO SENSITIVITY CONTROL FEATURE

1. Press the Menu button, and then use the Multi-selector to get to the Shooting menu.
2. Press the Multi-selector to the right to enter the menu, and then highlight ISO sensitivity settings (**A**).
3. Press the Multi-selector to the right to enter the ISO sensitivity settings screen.
4. Press the Multi-selector to the right to select the lowest ISO that you wish to use (ISO sensitivity), and press the OK button (**B**).
5. Press the Multi-selector down to highlight Auto ISO sensitivity control, and then move the Multi-selector to the right to select On to activate the feature (**C**).
6. Use the Multi-selector to choose Maximum sensitivity (**D**). This will be the upper limit of your ISO.
7. Finally, select the Minimum shutter speed that you want to use while shooting (**E**). This will be completely dependent on the speed necessary to stop the action you are shooting.

A

B

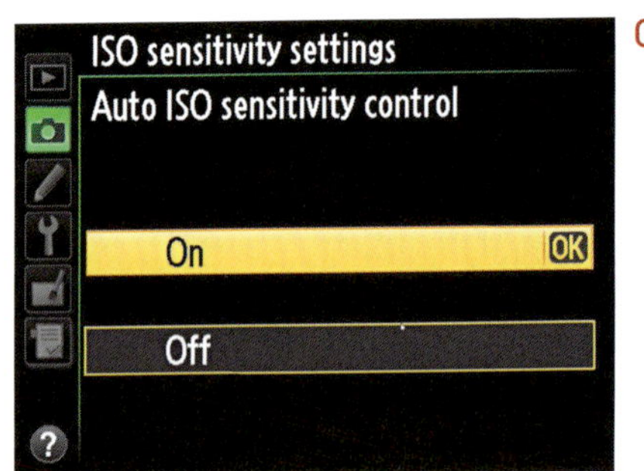

C

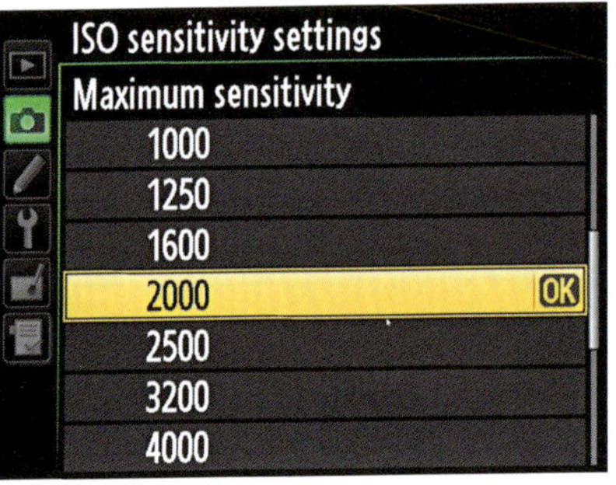

D

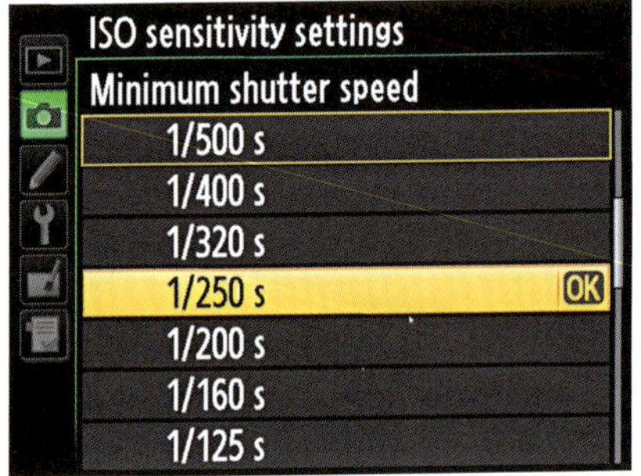

E

With everything set up, you can begin shooting without fear of constantly having to change the ISO. This technique is also helpful when working in varying light conditions. As you are shooting, you will notice the ISO Auto warning in the lower portion of the viewfinder, along with the adjusted ISO setting. With the improvements in high-ISO capture in the D600, I'm finding that I really love the flexibility this setting provides.

KEEP THEM IN FOCUS WITH CONTINUOUS-SERVO FOCUS AND AF FOCUS POINT SELECTION

With the exposure issue handled for the moment, let's move on to an area that is equally important: focusing. If you have browsed your manual, you know that there are several focus modes to choose from in the D600. To get the greatest benefit from each of them, it is important to understand how they work and the situations where each mode will give you the best opportunity to grab a great shot. Because we are discussing subject movement, our first choice is going to be Continuous-servo AF mode (AF-C). AF-C mode uses the focus points in the camera to track a moving subject and then lock in the focus when the shutter button is completely depressed. As the subject moves, the camera uses something called predictive focus tracking to anticipate where the subject will be moving and then adjust focus accordingly.

SELECTING AND SHOOTING IN CONTINUOUS-SERVO AF FOCUS MODE

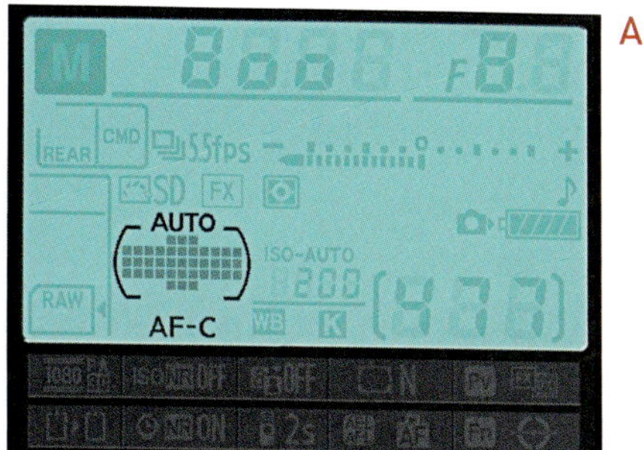

1. Press and hold the AF-mode button on the front of the camera.
2. Rotate the Main Command dial until the AF-C designation is visible in the viewfinder, the top control panel, or, after pressing the Info button, the rear LCD (**A**).
3. The camera will maintain the subject's focus as long as it remains within one of the focus points in the viewfinder or until you release the shutter button or take a picture.

You should take note that holding down the shutter button for long periods of time will cause your battery to drain much faster because the camera will be constantly focusing on the subject.

When using AF-C mode, you can change the AF-area mode to specify how the focus points are used. There are two modes to choose from.

Single-point AF. This mode allows you to select a single focus point. The camera will ignore all other points and utilize only the point you specify. To select a point, set the camera in Single-point AF mode by holding down the AF-mode button and rotating the Sub-command dial until you see the single-point designation. Next, use the Multi-selector to select the desired focus point, which will be highlighted in the viewfinder. You can lock in your point selection by rotating the lock lever to the L position.

Dynamic-area AF. This mode uses a focus point of your choosing as the primary focus but uses information from the surrounding points if your subject happens to move away from the point. You can select from three different areas: 9-point, 21-point, and 39-point. The area you use depends on how much subject movement there will be.

SETTING THE AF-AREA MODE TO DYNAMIC

1. To set the AF-area mode, press and hold the AF-mode button on the front of the camera.
2. Rotate the Sub-command dial until you see the desired setting in your viewfinder, control panel, or, after pressing the Info button, rear LCD.

Select a focus point, as described in the "Single-point AF" section. Pressing the button in the center of the Multi-selector will reset your focus point to the center position.

Note that the AF-area mode is used to select the method with which the camera will focus the lens. This is different from the AF points, which are a cluster of small points that are visible in the viewfinder and that are used to determine where you want the lens to focus (**Figure 5.7**).

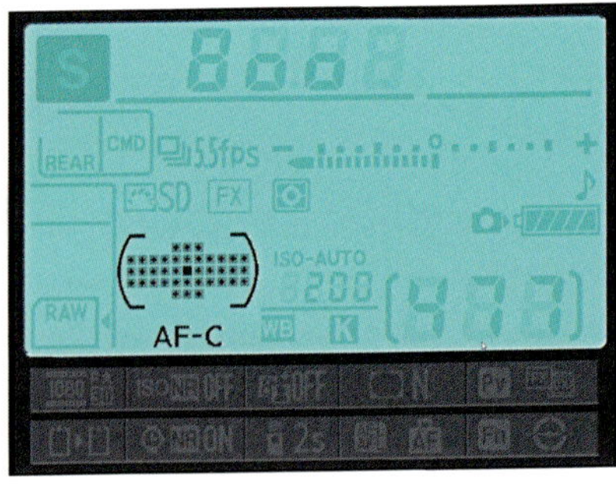

FIGURE 5.7

The Automatic Focus (AF) points are the 39 small boxes seen in the lower-left area of the info screen.

STOP AND GO WITH 3D-TRACKING AF

If you are going to be changing between a moving target and one that is still, you should consider using the 3D-tracking AF mode. This mode mixes the AF-S and Dynamic modes for shooting a subject that goes from stationary to moving without having to adjust your focus mode.

When you have a stationary subject, simply place your selected focus point on your subject and the camera will focus on it. If your subject begins to move out of focus, the camera will track the movement, keeping a sharp focus.

For example, suppose you are shooting a football game. The quarterback has brought the team to the line and is standing behind the center, waiting for the ball to be hiked. If you are using 3D-tracking AF mode, you can place your focus point on the quarterback and start taking pictures of him as he stands at the line. As soon as the ball is hiked and the action starts, the camera will switch to tracking mode and follow his movement within the frame. This can be a little tricky at first, but once you master it, it will make your action shooting effortless.

To select 3D-tracking, simply follow the same steps listed for selecting Dynamic-area AF mode but instead select 3D-tracking mode. It is important to know that 3D-tracking AF mode uses color and contrast to locate and then follow the subject, so this mode might be less effective when everything is similar in tone or color.

CHOOSING A FOCUS MODE

Selecting the proper focus mode depends largely on what type of subject you are photographing. Single-point is typically best for stationary subjects. It allows you to determine exactly where you want your focus to be and then recompose your image while holding the focus in place. If you are taking pictures of an active subject who is moving quickly, trying to set a focus point with Single-point can be difficult, if not impossible. This is when you will want to rely on the Dynamic-area and 3D-tracking modes to quickly assess the subject distance and set your lens focus. This can be especially helpful if the subject distance is varying constantly. Check out pages 97–100 of your manual to learn more about the autofocus features.

MANUAL FOCUS FOR ANTICIPATED ACTION

While I utilize the automatic focus modes for the majority of my shooting, there are times when I like to fall back on manual focus. This is usually when I know when and where the action will occur and I want to capture the subject as it crosses a certain plane of focus. This is useful in sports like motocross or auto racing, where the subjects are on a defined track and I know exactly where I want to capture the action. I could try tracking the subject, but sometimes the view can be obscured by a curve. By pre-focusing the camera, all I have to do is wait for the subject to approach my point of focus and then start firing the camera.

Take a look at **Figure 5.8**. If you want to get up close and personal shooting baseball, then I highly suggest attending a minor league baseball game. My friend Dave Cleaveland had a press pass to shoot the Portland Sea Dogs and was kind enough to invite me along. We spent most of the game just inside the home team dugout and had a blast. Unfortunately, the game was called due to fog (yeah, Portland, Maine, is a port town after all), but not before we got some awesome action shots. We were close to first base, so with the falling light level and increasing fog I used the Single-point focus method to focus on the exact spot that I wanted and then switched the lens to manual focus and waited for the play. As soon as the runner started moving, I started firing in continuous mode to try to nail the peak of action (he was safe). Many thanks to Dave and the Sea Dogs for a great night!

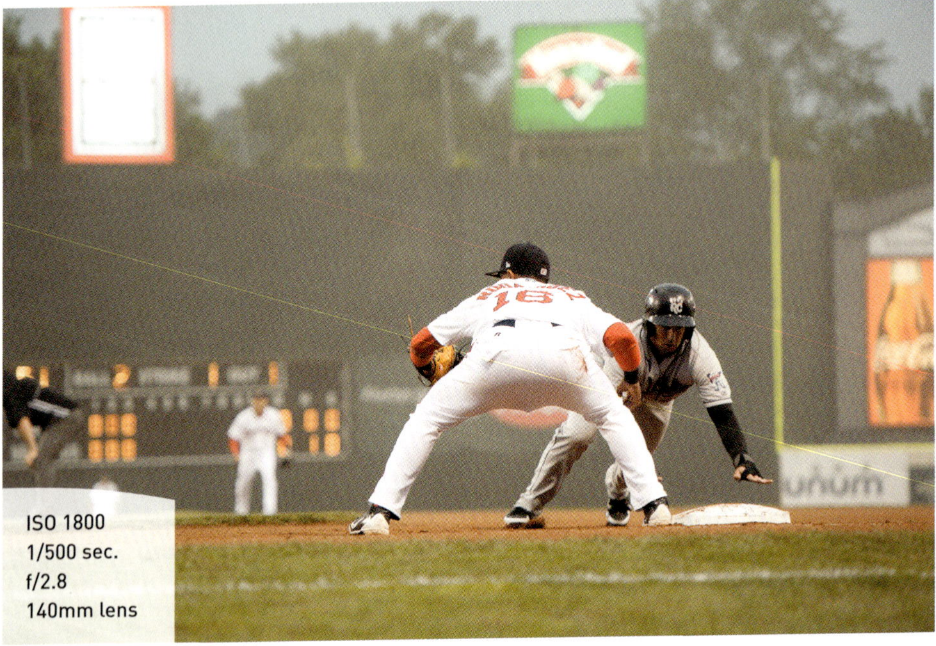

FIGURE 5.8
Pre-focus the camera on a point where you know the subject will be, and start shooting right before they get there.

When you want to use manual focus, just rotate the Focus-mode selector to the M position or set the focus switch on your lens to M (as discussed in Chapter 1). The camera will be able to assist you in focusing your camera using the focus points. Simply move the focus point over the area where you want the camera to focus, press the shutter button halfway to wake the rangefinder, and then turn the focus ring on your lens. When the camera is focused, you will see a circular in-focus indicator in the bottom of your viewfinder. The camera will hold this focus until you rotate the focus ring again or reactivate the AF system.

DRIVE MODES

The drive mode determines how fast your camera will take pictures. Single-frame is for taking one photograph at a time. With every full press of the shutter release button, the camera will take a single image. Continuous mode allows for a more rapid capture rate. Think of it like a machine gun. When you are using continuous mode, the camera will continue to take pictures as long as the shutter release button is held down.

KEEPING UP WITH THE CONTINUOUS SHOOTING MODE

Getting great focus is one thing, but capturing the best moment on the sensor can be difficult if you are shooting just one frame at a time. In the world of sports, and in life in general, things move pretty fast. If you blink, you might miss it. The same can be said for shooting in Single-frame mode. Fortunately, your D600 comes equipped with a Continuous High (CH)—or "burst"—shooting mode that lets you capture a series of images at up to 5.5 frames a second (**Figure 5.9**). You can also select Continuous Low (CL), which allows the user to customize the desired frames per second in the Custom Setting menu.

FIGURE 5.9
Using continuous mode means that you are sure to capture the peak of the action. The continuous shooting mode causes the camera to keep taking images for as long as you hold down the shutter release button. In Single-frame mode, you have to release the button and then press it again to take another picture.

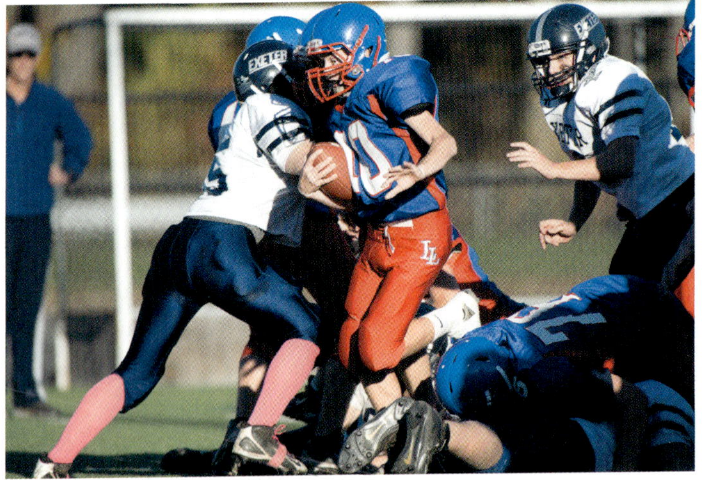

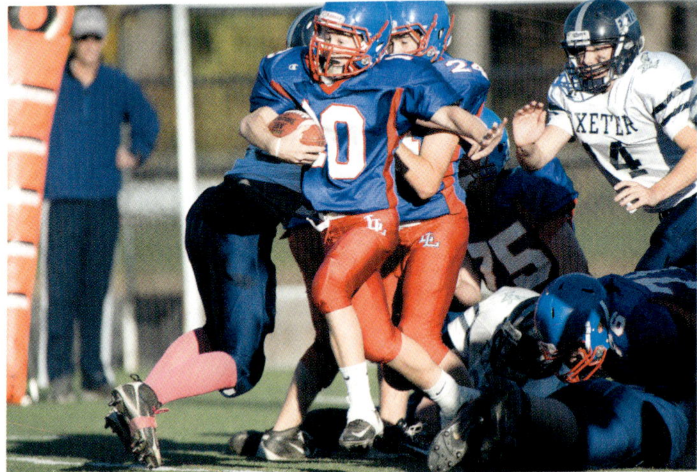

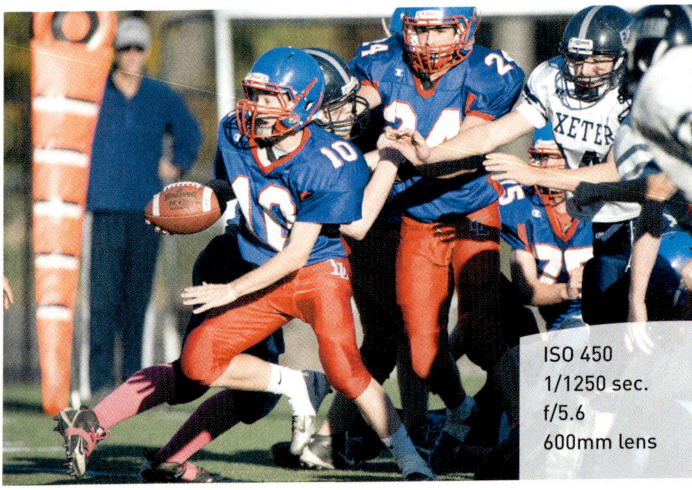

ISO 450
1/1250 sec.
f/5.6
600mm lens

SETTING UP AND SHOOTING IN CONTINUOUS SHOOTING MODE

1. Press the Mode dial lock release (on the top left of your camera).
2. While pressing the Mode dial lock release, simply turn the Release Mode dial to either CL or CH. CH will provide up to 5.5 frames per second, and CL will provide one to five frames per second, based on the user's preference. To set up CL, go to D5 in your Custom Setting menu. (For more on this, refer to page 229 of your user manual.)

Your camera has an internal memory, called a "buffer," where images are stored while they are being processed prior to being moved to your memory card. When the buffer fills up, the camera will stop shooting until space is made for new images. The camera readout in the viewfinder tells you how many frames are available in burst mode. Just look in the lower-right corner of the viewfinder to see the maximum number of images for burst shooting. As you shoot, the number will go down and then back up as the images are written to the memory card.

A SENSE OF MOTION

Shooting action isn't always about freezing the action. There are times when you want to convey a sense of motion so that the viewer can get a feel for the movement and flow of an event. Two techniques you can use to achieve this effect are panning and motion blur.

PANNING

Panning has been used for decades to capture the speed of a moving object as it moves across the frame. It doesn't work well for subjects that are moving toward or away from you. Panning is achieved by following your subject across your frame, moving your camera along with the subject, and using a slower-than-normal shutter speed so that the background (and sometimes even a bit of the subject) has a sideways blur but the main portion of your subject is sharp and blur-free. The key to a great panning shot is selecting the right shutter speed: too fast and you won't get the desired blurring of the background; too slow and the subject will have too much blur and will not be recognizable. Practice the technique until you can achieve a smooth motion with your camera that follows along with your subject. The other thing to remember when panning is to follow through even after the shutter has closed. This will keep the motion smooth and give you better images.

In **Figure 5.10**, I used the panning technique to follow this plane as it took off in front of me. I set the camera to the continuous shooting mode, I used Shutter Priority mode to select a shutter speed of 1/60 of a second, and the focus mode was on Dynamic. Even though my aperture was f/10, I knew that the panning motion would blur my background.

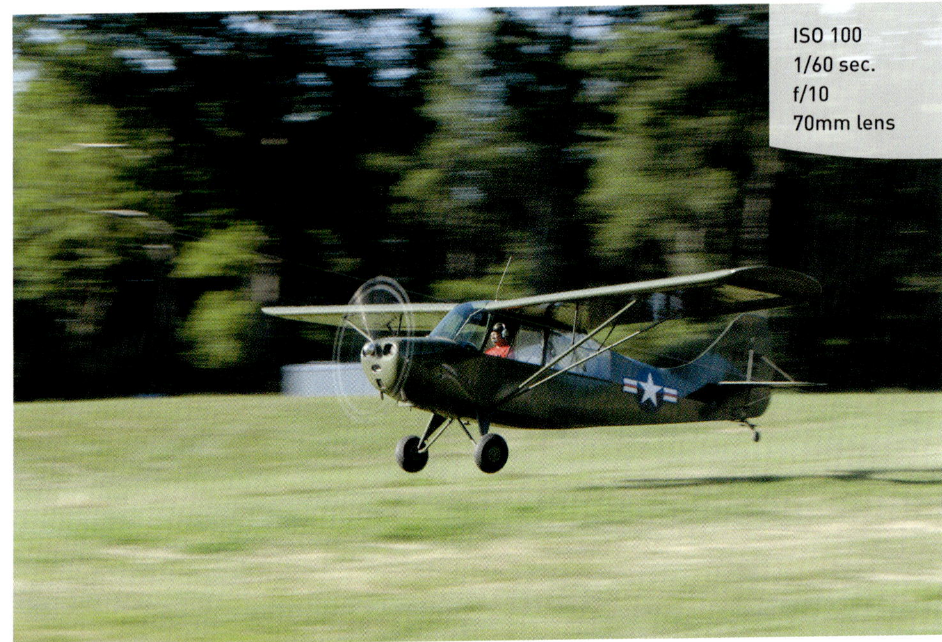
ISO 100
1/60 sec.
f/10
70mm lens

FIGURE 5.10
Following the subject as it moves across the field of view allows for a slower shutter speed and adds a sense of motion by blurring the background.

MOTION BLUR

Another way to let the viewer in on the feel of the action is to simply include some blur in the image. This isn't accidental blur from choosing the wrong shutter speed. This blur is more exaggerated, and it tells a story. In **Figure 5.11**, I was watching my son go around the racetrack. I took many shots with a nice fast shutter speed and froze him in his tracks, but I decided to slow down the shutter speed and let the motion tell part of the story too.

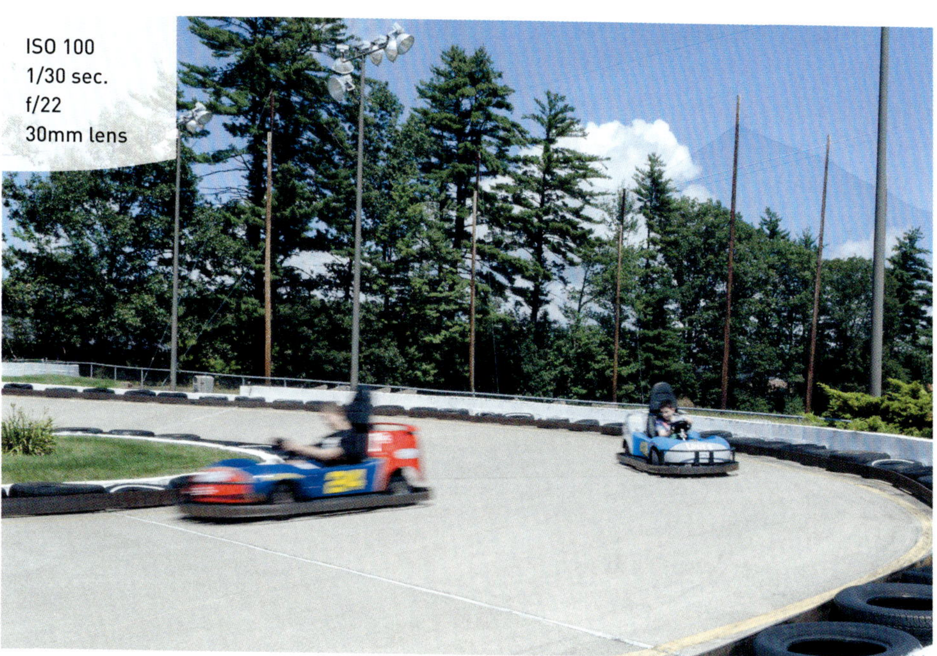

FIGURE 5.11 The movement of the go-karts coupled with the slow shutter speed conveys a sense of action in the shot.

Just as in panning, there is no preordained shutter speed to use for this effect. It is simply a matter of trial and error until you have a look that conveys the action. I try to get some area of the subject that is frozen. The key to this technique is the correct shutter speed combined with keeping the camera still during the exposure. You are trying to capture the motion of the subject, not of the photographer or the camera, so use a good shooting stance or even a tripod.

TIPS FOR SHOOTING ACTION

GIVE THEM SOMEWHERE TO GO

Whether you are shooting something as simple as your child's soccer match or as complex as the aerial acrobatics of a motorcycle jumper, where you place the subject in the frame is just as important as how well you expose the image. A poorly composed shot can completely ruin a great moment by not holding the viewer's attention.

The one mistake I see many times in action photography is that the photographer doesn't use the frame properly. If you are dealing with a subject that is moving horizontally across your field of view, give the subject somewhere to go by placing them to the side of the frame, with their motion leading toward the middle of the frame (**Figure 5.12**). This offsetting of the subject will introduce a sense of direction and anticipation for the viewer. Unless you are going to completely fill the image with the action, try to avoid placing your subject in the middle of the frame.

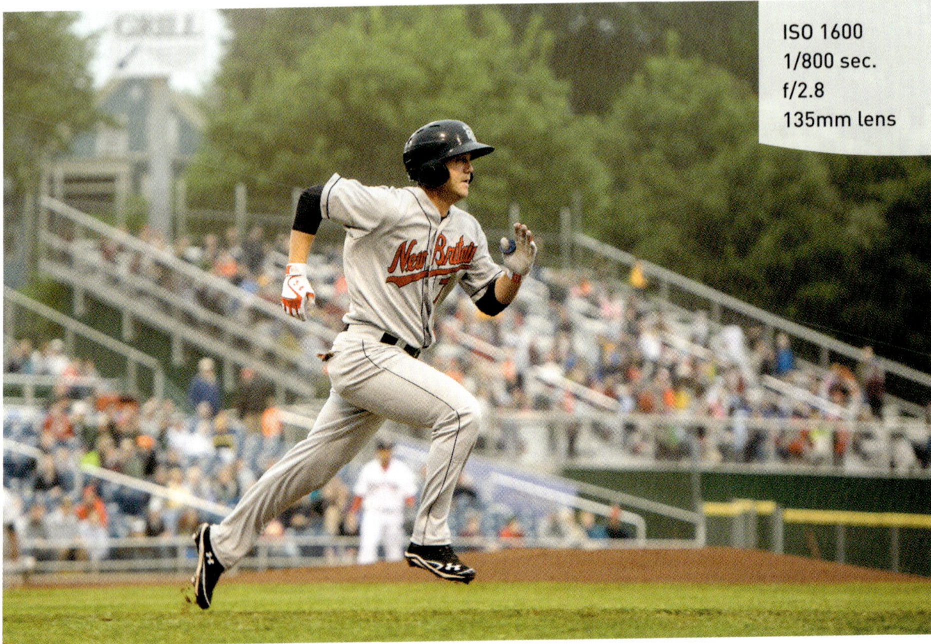

FIGURE 5.12
Try to leave space in front of your subject to lead the action in a direction.

GET IN FRONT OF THE ACTION

Here's another one. When shooting action, show the action coming toward you (**Figure 5.13**). Don't shoot the action going away from you. People want to see faces. Faces convey the action, the drive, the sense of urgency, and the emotion of the moment. So if you are shooting action involving people, always position yourself so that the action is either coming at you or at least perpendicular to your position.

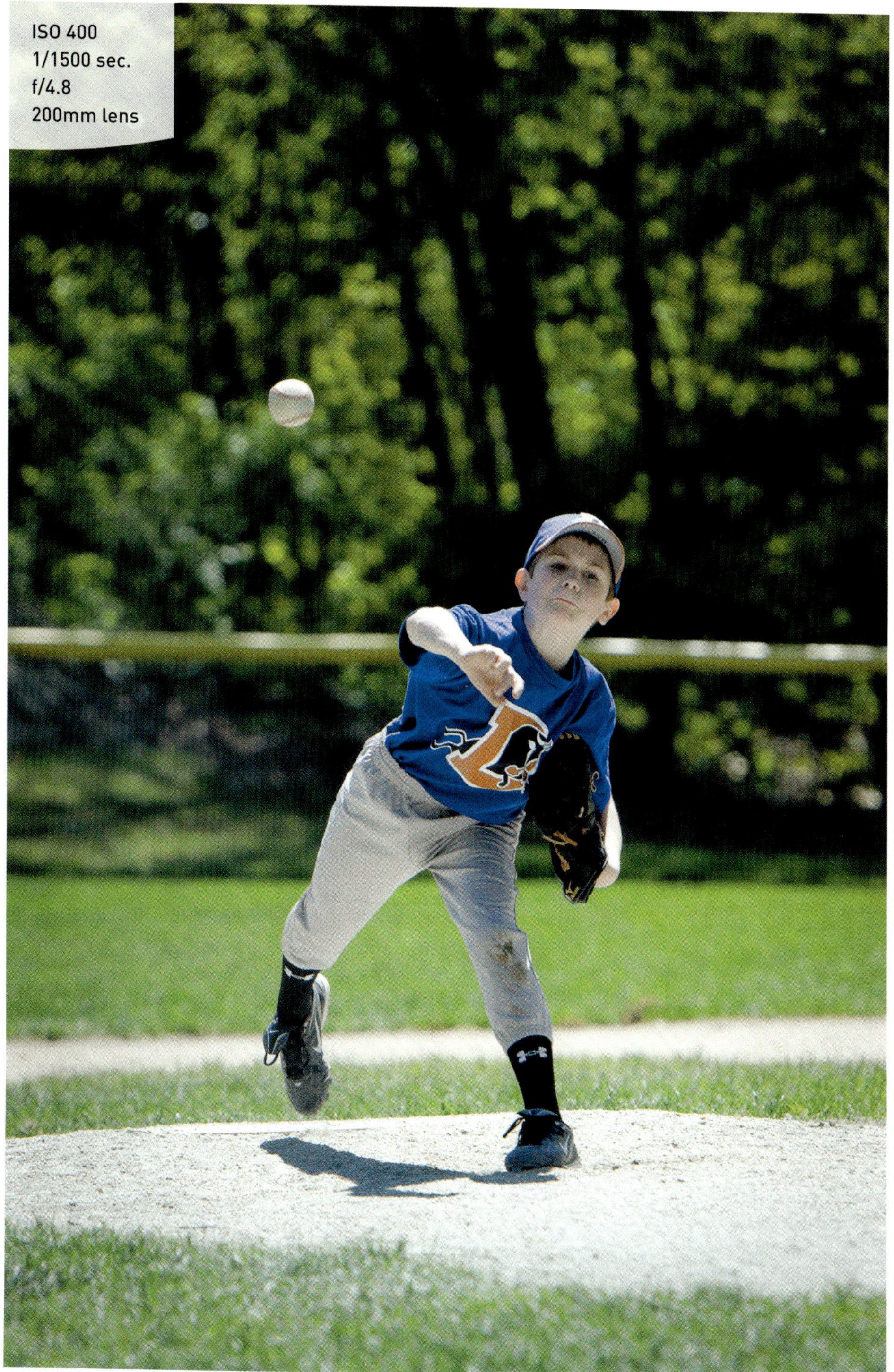

FIGURE 5.13
Shooting from the front with a telephoto gives a feeling that the action is coming right at you.

SHOOT IN MANUAL MODE TO LOCK IN YOUR EXPOSURE

The Aperture Priority and Shutter Priority modes are great, but sometimes it pays to just do things yourself. If you find yourself shooting in an environment where the action is moving across backgrounds that will play havoc with your meter readings, you might be better off setting up your shot in Manual mode.

I attended a local festival where there were people dressed in medieval armor demonstrating how knights fought in that time period. The meter was having trouble with the shiny armor, so after doing some trial and error in Manual mode, I settled on a combination of settings that would freeze the action, blur the distracting background, and not blow out the highlights on the armor (**Figure 5.14**).

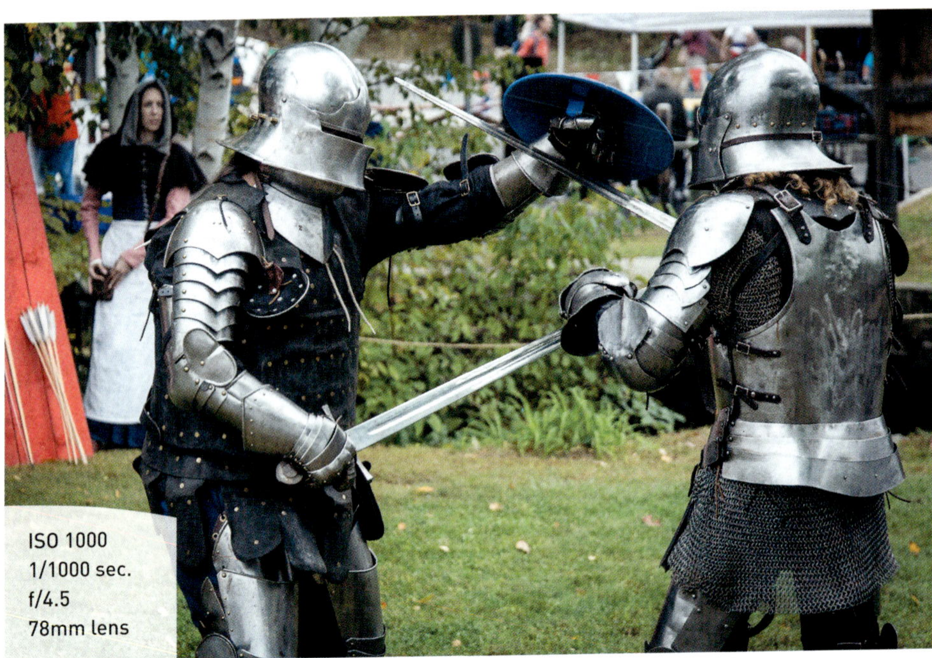
ISO 1000
1/1000 sec.
f/4.5
78mm lens

FIGURE 5.14 Sometimes it pays to shoot in Manual mode.

Chapter 5 Assignments

The mechanics of motion

For this first assignment, you need to find some action. Explore the relationship between the speed of an object and its direction of travel. Use the same shutter speed to record your subject moving toward you and across your view. Try using the same shutter speed for both to compare the difference made by the direction of travel.

Wide vs. telephoto

Just as with the first assignment, photograph a subject moving in different directions, but this time, use a wide-angle lens and then a telephoto. Check out how the telephoto setting on the zoom lens will require faster shutter speeds than the lens at its wide-angle setting.

Getting a feel for focusing modes

We discussed two different ways to autofocus for action: Dynamic and 3D-tracking. Starting with Dynamic mode, find a moving subject and get familiar with the way the mode works.

Now repeat the process using the 3D-tracking AF mode. The point of the exercise is to become familiar enough with the two modes to decide which one to use for the situation you are photographing.

Anticipating the spot using manual focus

For this assignment, you will need to find a subject that you know will cross a specific line that you can pre-focus on. A street with moderate traffic works well for this. Focus on a spot on the street that the cars will travel across (don't forget to set your lens for manual focus). To do this right, you need to set the drive mode on the camera to continuous mode. When a car approaches the spot, start shooting. Try shooting in three- or four-frame bursts.

Following the action

Panning is a great way to show motion. To begin, find a subject that will move across your path at a steady speed and practice following it in your viewfinder from side to side. With the camera in Shutter Priority mode, set your shutter speed to 1/30 of a second and the focus mode to Dynamic. Now pan along with the subject and shoot as it moves across your view. Experiment with different shutter speeds and focal lengths. Panning takes some time to get a feel for, so try it with different types of subjects moving at different speeds.

Feeling the movement

Instead of panning with the motion, use a stationary camera position and adjust the shutter speed until you get a blurred effect that gives the sense of motion but still allows you to identify the subject. There is a big difference between a slightly blurred photo that looks like you just picked the wrong shutter speed and one that looks intentional for the purpose of showing motion. Just as with panning, it will take some experimentation to find the shutter speed that achieves the desired effect.

Share your results with the book's Flickr group!

www.flickr.com/groups/d600fromsnapshotstogreatshots

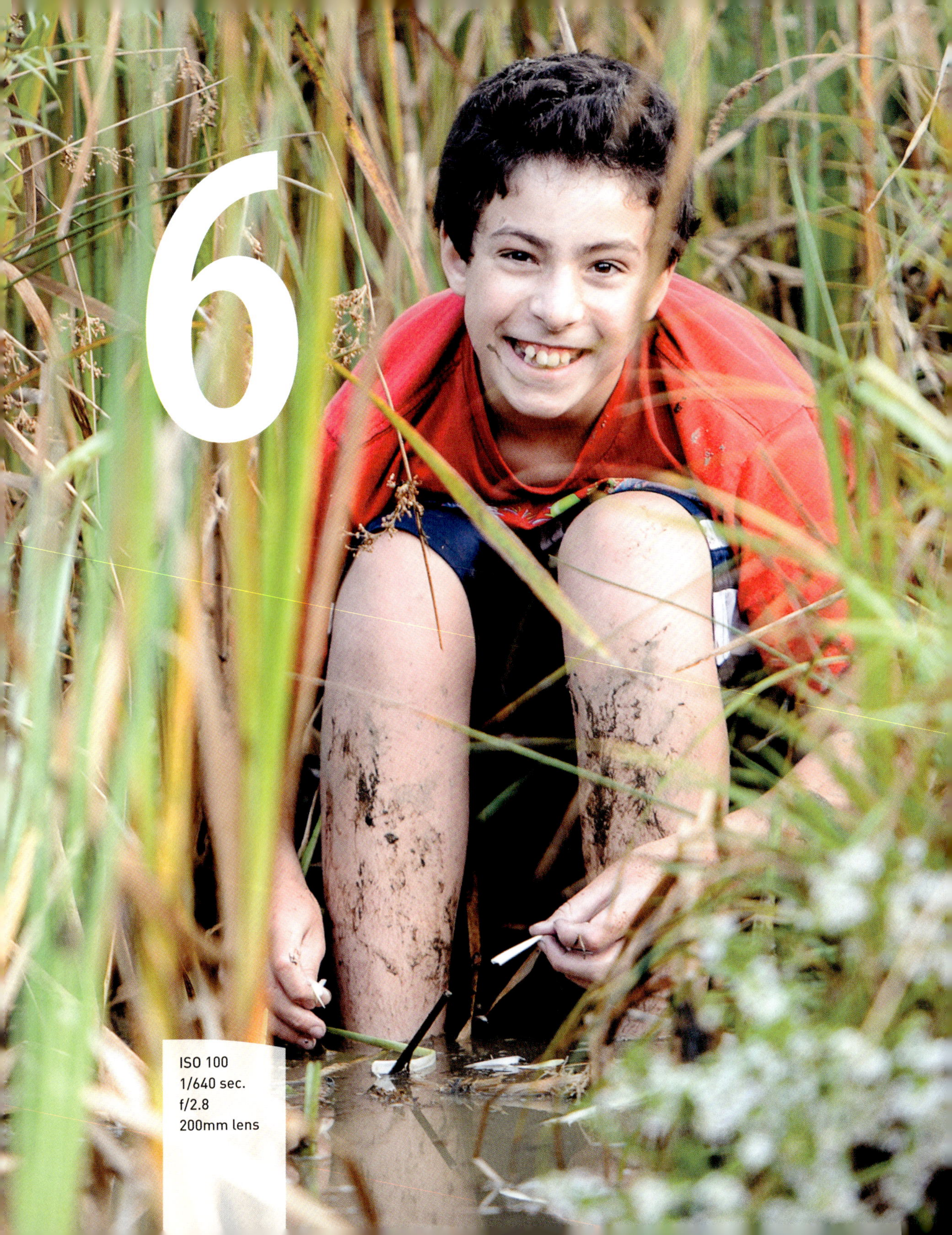

6

ISO 100
1/640 sec.
f/2.8
200mm lens

Perfect Portraits

SETTINGS AND FEATURES TO MAKE GREAT PORTRAITS

Taking pictures of people is one of the great joys of photography. You will experience a great sense of accomplishment when you capture the spirit and personality of someone in a photograph. At the same time, you have a great responsibility because the person in front of the camera is depending on you to make them look good. You can't always change how someone looks, but you can control the way you photograph that individual. In this chapter, we will explore some camera features and techniques that can help you create great portraits.

PORING OVER THE PICTURE

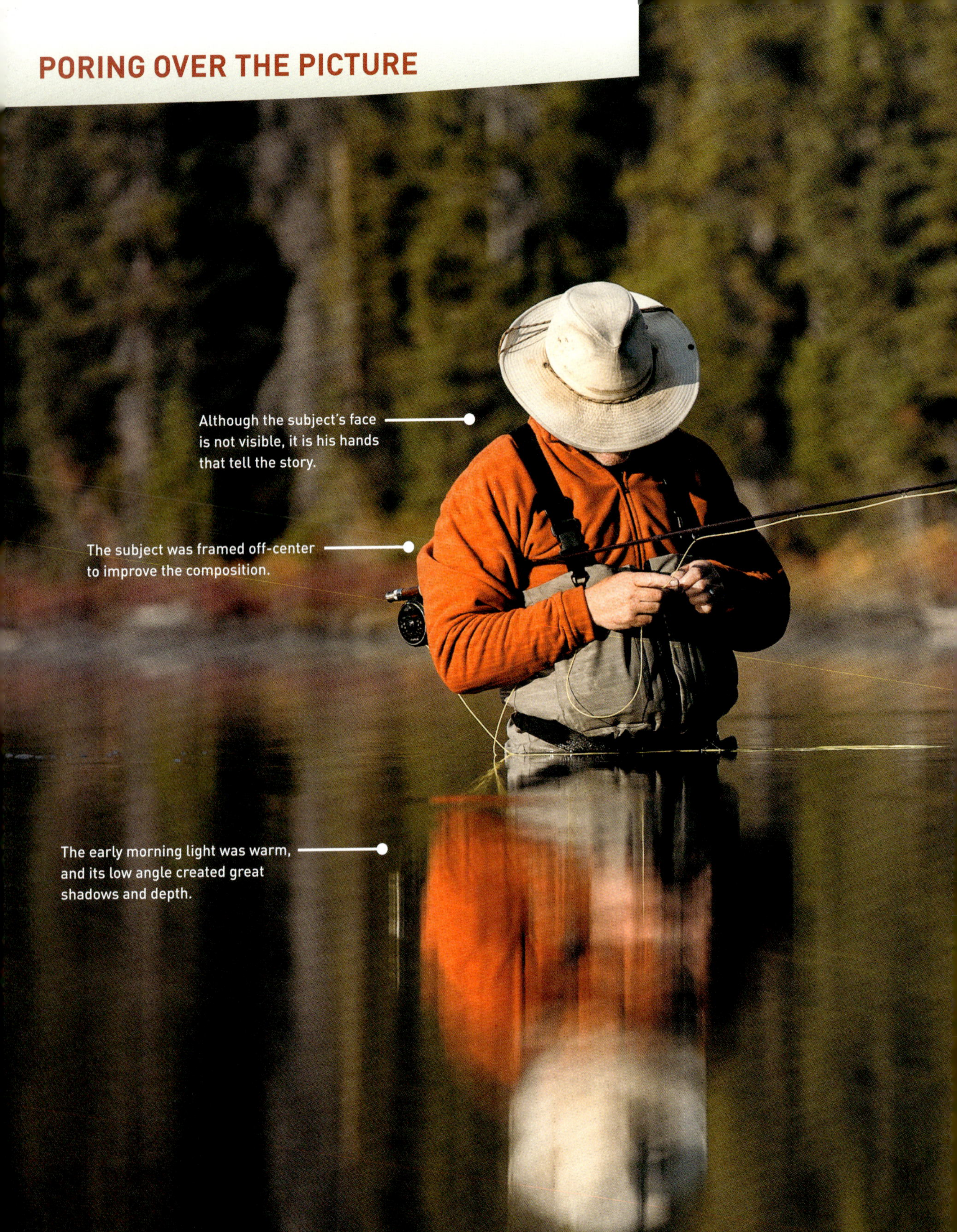

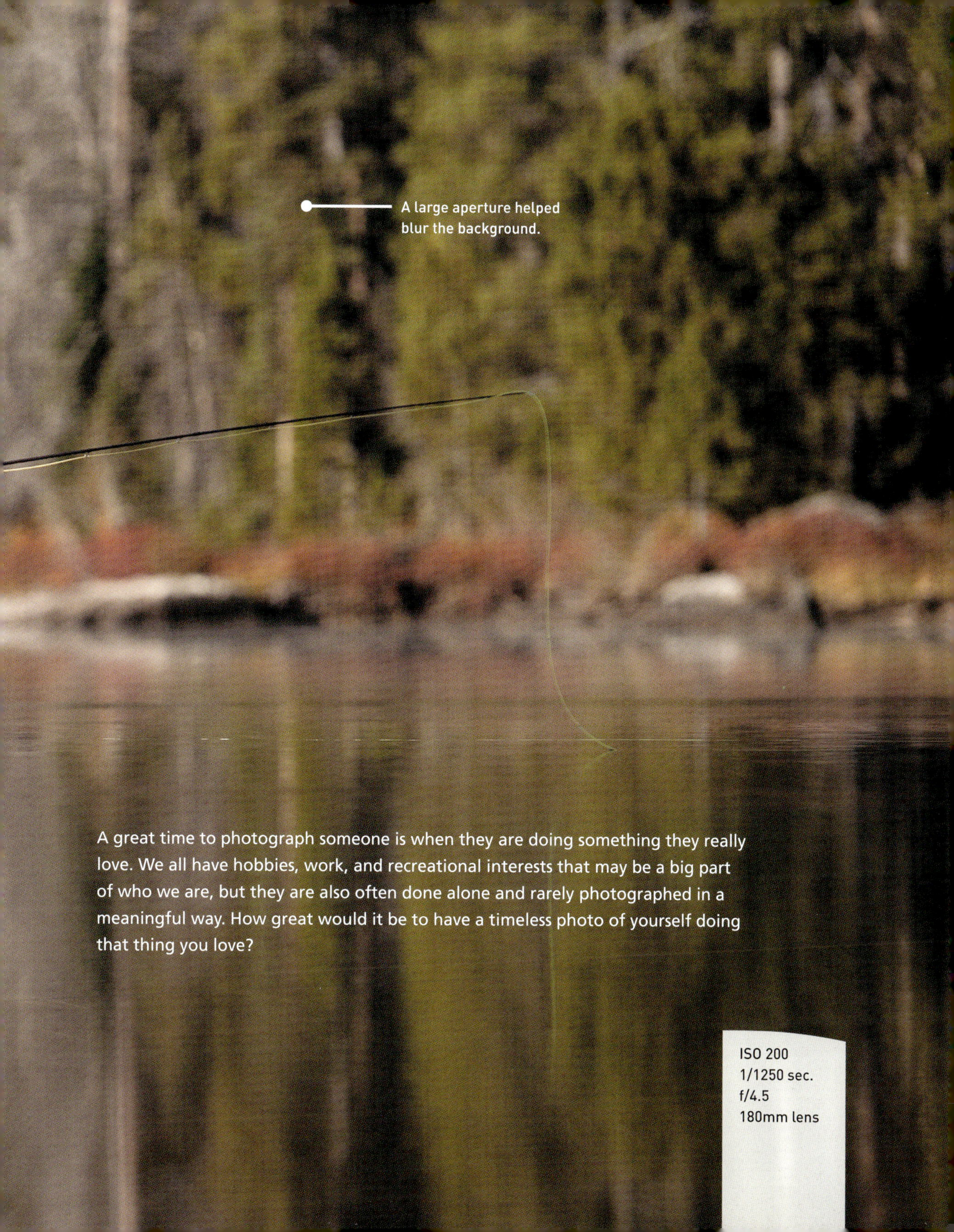

A large aperture helped blur the background.

A great time to photograph someone is when they are doing something they really love. We all have hobbies, work, and recreational interests that may be a big part of who we are, but they are also often done alone and rarely photographed in a meaningful way. How great would it be to have a timeless photo of yourself doing that thing you love?

ISO 200
1/1250 sec.
f/4.5
180mm lens

AUTOMATIC PORTRAIT MODE

In Chapter 3, we reviewed all of the automatic scene modes. One of them, Portrait mode, is dedicated to shooting portraits. While this is not my preferred camera setting, it is a great jumping-off point for those who are just starting out. The key to using this mode is to understand what is going on with the camera so that when you venture further into portrait photography, you can expand on the settings and get the most from your camera and, more importantly, your subject.

Whether you are photographing an individual or a group, the emphasis should always be on the subject. Portrait mode uses a larger aperture setting to keep the depth of field very narrow, which means that the background will appear slightly blurred or out of focus. To take full advantage of this effect, use a medium- to telephoto-length lens. Also, keep a pretty close distance to your subject. If you shoot from too far away, the narrow depth of field will not be as effective.

USING APERTURE PRIORITY MODE

If you took a poll of portrait photographers to see which shooting mode was most often used for portraits, the answer would certainly be Aperture Priority (A) mode. Selecting the right aperture is important for placing the most critically sharp area of the photo on your subject, while simultaneously blurring all of the distracting background clutter (**Figure 6.1**). Not only will a large aperture give the narrowest depth of field, it will also allow you to shoot in lower light levels at lower ISO settings.

This isn't to say that you have to use the largest aperture on your lens. A good place to begin is f/5.6. This will give you enough depth of field to keep the entire face in focus, while providing enough blur to eliminate distractions in the background. This isn't a hard-and-fast setting; it's just a good number to start with. Your aperture might change depending on the focal length of the lens you are using and on the amount of blur that you want for your foreground and background elements.

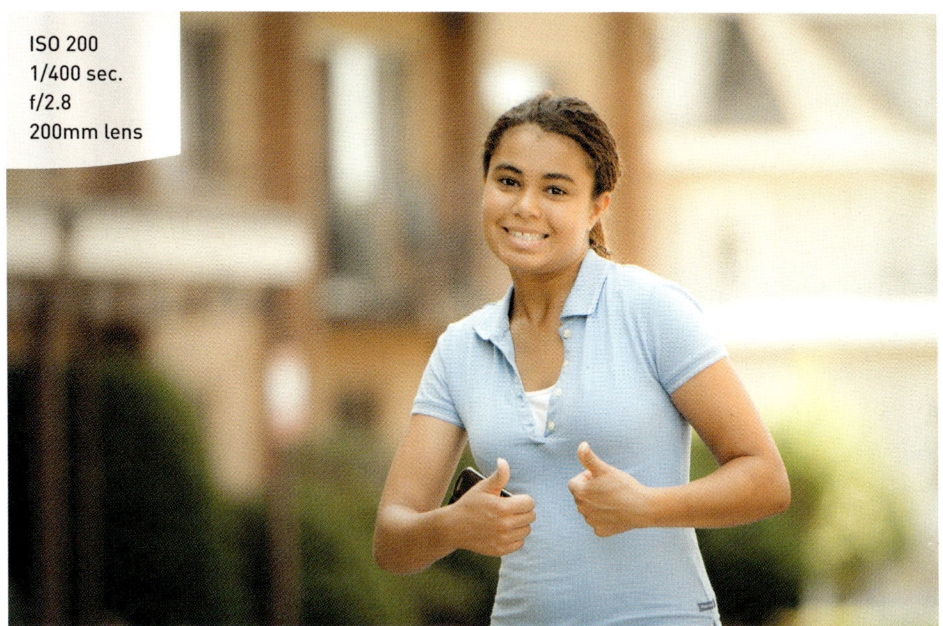

FIGURE 6.1
Using a wide aperture, especially with a longer lens, blurs distracting background details.

GO WIDE FOR ENVIRONMENTAL PORTRAITS

There will be times when your subject's environment is of great significance to the story you want to tell. This might mean using a smaller aperture to get more detail in the background or foreground. By using Aperture Priority mode, you can set your aperture to a higher f-stop, such as f/8 or f/11, and include the important details of the scene that surrounds your subject.

Using a wider-than-normal lens can also assist in getting more depth of field as well as showing the surrounding area. A wide-angle lens requires less stopping down of the aperture (making the aperture smaller) to achieve an acceptable depth of field. This is because wide-angle lenses cover a greater area, so the depth of field appears to cover a greater percentage of the scene.

A wider lens might also be necessary to relay more information about the scenery (**Figure 6.2**). Select a lens length that is wide enough to tell the story but not so wide that you distort the subject. There's little in the world of portraiture quite as unflattering as giving someone a big, distorted nose (unless you are going for that sort of look). When shooting a portrait with a wide-angle lens, keep the subject away from the edge of the frame. This will reduce the distortion, especially in very wide focal lengths. As the lens length increases, distortion will be reduced. I generally don't like to go wider than about 24mm for portraits.

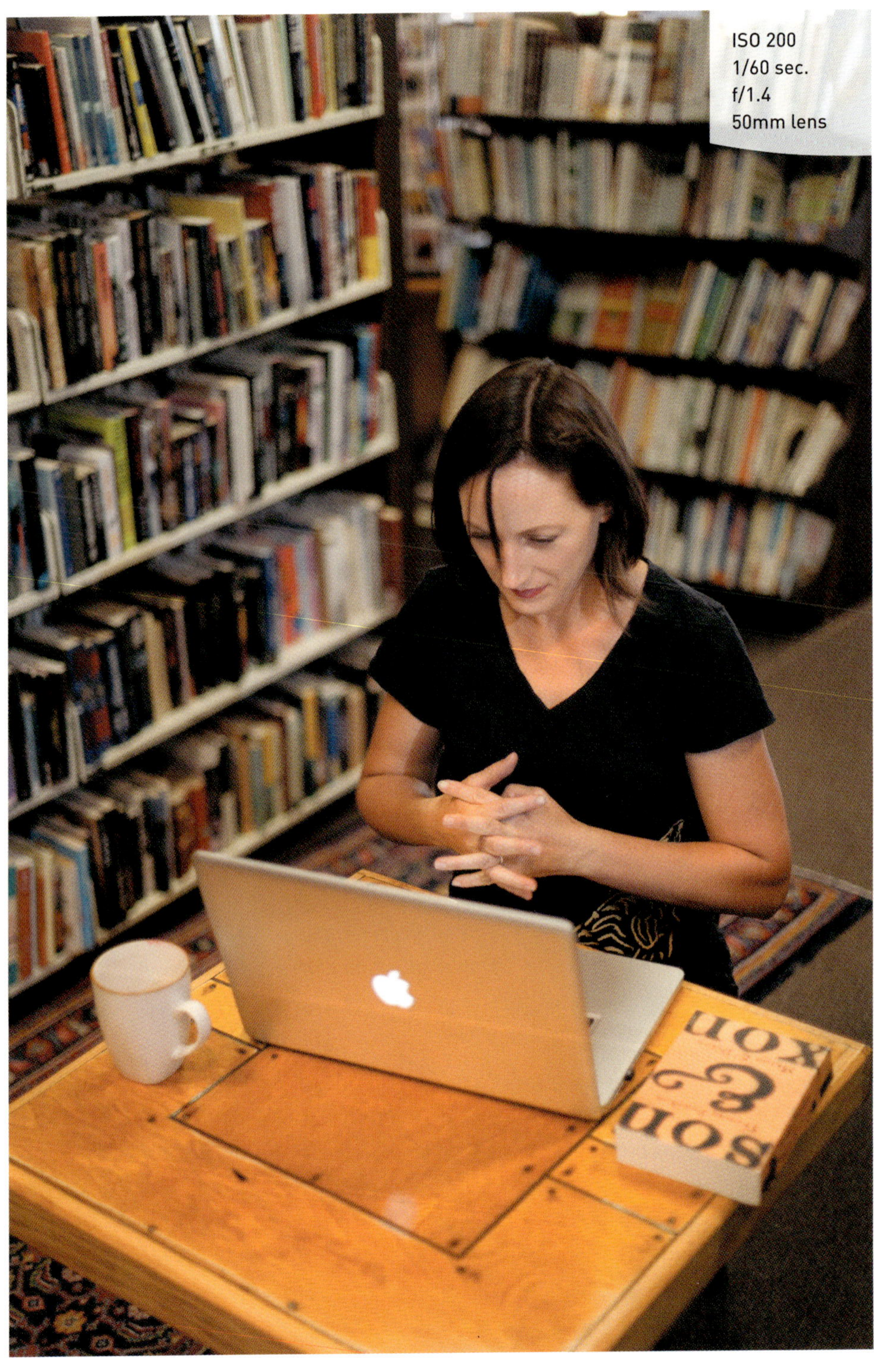

ISO 200
1/60 sec.
f/1.4
50mm lens

FIGURE 6.2
A wider lens allows you to capture more of the environment in the scene without having to increase the distance between you and the subject.

METERING BASICS

There are multiple metering modes in your camera, but the way they work is very similar. A light meter measures the amount of light being reflected off your subject and then renders a suggested exposure value based on the brightness of the subject and the ISO setting of the sensor. To establish this value, the meter averages all of the brightness values to come up with a middle tone, sometimes referred to as 18 percent gray. The exposure value is then rendered based on this middle gray value. This means that a white wall would be underexposed and a black wall would be overexposed in an effort to make each one appear gray. To assist with special lighting situations, the D600 has three metering modes: Matrix (**Figure 6.3**), which uses the entire frame; Spot (**Figure 6.4**), which takes specific readings from small areas (often used with a gray card); and Center-weighted (**Figure 6.5**), which looks at the entire frame but places most of the exposure emphasis on the center of the frame.

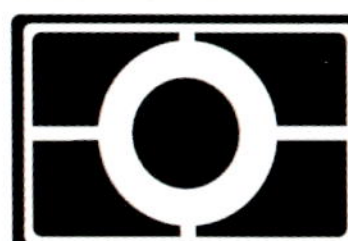

FIGURE 6.3
The Matrix metering mode uses the entire frame.

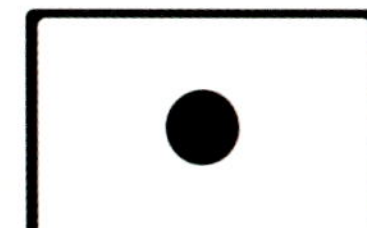

FIGURE 6.4
The Spot metering mode uses a very small area of the frame.

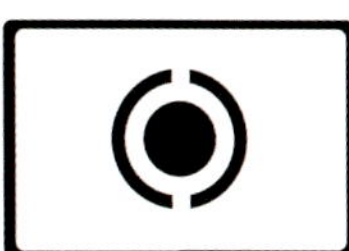

FIGURE 6.5
The Center-weighted metering mode looks at the entire frame but emphasizes the center of it.

METERING MODES FOR PORTRAITS

For most portrait situations, the Matrix metering mode is ideal. (For more on how metering works, see the "Metering Basics" sidebar.) This mode measures light values from all portions of the viewfinder and then establishes a proper exposure for the scene. The only problem that you might encounter when using this metering mode is when you have very light or very dark backgrounds in your portrait shots.

In those instances, the meter might be fooled into using the wrong exposure information because it will be trying to lighten or darken the entire scene based on the prominence of dark or light areas (**Figure 6.6**). You can deal with this in one of two ways. You can use exposure compensation, which we cover in Chapter 7, to dial in adjustments for over- and underexposure. Or you can change the metering mode to

Center-weighted metering. The Center-weighted metering mode uses only the center area of the viewfinder (about 9 percent) to get its exposure information. This is the best way to achieve proper exposure for most portraits; metering off skin tones, averaged with hair and clothing, will often give a more accurate exposure (**Figure 6.7**). This metering mode is also great to use when the subject is strongly backlit.

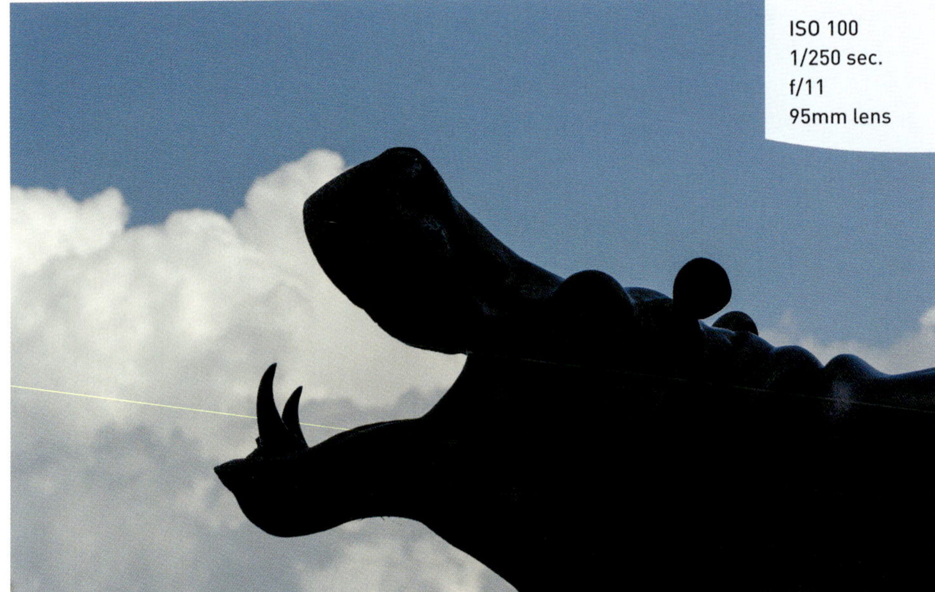

ISO 100
1/250 sec.
f/11
95mm lens

FIGURE 6.6
The bright background fooled the meter into choosing a slightly underexposed setting for this photo.

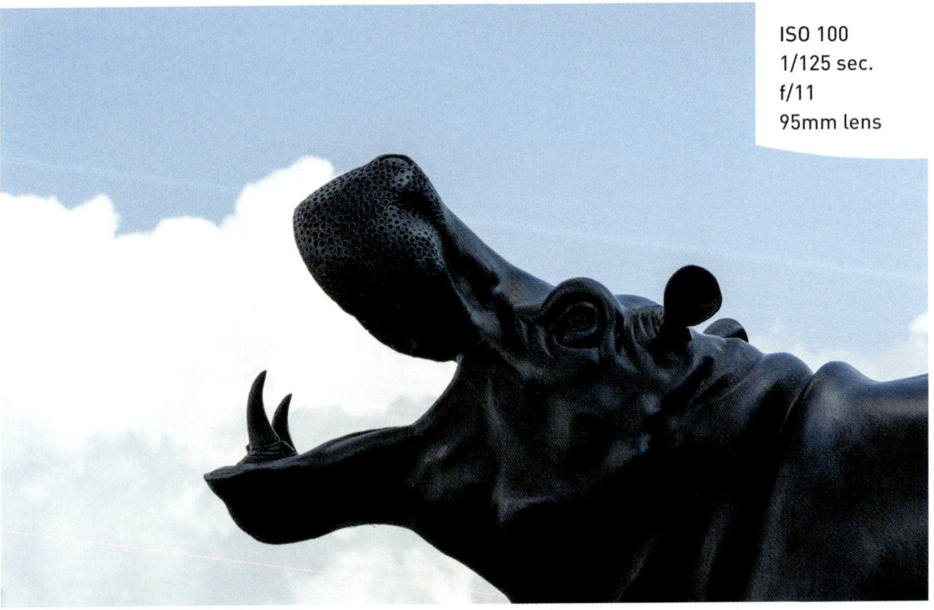

ISO 100
1/125 sec.
f/11
95mm lens

FIGURE 6.7
When I switched to the Center-weighted metering mode, my camera was able to ignore much of the background and add a little more time to the exposure.

SETTING YOUR METERING MODE TO CENTER-WEIGHTED METERING

1. Press and hold the Metering button, located on the top-right side of your camera.
2. Hold down the Metering button while rotating the Main Command dial to the Center-weighted metering icon, and then release.

USING THE AE-L (AUTO EXPOSURE LOCK) FEATURE

There will often be times when your subject is not in the center of the frame but you still want to use the Center-weighted metering mode. So how can you get an accurate reading if the subject isn't in the center? Try using the AE-L (Auto Exposure Lock) feature to hold the exposure setting while you recompose.

AE Lock lets you use the exposure setting from any portion of the scene that you think is appropriate, and then lock that setting in regardless of how the scene looks when you recompose. An example of this would be when you're shooting a photograph of someone and a large amount of blue sky appears in the picture. Normally, the meter might be fooled by all that bright sky and try to reduce the exposure. Using AE Lock, you can establish the correct metering by zooming in on the subject (or even pointing the camera toward the ground), taking the meter reading and locking it in with the AE-L feature, and then recomposing and taking your photo with the locked-in exposure.

Manual Callout

There is a way to lock in your AE-L reading so that you can continue shooting without having to hold in the AE-L button. This involves changing the button function in the Custom Setting menu, but I prefer to leave this feature turned off because I would, more often than not, forget that it is on and end up using the wrong metering for a new subject. If you want to learn more about this feature, check out page 244 of your manual.

SHOOTING WITH THE AE LOCK FEATURE

1. Find the AE-L/AF-L button (which we'll call AE-L for short) on the back of the camera and place your thumb on it.
2. While looking through the viewfinder, place the focus point on your subject, press the shutter release button halfway to get a meter reading, and focus the camera.

3. Press and hold the AE-L button to lock in the meter reading. You should see the AE-L indicator in the viewfinder.
4. While pressing in the AE-L button, recompose your shot and take the photo.
5. To take more than one photo without having to take another meter reading, just hold down the AE-L button until you are done using the meter setting.

FOCUSING: THE EYES HAVE IT

It has been said that the eyes are the windows to the soul, and nothing could be truer when you are taking a photograph of someone (**Figure 6.8**). You could have the perfect composition and exposure, but if the eyes aren't sharp the entire image suffers. While there are many different focusing modes to choose from on your D600, for portrait work you can't beat AF-S (Single-Servo AF) mode using a single focusing point. AF-S focusing will establish a single focus for the lens and then hold it until you take the photograph; the other focusing modes continue focusing until the photograph is taken. The single-point selection lets you place the focusing point right on your subject's eye and set that spot as the critical focus spot. Using AF-S mode lets you get that focus and recompose all in one motion.

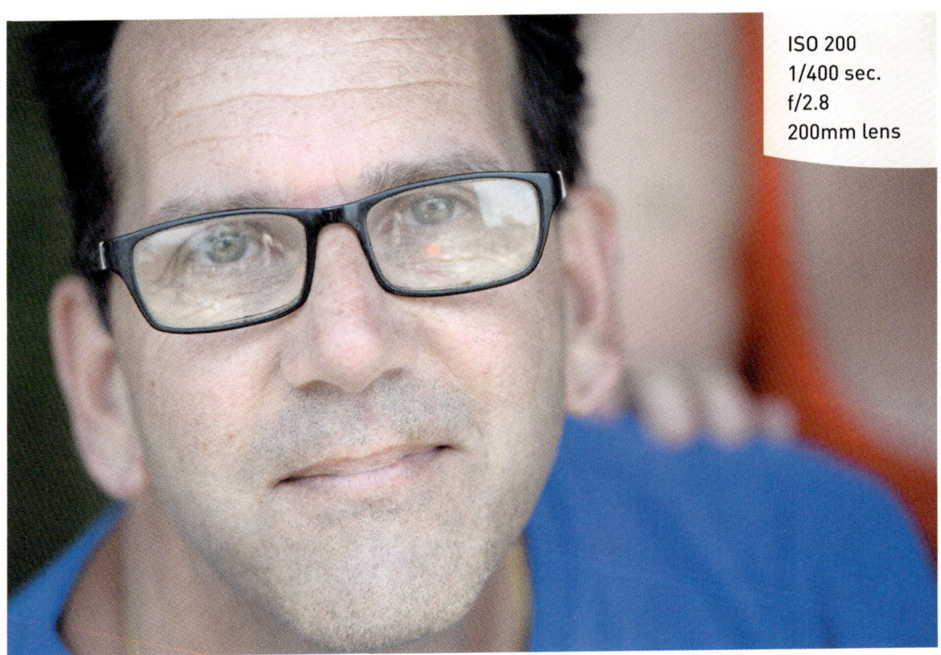

ISO 200
1/400 sec.
f/2.8
200mm lens

FIGURE 6.8
When photographing people, you should almost always place the emphasis on the eyes. (Photo by Raymond Paragian, my nephew.)

SETTING YOUR FOCUS TO A SINGLE POINT

1. Press and hold the Focus-mode selector, near the lens on the front of the camera.
2. While holding the button, rotate the Sub-command dial with your index finger.
3. Select the Single Point icon on the control panel or information screen (**A**) and release the Focus-mode selector button.

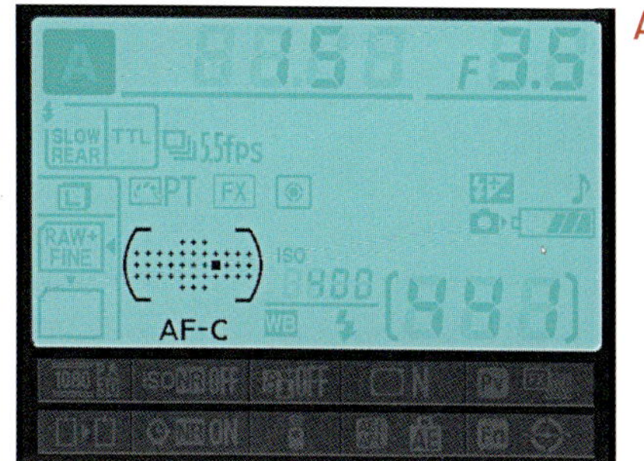

A

SETTING UP FOR AF-S FOCUS MODE

1. Press and hold the Focus-mode selector, near the lens on the front of the camera.
2. While holding the button, rotate the Main Command dial with your thumb.
3. Release the Focus-mode selector when AF-S is displayed in the control panel.
4. When you are back in shooting mode, use the Multi-selector to move the focus point to one of the 39 available positions. This is visible while looking through the viewfinder but also on the information screen (**B**).

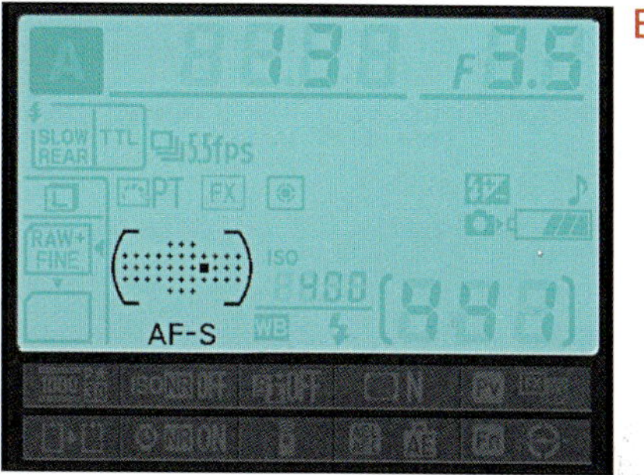

B

Now, to shoot using this focus point, place that point on one of your subject's eyes and press the shutter button halfway until you hear or see the focus indicator chirp. While still holding the shutter button down halfway, recompose if necessary and take your shot.

I typically use the center point for focus selection. I find it easier to place that point directly on the location where my critical focus should be established and then recompose the shot. Even though the single point can be selected from any of the focus points, it typically takes longer to figure out where that point should be in relation to my subject. By using the center point, I can quickly establish focus and get on with my shooting.

KEEPING THE FOCUS WHERE IT COUNTS

A common mistake is to focus on the center of the face or the nose. This will give you a portrait in which the nose is in focus but not the eyes, especially with a large aperture and shallow depth of field. Try to get into the habit of focusing on the eyes and then recomposing the image.

CLASSIC BLACK AND WHITE PORTRAITS

There is something timeless about a black and white portrait. It eliminates the distraction of color and puts all the emphasis on the subject. To get great black and whites without having to resort to image-processing software, set your picture control to Monochrome (**Figure 6.9**). You should know that the picture controls are automatically applied when shooting with the JPEG file format. If you are shooting in RAW, the picture that shows up on your rear LCD display will look black and white, but it will appear as a color image when you open it in non-Nikon RAW processing software (like Adobe Photoshop Lightroom or Apple Aperture). This is because the nature of RAW data is that the camera hasn't processed it. If you're using Nikon's ViewNX2 or Capture NX2 software, you'll see the assigned picture control when you first open the photo, but you can use the software to apply any picture control to your RAW photo.

The real key to using the Monochrome picture control is to customize it for your portrait subject. The control can be changed to alter the sharpness and contrast. For women, children, puppies, and anyone else who should look somewhat soft, set the Sharpness setting to 0 or 1. For old cowboys, longshoremen, and anyone else who you want to look really detailed, try a setting of 6 or 7. I typically like to leave Contrast at a setting of around –1 or –2. This gives me a nice range of tones throughout the image.

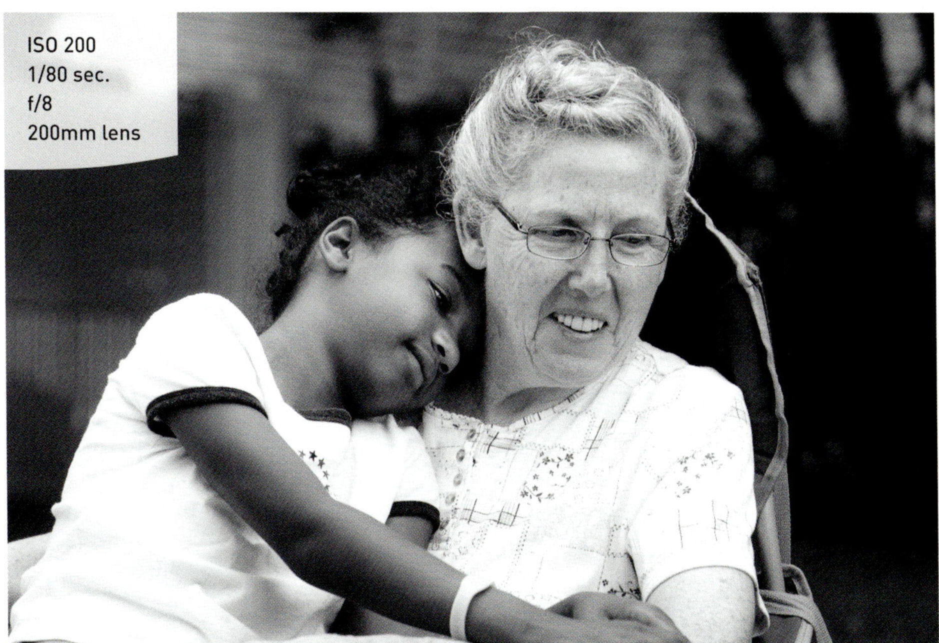

FIGURE 6.9
Getting high-quality black and white portraits can be as simple as setting the picture control to Monochrome.

The other adjustment that you should try is to change the picture control's Filter effect from None to one of the four available settings (Yellow, Orange, Red, and Green). Using the filters will have the effect of either lightening or darkening the skin tones. The Red and Yellow filters usually lighten skin, while the Green filter can make skin appear a bit darker. Experiment to see which one works best for your subject.

SETTING YOUR PICTURE CONTROL TO MONOCHROME

1. Press the Retouch/Picture Control button on the back of the camera to bring up the Set Picture Control screen, highlight Monochrome, and press OK (**A**).

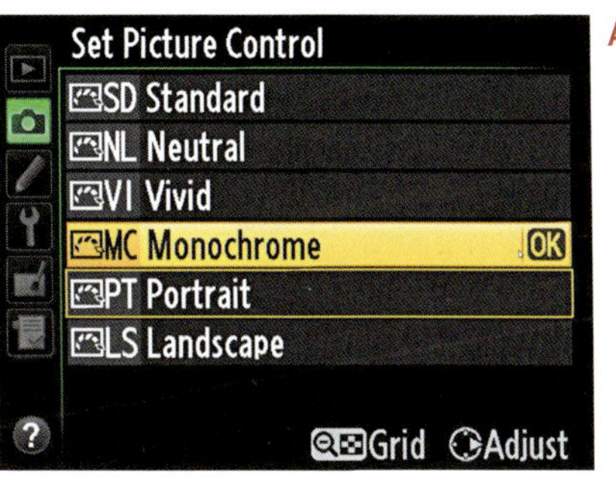

A

CUSTOMIZING YOUR MONOCHROME PICTURE CONTROL

1. Follow the previous step to get to the Picture Control menu and highlight Monochrome, but instead of pressing the OK button, press the Multi-Selector to the right to enter the customization menu (**A**).
2. Once you have modified the settings, press the OK button to save your changes. When you return to the Picture Control menu, you will now see a small star next to the MC. This is your clue that you have altered the default settings for that particular control (**B**).

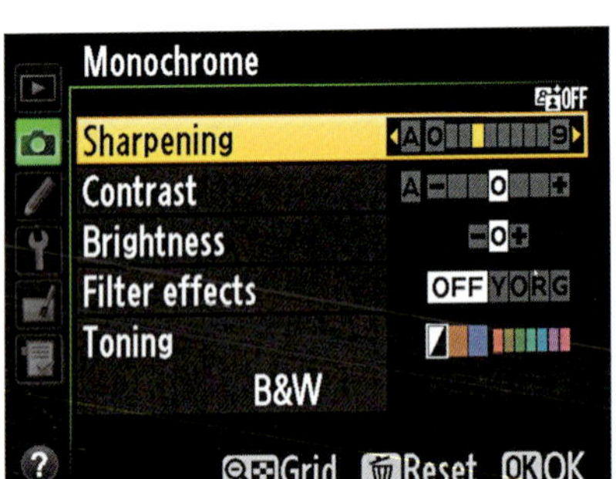

A

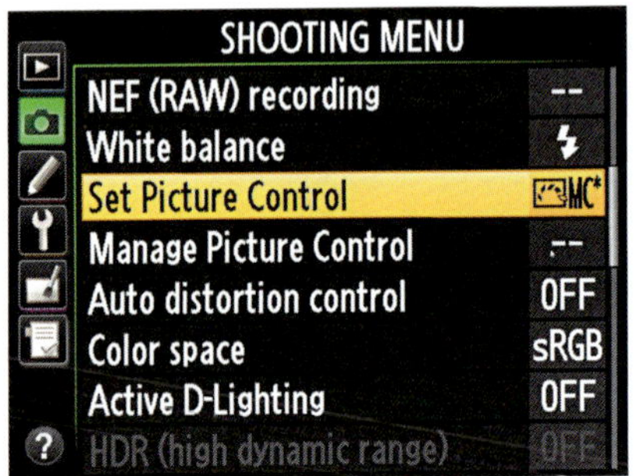

B

THE PORTRAIT PICTURE CONTROL FOR BETTER SKIN TONES

As long as we are talking about picture controls for portraits, there is another control on your D600 that has been tuned specifically for this type of shooting. Unsurprisingly enough, it's called Portrait. To set this control on your camera, simply follow the same directions as earlier, except this time, select the Portrait control (PT) instead of Monochrome. There are also individual options for the Portrait control that, like the Monochrome control, include sharpness and contrast. You can also change the saturation (how intense the colors will be) and the hue, which lets you change the skin tones from more reddish to more yellowish. I prefer brighter colors, so I like to boost the Saturation setting to +2 and leave everything else at the defaults. You won't be able to use the same adjustments for everyone, especially when it comes to color tone, so do some experimenting to see what works best.

DETECT FACES WITH LIVE VIEW

Face detection is becoming commonplace in digital cameras. Your D600 has two autofocus modes for Live View: single-servo (AF-S) and full-time servo (AF-F). Within those two autofocus modes there are four Live View–specific AF-area modes: Wide Area, Normal Area, Subject Tracking, and Face Priority. When you turn on Live View with Face Priority focusing, the camera does an amazing thing: it zeroes in on any face appearing on the LCD and places a box around it. I'm not sure how it works; it just does. You can use Face Priority with AF-S or AF-F, but I prefer to use AF-S so that I am always in control of when the camera grabs focus. Face Priority mode is probably the slowest of the Live View focusing area modes, so use it with a tripod or when your subjects are going to remain fairly still.

A whole chapter in your manual is dedicated to using Live View. It can be found on pages 49–56.

SETTING UP AND SHOOTING WITH LIVE VIEW AND FACE PRIORITY FOCUSING

1. Activate the Live View function by rotating the Live View selector switch to the camera icon and pressing the Lv button.
2. Press and hold the Focus-mode selector, near the lens on the front of the camera, and rotate the Main Command dial to choose the AF-S autofocus mode (**A**).
3. While holding the button, rotate the Sub-command dial with your index finger to choose Face Priority (**B**).
4. Point your camera at a person, and watch as the frame appears over the face in the LCD.
5. Depress and hold the shutter release button halfway to focus on the face, and wait until you hear the confirmation chirp.
6. Press the shutter button fully to take the photograph.

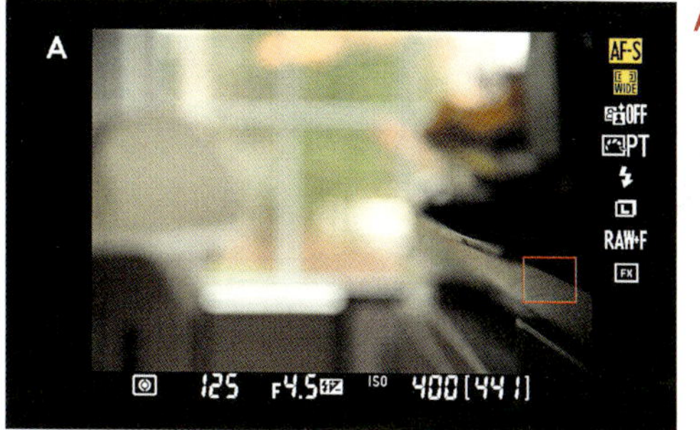

A

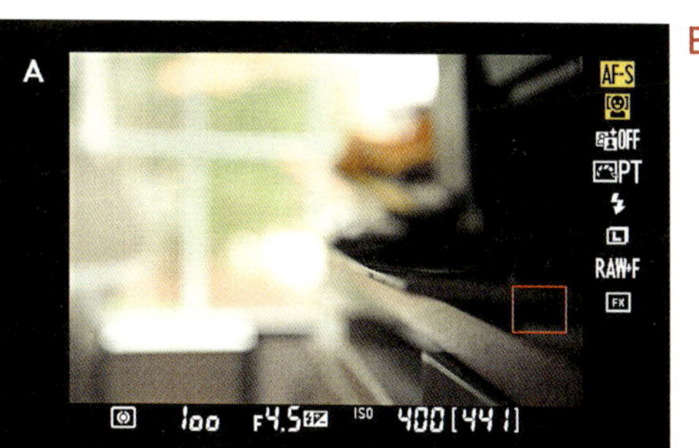

B

USE FILL FLASH FOR REDUCING SHADOWS

A common problem when taking pictures of people outside, especially during the midday hours, is that the overhead sun can create dark shadows under the eyes and chin. You could have your subject turn his or her face to the sun, but that is usually considered cruel and unusual punishment. So how can you have your subject's back to the sun and still get a decent exposure of the face? Try turning on your flash to fill in the shadows (**Figure 6.10**).

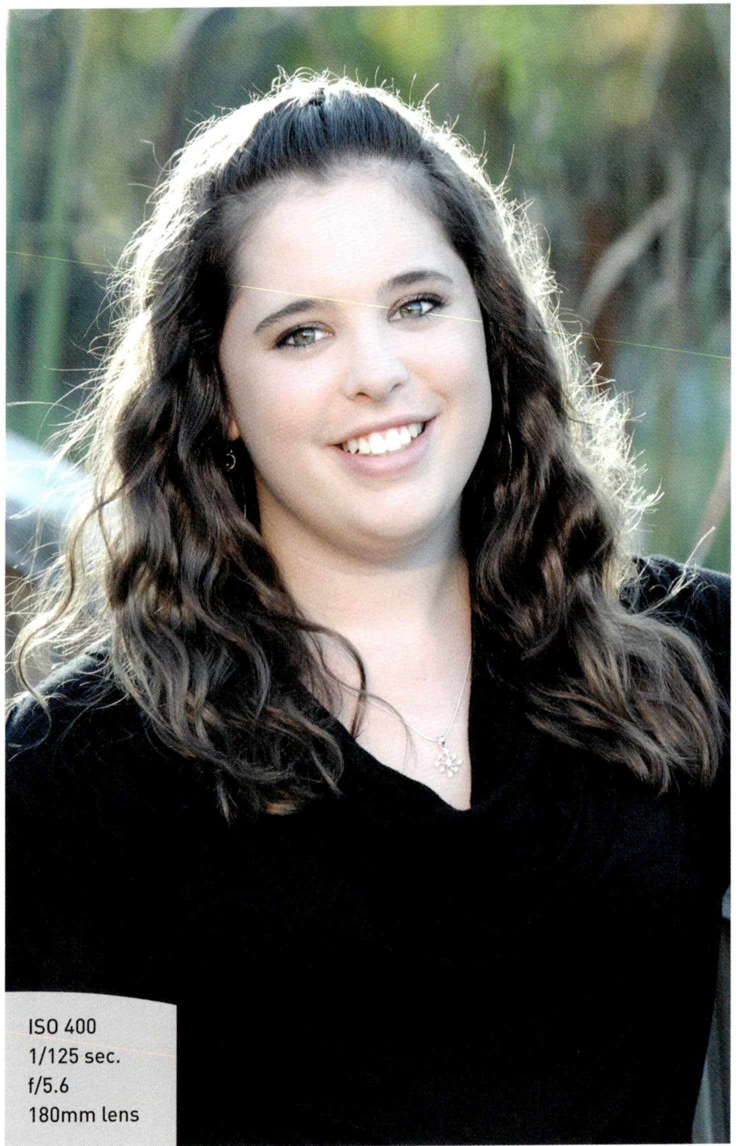
ISO 400
1/125 sec.
f/5.6
180mm lens

FIGURE 6.10
I used fill flash to lighten the subject, who was standing in a shaded area with strong light behind her.

CATCHLIGHT

A *catchlight* is that little sparkle that adds life to the eyes. When you are photographing a person with a light source in front of them, you will usually get a reflection of that light in the eye, be it your flash, the sun, or something else brightly reflecting in the eye. The light is reflected off the surface of the eyes as bright highlights and serves to bring attention to the eyes.

This also works well when you are photographing someone wearing a ball cap. The bill of the hat tends to create heavy shadows over the eyes, and the fill flash will lighten up those areas while providing a really nice catchlight in the eyes.

The key to using the flash as a fill is to not use it on full power. If you do, the camera will try to balance the flash with the daylight, and you will get a very flat and featureless face.

SETTING UP AND SHOOTING WITH FILL FLASH

1. Press the pop-up flash button to raise your pop-up flash into the ready position.
2. Press and hold the flash compensation button on the front of the camera, and then rotate the Sub-command dial to reduce the flash exposure by –0.3. Look in the control panel to see the compensation readout.
3. Take a photograph and check your playback LCD to see if it looks good. If it doesn't, try reducing power in 1/3-stop increments.

One problem that can quickly surface when using the on-camera flash is red-eye. Not to worry, though—we will talk about that in Chapter 8.

PORTRAITS ON THE MOVE

Not all portraits are shot with the subject sitting in a chair, posed and ready for the picture. Sometimes you might want to get an action shot that says something about the person, similar to an environmental portrait. Children, especially, just like to move. Why fight it? Set up an action portrait instead.

For the photo in **Figure 6.11**, I set my camera to Shutter Priority mode. This shot was all about movement and I wanted to make sure that I had a fairly high shutter speed to freeze the action, so I set it to 1/1250 of a second. I set the focus mode to AF-C and the release mode to Continuous high speed, and I just let it rip. There were quite a few throwaway shots, but I was able to capture one that conveyed the energy and fun.

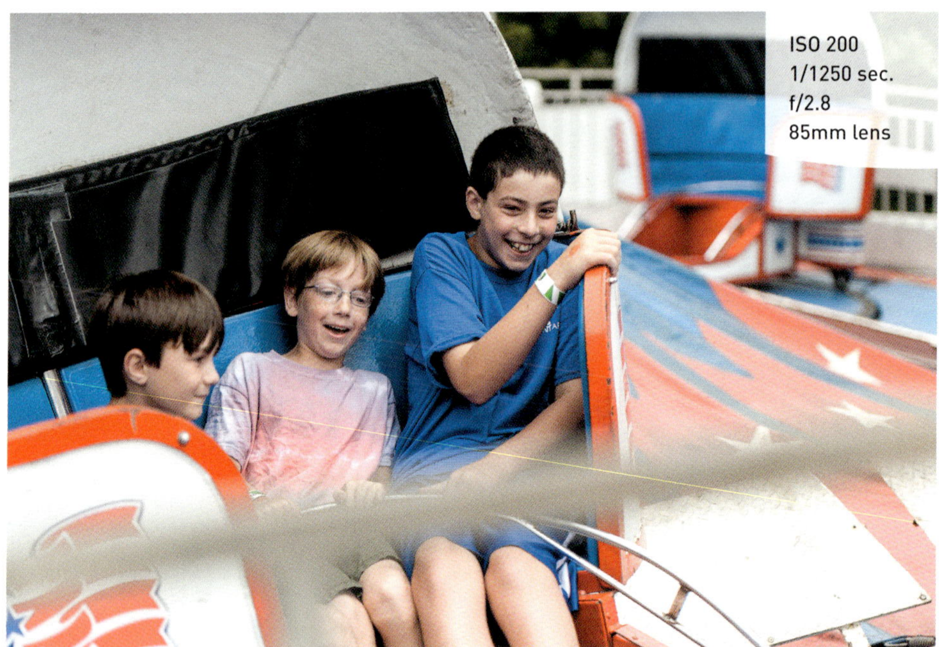

FIGURE 6.11
A fast shutter speed to stop the action—and a large aperture to isolate the subjects from the clutter—worked great in this situation.

TIPS FOR SHOOTING BETTER PORTRAITS

Before we get to the assignments for this chapter, I thought it might be a good idea to leave you with a few extra pointers on shooting portraits that don't necessarily have anything specific to do with your camera. There are entire books that cover things like portrait lighting, posing, and so on, but here are a few pointers that will make your people pics look a lot better.

AVOID THE CENTER OF THE FRAME

This falls under the category of composition. Place your subject to the side of the frame (**Figure 6.12**)—it just looks more interesting than plunking them smack dab in the middle (**Figure 6.13**).

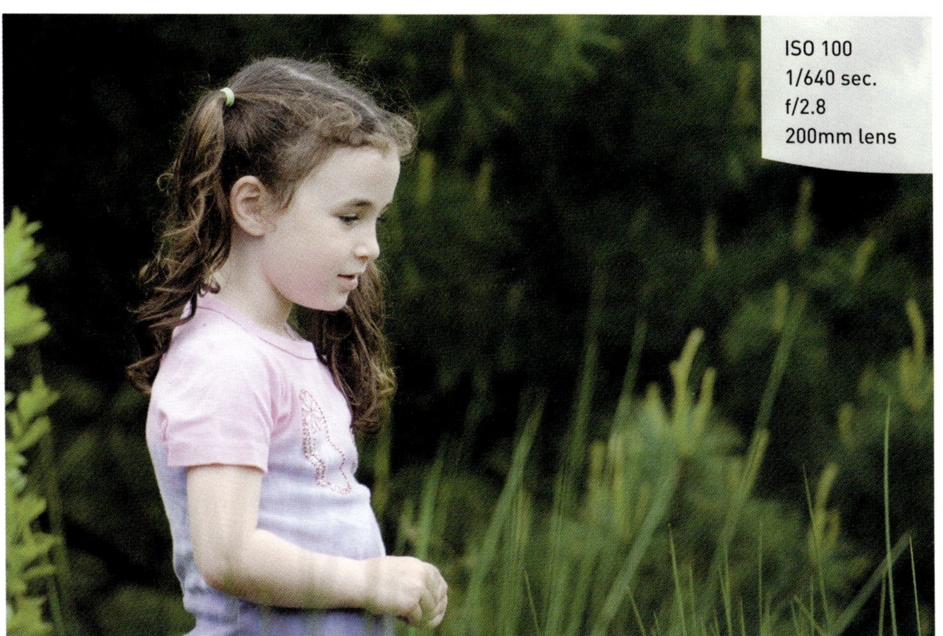

FIGURE 6.12
Try cropping in a bit, and place the subject off-center to improve the shot.

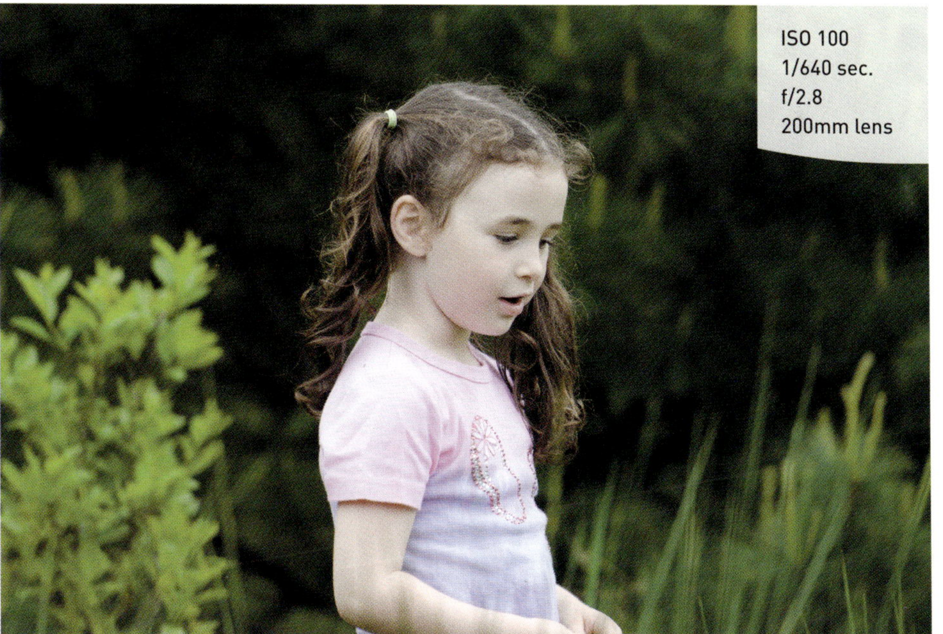

FIGURE 6.13
Having the subject in the middle of the frame with so much empty space on the sides can make for a less-than-interesting portrait.

CHOOSE THE RIGHT LENS

Choosing the correct lens can make a huge impact on your portraits. A wide-angle lens can distort the features of your subject, which can lead to an unflattering portrait (**Figure 6.14**). Select a longer focal length if you will be close to your subject (**Figure 6.15**).

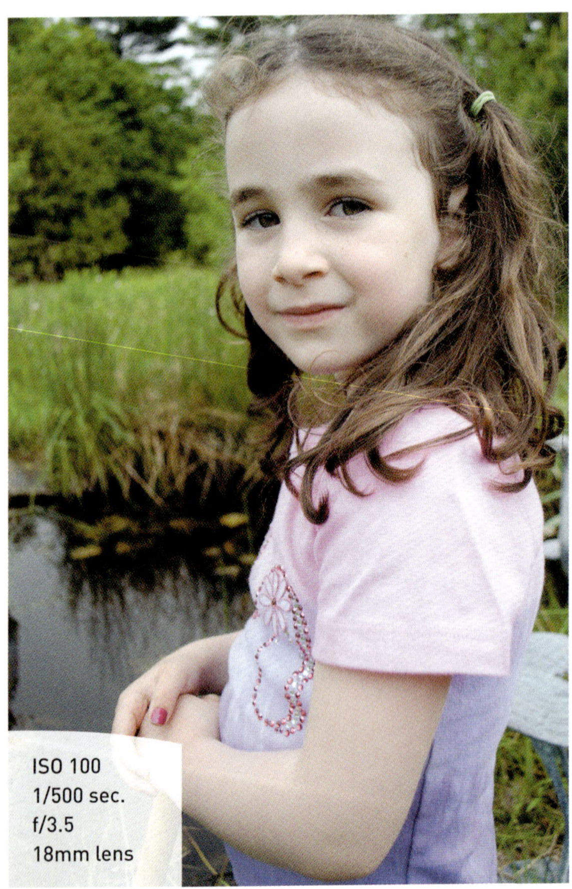

FIGURE 6.14
At this close distance, the 18mm lens is distorting the subject's face.

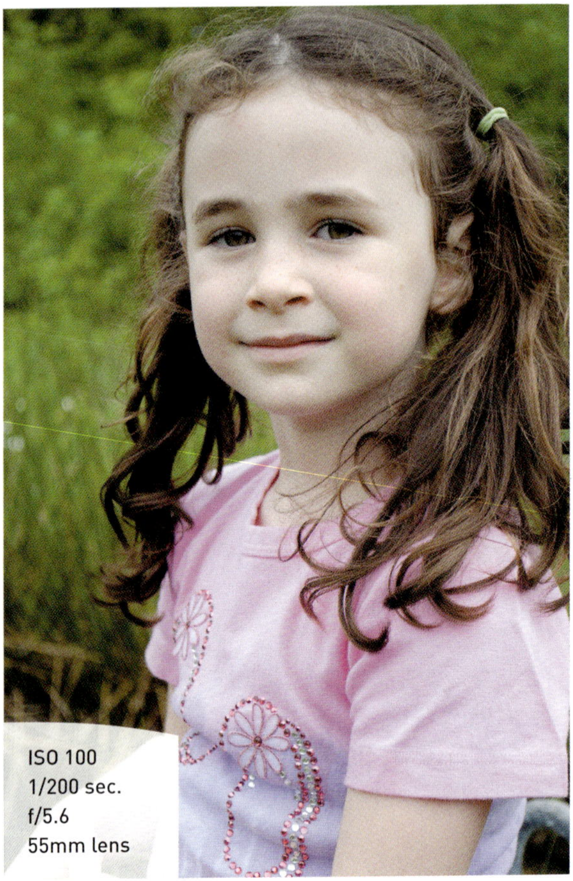

ISO 100
1/200 sec.
f/5.6
55mm lens

FIGURE 6.15
By zooming out to 55mm, I am able to remove the distortion for a much better photo.

DON'T CUT THEM OFF AT THE JOINT

There is an old rule about photographing people: never crop the picture at a joint. This means no cropping at the ankles or the knees. If you need to crop at the legs, the proper place to crop is mid-shin or mid-thigh (**Figure 6.16**).

USE THE FRAME

Have you ever noticed that most people are taller than they are wide? Turn your camera vertically for a more pleasing composition (**Figure 6.17**).

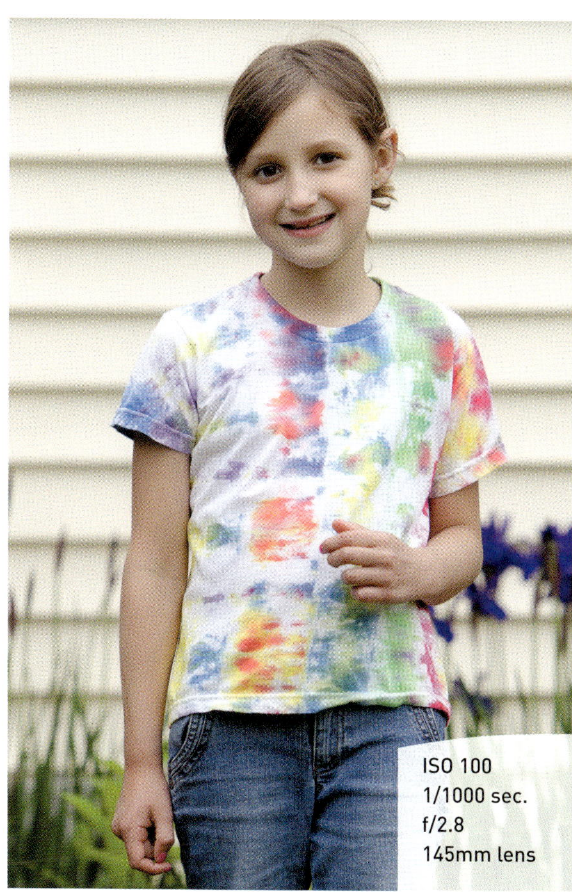

ISO 100
1/1000 sec.
f/2.8
145mm lens

FIGURE 6.16
A good crop for people is at mid-thigh or mid-shin.

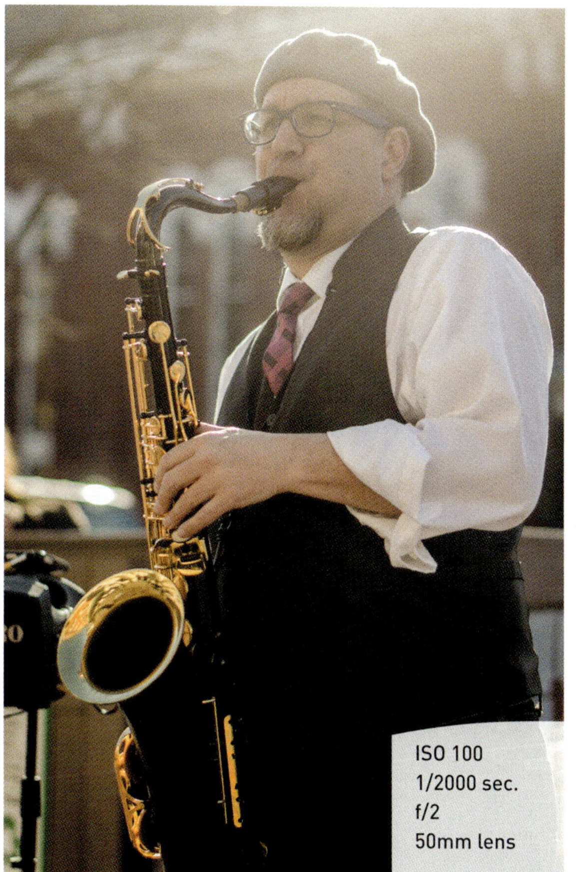

ISO 100
1/2000 sec.
f/2
50mm lens

FIGURE 6.17
Get in the habit of turning your camera to a vertical position when shooting portraits. This is also referred to as portrait orientation.

SUNBLOCK FOR PORTRAITS

The midday sun can be harsh and can do unflattering things to people's faces (**Figure 6.18**). If you can, find a shady spot out of the direct sunlight. You will get softer shadows, smoother skin tones, and better detail (**Figure 6.19**). This holds true for overcast skies as well. Just be sure to adjust your white balance accordingly.

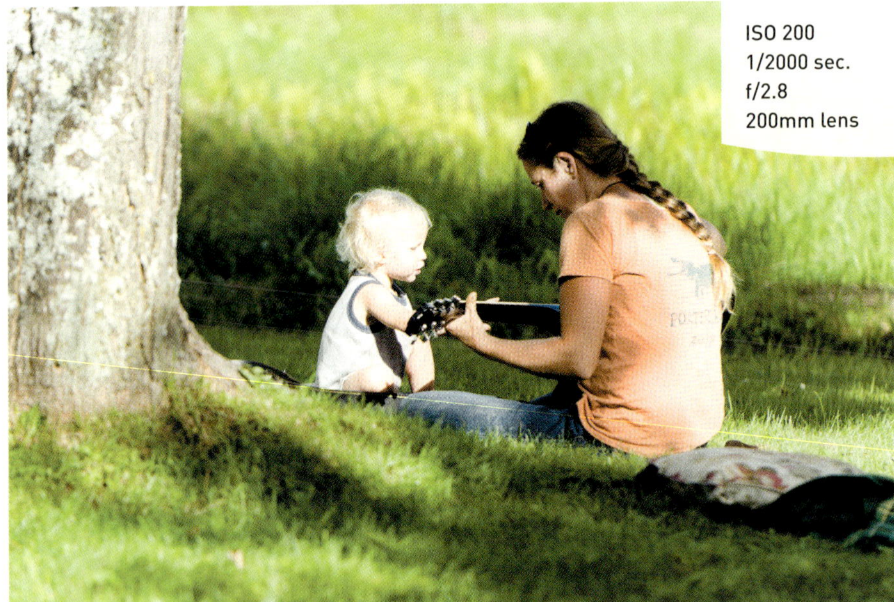

ISO 200
1/2000 sec.
f/2.8
200mm lens

FIGURE 6.18
The dappled sunlight can result in overexposure in the highlights.

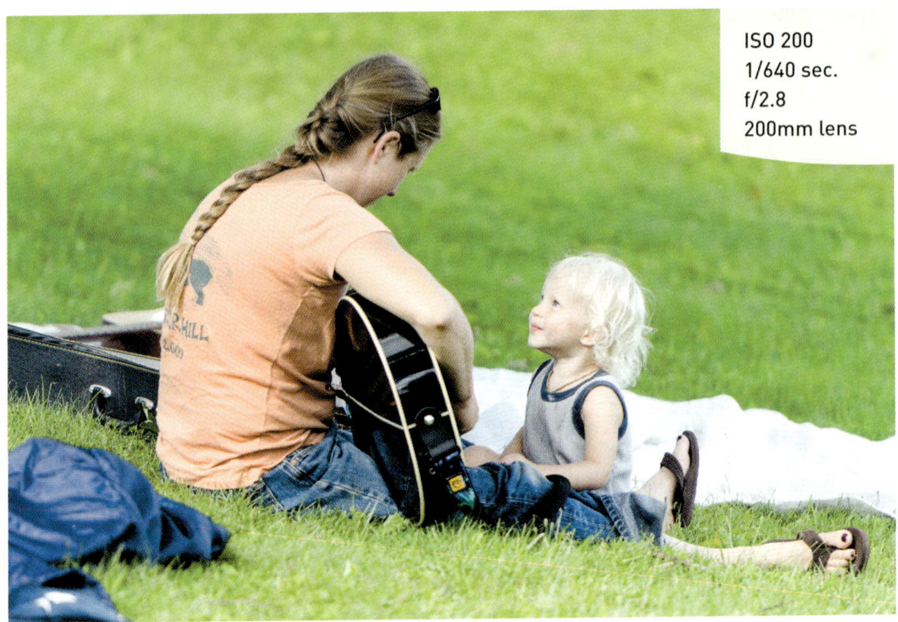

ISO 200
1/640 sec.
f/2.8
200mm lens

FIGURE 6.19
By waiting for a cloud to pass in front of the sun and changing my position, I was able to get a much more even and pleasing result.

GIVE THEM A HEALTHY GLOW

Nearly everyone looks better with a warm, healthy glow. Some of the best light of the day happens just a little before sundown, so shoot at that time if you can (**Figure 6.20**).

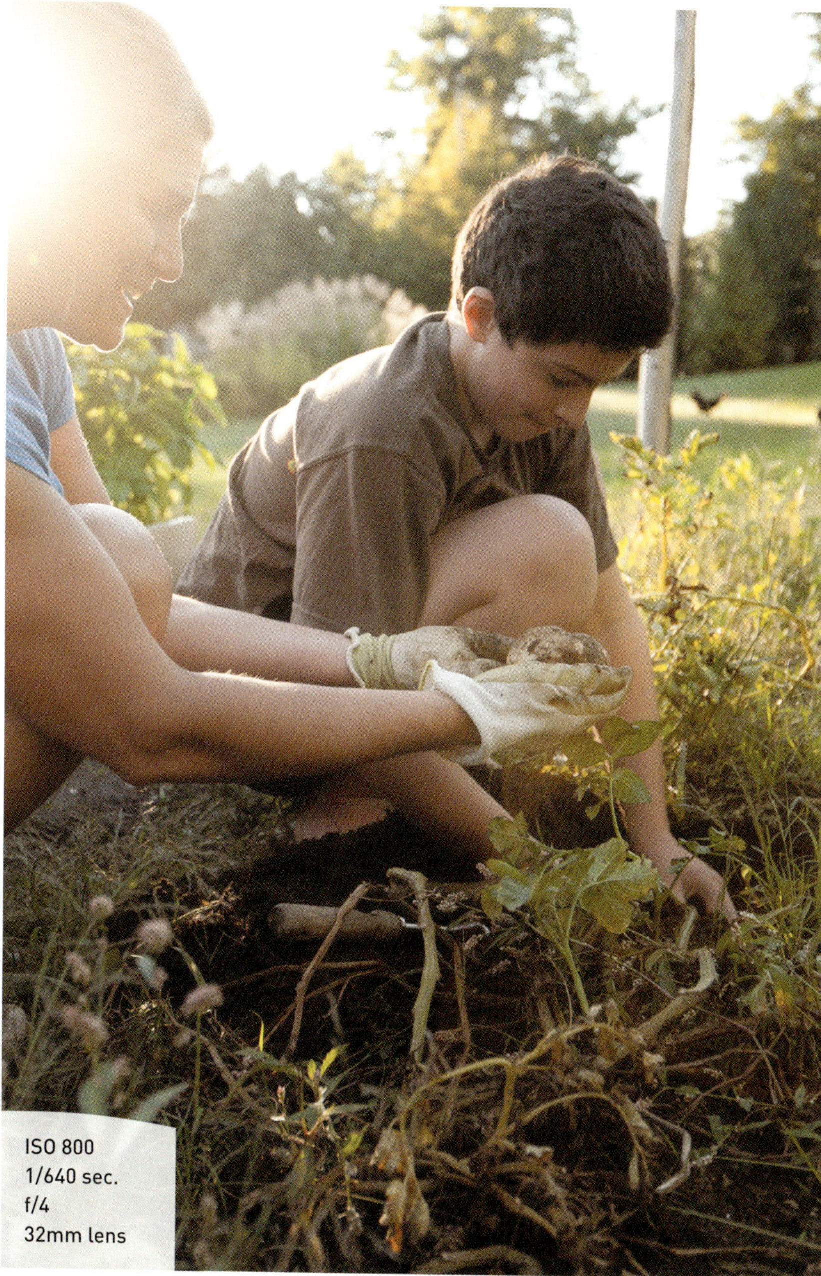

ISO 800
1/640 sec.
f/4
32mm lens

FIGURE 6.20
You just can't beat the glow of the late afternoon sun for adding warmth to your portraits.

KEEP AN EYE ON YOUR BACKGROUND

Sometimes it's easy to get so caught up in taking a great shot that you forget about the smaller details. Try to keep an eye on what is going on behind your subject so they don't end up with things popping out of their heads (**Figures 6.21** and **6.22**).

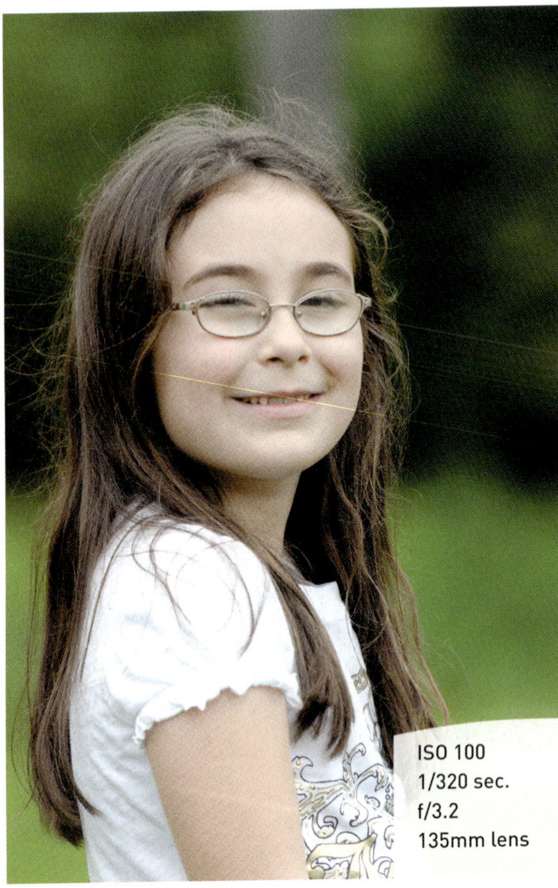

ISO 100
1/320 sec.
f/3.2
135mm lens

FIGURE 6.21
The fence post in the background is coming right out of the subject's head.

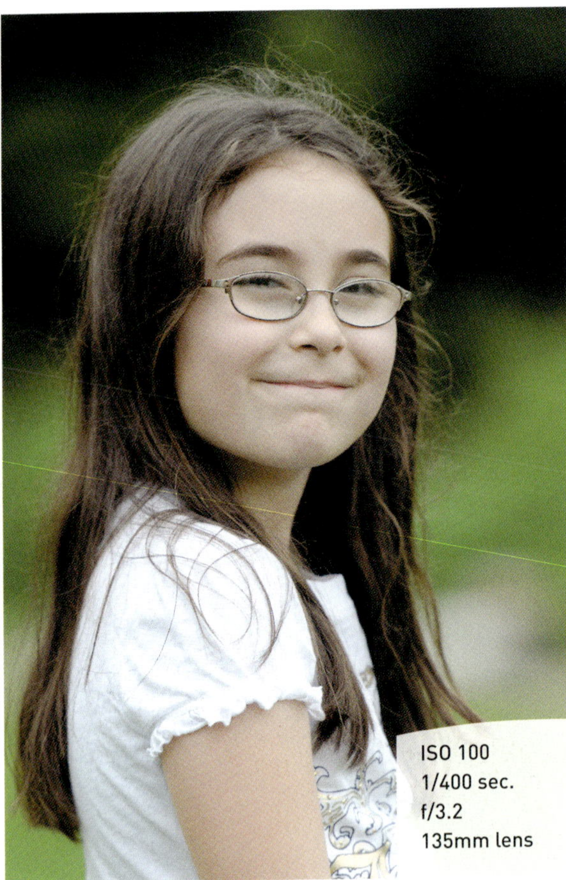

ISO 100
1/400 sec.
f/3.2
135mm lens

FIGURE 6.22
By moving the camera a little to the left, I was able to remove the post from the scene.

FRAME THE SCENE

Using elements in the scene to create a frame around your subject is a great way to draw the viewer in. You don't have to use a window frame to do this. Just look for elements in the foreground that could be used to force the viewer's eye toward your subject (**Figure 6.23**).

GET DOWN ON THEIR LEVEL

If you want better pictures of children, don't shoot from an adult's eye level. Getting the camera down to the child's level will make your images look more personal (**Figure 6.24**).

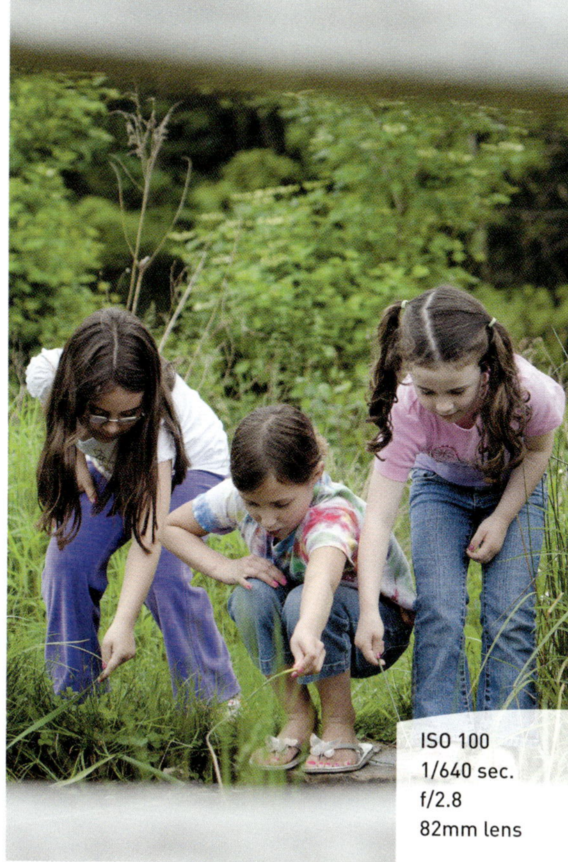

ISO 100
1/640 sec.
f/2.8
82mm lens

FIGURE 6.23
While a fence coming out of a person's head is unattractive, it can make a great frame for the subject.

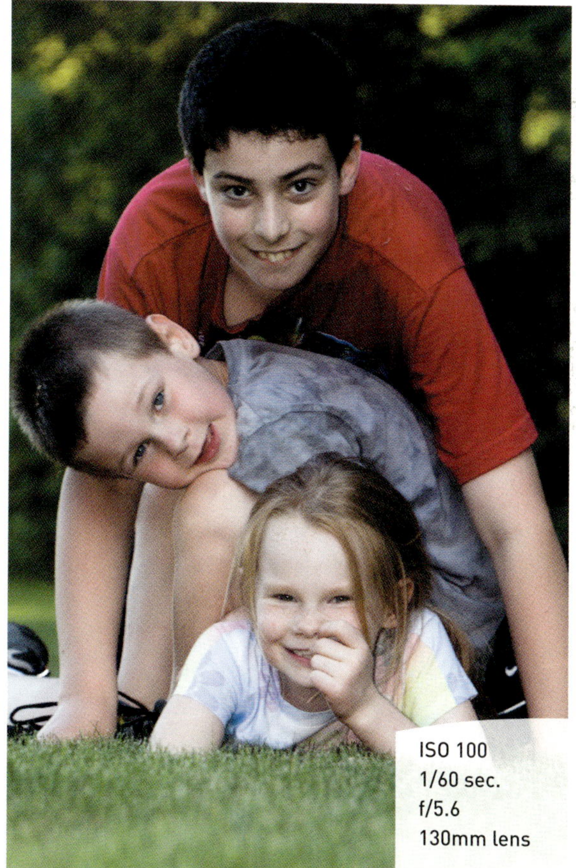

ISO 100
1/60 sec.
f/5.6
130mm lens

FIGURE 6.24
Sometimes taking photographs of children means getting low to the ground, but the result is a much better image.

ELIMINATE SPACE BETWEEN YOUR SUBJECTS

One of the problems you can encounter when taking portraits of more than one person is that of personal space. What feels like a close distance to the subjects can look impersonal to the viewer. Have your subjects move close together, eliminating any open space between them (**Figure 6.25**).

MORE THAN JUST A PRETTY FACE

Most people think of a portrait as a photo of someone's face. Don't ignore other aspects of your subject that reflect his or her personality—hands, especially, can go a long way toward describing someone (**Figure 6.26**).

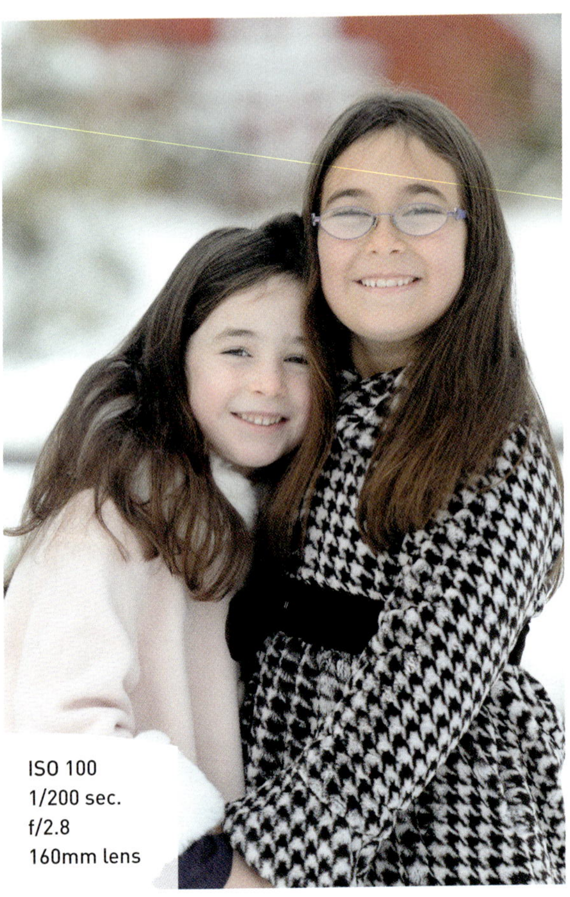

ISO 100
1/200 sec.
f/2.8
160mm lens

FIGURE 6.25

Getting your subjects to move in close together can sometimes be a challenge, but the results are worth the effort.

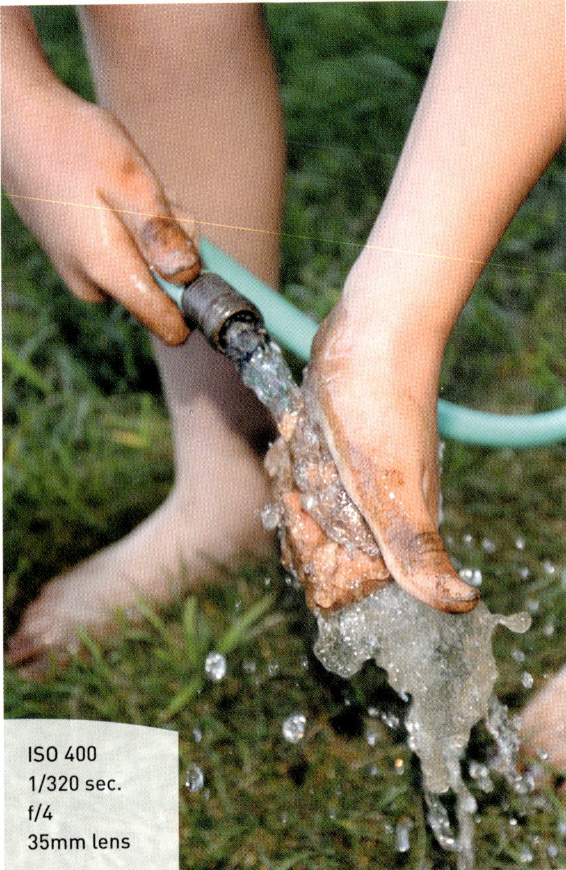

ISO 400
1/320 sec.
f/4
35mm lens

FIGURE 6.26

There's more to a person than just a face. My son loves to be barefoot outside, playing in the dirt. When I saw him cleaning up at the end of an afternoon in the garden, I had to capture the moment.

Chapter 6 Assignments

Depth of field in portraits

Let's start with something simple. Grab your favorite person and start experimenting with using different aperture settings. Shoot wide open (the widest your lens goes, such as f/3.5 or f/5.6) and then really stopped down (like f/22). Look at the difference in the depth of field and how it plays an important role in placing the attention on your subject. (Make sure you don't have your subject standing against the background. Give some distance so that there is a good blurring effect of the background at the wide f-stop setting.)

Discovering the qualities of natural light

Pick a nice sunny day and try shooting some portraits in the midday sun. If your subject is willing, have them turn so the sun is in their face. If they are still speaking to you after blinding them, have them turn their back to the sun. Try this with and without the fill flash so you can see the difference. Finally, move them into a completely shaded spot and take a few more.

Picking the right metering method

Find a very dark or light background and place your subject in front of it. Now take a couple of shots, giving a lot of space around your subject for the background to show. Now switch metering modes and use the AE Lock feature to get a more accurate reading of your subject. Notice the differences in exposure between the metering methods.

Picture controls for portraits

Have some fun playing with the different picture controls. Try the Portrait control as compared to the Standard. Then try out Monochrome and play with the different color filter options to see how they affect skin tones.

Share your results with the book's Flickr group!

www.flickr.com/groups/d600fromsnapshotstogreatshots

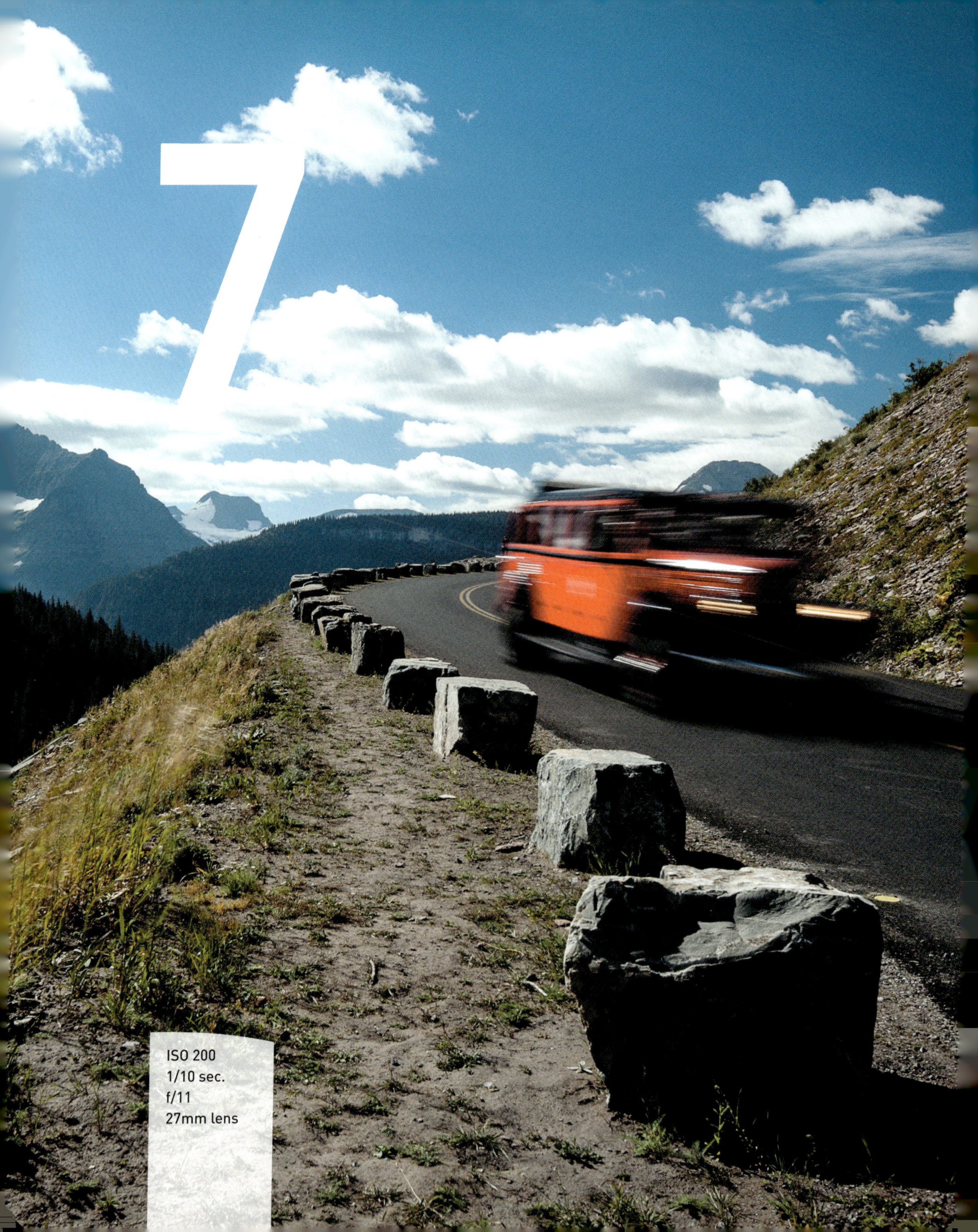

7

ISO 200
1/10 sec.
f/11
27mm lens

Landscape Photography

TIPS, TOOLS, AND TECHNIQUES TO GET THE MOST OUT OF YOUR LANDSCAPE PHOTOGRAPHY

There has always been something about shooting landscapes that has brought a sense of joy to my photography. It might have something to do with being outdoors and working at the mercy of Mother Nature. Maybe it's the way it challenges me to visualize the landscape and try to capture it with my camera. It truly is a celebration of light, composition, and the world we live in.

In this chapter, we will explore some of the features of the D600 that not only improve the look of your landscape photography, but also make it easier to take great shots. We will also explore some typical scenarios and discuss methods to bring out the best in your landscape photography.

PORING OVER THE PICTURE

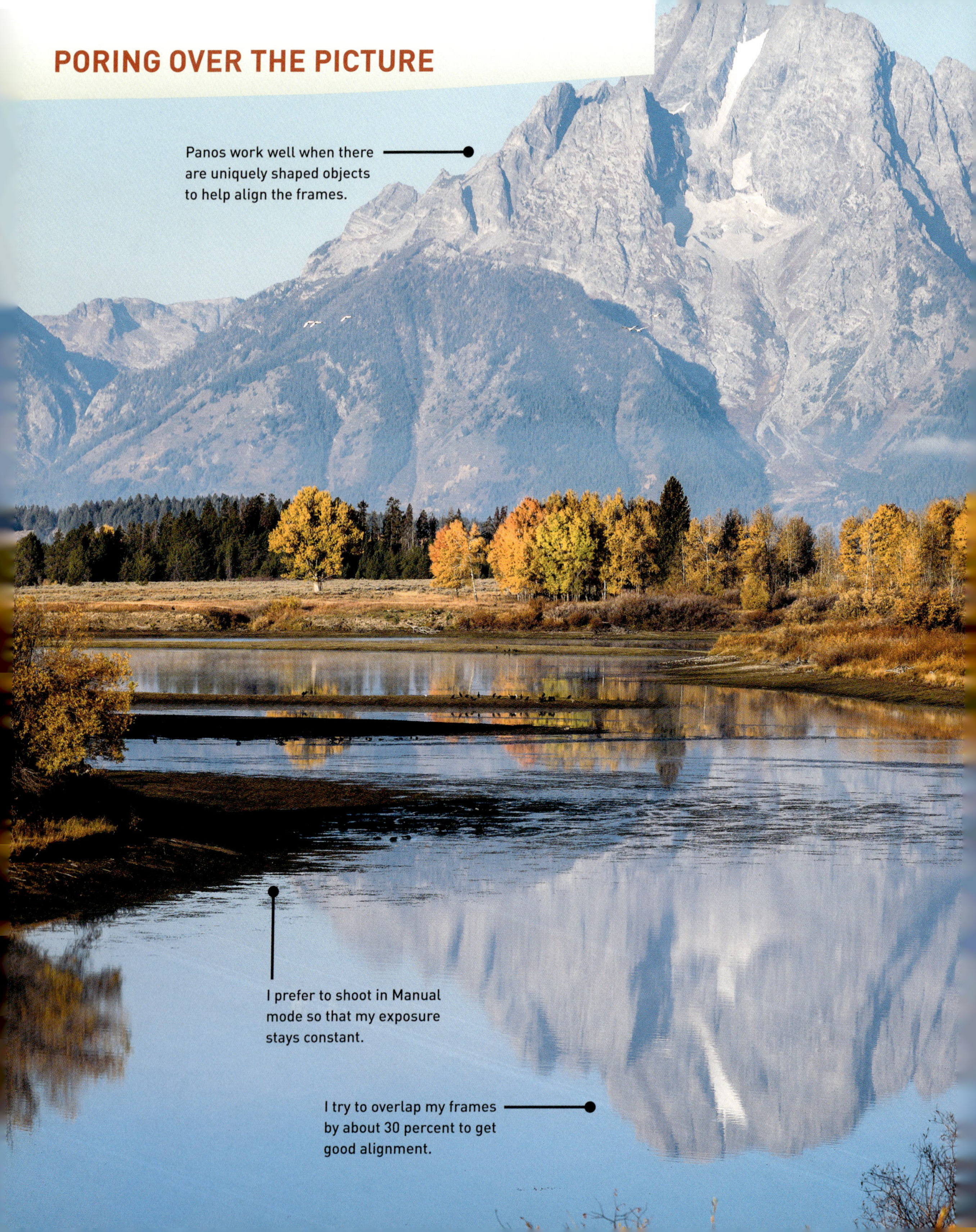

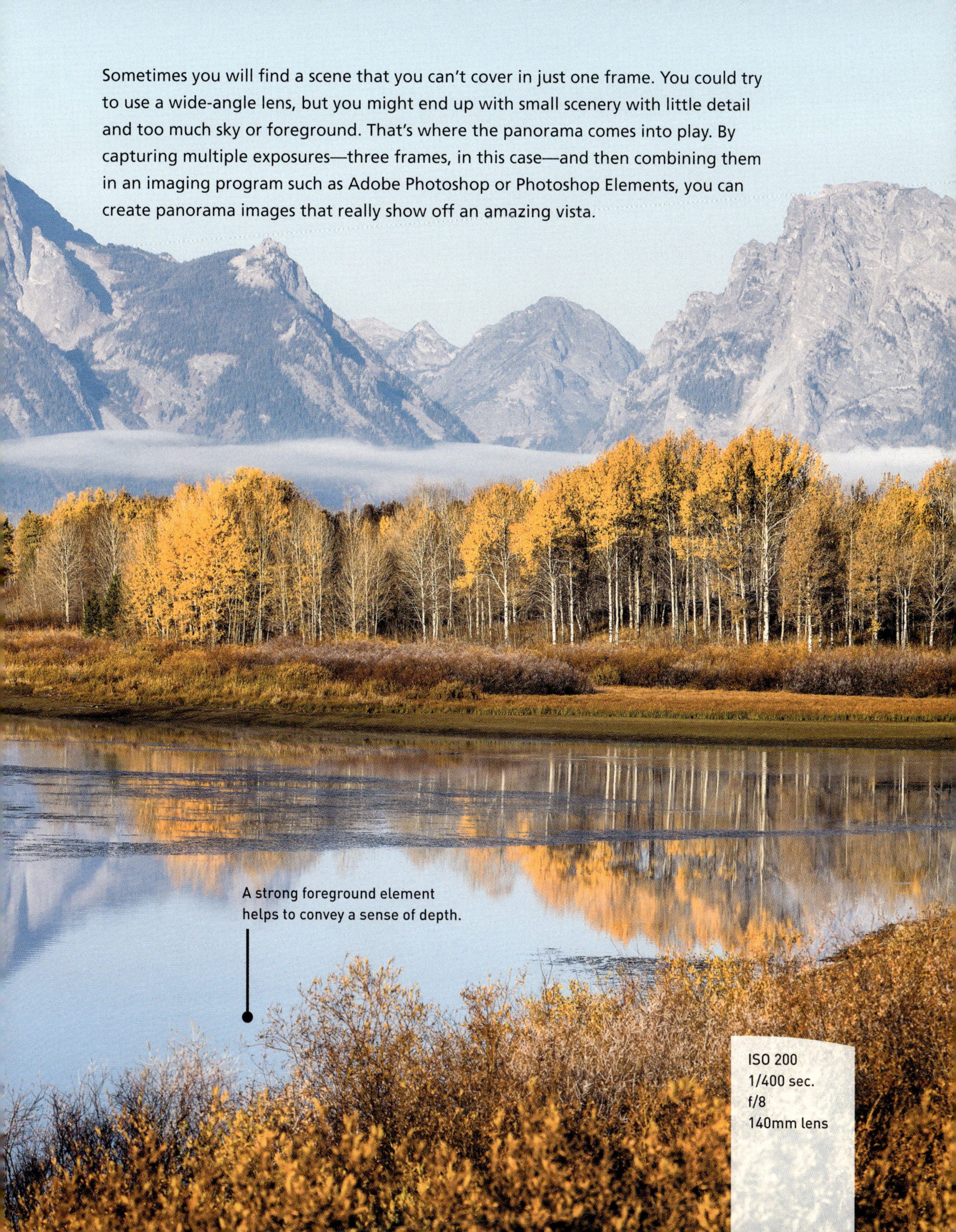

Sometimes you will find a scene that you can't cover in just one frame. You could try to use a wide-angle lens, but you might end up with small scenery with little detail and too much sky or foreground. That's where the panorama comes into play. By capturing multiple exposures—three frames, in this case—and then combining them in an imaging program such as Adobe Photoshop or Photoshop Elements, you can create panorama images that really show off an amazing vista.

A strong foreground element helps to convey a sense of depth.

ISO 200
1/400 sec.
f/8
140mm lens

SHARP AND IN FOCUS: USING TRIPODS

Throughout the previous chapters, we have concentrated on using the camera to create great images. We will continue that trend in this chapter, but there is one additional piece of equipment that is crucial in the world of landscape shooting: the tripod. There are a couple of reasons why tripods are so critical to your landscape work, the first being the time of day that you will be working. For reasons that will be explained later, the best light for most landscape work happens at sunrise and just before sunset. While this is the best time to shoot, it's also kind of dark. That means you'll be working with slow shutter speeds. Slow shutter speeds mean camera shake. Camera shake equals bad photos.

The second reason is also related to the amount of light that you're gathering with your camera. When taking landscape photos, you will usually want to be working with very small apertures, as they give you lots of depth of field. This also means that, once again, you will be working with slower-than-normal shutter speeds.

Slow shutter = camera shake = bad photos.

Do you see the pattern here? The one tool you want in your in your arsenal to truly defeat camera shake and ensure tack-sharp photos is a good tripod (**Figure 7.1**).

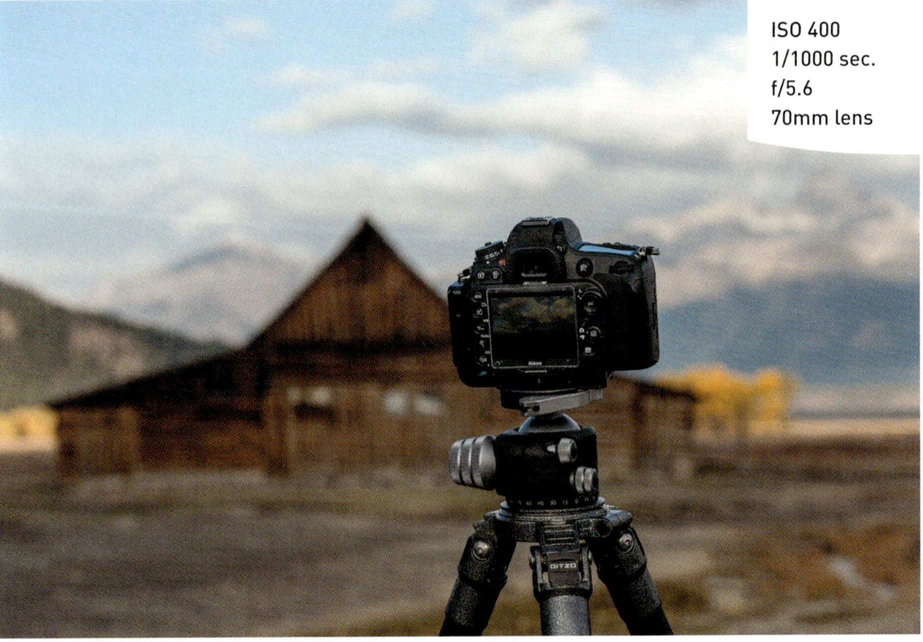

ISO 400
1/1000 sec.
f/5.6
70mm lens

FIGURE 7.1
A sturdy tripod is the key to sharp landscape photos.

So what should you look for in a tripod? Well, first make sure it is sturdy enough to support your camera and any lens that you might want to use. Next, check the height of the tripod. Bending over all day to look through the viewfinder of a camera on a short tripod can wreak havoc on your back. Finally, think about getting a tripod that utilizes a quick-release head. This usually employs a plate that screws into the bottom of the camera and then quickly snaps into place on the tripod. This will be especially handy if you are going to move between shooting by hand and using the tripod. You'll find more information about tripods in Chapter 11.

TRIPOD STABILITY

Many tripods have a center column that allows the user to extend the height of the camera above the point where the tripod legs join together. This might seem like a great idea, but the reality is that the farther you raise that column, the less stable your tripod becomes. Think of a tall building that sways near the top. To get the most solid base for your camera, always try to use it with the center column at its lowest point so that your camera is right at the apex of the tripod legs.

VR LENSES AND TRIPODS DON'T MIX

If you are using Vibration Reduction (VR) lenses on your camera, you need to remember to turn this feature off when you use a tripod (**Figure 7.2**). This is because the Vibration Reduction can, while trying to minimize camera movement, actually create movement when the camera is already stable. To turn off the VR feature, just slide the VR selector switch on the side of the lens to the Off position.

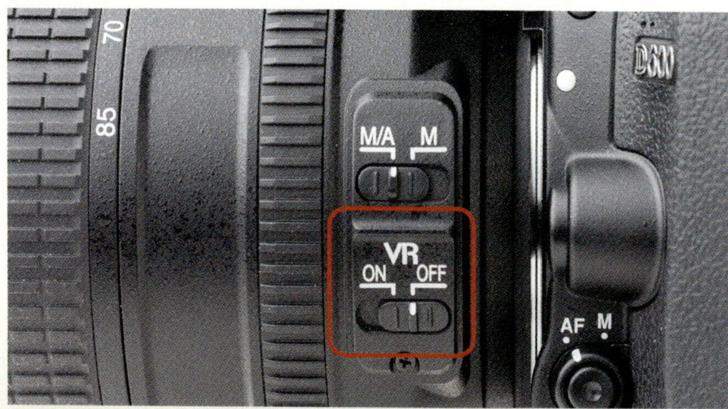

FIGURE 7.2 Turn off the Vibration Reduction feature when using a tripod.

SELECTING THE PROPER ISO

For most landscape scenes, the ISO is the one factor that should be increased only as a last resort. While it is easy to select a higher ISO to get a smaller aperture, the noise that it can introduce into your images can be harmful. Not only is the noise visible as large grainy artifacts, but it can also be multicolored, which further degrades the image quality and color balance.

Take a look at **Figures 7.3** and **7.4**, which show a photograph taken with an ISO of 1600. The purpose was to shorten the shutter speed and still use a small aperture setting of f/11. The problem is that the noise level is so high that, in addition to being distracting, it is obscuring fine details in the shadows.

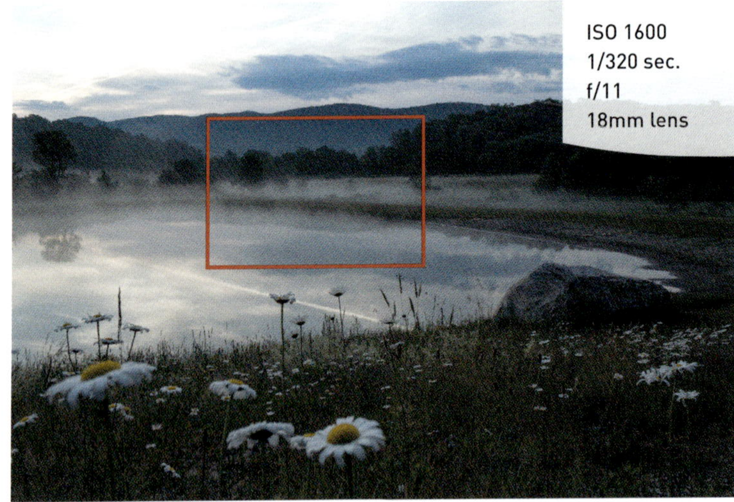

ISO 1600
1/320 sec.
f/11
18mm lens

FIGURE 7.3
A high ISO setting created a lot of digital noise in the shadows.

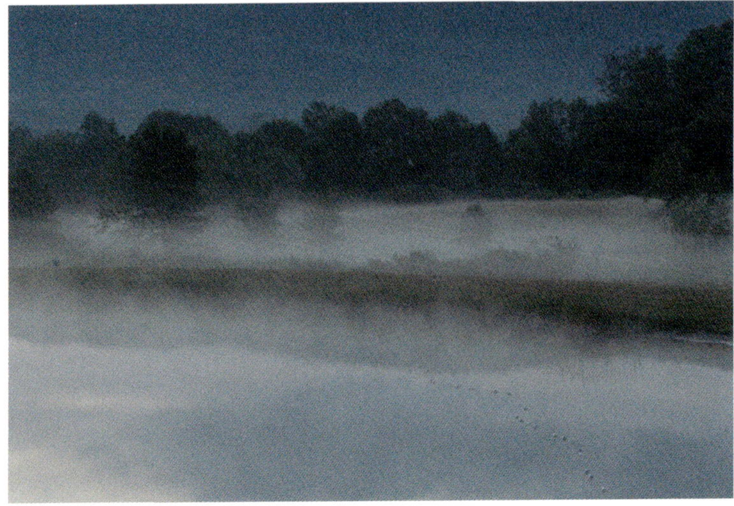

FIGURE 7.4
When the image is enlarged, the noise is even more apparent.

Now check out another image that was taken in the same light but with a much lower ISO setting (**Figures 7.5** and **7.6**). As you can see, the noise levels are much lower, which means that my blacks look black, and the fine details are beautifully captured.

When you're shooting landscapes, set your ISO to the lowest possible setting at all times. Between the use of Vibration Reduction lenses (if you are shooting handheld) and a good tripod, there should be few circumstances where you would need to shoot landscapes with anything above an ISO of 400.

As you start shooting with shutter speeds that exceed 1 second, the level of image noise can increase. Your camera has a feature called Long Exposure Noise Reduction that you can turn on to combat noise from long exposures and high ISOs.

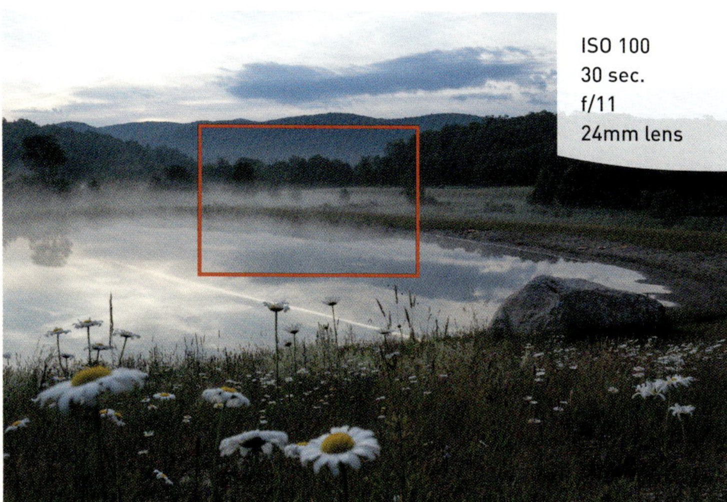

ISO 100
30 sec.
f/11
24mm lens

FIGURE 7.5
By lowering the ISO to 100, I was able to avoid the noise and capture a clean image.

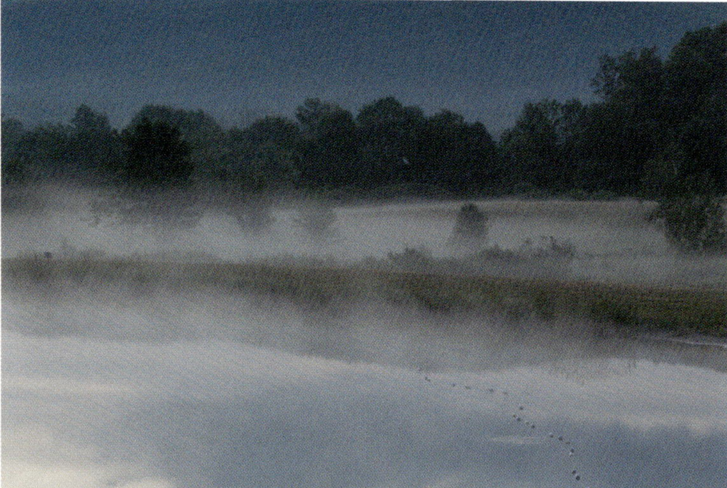

FIGURE 7.6
Zooming in shows that the noise levels for this image are almost nonexistent.

SETTING UP LONG EXPOSURE NR

1. Press the Menu button, then use the Multi-selector to get to the Shooting menu.
2. Using the Multi-selector, locate the Long exposure NR menu item and then press OK (**A**). Change this option to On (**B**) and press the OK button.

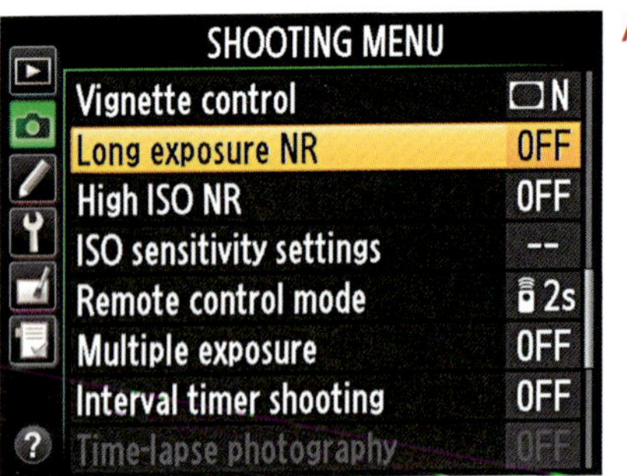

A

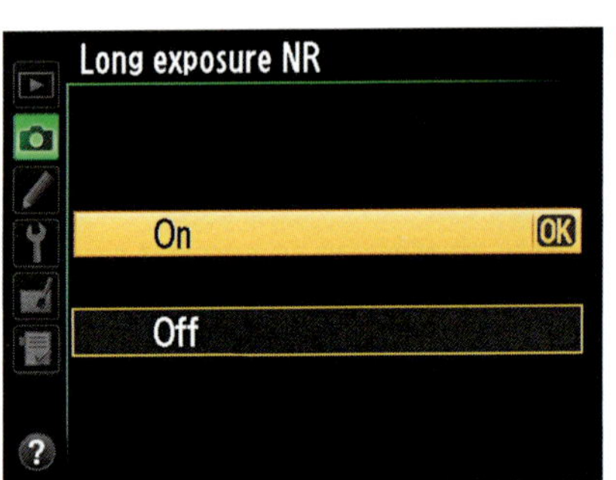

B

That's all there is to it. Now when you shoot, your camera will be aware of the settings and work toward minimizing unwanted noise in your images.

SELECTING A WHITE BALANCE

This probably seems like a no-brainer. If it's sunny, select Daylight. If it's overcast, choose the Shade or Cloudy setting. Those choices wouldn't be wrong for those circumstances, but why limit yourself? Sometimes you can actually change the mood of the photo by selecting a white balance that doesn't quite fit the light for the scene that you are shooting.

Figure 7.7 is an example of a correct white balance. It was late afternoon and the sun was starting to move low in the sky, giving everything that warm afternoon glow. The white balance for this image was set to Daylight.

But what if I want to make the scene look like it was shot in the early morning hours? Simple, I just change the white balance to Fluorescent, which is a much cooler setting (**Figure 7.8**).

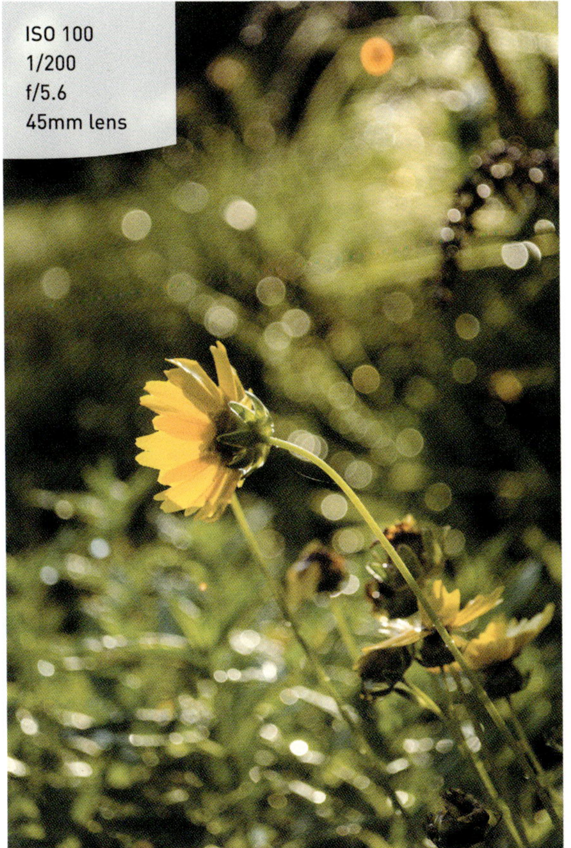

FIGURE 7.7
Using the "proper" white balance yields predictable results.

ISO 100
1/200
f/5.6
45mm lens

FIGURE 7.8
Changing the white balance to Fluorescent gives the impression that the picture was taken at a different time of day than it really was.

So how do you know what a good white balance selection is? You could just take a guess, but an easier way is to take the shots, review them on the LCD, and keep the one you like. I actually prefer to preview the effect using the Live View function. Live View will display the scene you are getting ready to shoot and will do so using the current white balance settings. If you hold the WB button and turn the Main Command dial while Live View is turned on, the changes in white balance will be displayed in the preview monitor. To activate Live View, press the LV button on the back of the camera. When you are done, press the LV button again to turn it off.

USING THE LANDSCAPE PICTURE CONTROL

When shooting landscapes, I always look for great color and contrast. This is one of the reasons that so many landscape shots are taken in the early morning or during sunset. The light is much more vibrant and colorful at these times of day and adds a sense of drama to an image. There are also much longer and deeper shadows because of the angle of the light. These shadows are what give depth to your image.

Manual Callout

Check out pages 129–136 in your camera manual for more information on setting picture controls.

You can help boost vibrancy and contrast, especially in the less-than-golden hours of the day, by using the Landscape picture control (**Figure 7.9**). Just as in the Landscape mode found in the automatic scene modes, you can set up your landscape shooting so that you capture images with increased sharpness and a slight boost in blues and greens. This control will add some pop to your landscapes without the need for additional processing in any software.

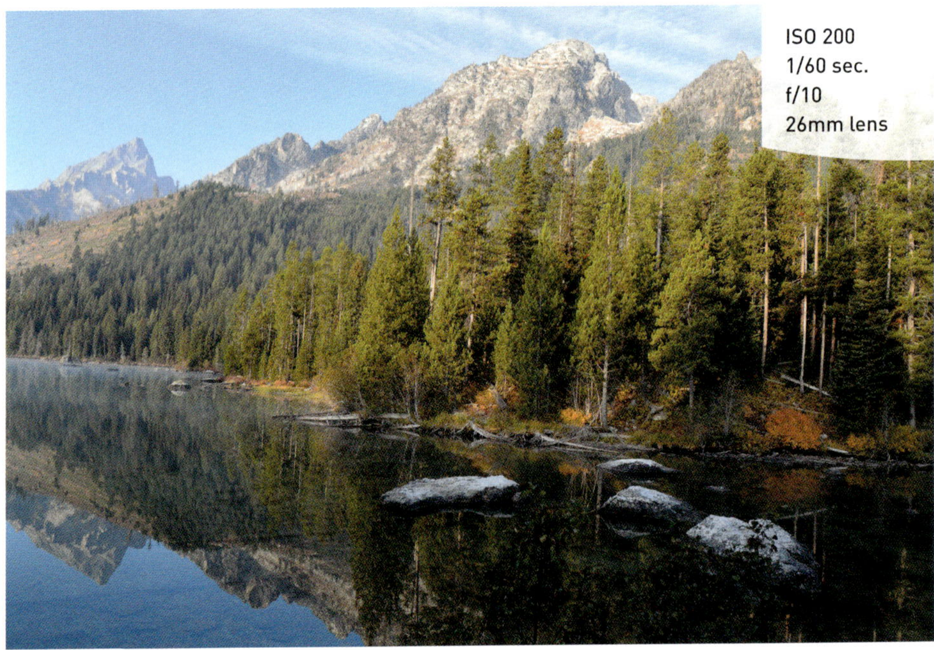

FIGURE 7.9
Using the Landscape picture control can add sharpness and more vivid color to skies and vegetation.

SETTING UP THE LANDSCAPE PICTURE CONTROL

1. You can set the Landscape picture control by using the menu system, but there is an easier method. To quickly access the controls, press the Picture Control button on the back of the camera (**A**).
2. Look at the rear LCD monitor, use the Multi-selector to choose Landscape, and press OK when done (**B**).

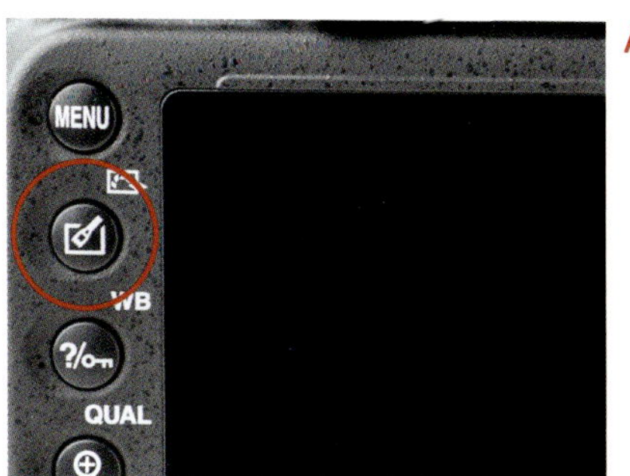

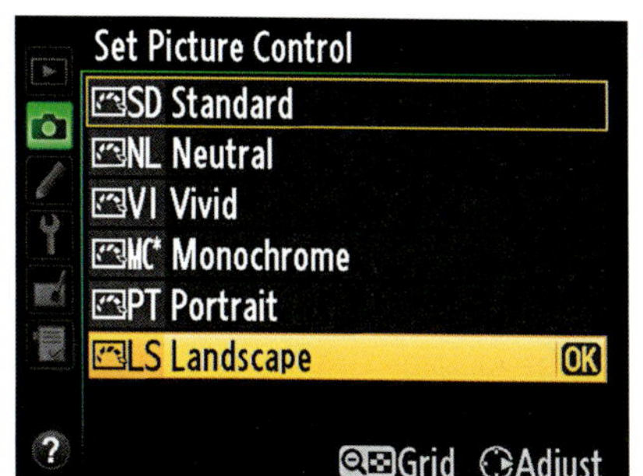

The camera will now apply the Landscape picture control to all of your photos. This style will be locked into the camera even after turning it off and back on again, so make sure to change it back to Standard when you are done with your landscape shoot.

PICTURE CONTROLS FOR RAW FILES

When you set up the picture control, the camera will apply the changes to your file as it is saved and show you the result on your LCD monitor. If you are shooting with the RAW format and set a picture control, the picture control adjustments will show up on your LCD monitor but will go away completely if you open the image for processing in non-Nikon software. You can, however, use Nikon software—like ViewNX 2 or CaptureNX 2—to change the picture control adjustments. That's because, although a RAW file has no camera processing applied, Nikon software will recognize the camera's style settings as a starting place. Non-Nikon programs—like Adobe Camera Raw and Photoshop Lightroom—don't understand the in-camera style settings but will let you use the software's own adjustments to add the look of the picture control back to your RAW file. Check your software manual for more info.

TAMING BRIGHT SKIES WITH EXPOSURE COMPENSATION

Balancing exposure in scenes that have a wide contrast in tonal ranges can be extremely challenging. The one thing you should try to avoid is overexposing your skies to the point of blowing out your highlights (unless, of course, that is the look you are going for). It's one thing to have white clouds, but it's a completely different and bad thing to have no detail at all in those clouds. This usually happens when the camera is trying to gain exposure in the darker areas of the image (**Figure 7.10**). The one way to tell if you have blown out your highlights is to turn on the Highlight Alert, or "blinkies," feature on your camera (see the "How I Shoot" section in Chapter 4). When you take a shot where the highlights are exposed beyond the point of having any detail, that area will blink in your LCD display if you have set up the Highlights display option. It is up to you to determine if that particular area is important enough to regain detail by altering your exposure. If the answer is yes, then the easiest way to go about it is to use exposure compensation.

With this feature, you can force your camera to choose an exposure that ranges, in 1/3-stop increments, from five stops over to five stops under the metered exposure (**Figure 7.11**).

HIGH-KEY AND LOW-KEY IMAGES

When you hear someone refer to a subject as being *high key,* it usually means that the entire image is composed of a very bright subject with very few shadow areas—think snow or beach. It makes sense, then, that a *low-key* subject has very few highlight areas and a predominance of shadow areas. Think of a cityscape at night as an example of a low-key photo.

USING EXPOSURE COMPENSATION TO REGAIN DETAIL IN HIGHLIGHTS

1. Activate the camera meter by lightly pressing the shutter release button.
2. Using your index finger, press and hold the Exposure Compensation button, and change the over/underexposure setting by rotating the Main Command dial.
3. Rotate the Main Command dial to the left one click, and take another picture (each click of the Main Command dial is a 1/3-stop exposure change).
4. If the blinkies are gone, you are good to go. If not, keep subtracting from your exposure by 1/3 of a stop until you have a good exposure in the highlights.

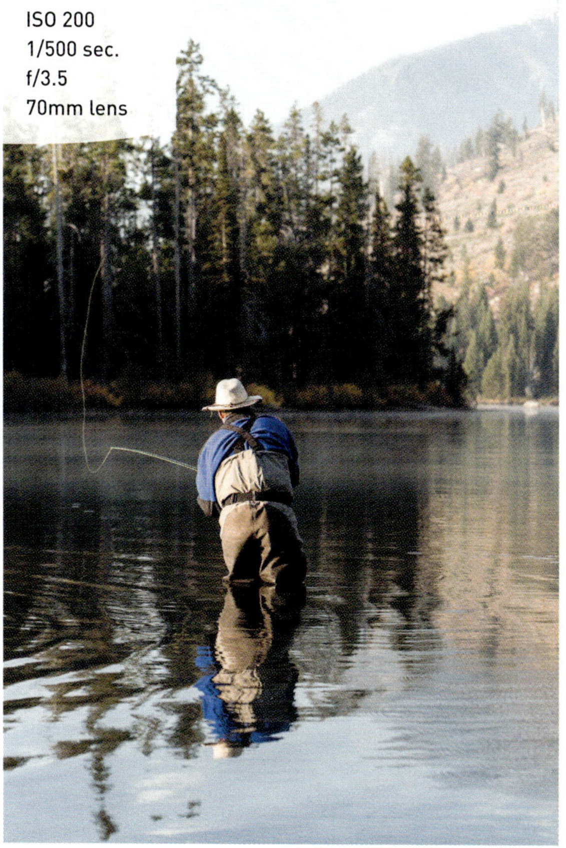

FIGURE 7.10
The dark shadows from the trees caused the meter to overexpose the sky and the fisherman's hat.

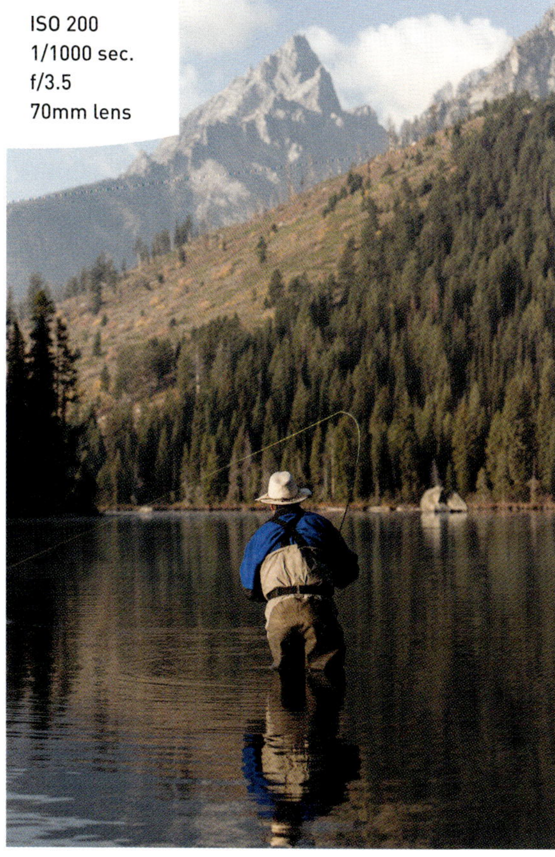

FIGURE 7.11
A compensation of one stop of underexposure brought back the detail in the sky.

I generally keep my camera set to –1/3 stop for most of my landscape work unless I am working with a location that is very dark or low key.

Note that any exposure compensation will remain in place even after turning the camera off and then on again. Don't forget to reset it once you have successfully captured your image. Also, exposure compensation works across all of the shooting modes. If you change between modes (e.g., from Program to Aperture Priority), the camera will hold the compensation you set in the previous mode.

SHOOTING BEAUTIFUL BLACK AND WHITE LANDSCAPES

There's nothing as timeless as a beautiful black and white landscape photo. For many, it is the purest form of photography. The genre conjures up thoughts of Ansel Adams out in Yosemite Valley, capturing stunning monoliths with his 8x10 view camera. Well, just because you are shooting with a digital camera doesn't mean you can't create your own stunning photos using the power of the Monochrome picture control. (See the "Classic Black and White Portraits" section of Chapter 6 for instructions on setting up this feature.) Not only can you shoot in black and white, you can also customize the camera to apply built-in software filters to lighten or darken different elements within your scene, as well as add contrast and definition.

The four filter colors are red, yellow, green, and orange. The most typically used filters in black and white photography are red and yellow. This is because the color of these filters will darken opposite colors and lighten similar colors. So if you want to darken a blue sky, you would use a yellow filter, because blue is the opposite of yellow. To darken green foliage, you would use a red filter. Check out the series of shots in **Figure 7.12** with different filters applied.

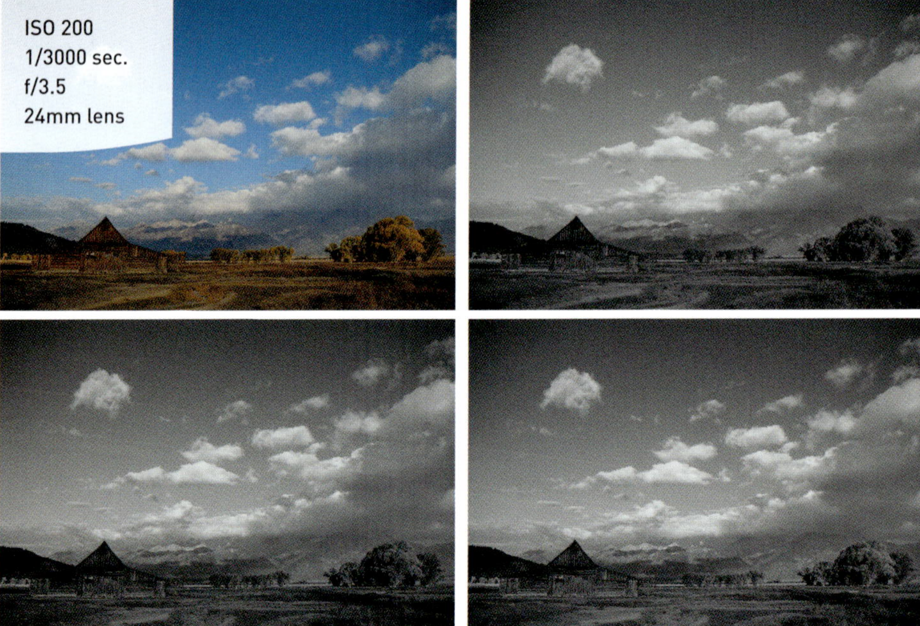

FIGURE 7.12 Adding color filter settings to the Monochrome picture control allows you to lighten or darken elements in your scene. The top-right image has no filter applied to it. The bottom left has a green filter, and the bottom right has a yellow filter.

You can see that there is no real difference in contrast between the color image and the black and white image with no filter. The green filter has the effect of darkening the skies slightly and giving a significantly lighter look to the vegetation. Using the yellow filter makes the vegetation a little lighter but dramatically darkens the sky. There is no right or wrong to choosing a filter for your black and white shots—it's pretty much whatever you prefer. In this instance, I think I prefer the image with the green filter.

Other options in the Monochrome picture control enable you to adjust the sharpness and contrast and even add some color toning (like sepia) to the final image. This information is also in the "Classic Black and White Portraits" section of Chapter 6. I like to have Sharpness set to 5 and Contrast set to +1 for my landscape images. This gives an overall look to the black and white image that is reminiscent of the classic black and white films. Experiment with the various settings to find the combination that is most pleasing to you. Just remember that the Monochrome picture control is automatically applied and saved to a JPEG file but can be lost when you open your RAW files (see the sidebar "Picture Controls for Raw Files," earlier in this chapter).

THE GOLDEN LIGHT

If you ask professional landscape photographers what their favorite time of day to shoot is, chances are they will tell you it's the hours surrounding daybreak and sunset (**Figures 7.13** and **7.14**). The reason for this is that the light is coming from a very low angle to the landscape, which creates shadows and gives depth and character. There is also a quality to the light that seems cleaner and is more colorful than the light you get when shooting at midday. One thing that can dramatically improve any morning or evening shot is the presence of clouds. The sun will fill the underside of the clouds with a palette of colors and add drama to your image.

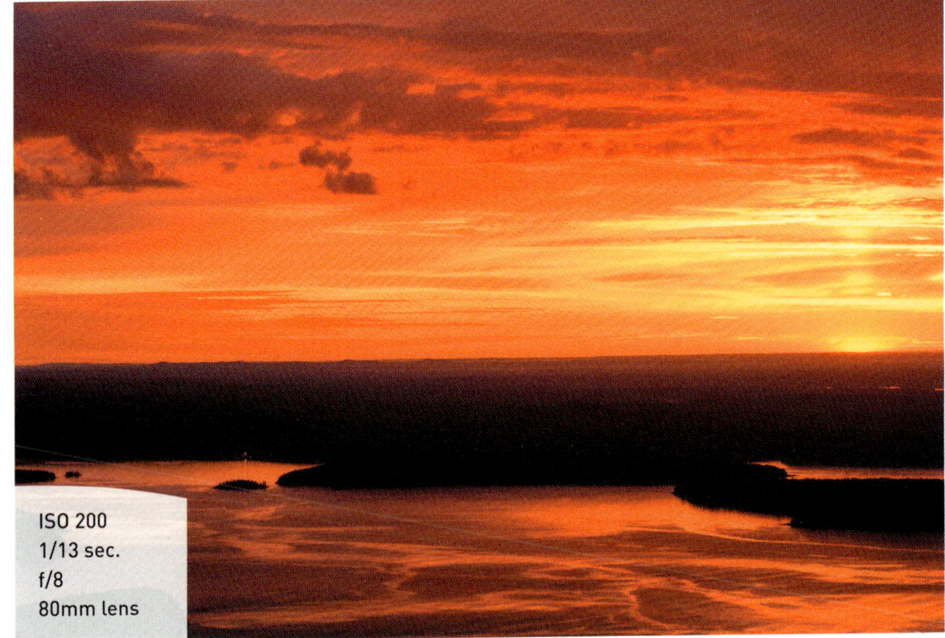

ISO 200
1/13 sec.
f/8
80mm lens

FIGURE 7.13
The few minutes just prior to sunrise can add great colors to a partly cloudy sky. This is the view from Cadillac Mountain in Acadia National Park, the first point on the East Coast to see the sunrise.

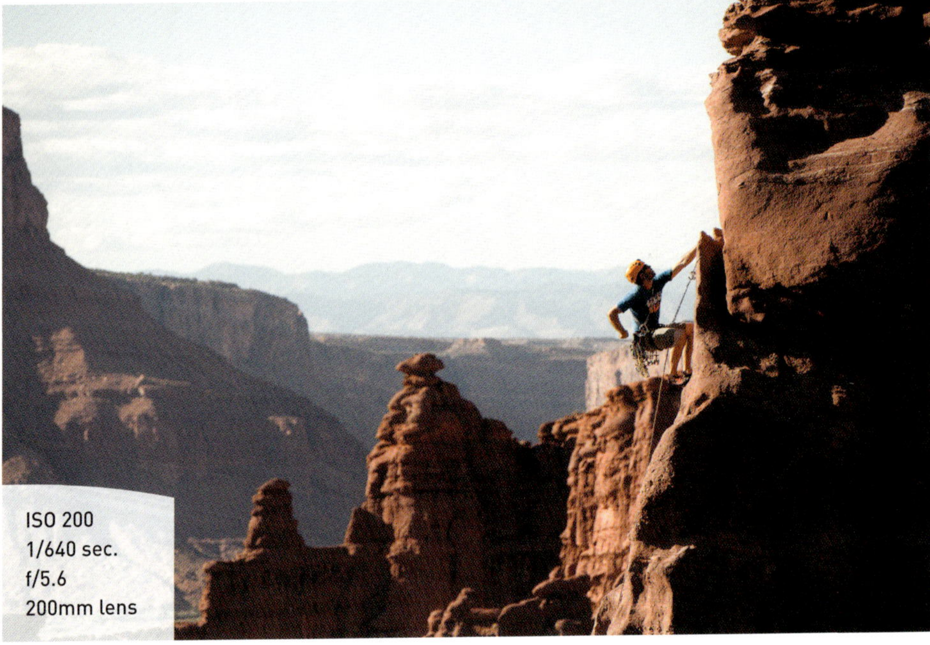

ISO 200
1/640 sec.
f/5.6
200mm lens

FIGURE 7.14
Late afternoon sun is usually warmer and adds drama and warmth.

WARM AND COOL COLOR TEMPERATURES

These two terms are used to describe the overall color cast of an image. Reds and yellows are said to be *warm*, which is usually the look that you get from the late afternoon sun. Blue is usually the predominant color when talking about a *cool* cast.

WHERE TO FOCUS

Large landscape scenes are great fun to photograph, but they can present a problem: where exactly do you focus when you want everything to be sharp? Since our goal is to create a great landscape photo, we will need to concentrate on how to best create an image that is tack sharp, with a depth of field that renders great focus throughout the scene.

I have already stressed the importance of a good tripod when shooting landscapes. The tripod lets you concentrate on the aperture portion of the exposure without worrying about how long your shutter will be open. This is because the tripod provides the stability to handle any shutter speed you might need when shooting at small apertures. I find that for most of my landscape work I set my camera to Aperture Priority mode and the ISO to 200 (for a clean, noise-free image).

But shooting with the smallest aperture on your lens doesn't necessarily mean that you will get the proper sharpness throughout your image. The real key is knowing where in the scene to focus your lens to maximize the depth of field for your chosen aperture. To do this, you must utilize something called the "hyper focal distance" of your lens.

Hyper focal distance, also referred to as HFD, is the point of focus that will give you the greatest acceptable sharpness from a point near your camera all the way out to infinity. If you combine good HFD practice with a small aperture, you will get images that are sharp to infinity.

There are a couple of ways to do this, and the one that is probably the easiest is, as you might guess, the one that is most widely used by working pros. When you have your shot all set up and composed, focus on an object that is about one-third of the distance into your frame (**Figure 7.15**). It is usually pretty close to the proper distance and will render favorable results. When you have the focus set, take a photograph and then zoom in on the preview on your LCD to check the sharpness of your image.

FIGURE 7.15 To get maximum focus from near to far, the focus was set about a third of the way up the stone wall on the left.

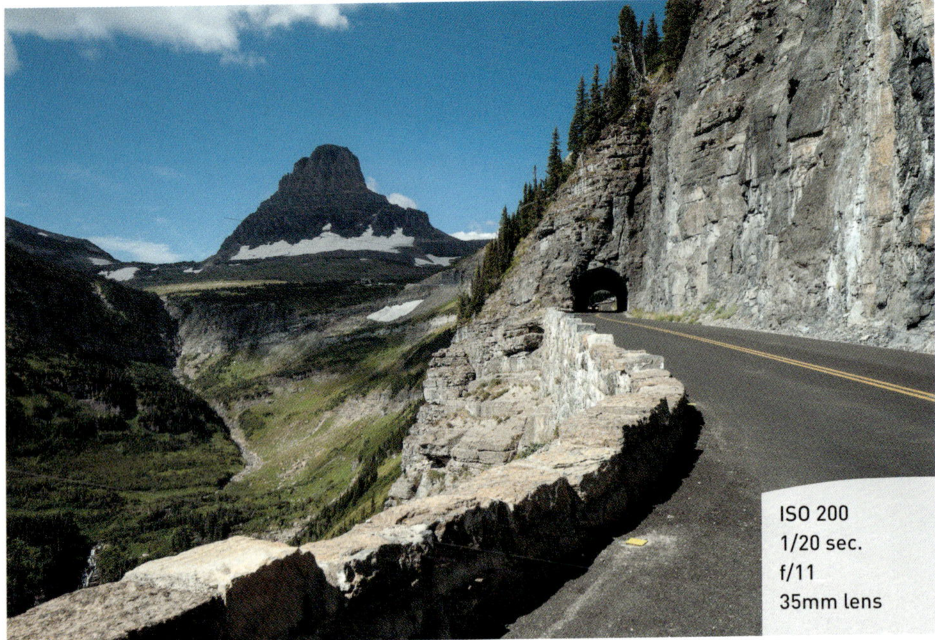

ISO 200
1/20 sec.
f/11
35mm lens

One thing to remember is that as your lens gets wider in focal length, your HFD will be closer to the camera position. This is because the wider the lens, the greater depth of field you can achieve. This is yet another reason why a good wide-angle lens is indispensable to the landscape shooter.

TACK SHARP

Here's one of those terms that photographers like to throw around. *Tack sharp* refers not only to the focus of an image but also to the overall sharpness of the image. This usually means that there is excellent depth of field in terms of sharp focus for all elements in the image. It also means that there is no sign of camera shake, which can give soft edges to subjects that should look nice and crisp. To get your images tack sharp, use a small depth of field, don't forget your tripod, use the self-timer to activate the shutter if no cable release is handy, and practice achieving good hyper focal distance (HFD) when picking your point of focus.

EASIER FOCUSING

There's no denying that the automatic focus features on the D600 are great, but sometimes it just pays to turn them off and focus manually. This is especially true if you are shooting on a tripod: once you have your shot composed in the viewfinder and you are ready to focus, chances are that the area you want to focus on is not going to be in the area of one of the focus points. Often this is the case when you have a foreground element that is fairly low in the frame. You could use a single focus point set low in your viewfinder and then pan the camera down until it rests on your subject. But then you would have to press the shutter button halfway to focus the camera and then try to recompose and lock down the tripod. It's no easy task.

But you can have the best of both worlds by having the camera focus for you, then switching to manual focus to comfortably recompose your shot (**Figure 7.16**).

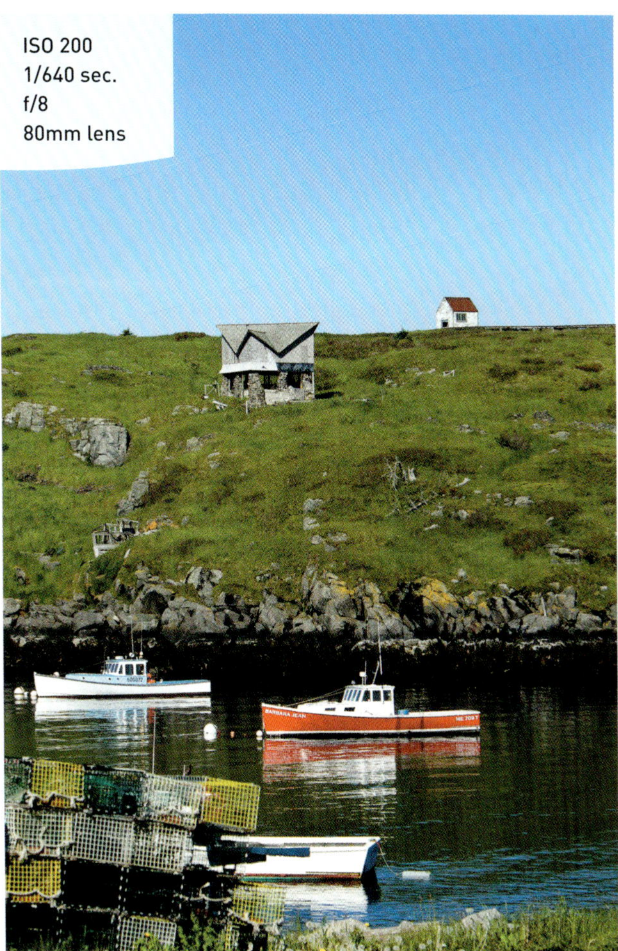

FIGURE 7.16
Using the HFD (hyper focal distance) one-third rule, I focused on the red lobster boat, then switched the lens to manual focus before recomposing for the final shot.

GETTING FOCUSED WHILE USING A TRIPOD

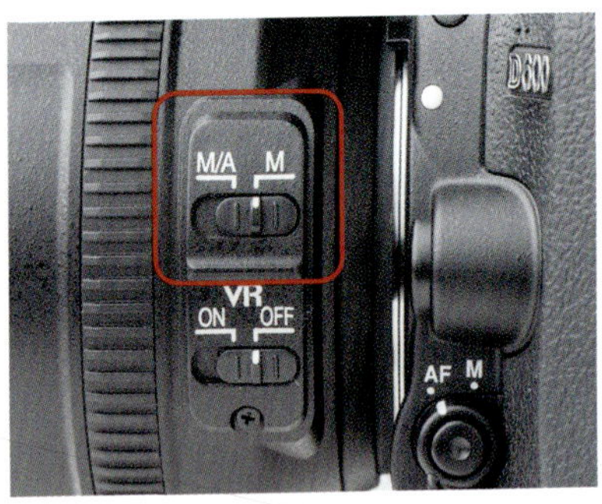

1. Set up your shot and find the area that you want to focus on.
2. Pan your tripod head so that your active focus point is on that spot.
3. Press the shutter button halfway to focus the camera.
4. Switch the camera to manual focus by sliding the switch on the lens barrel from M/A to M.
5. Recompose the composition on the tripod, and then take the shot.

The camera will fire without trying to refocus the lens. This works especially well for wide-angle lenses, which can be difficult to focus in Manual mode.

MAKING WATER FLUID

There's little that is quite as satisfying for the landscape shooter as capturing a silky waterfall shot. Creating the smooth-flowing effect is as simple as adjusting your shutter speed to allow the water to be in motion while the shutter is open. The key is to have your camera on a stable platform (such as a tripod) so that you can use a shutter speed that's long enough to work (**Figure 7.17**). To achieve a great effect, use a shutter speed that is at least 1/15 of a second or longer.

SETTING UP FOR A WATERFALL SHOT

1. Attach the camera to your tripod, then compose and focus your shot.
2. Make sure the ISO is set to 100.
3. Using Aperture Priority mode, set your aperture to the smallest opening (such as f/22 or f/36).
4. Press the shutter button halfway so the camera takes a meter reading.
5. Check to see if the shutter speed is 1/15 of a second or slower.
6. Take a photo and then check the image on the LCD.

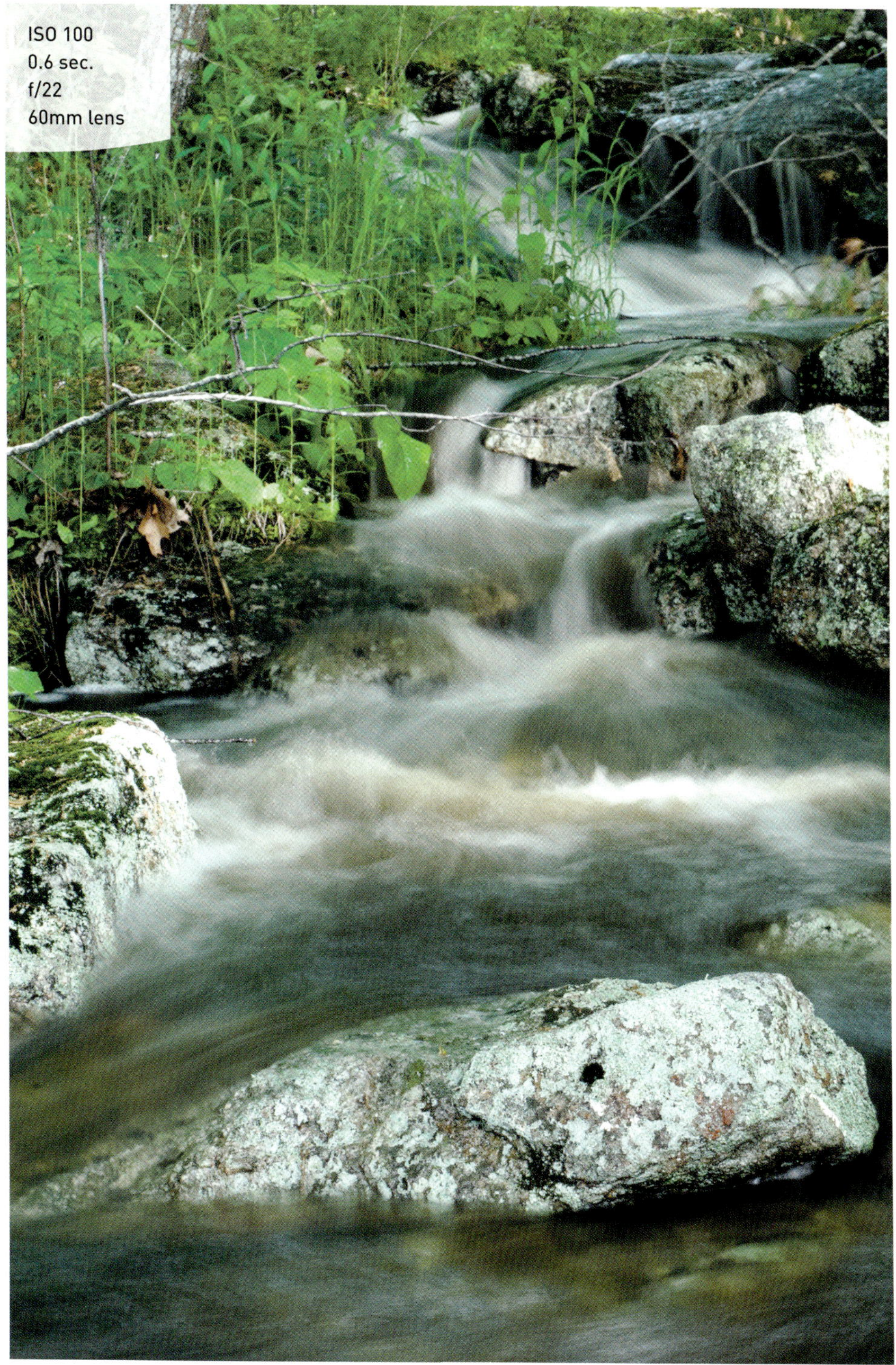

FIGURE 7.17
This stream was in the shade of the forest, but it was still pretty bright. Using f/22 allowed me to get the slower shutter speed I needed.

You can also use Shutter Priority mode for this effect by dialing in the desired shutter speed and having the camera set the aperture for you. I prefer to use Aperture Priority to ensure that I have the greatest depth of field possible.

If the water is blinking on the LCD, indicating a loss of detail in the highlights, then use the exposure compensation feature (as discussed earlier in this chapter) to bring details back into the waterfall. You will need to have the Highlight Alert feature turned on to check for overexposure (see "How I Shoot" in Chapter 4).

There is a possibility that you will not be able to have a shutter speed that is long enough to capture a smooth, silky effect, especially if you are shooting in bright daylight conditions. To overcome this obstacle, you need a filter for your lens—either a polarizing filter or a neutral density filter (or both). The polarizing filter redirects wavelengths of light to create more vibrant colors, reduce reflections, and darken blue skies. It also lengthens exposure times by about two stops due to the darkness of the filter (this amount can vary depending on the brand of filter used). It is a handy filter for landscape work. The neutral density filter is typically just a dark piece of glass that serves to darken the scene by one, two, or three stops (**Figure 7.18**). This allows you to use slower shutter speeds during bright conditions. Think of it as sunglasses for your camera lens. You will find more discussion on filters in Chapter 11.

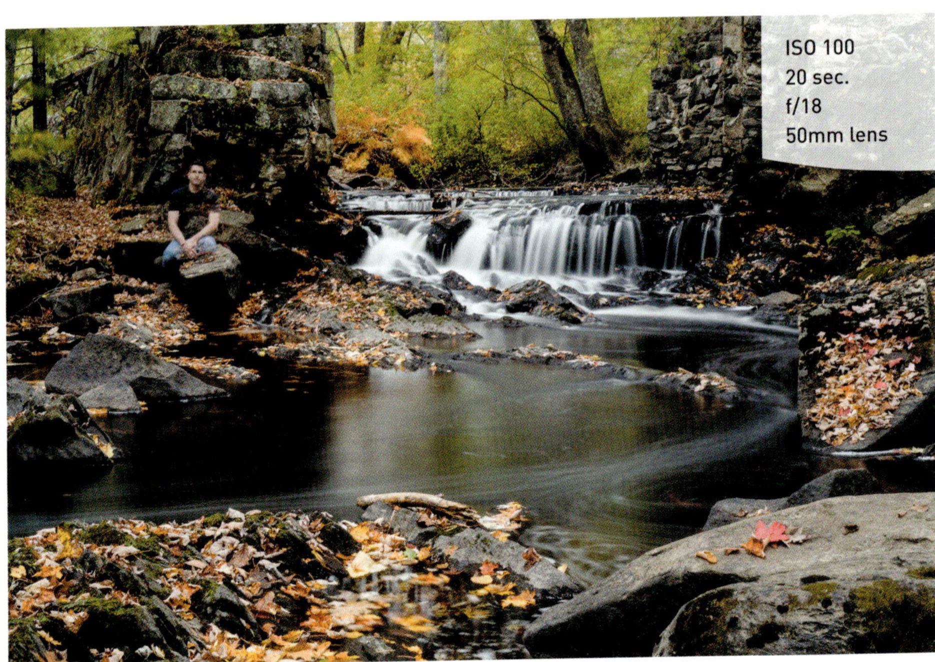

FIGURE 7.18
I used a neutral density filter and a polarizing filter together to add four stops of exposure, thus allowing for a longer exposure time (so long I had time to get in it).

DIRECTING THE VIEWER: A WORD ABOUT COMPOSITION

As a photographer, it's your job to lead the viewer through your image. You accomplish this by utilizing the principles of composition—the arrangement of elements in the scene that draw the viewer's eyes through your image and hold their attention. As the director of this viewing, you need to understand how people see, and then use that information to focus their attention on the most important elements in your image.

There is a general order at which we look at elements in a photograph. The first is brightness. The eye wants to travel to the brightest object within a scene. So if you have a bright sky, it's probably the first place the eye will travel to. The second order of attention is sharpness. Sharp, detailed elements will get more attention than soft, blurry areas. Finally, the eye will move to vivid colors while leaving the dull, flat colors for last. It is important to know these essentials in order to grab—and keep—the viewer's attention and then direct them through the frame.

In **Figure 7.19**, the eye is drawn to the bright moon in the upper third of the frame. From there, it is pulled toward the color and detail of the foliage that is anchoring the lower portion of the image. The eye moves around the slope at the bottom of the frame, where it is then lifted back up to the distant mountains and sky, right back to the beginning. The elements within the image all help to keep the eye moving but never leave the frame.

FIGURE 7.19
The composition of the elements pulls the viewer's eyes around the image, leading from one element to the next in a circular pattern.

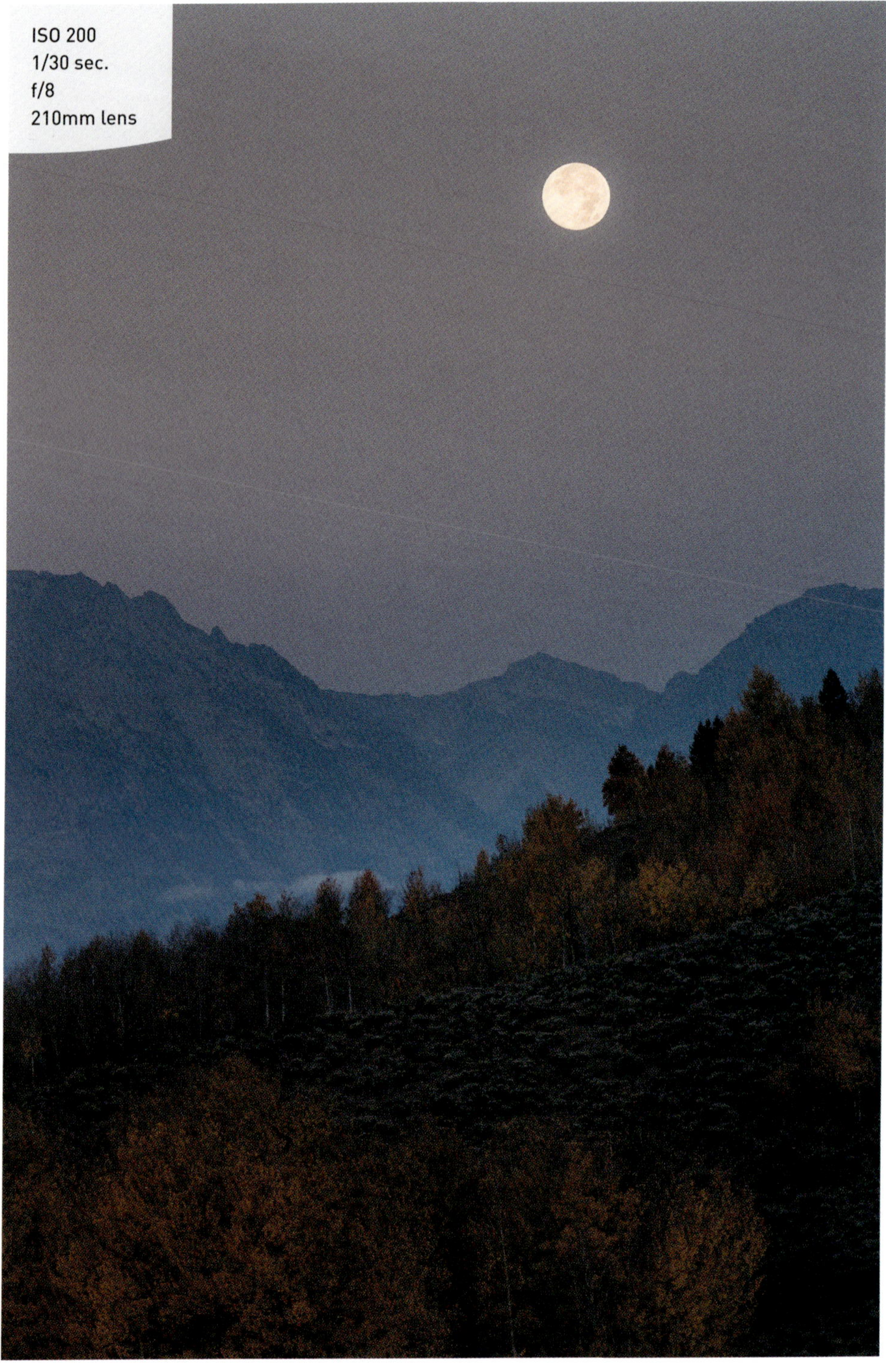

ISO 200
1/30 sec.
f/8
210mm lens

RULE OF THIRDS

There are quite a few philosophies concerning composition. The easiest one to begin with is known as the "rule of thirds." Using this principle, you simply divide your viewfinder into thirds by imagining two horizontal and two vertical lines that divide the frame equally.

The key to using this method of composition is to have your main subject located at or near one of the intersecting points (**Figure 7.20**).

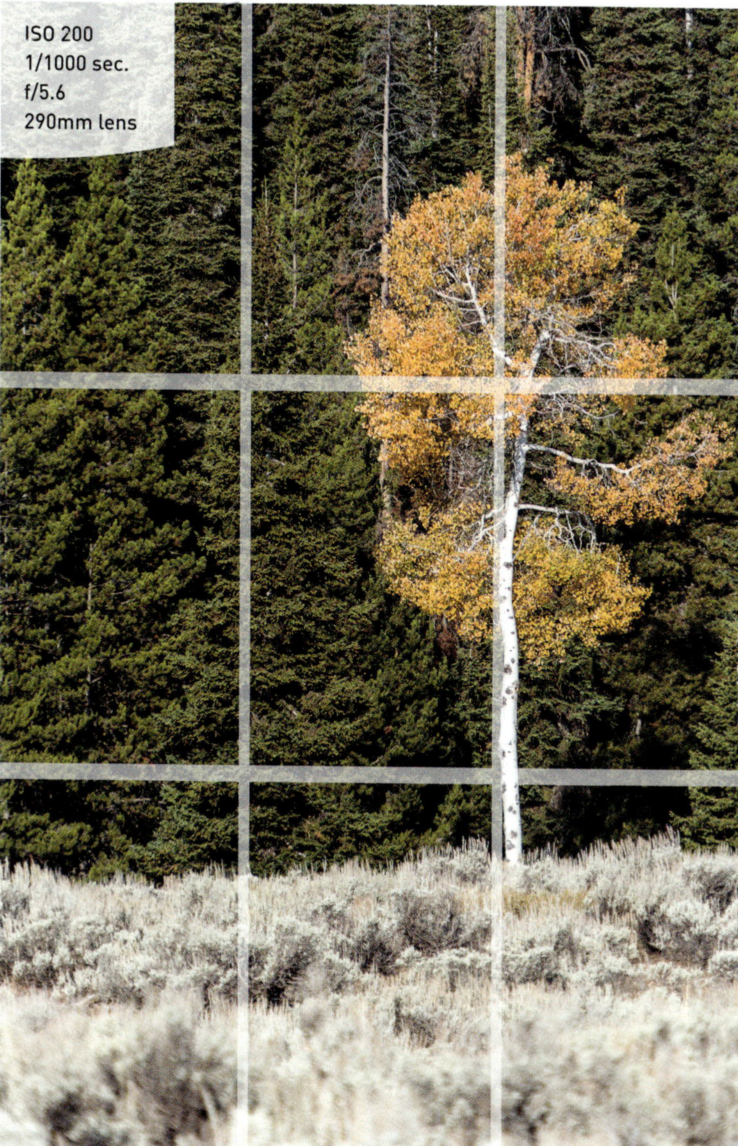

FIGURE 7.20
Placing the birch tree in the right-third of the image creates a much more interesting composition than having it dead center in the frame. Additionally, the horizon line is running across the bottom third of the frame.

By placing your subject near these intersecting lines, you are giving the viewer space to move within the frame. The one thing you don't want to do is place your subject smack dab in the middle of the frame. This is sometimes referred to as "bull's-eye" composition, and it requires the right subject matter for it to work. It's not always wrong, but it will usually be less appealing and may not hold the viewer's attention.

Speaking of the middle of the frame: the other general rule of thirds deals with horizon lines. Generally speaking, you should position the horizon one-third of the way up or down in the frame. Splitting the frame in half by placing your horizon in the middle of the picture is akin to placing the subject in the middle of the frame; it doesn't lend a sense of importance to either the sky or the ground.

The D600 has a visual tool for assisting you in composing your photo in the viewfinder: a grid overlay. The grid can be turned on using the camera menu system so that three horizontal and three vertical grid lines appear in the viewfinder. This won't necessarily help with aligning things in thirds, but it will help you keep your horizons straight and give you some visual alignment cues.

USING A GRID OVERLAY IN THE VIEWFINDER

1. Press the Menu button, then use the Multi-selector to navigate to the Custom Setting menu and select d Shooting/display. Press OK (**A**).
2. Highlight d2 Viewfinder grid display, press OK, set the feature to On, and press OK once again to lock in your changes (**B**).

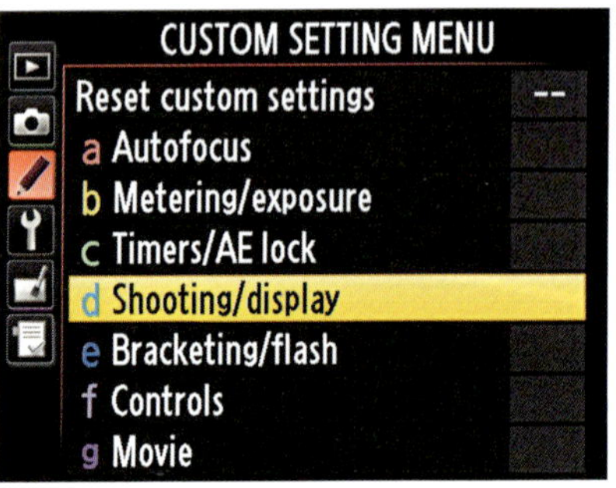

A

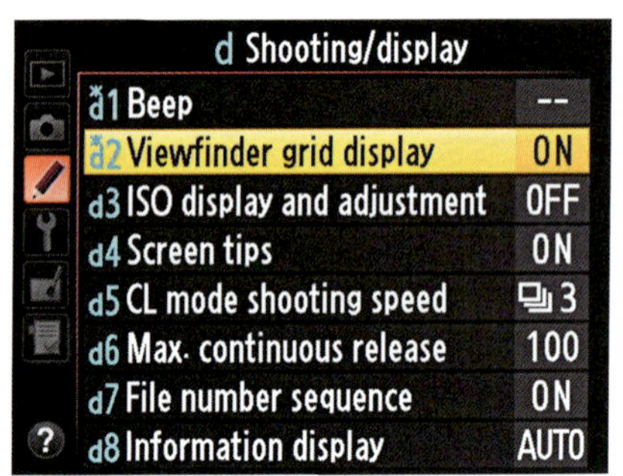

B

Now when you look through the viewfinder you will see a grid overlay. Don't ask me how they do that, but it is a very cool feature. When using the Live View mode for shooting, you can turn on the grid feature by pressing the Info button until the grid appears in the LCD monitor.

CREATING DEPTH

Because a photograph is a flat, two-dimensional space, you need to create a sense of depth by using the elements in the scene to create a three-dimensional feel. This is accomplished by including different and distinct spaces for the eye to travel: a foreground, middle ground, and background. By using these three spaces, you draw the viewer in and render depth to your image.

The salt marsh scene in **Figure 7.21** illustrates this well. The fallen tree strongly defines the foreground area. The misty marsh leading to the forest helps separate the tree from the middle ground, and the sky full of puffy clouds and color creates a perfect backdrop for the scene.

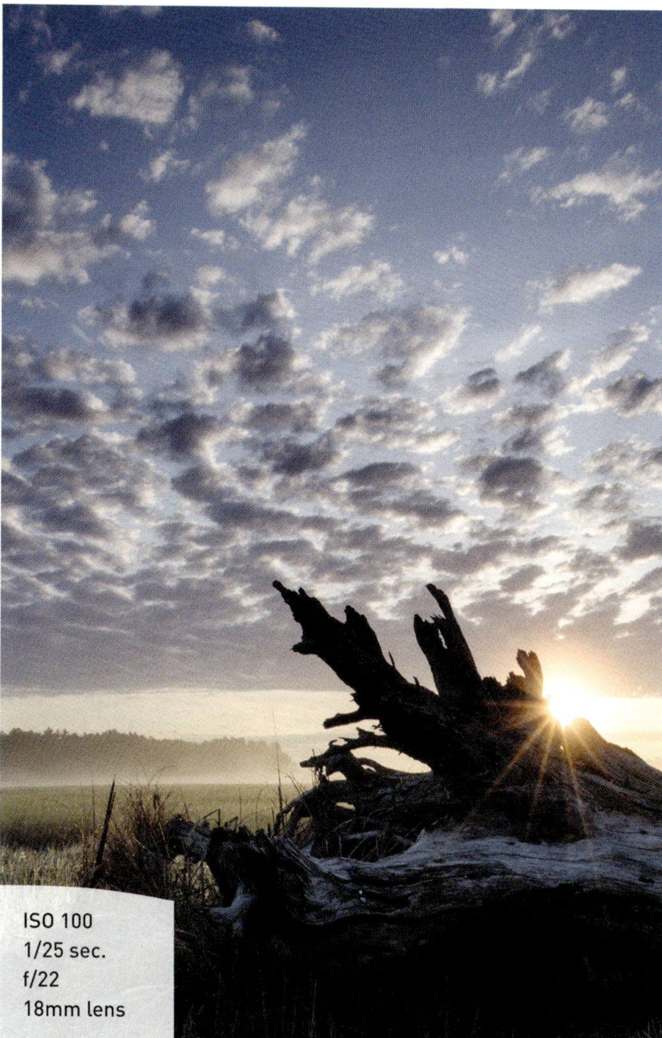

FIGURE 7.21
The fallen tree, misty marsh, and sky all add to the feeling of depth in this image.

Chapter 7 Assignments

We've covered a lot of ground in this chapter, so it's definitely time to put this knowledge to work and get familiar with these new camera settings and techniques.

Comparing depth of field: Wide-angle vs. telephoto

Practice using the hyper focal distance of your lens to maximize the depth of field. You can do this by picking a focal length to work with on your lens.

If you have a zoom lens, try using the longest length. Compose your image and find an object to focus on. Set your aperture to f/22 and take a photo.

Now do the same thing with the zoom lens at its widest focal length. Use the same aperture and focus point.

Review the images and compare the depth of field when using a wide-angle lens as opposed to a telephoto lens. Try this again with a large aperture as well.

Applying hyper focal distance to your landscapes

Pick a scene that has objects that are near the camera position as well as something that is clearly defined in the background. Try using a wide to medium-wide focal length for this (18–35mm). Use a small aperture and focus on the object in the foreground; then recompose and take a shot.

Without moving the camera position, use the object in the background as your point of focus and take another shot.

Finally, find a point that is one-third of the way into the frame from near to far and use that as the focus point.

Compare all of the images to see which method delivered the greatest range of depth of field from near to infinity.

Placing your horizons

Find a location with a defined horizon. Using the rule-of-thirds grid overlay, shoot the horizon along the top third of the frame, in the middle of the frame, and along the bottom third of the frame.

Share your results with the book's Flickr group!

www.flickr.com/groups/d600fromsnapshotstogreatshots

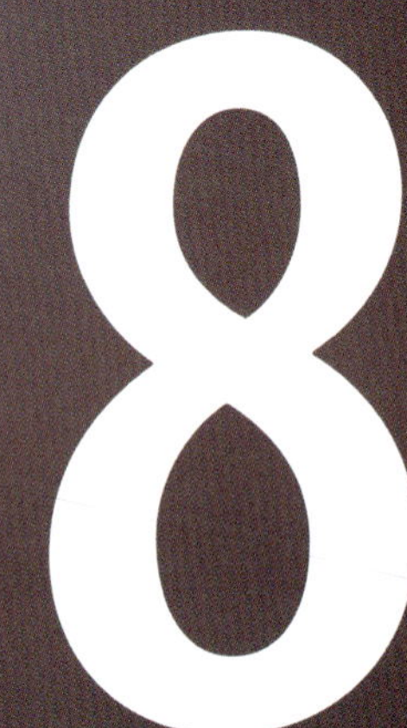

ISO 100
2 sec.
f/4
98mm lens

Mood Lighting

SHOOTING WHEN THE LIGHTS GET LOW

There is no reason to put your camera away when the sun goes down. Your D600 has some great features that let you work with available light as well as the built-in flash. In this chapter, we will explore ways to push your camera's technology to the limit in order to capture great photos in difficult lighting situations. We will also explore the use of flash and how best to utilize your built-in flash features to improve your photography. But let's first look at working with low-level available light.

PORING OVER THE PICTURE

If you ever have a chance to learn how to paint with light with Dave Black (www.daveblackphotography.com), I highly recommend jumping on the opportunity. All the light you see in this scene came from one very small LED flashlight that I used to paint different areas of the photo over a 15-second exposure during one of Dave's recent classes. Illuminating a scene in this way is a great way to learn about using directional light to add interest and dimension to your photographs. Plus, it's a whole lot of fun!

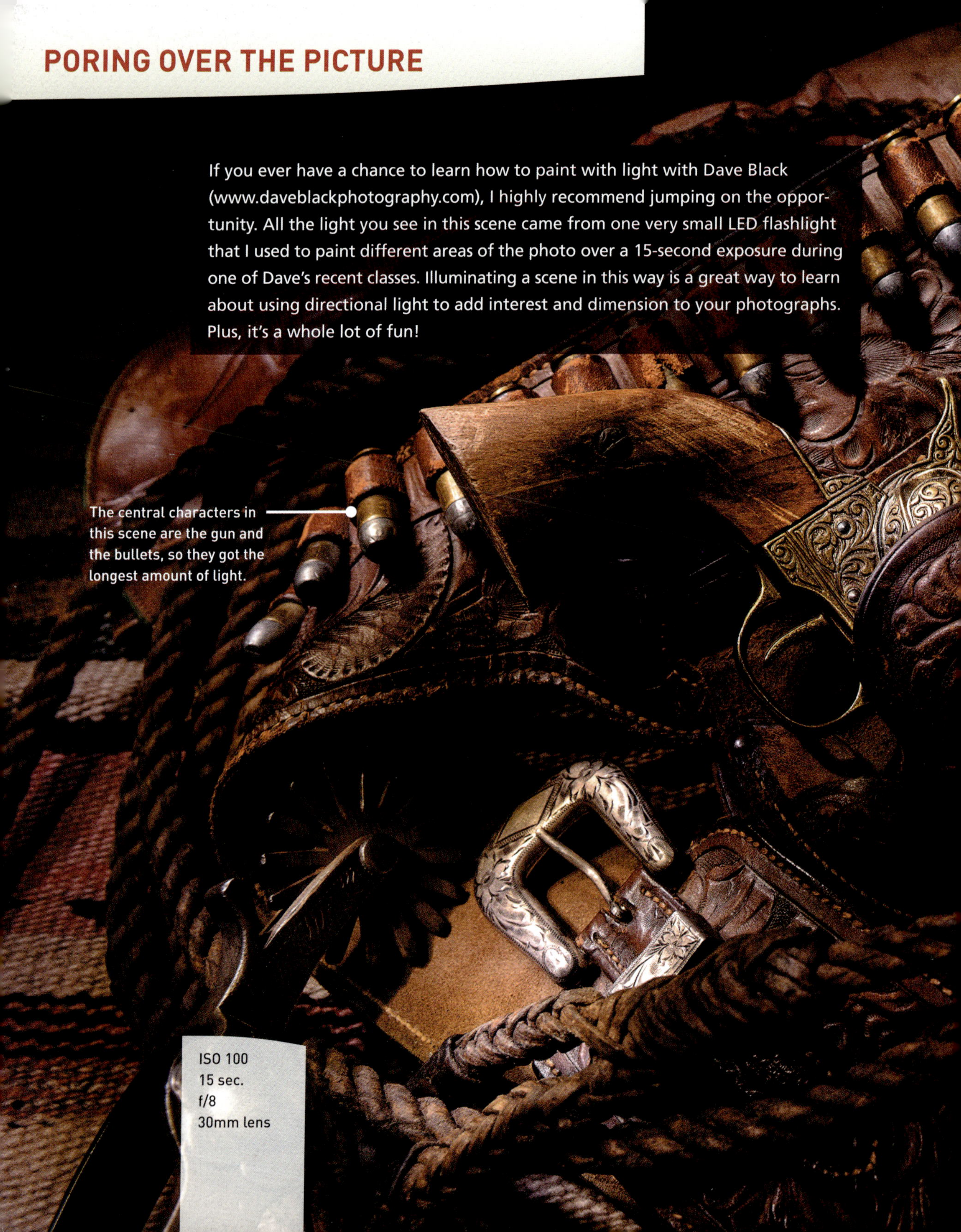

The central characters in this scene are the gun and the bullets, so they got the longest amount of light.

ISO 100
15 sec.
f/8
30mm lens

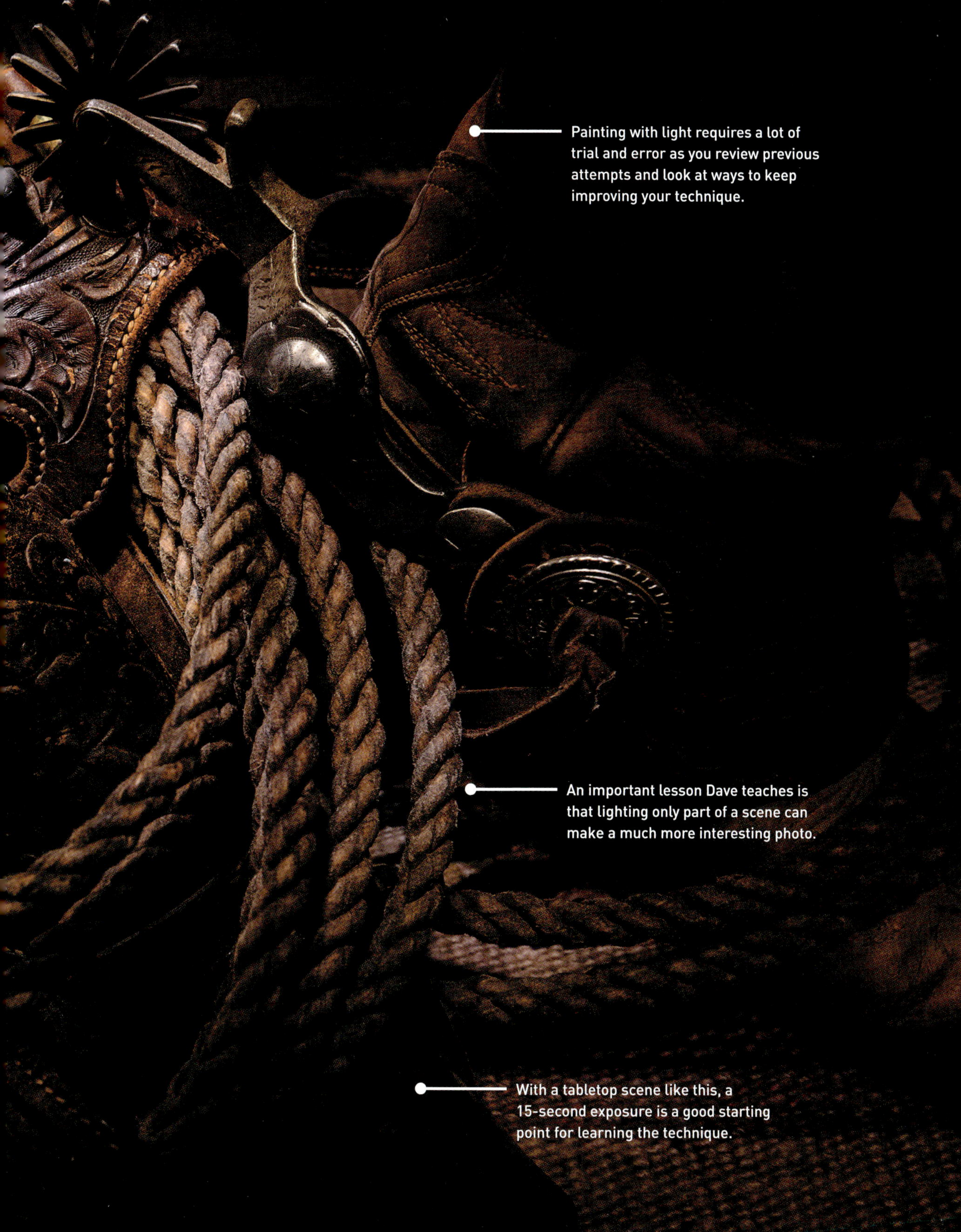
Painting with light requires a lot of trial and error as you review previous attempts and look at ways to keep improving your technique.
An important lesson Dave teaches is that lighting only part of a scene can make a much more interesting photo.
With a tabletop scene like this, a 15-second exposure is a good starting point for learning the technique.

RAISING THE ISO: THE SIMPLE SOLUTION

Let's begin with the obvious way to keep shooting when the lights get low: raising the ISO (**Figure 8.1**). By now you know how to change the ISO by using the ISO button and the Main Command dial. In typical shooting situations, you should keep the ISO in the 100–1600 range. This will keep your pictures nice and clean by keeping the digital noise to a minimum. But as the available light gets low, you might find yourself working in the higher ranges of the ISO scale, which could lead to more noise in your image.

How much noise is too much is subjective. Some people have a higher tolerance for noise than others, and sometimes the output destination or subject matter determines the acceptable level of noise. If I'm shooting a night sporting event, for example, I am much more tolerant of higher noise levels if that is what allows me to stop action and get the shot. But if I'm doing a long exposure of moving water, I prefer it to be as clean as possible, so I keep the ISO low. You'll have your own reasons and tolerance levels, so experiment with different ISO settings and get a feel for what works for your needs and output destinations.

You could use the flash, but that has a limited range (15–20 feet) that might not work for you. Or you could be in a situation where flash is prohibited or at least frowned upon, like at a wedding or in a museum.

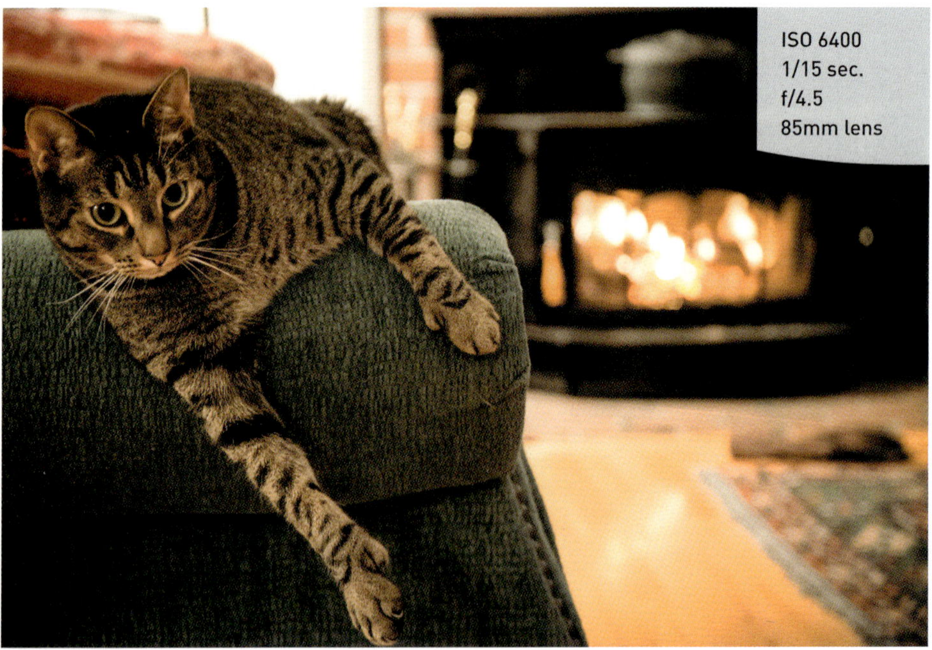

ISO 6400
1/15 sec.
f/4.5
85mm lens

FIGURE 8.1
The size of the cat's pupils give an indication of how low the light was.

And what about a tripod in combination with a long shutter speed? That is also an option, and we'll cover it a little further into the chapter. The problem with using a tripod and a slow shutter speed in low-light photography, though, is that it performs best when subjects aren't moving. Besides, try to set up a tripod in a museum and see how quickly you grab the attention of the security guards.

So if the only choice to get the shot is to raise the ISO, you'll want to consider the High ISO Noise Reduction feature. This shooting menu function is set to Normal by default, but as you start using higher ISO values you might consider changing it to the High setting.

It is important to keep in mind that High ISO Noise Reduction is applied only to in-camera JPEGs, so raising it to the High setting slightly increases the processing time for your images, and if you are shooting in continuous mode you might see a little reduction in the speed of your frames per second. If you are shooting in RAW mode, then this setting is recorded in the metadata of the photo and used by Nikon's post-processing software, but it is invisible to third-party post-processing software. So if you are shooting in RAW, you will be doing most of your noise reduction in post-processing software. (Chapter 7 explains how to set the Long Exposure Noise Reduction feature, which is applied equally to JPEG and RAW photos.)

To see the effect of noise reduction, zoom in and take a closer look (**Figures 8.2** and **8.3**).

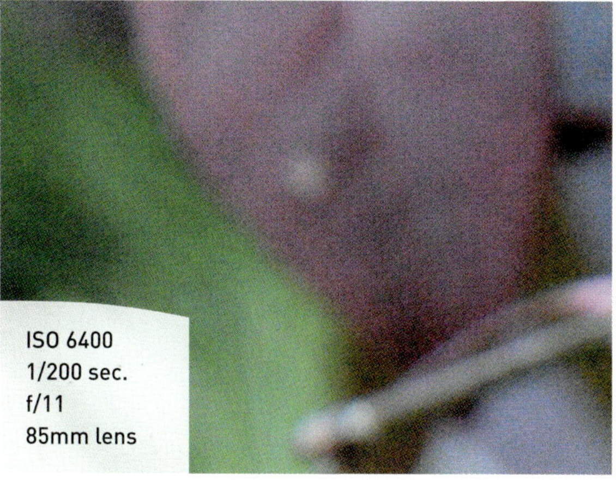

ISO 6400
1/200 sec.
f/11
85mm lens

FIGURE 8.2
Here is an enlargement of a shot without High ISO Noise Reduction.

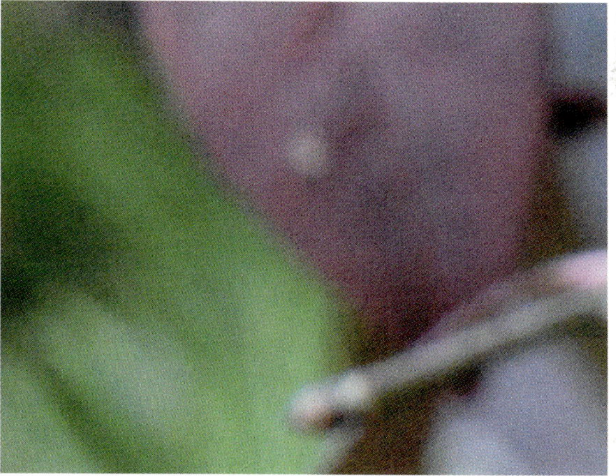

FIGURE 8.3
Here is the same subject photographed with High ISO Noise Reduction set to High. While it doesn't get rid of all the noise, it certainly reduces it and improves the look of the image.

NOISE REDUCTION SAVES SPACE

When you're shooting at very high ISO settings, running noise reduction can save you space on your memory card. If you are saving your photos as JPEGs, the camera will compress the information in the image to take up less space. But excessive noise can literally add megabytes to the file size. This is because the camera has to deal with more information: it views the noise in the image as photo information and, therefore, tries not to lose that information during the compression process. That means that more noise equals bigger files. So not only will turning on noise reduction improve the look of your image, it will also save you some space so you can take a few more shots.

USING VERY HIGH ISOS

Is ISO 6400 just not enough for you? Well, in that case, you will need to set your camera to one of the expanded ISO settings. These settings open up another two stops of ISO, raising the new limit to 25600. The new settings will not appear in your ISO scale as numbers, but as H 0.3 for 8000, H 0.7 for 10000, H 1.0 for 12800, and H 2.0 for 25600.

USING THE HIGHER ISO SETTINGS

1. Press and hold the ISO button. Then rotate the Command dial while observing the viewfinder, the control panel, or the information screen (**A**). Rotate the dial until you reach the H settings, then release the ISO button.
2. Select H 0.3, H 0.7, H 1.0, or H 2.0 (**B**).

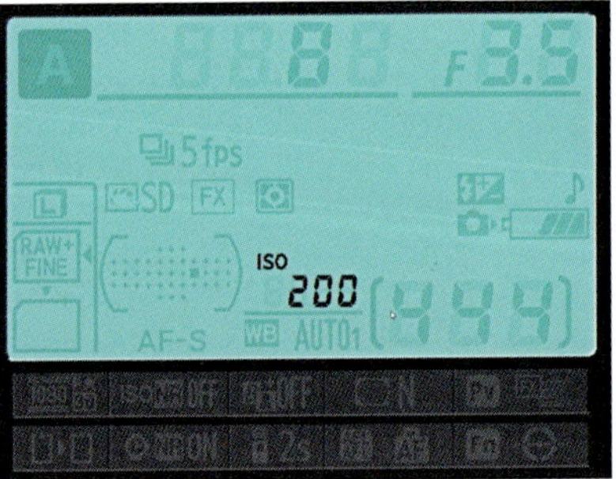

A

B

A word of warning about the expanded ISO settings: Although it is great to have these high ISO settings available during low-light shooting, they should always be your last resort. Even with the High ISO Noise Reduction turned on, the amount of visible noise will be extremely high. Try to avoid using high ISO whenever you can, but don't skip an opportunity for a terrific shot because you're afraid to use a higher ISO (**Figure 8.4**). The D600 does remarkably well at 1600 and below, so experiment a little. Remember: a picture never taken is far worse than one with a little noise!

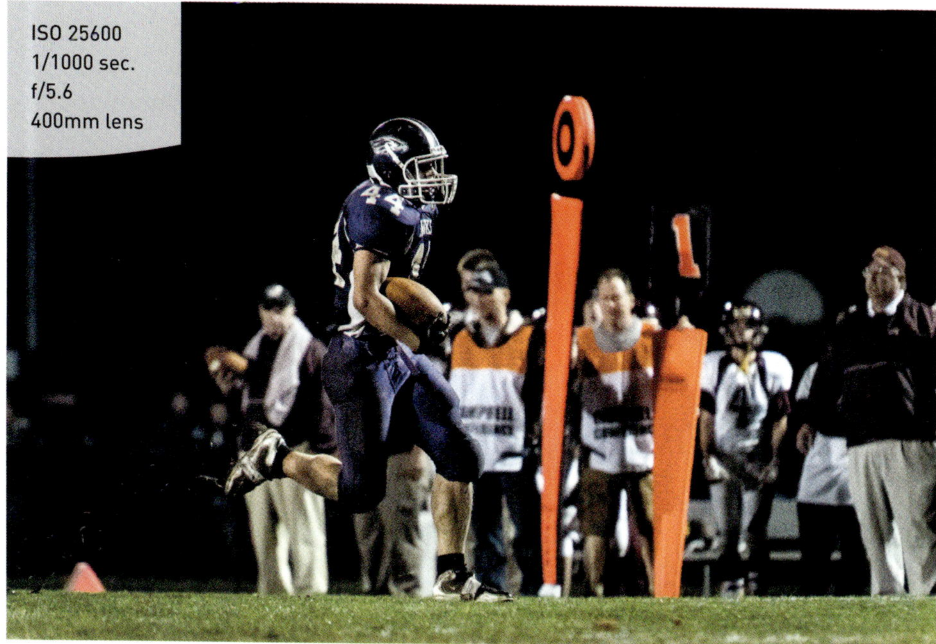

FIGURE 8.4
The only way to get a fast-enough shutter speed during this night football game was to raise the ISO to 25600.

STABILIZING THE SITUATION

If you purchased your camera with the Vibration Reduction (VR) lens, you already own a great tool to squeeze two stops of exposure out of your camera when shooting without a tripod. Typically, the average person can handhold a camera down to about 1/60 of a second before blurriness results due to hand shake. As the length of the lens is increased (or zoomed), the ability to handhold at slow shutter speeds (1/60 and slower) and still get sharp images is reduced (**Figure 8.5**).

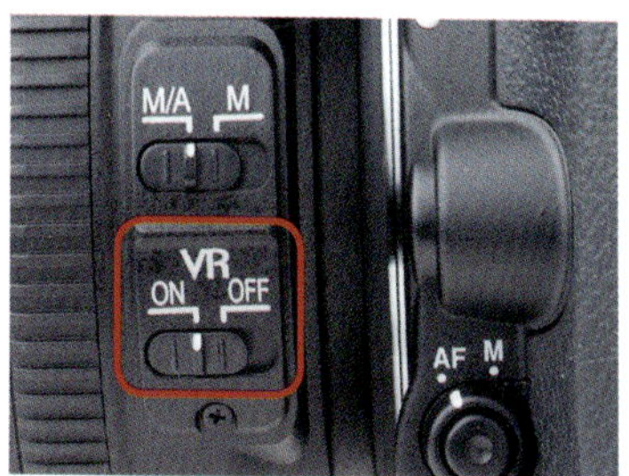

FIGURE 8.5
Turning on the VR switch helps you shoot in low-light conditions.

The Nikon VR lenses contain small gyro sensors and servo-actuated optical elements, which correct for camera shake and stabilize the image. The VR function is so good that it is possible to improve your handheld photography by two or three stops, meaning that if you are pretty solid at a shutter speed of 1/60 of a second, the VR feature will let you shoot at 1/15, and possibly even 1/8, of a second (**Figures 8.6** and **8.7**). When you're shooting in low-light situations, make sure you set the VR switch on the side of your lens to the On position.

ISO 200
1/10 sec.
f/11
85mm lens

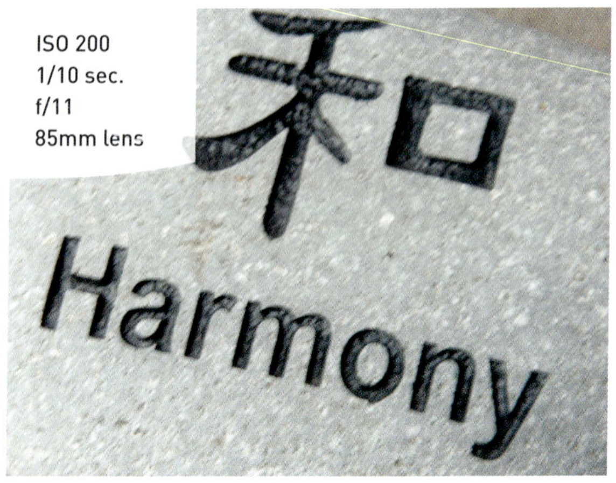

FIGURE 8.6
This image was shot handheld with the VR turned off.

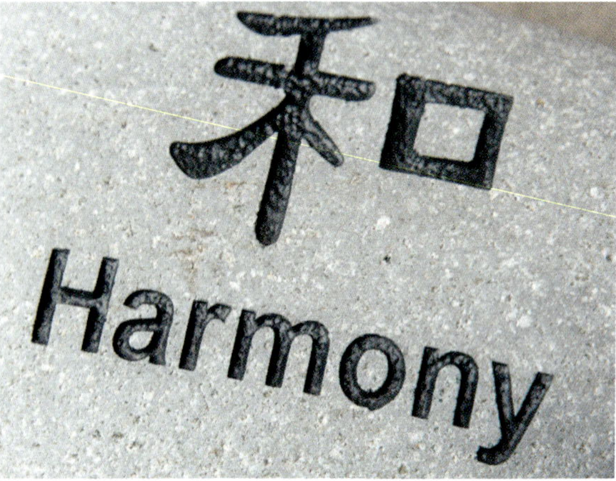

FIGURE 8.7
Here is the same subject shot with the same camera settings, but this time I turned the VR on.

HANDS OFF FOR SHARPER IMAGES

Whether you are shooting with a tripod or resting your camera on a wall, you can increase the sharpness of your pictures by taking your hands out of the equation. Whenever you use your finger to depress the shutter release button, you are increasing the chances that there will be a little bit of shake in your image. To eliminate this possibility, try setting your camera up to use the self-timer or the Exposure Delay mode (or even both together). Self-timer mode is the most commonly used, so let's look at that first.

1. To turn on the self-timer, simply press the Release Mode dial lock and rotate the Release Mode dial to Self-timer.
2. Press the Menu button to find the Custom Setting menu. Highlight and select C Timers/AE Lock, then press OK (**A**).
3. Select C3 Self-timer, and click OK (**B**).

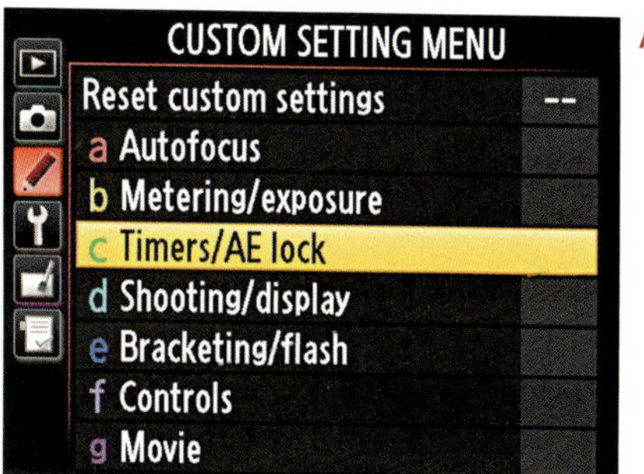

A

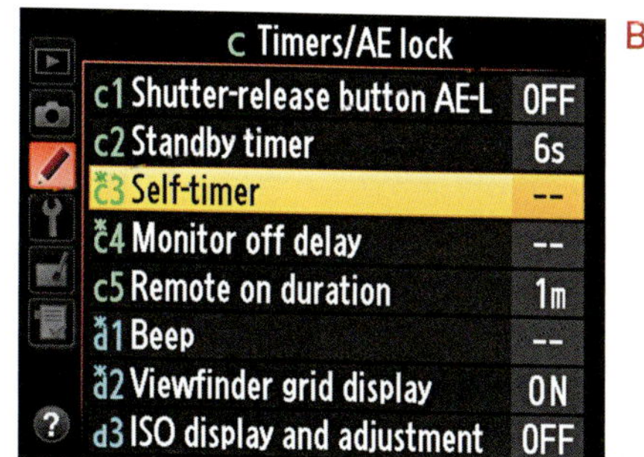

B

4. Choose the length of self-timer delay: 2, 5, 10, or 20 seconds (**C**). 5 seconds is ample time to quiet the tripod vibration caused by your actions.

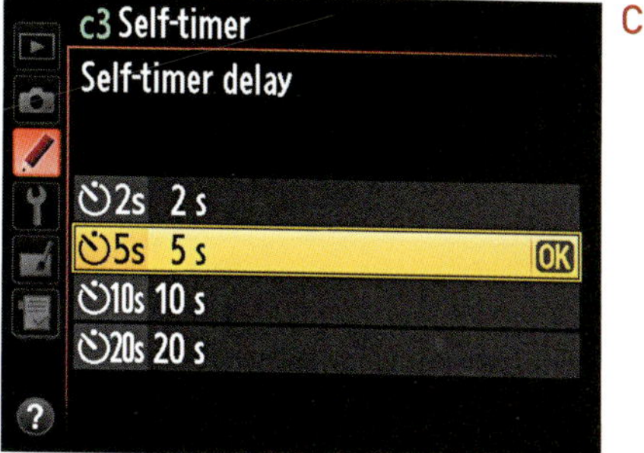

C

5. Choose the number of shots, from one to nine, that you want the camera to take when you press the shutter button. This can be handy when used in conjunction with the Auto bracket feature (covered in Chapter 9) or for group photos when you want to take multiple shots to ensure that you get a frame with everyone's eyes open.
6. Choose the time interval between shots: 0.5, 1, 2, or 3 seconds.

Now all you have to do is press the shutter button, and the camera will take the shot based on your settings. The self-timer is great, but it doesn't do anything to help with the vibration caused by the camera's mirror slapping up when a photo is taken. This is where Exposure Delay mode can help. Exposure Delay mode works with any of the other release modes, and when turned on it delays the shutter from 1–3 seconds after the mirror is moved up out of the way. Here's how to set it up:

1. Choose your desired release mode.
2. Press the Menu button to find the Custom Setting menu. Highlight and select D Shooting/display, then press OK (**A**).
3. Select D10 Exposure delay mode, and press OK (**B**).

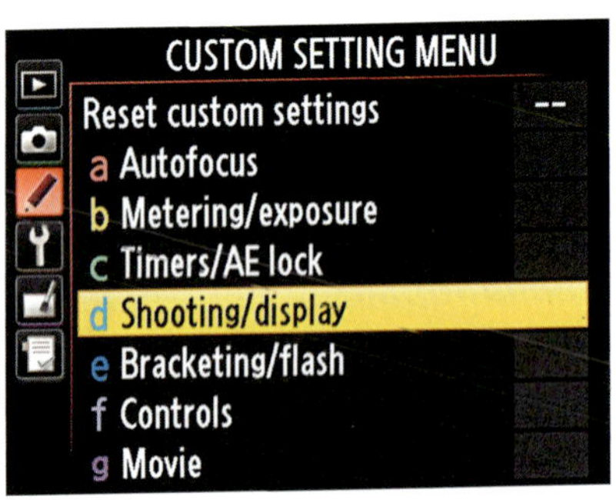

A

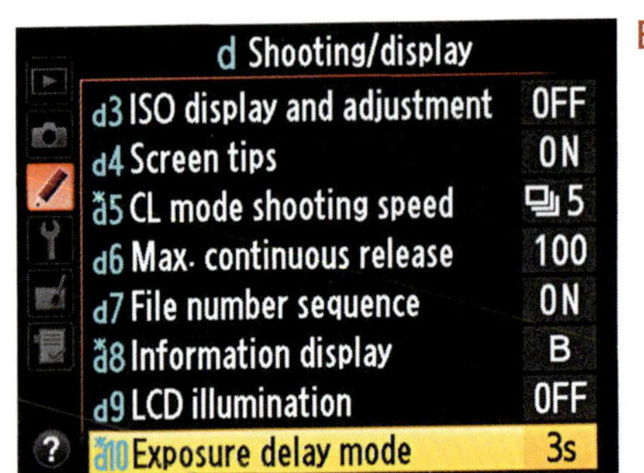

B

4. Choose the length of delay (1, 2, or 3 seconds) and press OK (**C**).

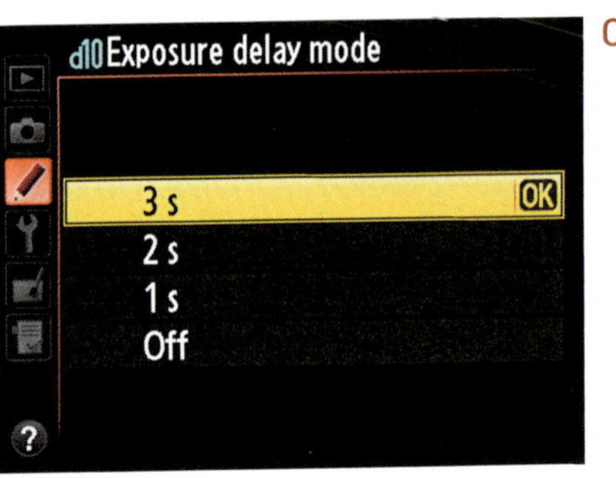

C

On a recent outing, I forgot to bring my remote release. So while taking some pre-dawn shots, I opted for a 5-second self-timer coupled with a 3-second exposure delay. It worked really well, and I was glad to have those options, though I still prefer a remote release. Make sure you switch out of self-timer mode and turn off the exposure delay when your shooting session is done.

FOCUSING IN LOW LIGHT

The D600 has a great focusing system, but occasionally the light levels might be too low for the camera to achieve an accurate focus. There are a few things you can do to overcome this obstacle.

First, you should know that the camera utilizes contrast in the viewfinder to establish a point of focus. This is why your camera will not be able to focus when you point it at a white wall or a cloudless sky. It simply can't find any contrast in the scene to work with. Knowing this, you might be able to use a single focus point in AF-S mode to find an area of contrast that is at the same distance as your subject. You can then hold that focus by holding down the shutter button halfway (or by pressing the AF-ON button) and recomposing your image.

Then there are those times when there just isn't anything there for you to focus on. A perfect example of this would be a fireworks display. If you point your lens to the night sky in any automatic focus (AF) mode, it will just keep searching for—and not finding—a focus point. On these occasions, you can simply turn off the autofocus feature and manually focus the lens (**Figure 8.8**). Look for the A/M switch on the side of the lens and slide it to the M position. Don't forget to put it back in A mode at the end of your shoot.

ISO 400
30 sec.
f/22
28mm lens

FIGURE 8.8
Focusing in low light is best done in manual focus mode.

SHOOTING LONG EXPOSURES

We have covered some of the techniques for shooting in low light, so let's go through the process of capturing a night or low-light scene for maximum image quality (**Figure 8.9**). The first thing to consider is that in order to shoot in low light with a low ISO, you will need to use shutter speeds that are longer than you could possibly handhold (longer than 1/15 of a second). This will require the use of a tripod or stable surface for you to place your camera on. For maximum quality, the ISO should be low—somewhere below 400. The Long Exposure Noise Reduction feature should be turned on to minimize the effects of exposing for longer durations (to set this up, see Chapter 7).

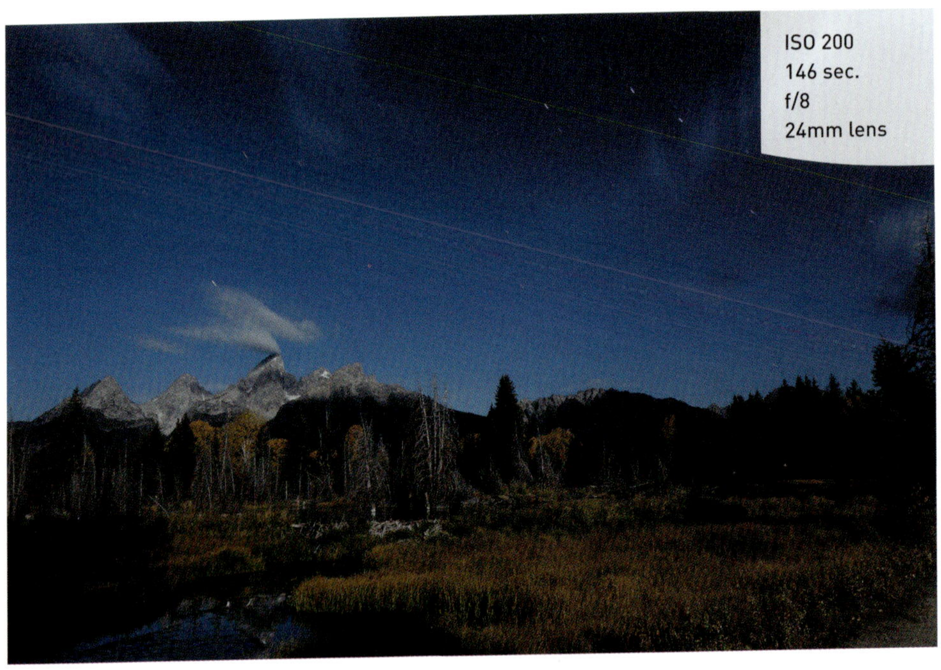

FIGURE 8.9
A very long exposure and a tripod were necessary for this moonlit view of the Grand Tetons.

Once you have the noise reduction turned on, set your camera to Aperture Priority (A) mode. That way, you can concentrate on the aperture that you believe is most appropriate and let the camera determine the best shutter speed (I discuss the Bulb setting in Manual mode in Chapter 9).

If it is too dark for the autofocus to function properly, try focusing manually. Finally, consider using a remote cable (see Chapter 11) to activate the shutter. If you don't have a remote of some sort, use the self-timer or the Exposure Delay mode discussed earlier. Once you shoot the image, you may notice some lag time before it is displayed on the rear LCD. This is due to the noise-reduction process, which can take anywhere from a fraction of a second up to 30 seconds, depending on the length of the exposure. Typically, the noise-reduction process will take the same amount of time as the exposure itself.

USING THE BUILT-IN FLASH

There are going to be times when you have to turn to your camera's built-in flash to get the shot. The pop-up flash on the D600 is not extremely powerful, but with the camera's advanced metering system it does a pretty good job of lighting up the night...or just filling in the shadows.

If you are working with one of the automatic scene modes, the flash should automatically activate when needed. If, however, you are working in one of the professional modes, you will first have to turn on the flash. To do this, just press the pop-up flash button located on the front of the camera (**Figure 8.10**). Once the flash is up, it is ready to go (**Figure 8.11**). It's that simple.

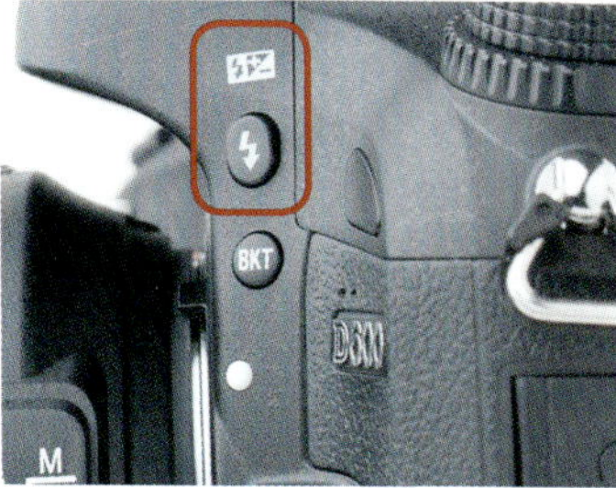

FIGURE 8.10
A quick press of the pop-up flash button will release the built-in flash up to its ready position.

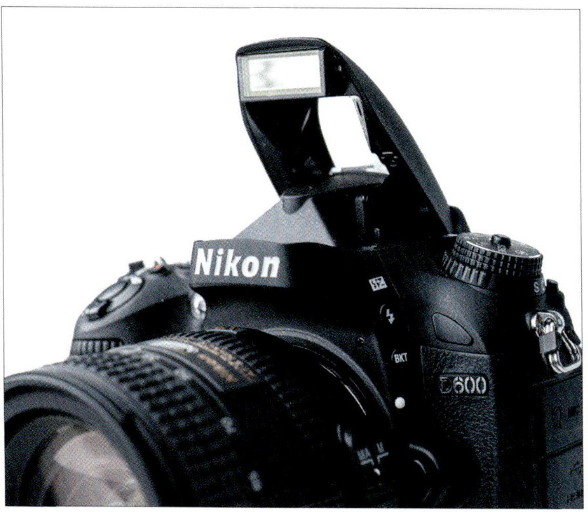

FIGURE 8.11
The pop-up flash in its ready position.

FLASH RANGE

Because the pop-up flash is fairly small, it does not have enough power to illuminate a large space (**Figure 8.12**). The effective distance varies depending on the ISO and aperture setting. At ISO 200 and f/4, the range is about 14 feet. This range can be extended to as far as 28 feet when the camera is set to an ISO of 800 at the same f-stop. Check out page 147 of your manual for a chart that shows the effective flash range for various ISO and aperture settings.

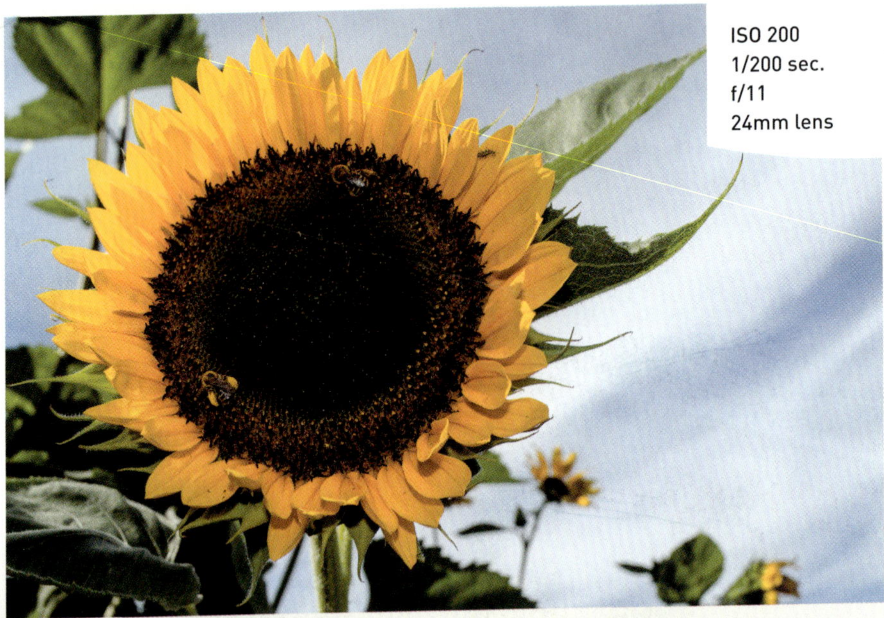

ISO 200
1/200 sec.
f/11
24mm lens

FIGURE 8.12
The pop-up flash was used as a fill flash to illuminate the front of the sunflowers. This is very handy when you are shooting with the sun coming in from behind your subjects.

SHUTTER SPEEDS

The standard flash synchronization speed for your camera is between 1/60 and 1/200 of a second. When you are working with the built-in flash in Program mode, the camera will typically adjust the shutter speed between these settings depending on the amount of ambient light.

The real key to using the flash to get great pictures is to control the shutter speed. The goal is to balance the light from the flash with the existing light so that everything in the picture has an even illumination. Let's take a look at the shutter speeds for the other modes.

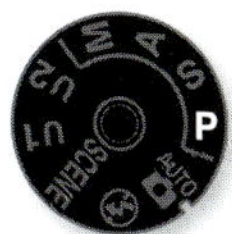

Program (P): The shutter speed stays at 1/60 of a second. The only adjustment you can make in this mode is overexposure or underexposure using the Exposure Compensation setting or the Flash Compensation settings.

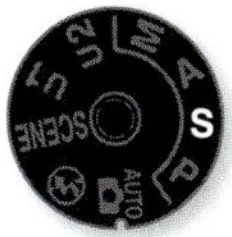

Shutter Priority (S): You can adjust the shutter speed to as fast as 1/200 of a second all the way down to 30 seconds. The lens aperture will adjust accordingly, but at long exposures the lens will typically be set to its smallest aperture.

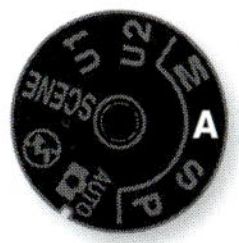

Aperture Priority (A): This mode will allow you to adjust the aperture but will adjust the shutter speed between 1/200 and 1/60 of a second in the standard flash mode.

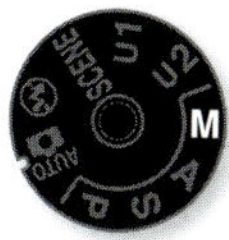

Manual (M): You can adjust the shutter speed to as fast as 1/200 of a second all the way down to 30 seconds. The lens aperture is adjusted independently, so you will need to do a little experimentation to see what works best.

FLASH SHUTTER SPEED

You can adjust the flash shutter speed in the menu so that a slower shutter speed can be used when you are in Program mode or Aperture Priority mode. You can select a speed from 1/60 of a second to 30 seconds. This setting also affects the red-eye, slow-sync, and rear-curtain sync settings. Check out page 235 in your manual for more information.

FLASH SYNC

The basic idea behind the term *flash synchronization (flash sync* for short) is that when you take a photograph using the flash, the camera needs to ensure that the shutter is fully open at the time that the flash goes off. This is not an issue if you are using a long shutter speed such as 1/15 of a second but does become more critical for fast shutter speeds. To ensure that the flash and shutter are synchronized so that the flash is going off while the shutter is open, the D600 implements a top sync speed of 1/200 of a second. This means that when you are using the flash, you will not be able to use any shutter speed faster than 1/200. If you did use a faster shutter speed, the shutter would actually start closing before the flash fired, which would cause a black area to appear in the frame where the light from the flash was blocked by the shutter. To learn about how to use faster shutter speeds with compatible accessory flash units using Auto FP high-speed sync, check out page 234 in your manual.

METERING MODES

The built-in flash uses a technology called TTL (Through The Lens) metering to determine the appropriate amount of flash power to output for a good exposure. When you depress the shutter button, the camera quickly adjusts focus while gathering information from the entire scene to measure the amount of ambient light. As you press the shutter button down completely, the flash uses that exposure information and fires a predetermined amount of light at your subject during the exposure.

The default setting for the flash meter mode is TTL. The meter can also be set to Manual mode. In Manual flash mode, you can determine how much power you want coming out of the flash, ranging from full power all the way down to 1/128 power. Each setting from full power on down will cut the power by half. This is the equivalent of reducing flash exposure by one stop with each power reduction. The benefit of using Manual mode is that the flash output is consistent every time and not dependent on the exposure reading.

SETTING THE FLASH TO THE MANUAL POWER SETTING

1. Press the Menu button, navigate to the Custom Setting menu, highlight the setting called e Bracketing/flash, and press OK (**A**).
2. Highlight the item labeled e3 Flash cntrl for built-in flash, and press OK (**B**).
3. Highlight the Manual option, and press OK (**C**).
4. Select the amount of flash power you want to use, and press OK (**D**).

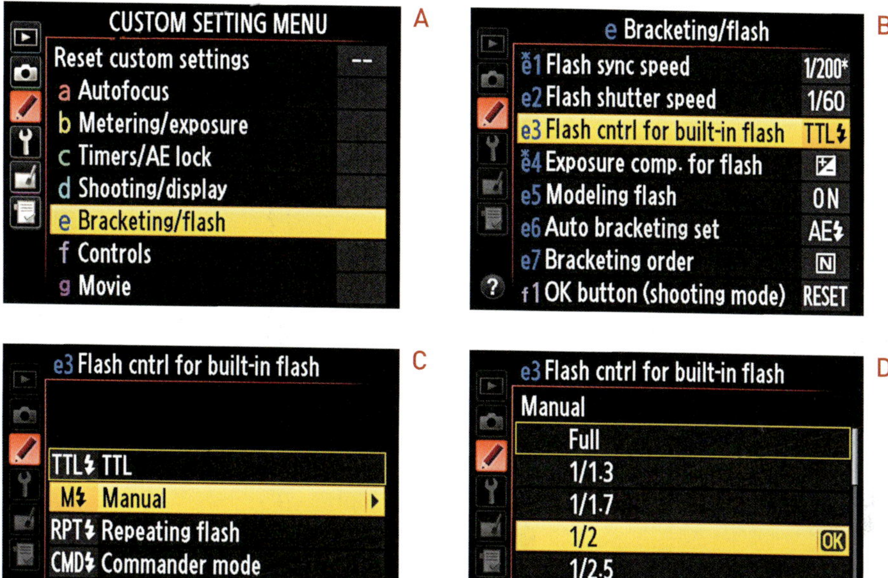

Don't forget to set the flash back to TTL when you are done, because the camera will hold this setting until you change it.

COMPENSATING FOR THE FLASH EXPOSURE

The TTL system will usually do an excellent job of balancing the flash and ambient light for your exposure, but it does have the limitation of not knowing what effect you want in your image. You may want more or less flash in a particular shot. You can achieve this by using the Flash Exposure Compensation feature.

Just as with exposure compensation, flash compensation allows you to dial in a change in the flash output in increments of 1/3 of a stop. You will probably use this most often to tone down the effects of your flash, especially when you are using the flash as a subtle fill light (**Figures 8.13** and **8.14**). The range of compensation goes from +1 stop down to –3 stops.

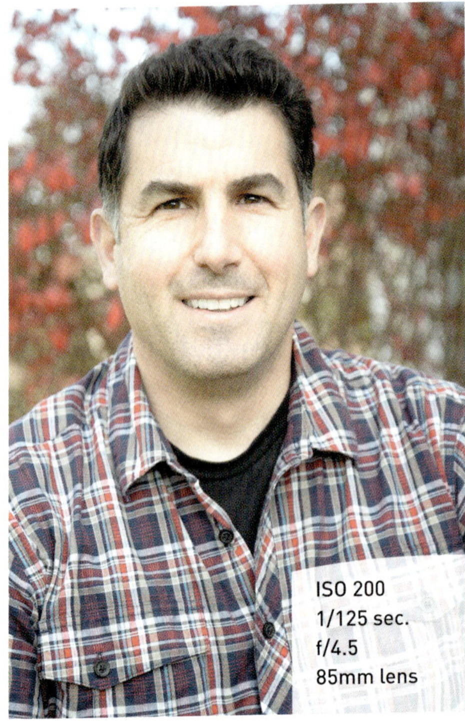

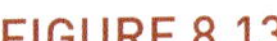

FIGURE 8.13
This shot was taken with the pop-up flash set to normal power. As you can see in the bright highlights on the cheeks and forehead, it was trying a little too hard to illuminate the subject.

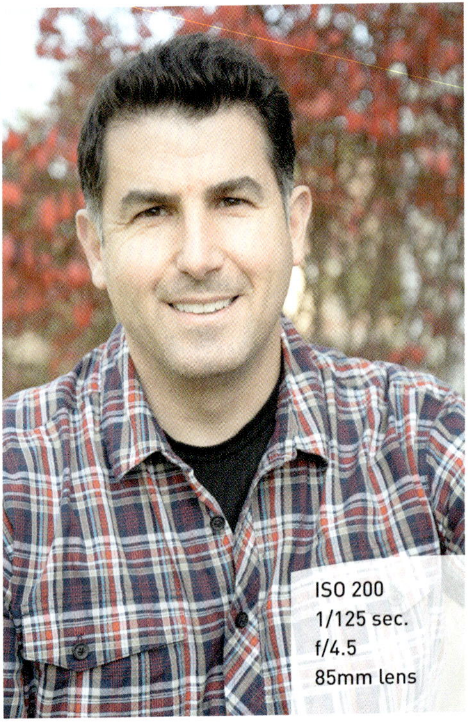

FIGURE 8.14
This image was made with the same camera settings. The difference is that the flash compensation was set to –1.0 stops, and it did a nice job of taking the edge off the flash to help it blend into the overall exposure.

USING THE FLASH EXPOSURE COMPENSATION FEATURE TO CHANGE THE FLASH OUTPUT

1. With the flash in the upright and ready position, press and hold the flash compensation button.
2. While holding down the button, rotate the Sub-command dial to set the amount of compensation you desire. Turning to the right increases the flash power 1/3 of a stop with each click of the dial. Turning left decreases the flash power.
3. Press the shutter button halfway to return to shooting mode, and then take the picture.
4. Review your image to see if more or less flash compensation is required, and repeat these steps as necessary.

You can view the amount of flash compensation in the control panel or in the viewfinder. You can also see the amount of compensation by activating the info screen prior to changing the compensation (**Figure 8.15**).

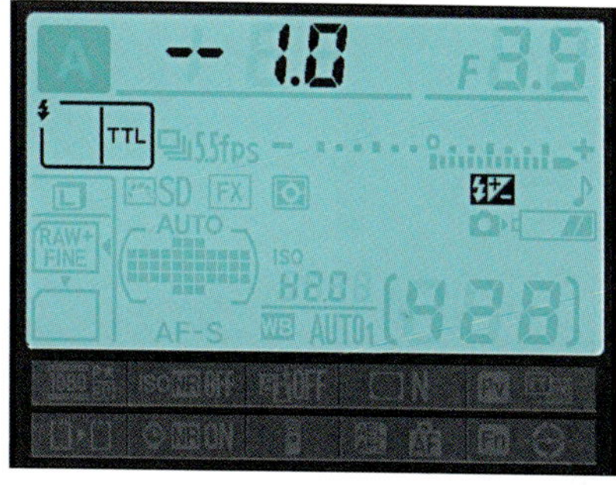

FIGURE 8.15
Using the info screen is an easy way to see how much compensation you have set.

The Flash Exposure Compensation feature does not reset itself when the camera is turned off, so whatever compensation you have set will remain in effect until you change it. Your only clue to knowing that the flash output is changed will be the presence of the Flash Exposure Compensation symbol in the viewfinder. It will disappear when a zero compensation is set.

REDUCING RED-EYE

We've all seen the result of using on-camera flashes when photographing people: the dreaded red-eye! This demonic effect is the result of the light from the flash entering the pupil and then reflecting back as an eerie red glow. The closer the flash is to the lens, the greater the chance that you will get red-eye. This is especially true when it is dark and the subject's pupils are fully dilated. There are two ways to combat this problem. The first is to get the flash away from the lens. That's not really an option, though, if you are using the pop-up flash. Therefore, you will need to turn to the Red-Eye Reduction feature.

This is a simple feature that shines a light from the camera at the subject, causing their pupils to shrink, thus eliminating or reducing the effects of red-eye (**Figure 8.16**).

The feature is set to Off by default and needs to be turned on by using the information screen or the flash compensation button.

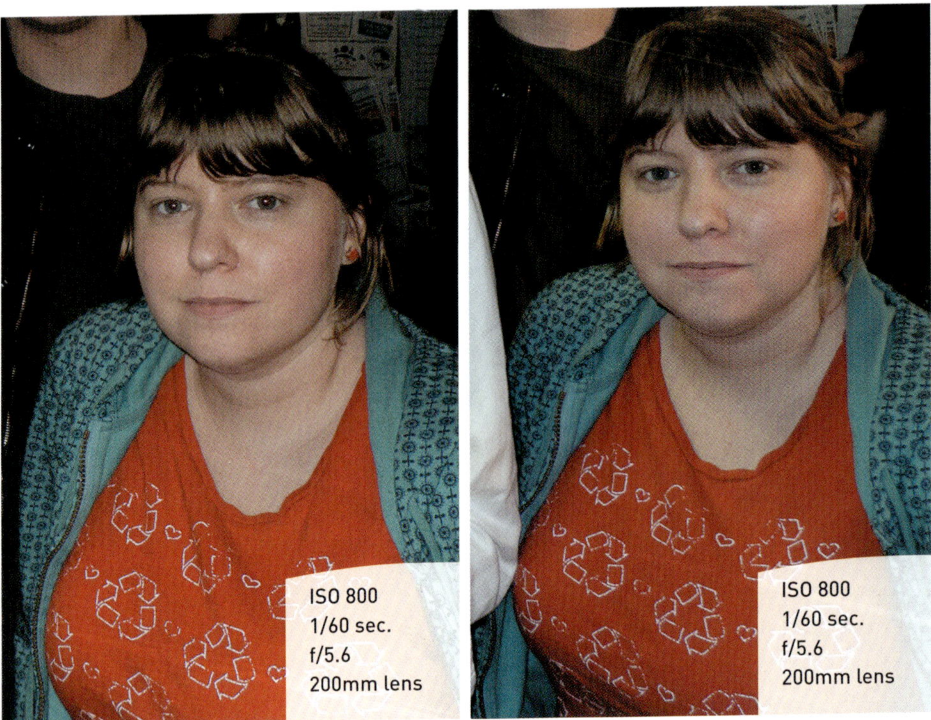

FIGURE 8.16
The picture on the left did not utilize Red-Eye Reduction, thus the glowing red eyes. Notice that the pupils on the image on the right, without red-eye, are smaller as a result of using the red-eye reduction lamp.

TURN ON THE LIGHTS!

When you're shooting indoors, another way to reduce red-eye—or just shorten the length of time that the reduction lamp needs to be shining into your subject's eyes—is to turn on a lot of lights. The brighter the ambient light levels, the smaller the subject's pupils will be. This will reduce the time necessary for the red-eye reduction lamp to shine. It will also allow you to take more candid pictures because your subjects won't be required to stare at the red-eye lamp while waiting for their pupils to reduce.

TURNING ON THE RED-EYE REDUCTION FEATURE

1. Press and hold the flash compensation button on the front of the camera.
2. Rotate the Main Command dial until you see the red-eye reduction symbol in the control panel or the information screen (**A**).
3. With red-eye reduction activated, compose your photo and then press the shutter release button to take the picture.

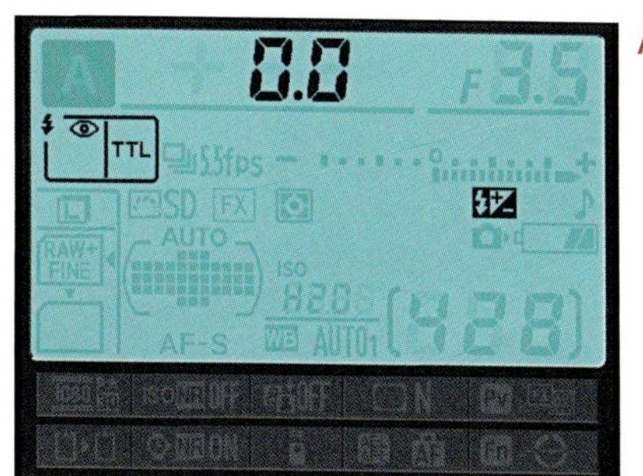

A

When red-eye reduction is activated, the camera will not fire the instant that you press the shutter release button. Instead, the red-eye reduction lamp will illuminate for a second or two and then fire the flash for the exposure. This is important to remember, as people have a tendency to move around, so you will need to instruct them to hold still for a moment while the lamp works its magic.

Truth be told, I rarely shoot with red-eye reduction turned on because of the time it takes before being able to take a picture. If I am after candid shots and have to use the flash, I will take my chances on red-eye and try to fix the problem in my image-processing software or even in the camera's retouching menu.

REAR CURTAIN SYNC

There are five flash synchronization modes in the D600: Front Curtain Sync, Red-Eye Reduction, Red-Eye Reduction with Slow Sync, Slow Sync, and Rear Curtain Sync. You may be asking, "What in the world does synchronization do, and what's with these 'curtains'?" Good question.

When your camera fires, there are two curtains that open and close to make up the shutter. The first, or front, curtain moves out of the way, exposing the camera sensor to the light. At the end of the exposure, the second, or rear, curtain moves in front of the sensor, ending that picture cycle. In flash photography, timing is extremely important because the flash fires in milliseconds and the shutter is usually opening in tenths or hundredths of a second. To make sure these two functions happen in order, the camera usually fires the flash just as the first curtain moves out of the way (see the "Flash Sync" sidebar, earlier in this chapter).

In Slow Sync mode, the camera knows to balance the flash with a longer shutter speed. In Rear Curtain Sync mode, the flash will not fire until just before the second shutter curtain ends the exposure. So why have this mode at all? Well, there might be times when you want to have a longer exposure to balance out the light from the background to go with the subject needing the flash. Rear Curtain Sync adds some creativity by capturing the movement of light with a longer exposure while freezing the subject with the flash. Imagine taking a photograph of a friend standing in Times Square at night with all the traffic moving about and the bright lights of the streets overhead. If the flash fires at the beginning of the exposure and then the objects around the subject move, those objects will often blur or even obscure the subject a bit. If the camera is set to Rear Curtain Sync mode, though, all of the movement is recorded using the existing light first, and then the subject is "frozen" by the flash at the end by the exposure.

There is no right or wrong to it. It's just a decision on what type of effect you would like to create. Many times, Rear Curtain Sync is used for artistic purposes or to record movement in the scene without it overlapping the flash-exposed subject (**Figure 8.17**). To make sure that the main subject is always getting the final pop of the flash, I leave my camera set to Rear Curtain Sync most of the time.

You can have a lot of fun with Rear Curtain Sync. **Figure 8.18** shows an example of a long exposure that recorded the light trail from a cool iPad app called Holographium (you type a word into the app and move the iPad across the frame during a long exposure to extrude the word across your photo), with a burst of flash at the end that gives a ghostly appearance to yours truly. As you can see, my friends and I were playing around with various light-emitting devices in the background.

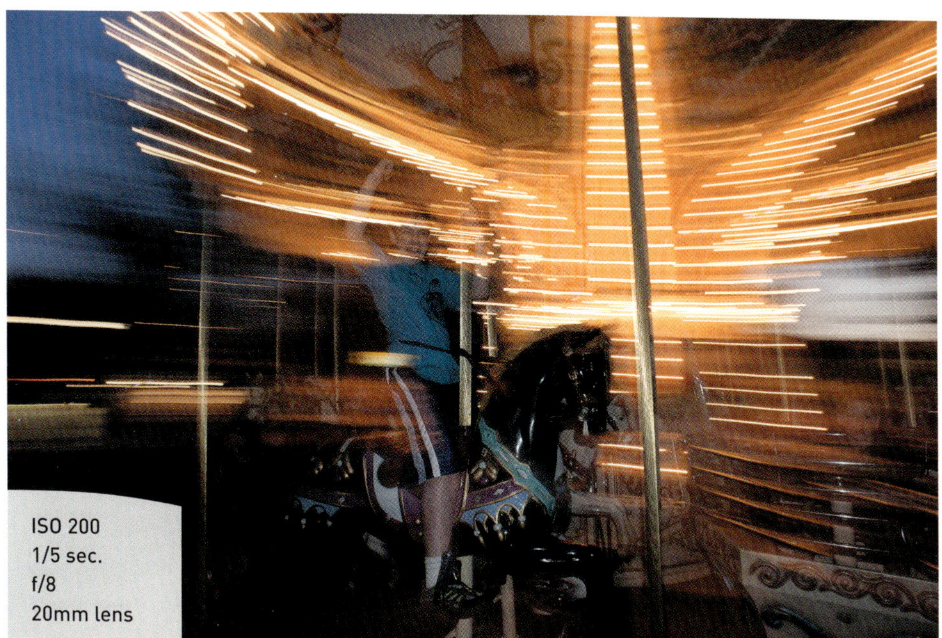

ISO 200
1/5 sec.
f/8
20mm lens

FIGURE 8.17
The effect of using Rear Curtain Sync is most evident during long flash exposures, such as in this photo of a barbarian charging into battle on a carousel.

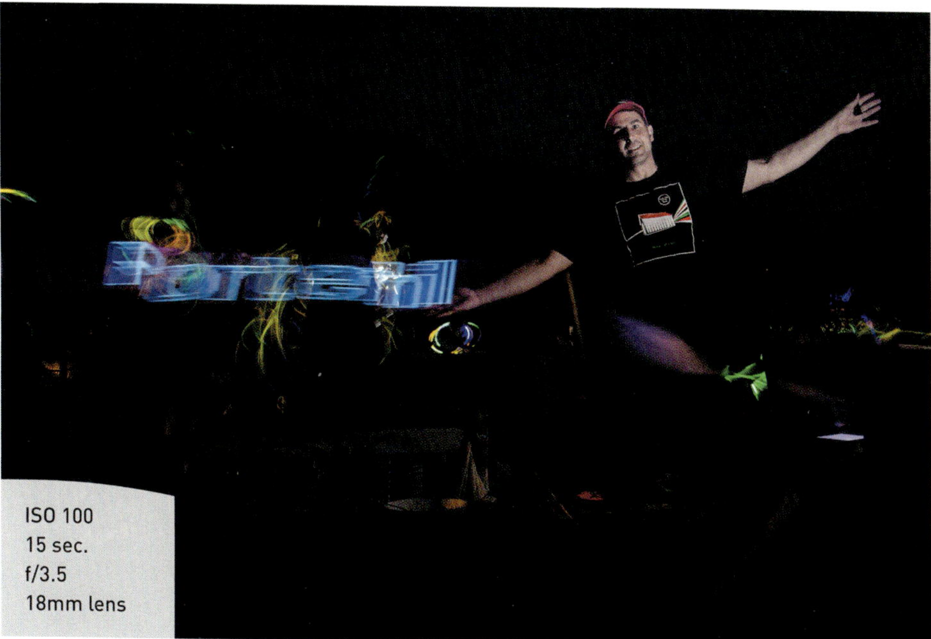

ISO 100
15 sec.
f/3.5
18mm lens

FIGURE 8.18
This effect is possible because the flash fired at the end of the exposure using Rear Curtain Sync.

If you intend to use a long exposure with Front Curtain Sync, you need to have your subject remain fairly still so that any movement that occurs after the flash goes off will be minimized in the image.

CHANGING THE FLASH SYNC MODE

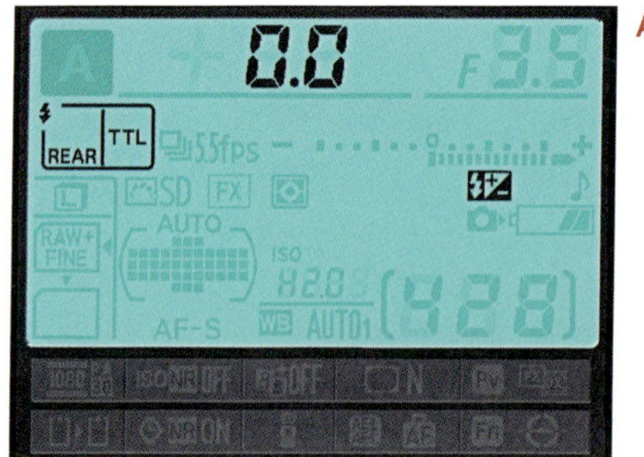

A

1. Press and hold the flash compensation button.
2. Rotate the Main Command dial to change the mode.
3. View the flash sync mode changes by looking at the control panel or information screen (**A**).

FLASH AND GLASS

If you find yourself in a situation where you want to use your flash to shoot through a window or display case, try placing your lens right against the glass so that the reflection of the flash won't be visible in your image (**Figures 8.19** and **8.20**). This is extremely useful in museums and aquariums.

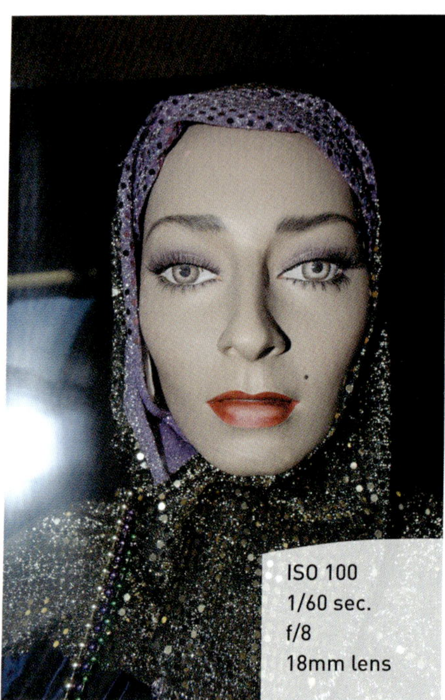

FIGURE 8.19 (left) The bright spot on the left of the frame is a result of the flash reflecting off the display glass.

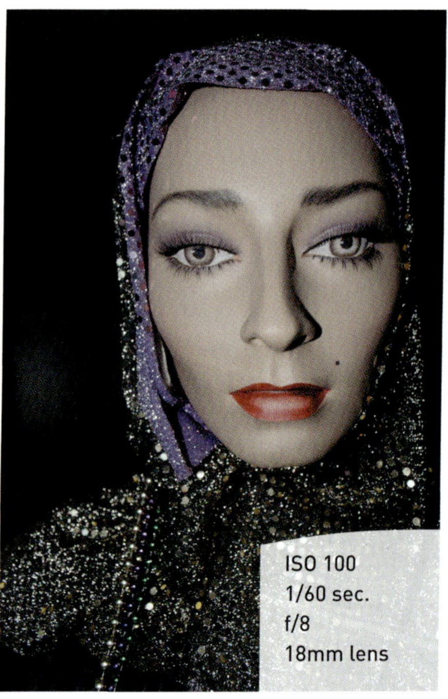

FIGURE 8.20 (right) To eliminate the reflection, place the lens against the glass or as close to it as possible. This might also require zooming the lens out a little.

DISABLING THE FLASH

Remember that if you are shooting in a professional mode, the only way to get the flash to fire is to first turn on the flash via the Pop-up Flash button. If you are shooting in an automatic scene mode, it will sometimes come on automatically, depending on the mode. For example, in Candlelight and Landscape modes it does not come on, whereas in Pet mode and Night Portrait mode it is automatically on. If the small flash icon appears on the control panel when you are shooting in a particular mode, it means that the setting calls for flash and it will fire automatically. If you don't wish to operate the flash in that mode, you will have to turn it off by pressing the Pop-up Flash/Flash mode button and rotating the Main Command dial to the Flash Off setting (the icon looks like a flash with a slash through it).

To disable the flash when shooting in Auto mode, turn the Mode dial to the Flash Off icon (a flash with a slash through it).

A FEW WORDS ABOUT EXTERNAL FLASH

We have discussed several ways to get control over the built-in pop-up flash on the D600. The reality is that, as flashes go, it will render only average results. For people photography, it is probably one of the most unflattering light sources that you could ever use. This isn't because the flash isn't good—it's actually very sophisticated for its size. The problem is that light should come from any direction besides the camera to best flatter a human subject. When the light emanates from directly above the lens, it gives the effect of becoming a photocopier. Imagine putting your face down on a scanner: the result would be a flatly lit, featureless photo.

> **Manual Callout**
>
> For more information on the use of external Speedlight flashes on your D600, check out pages 292–296 of your manual.

To really make your flash photography come alive with possibilities, you should consider buying an external flash, such as the Nikon SB-700 AF Speedlight. The SB-700 has a swiveling flash head and more power, and it communicates with the camera and the TTL system to deliver balanced flash exposures. I delve into accessory flash units, including how to control an external Speedlight using your camera's pop-up flash, in Chapter 11.

Chapter 8 Assignments

Now that we have looked at the possibilities of shooting after dark, it's time to put it all to the test. These assignments cover the full range of shooting possibilities, both with flash and without. Let's get started.

How steady are your hands?

It's important to know just what your limits are in terms of handholding your camera and still getting sharp pictures. This will change depending on the focal length of the lens you are working with. Wider-angle lenses are more forgiving than telephoto lenses, so check this out for your longest and shortest lenses. Using a zoom lens, set your lens to its longest focal length and then, with the camera set to ISO 100 and the mode set to Shutter Priority, turn off the VR and start taking pictures with lower and lower shutter speeds. Review each image on the LCD at a zoomed-in magnification to take note of when you start seeing visible camera shake in your images. It will probably be about 1 over the focal length (1/125 of a second for a 125mm lens length).

Now do the same for the wide-angle setting on the lens. My limit is about 1/30 of a second. These shutter speeds are with the Vibration Reduction feature turned off. If you have a VR lens, try it with and without the VR feature enabled to see just how slow you can set your shutter while getting sharp results.

Pushing your ISO to the extreme

Find a place to shoot where the ambient light level is low. This could be at night or indoors in a darkened room. Using the mode of your choice, start increasing the ISO from 100 until you get to 25600 (H 2.0). Make sure you evaluate the level of noise in your image, especially in the shadow areas. Only you can decide how much noise is acceptable in your pictures for a given subject matter and output destination.

Getting rid of the noise

Turn on the High ISO Noise Reduction feature and repeat the previous assignment. Find your acceptable limits with the noise reduction turned on. Also pay attention to how much detail is lost in your shadows with this function enabled.

Long exposures in the dark

If you don't have a tripod, find a stable place to set your camera outside and try some long exposures. Set your camera to Aperture Priority mode and then use the self-timer to activate the camera (this will keep you from shaking the camera while pressing the shutter button).

Shoot in an area that has some level of ambient light, be it a streetlight, traffic lights, or even a full moon. The idea is to get some late-night, low-light exposures.

Testing the limits of the pop-up flash

Wait for the lights to get low, and then press that pop-up flash button to start using the built-in flash. Try using the different shooting modes to see how they affect your exposures. Use the Flash Exposure Compensation feature to take a series of pictures while adjusting from –3 stops all the way to +1 stops so that you become familiar with how much latitude you will get from this feature.

Getting the red out

Find a friend with some patience and a tolerance for bright lights. Have them sit in a darkened room or outside at night and then take their picture with the flash. Now turn on the Red-Eye Reduction feature to see if you get better results. Don't forget to have them sit still while the red-eye lamp does its thing.

Getting creative with Rear Curtain Sync

Now it's time for a little creative fun. Set your camera up for Rear Curtain Sync and start shooting. Moving targets are best. Experiment with Shutter and Aperture Priority modes to lower the shutter speeds and exaggerate the effect. Try using a low ISO so the camera is forced to use longer shutter speeds. Be creative and have some fun!

Share your results with the book's Flickr group!

www.flickr.com/groups/d600fromsnapshotstogreatshots

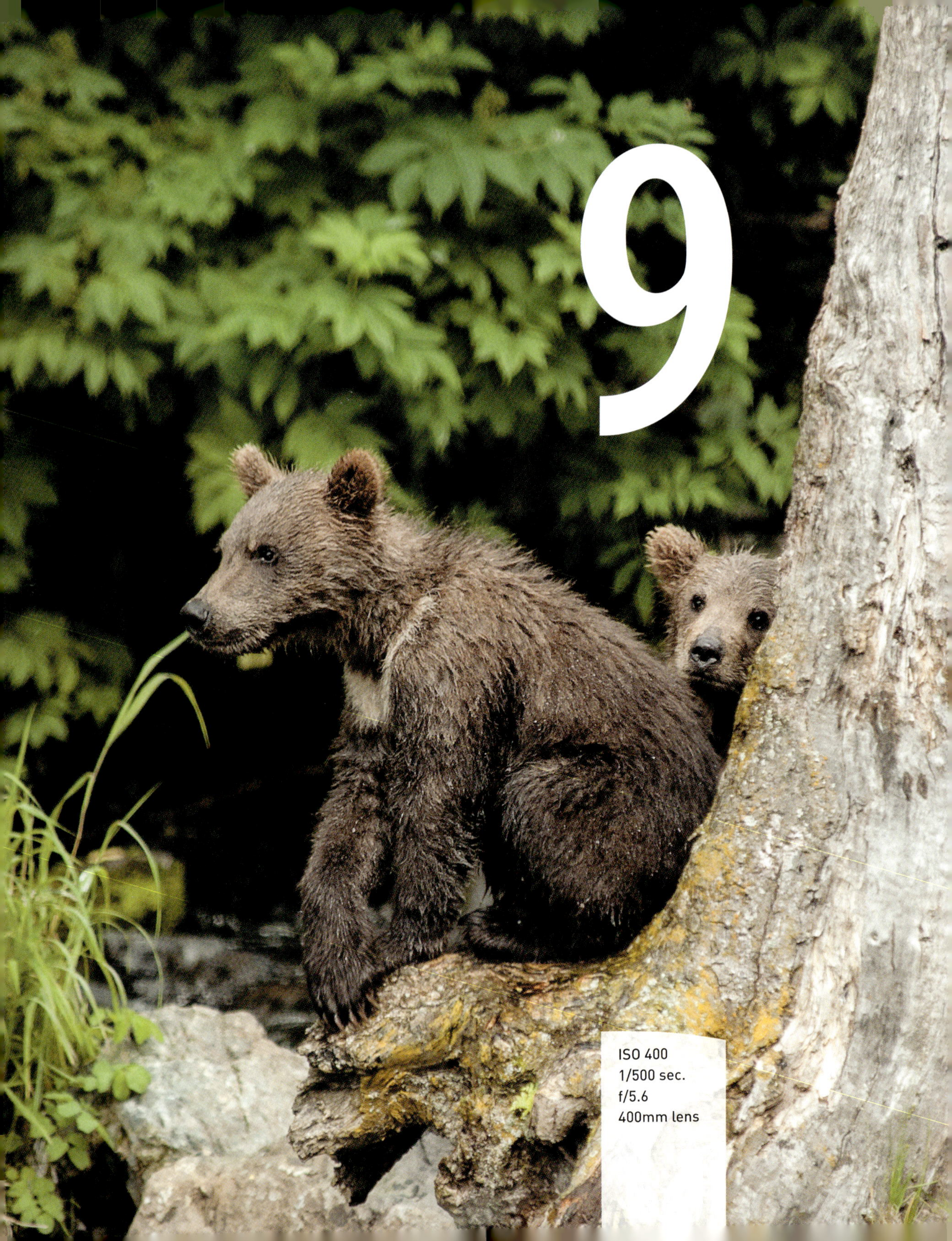

9

ISO 400
1/500 sec.
f/5.6
400mm lens

Advanced Techniques

IMPRESS YOUR FAMILY AND FRIENDS

We've covered a lot of ground in the previous chapters, especially on the general photographic concepts that apply to most of the shooting situations you might encounter. There are, however, some specific tools and techniques that will give you an added advantage in obtaining a great shot. This section also comes with a warning attached. All of the techniques and topics up to this point have been centered on your camera. But in this chapter, I discuss a few techniques—such as panoramas and high dynamic range (HDR) images—that require you to use image-processing software to complete the photograph. They are, however, important enough that you should know how to shoot for success should you choose to explore these popular techniques.

PORING OVER THE PICTURE

I had the idea to test the built-in HDR function of the D600 by photographing the inside of a church that contained a wide range in contrast, from dark shadows to the light of interior lighting and stained glass windows. While walking around Boston recently, I came across the beautiful and historic Church of the Covenant. After explaining what I had in mind to the church administrator, I was granted permission to spend a few minutes in the sanctuary and take some photos. Later in the chapter, I dive into the specifics of creating HDR images with and without the built-in HDR function, but I thought this image of a three-exposure HDR deserved a two-page spread. Many thanks to the church for letting me capture this beautiful scene.

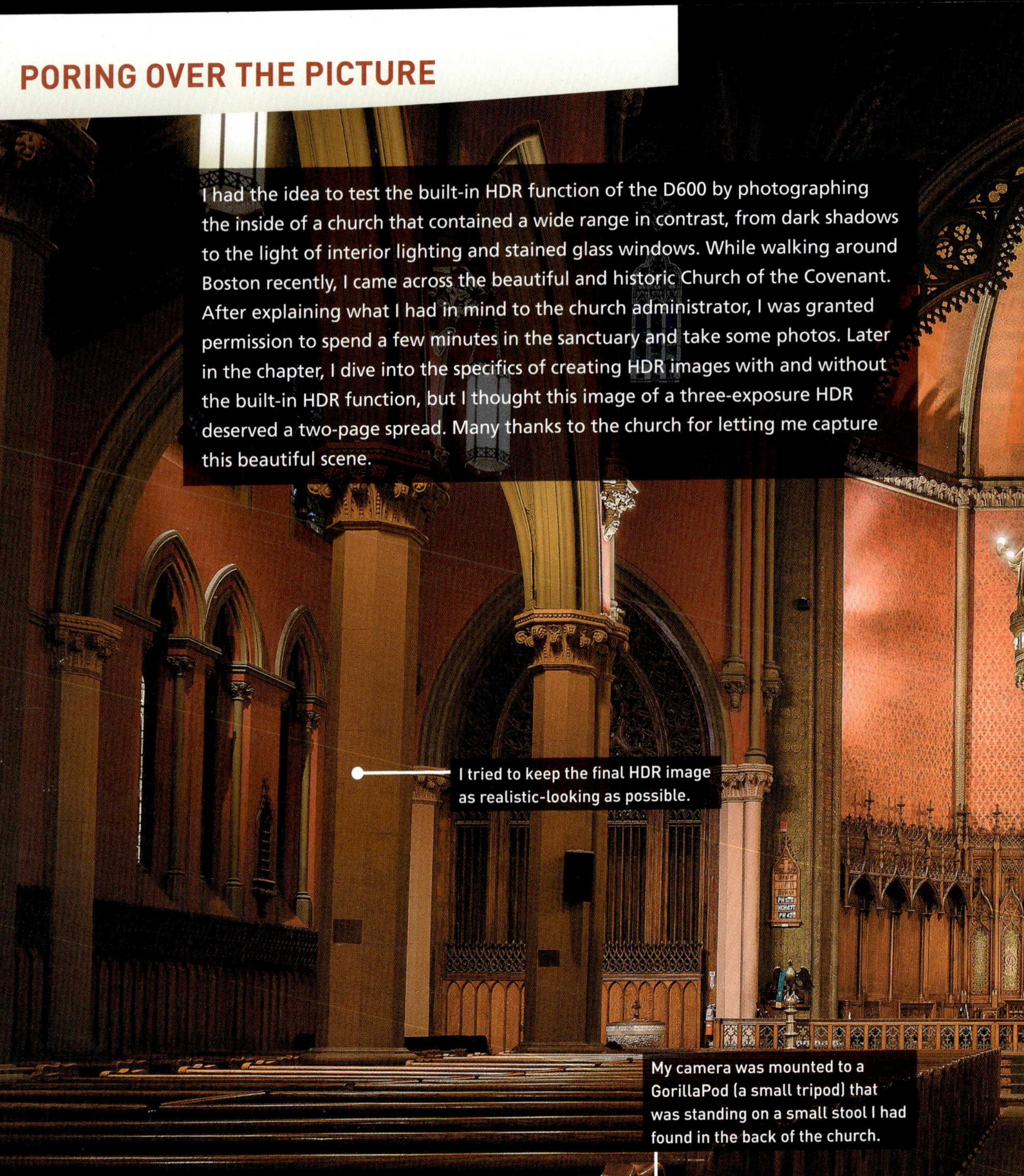

I tried to keep the final HDR image as realistic-looking as possible.

My camera was mounted to a GorillaPod (a small tripod) that was standing on a small stool I had found in the back of the church.

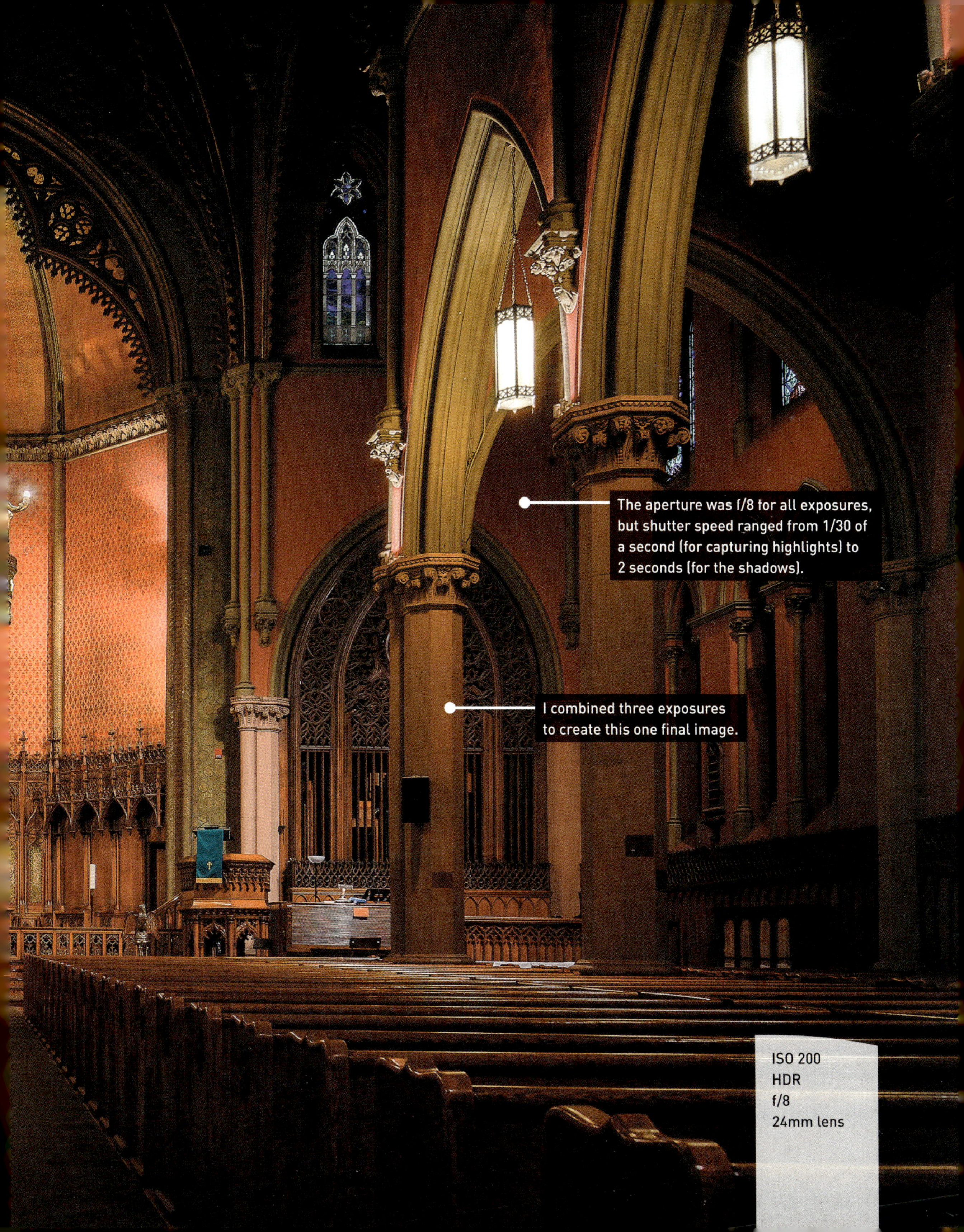

The aperture was f/8 for all exposures, but shutter speed ranged from 1/30 of a second (for capturing highlights) to 2 seconds (for the shadows).
I combined three exposures to create this one final image.
ISO 200
HDR
f/8
24mm lens

SPOT METER FOR MORE EXPOSURE CONTROL

Generally speaking, Matrix metering mode provides accurate metering information for the majority of your photography. It does an excellent job of evaluating the scene and then relating the proper exposure information to you. The only problem with this mode is that, like any metering mode on the camera, it doesn't know what it is looking at. There will be specific circumstances where you want to get an accurate reading from just a portion of a scene and discount the remaining area. To give you greater control of the metering operation, you can switch the camera to Spot metering mode. This allows you to take a meter reading from a very small circle while ignoring the rest of the viewfinder area. If you are using the Auto-Area AF focus mode, the Spot meter will use the center spot in the viewfinder. Otherwise, the meter location is based on whichever focus point you are using.

So when would you need to use this? Think of a person standing in front of a very light wall. In Matrix metering mode, the camera would see the entire scene and try to adjust the exposure information so that the background is exposed to render a darker wall in your image. This means that the scene would actually be underexposed, and your subject would then appear too dark. To correct this, you can place the camera in Spot metering mode and take a meter reading right off of—and *only* off of—your subject, ignoring the white wall altogether. The Spot metering will read the location where you have your focus point, placing all of the exposure information right on your point of interest.

Other situations that would benefit from Spot metering include:

- Snow or beach environments, where the overall brightness level of the scene could fool the meter
- Strongly backlit subjects that are leaving the subject underexposed
- Cases where the overall feel of a photo is too light or too dark

SETTING UP AND SHOOTING IN SPOT METERING MODE

1. Make sure the camera is in one of the professional shooting modes, as indicated by M, A, S, or P on the Mode dial. (You cannot change metering in the automatic modes.)
2. Press and hold the Metering button while rotating the Main Command dial with your thumb. Select Spot Metering by watching the control panel as you turn the Main Command dial.

3. Once you have selected Spot Metering, release the Metering button.
4. Now use the Multi-selector to move the focus point onto your subject, and take your photo. The meter reading will come directly from the location of the focus point.

Note that if you are using the Auto-Area AF focus mode, the camera will use the center focus point as the Spot metering location.

When using Spot metering mode, remember that the meter believes it is looking at a middle-gray value, so you might need to incorporate some exposure compensation of your own to the reading that you are getting from your subject. This will come from experience as you use the meter.

SPOT METERING FOR SUNRISE OR SUNSET

Capturing a beautiful sunrise or sunset is all about the sky. If there is too much foreground in the viewfinder, the camera's meter will deliver an exposure setting that is accurate for the darker foreground areas but leaves the sky looking overexposed, undersaturated, and generally just not very interesting (**Figure 9.1**).

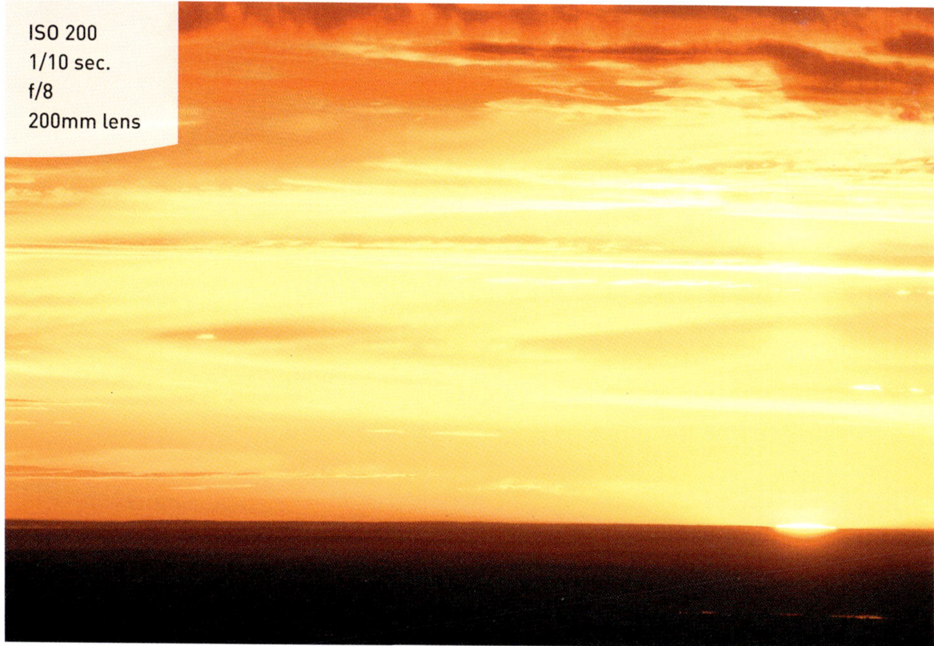

FIGURE 9.1
By metering with all the information in the frame, you get bright skies and more detail in the ground.

To gain more emphasis on the colorful sky, change the metering mode to Spot, point your camera at the brightest part of the sky, use the AE Lock to take your meter reading, and recompose. The result will be an exposure setting that underexposes the foreground but provides a darker, more dramatic sky (**Figure 9.2**).

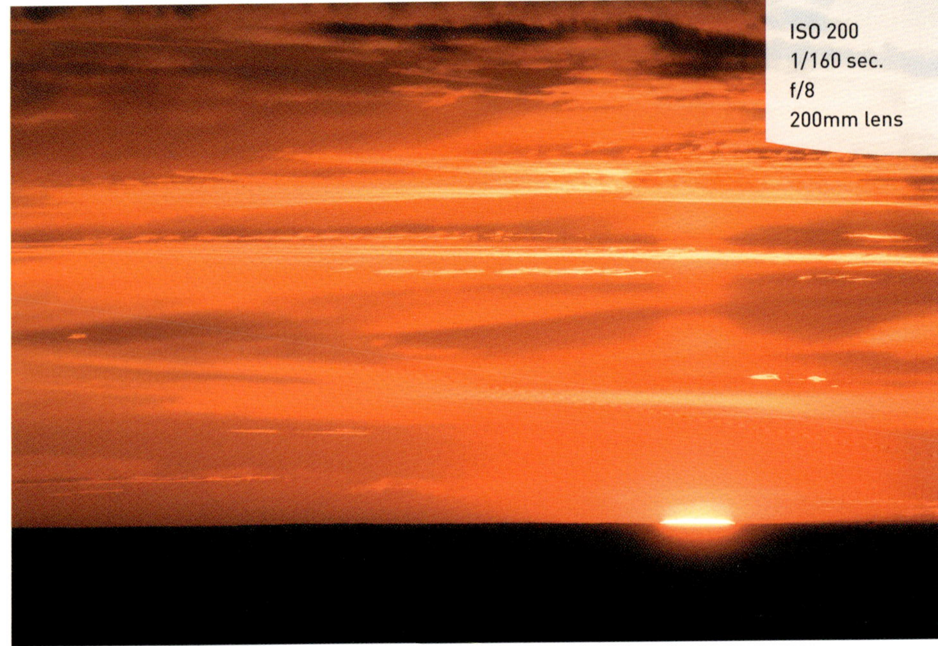

ISO 200
1/160 sec.
f/8
200mm lens

FIGURE 9.2
By taking the meter reading from the brightest part of the sky, you will get darker, more colorful sunsets.

USING AE-L

1. Point your camera toward a bright portion of the sky.
2. Press and hold the AE-L button with your thumb to activate the meter and lock the exposure.
3. While holding the button, recompose your photo and then take the shot. As long as you keep the AE-L button pressed, your exposure will not change.

MANUAL MODE

Probably one of the most advanced and yet most basic skills to master is shooting in Manual mode. With the power and utility of most of the semi-automatic modes, Manual mode almost never sees the light of day. I have to admit that I don't use it very often, but there are times when no other mode will do. One situation that works well with Manual is studio work with external flashes. I know that when I work with studio lights, my exposure will not change, so I use Manual to eliminate any automatic changes that might happen from shooting in Program, Shutter Priority, or Aperture Priority mode. In fact, every picture of the D600 camera in this book was taken using Manual mode.

Since working with studio strobes is a bit outside the scope of this book, I will concentrate on another way in which you will want to use Manual mode for your photography: long nighttime exposures.

BULB PHOTOGRAPHY

If you want to work with long shutter speeds that don't quite fit into one of the selectable shutter speeds, you can select Bulb. This setting is only available in Manual mode, and its sole purpose is to open the shutter at your command and then close it again when you decide. I can think of four scenarios where this would come in handy: shooting fireworks, shooting lightning, shooting exposures that exceed 30 seconds, and painting with light.

If you are photographing fireworks, you could certainly use one of the longer shutter speeds available in Shutter Priority mode, since they are available for exposure times up to 30 seconds. That is fine, but sometimes you don't need 30 seconds' worth of exposure and sometimes you need more.

If you open the shutter and then see a great burst of fireworks, you might decide that that is all you want for that particular frame, so you click the button to end the exposure (**Figure 9.3**). Set the camera to 30 seconds and you might get too many bursts, but if you shorten it to 10 seconds you might not get the one you want.

FIGURE 9.3
A great time to use the Bulb setting is when you're capturing fireworks.

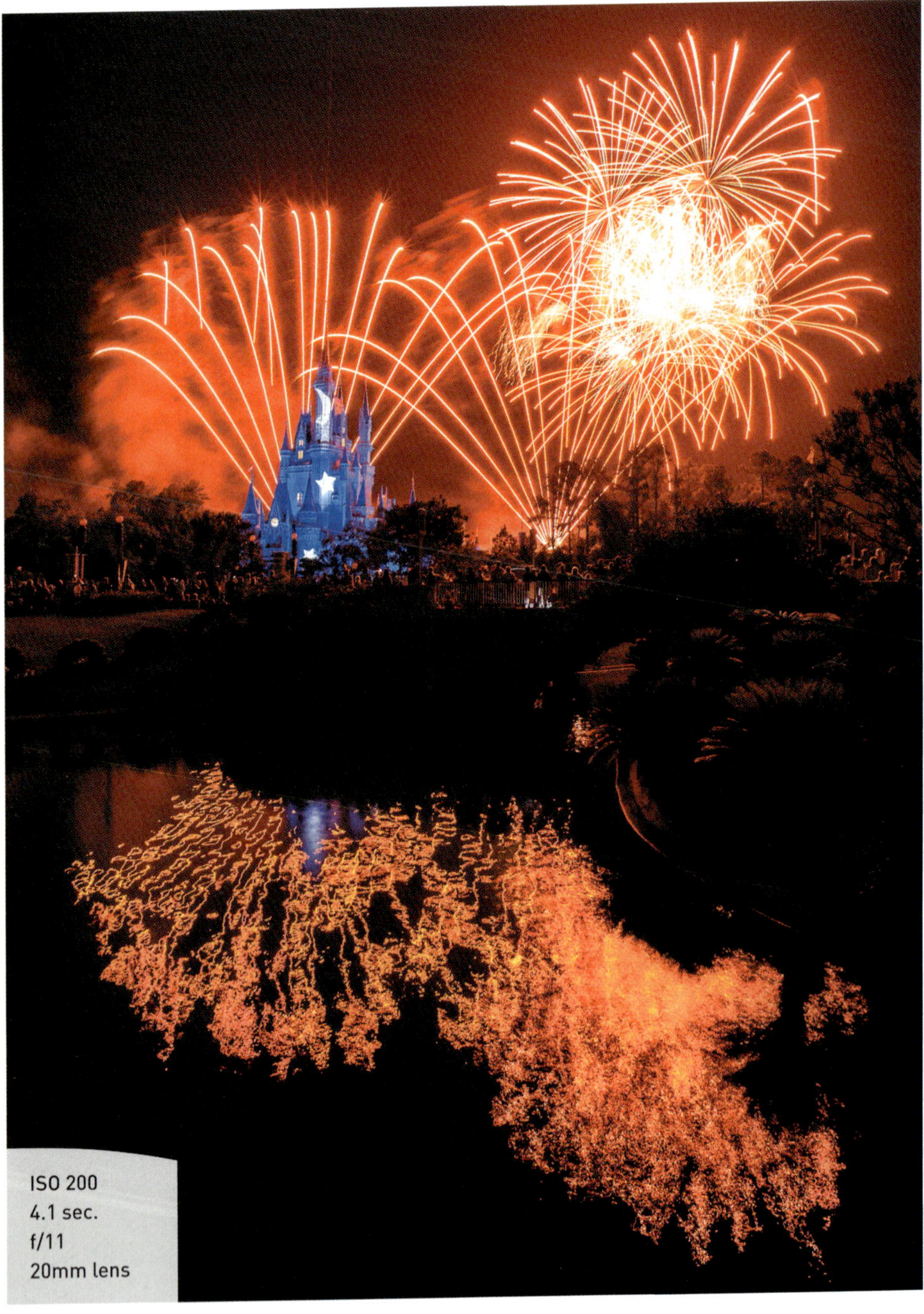

ISO 200
4.1 sec.
f/11
20mm lens

The same can be said for photographing a lightning storm. I have a friend who loves electrical storms, and he has some amazing shots that he captured using the Bulb setting. Lightning can be very tricky to capture, and using the Bulb setting to open and then close the shutter at will allows for more creativity, as well as more opportunity to get the shot.

Painting with light is a process in which you set your camera to Bulb, open the shutter, and then use a light source to "paint" your subject with light. This can be done with a handheld flash or even a flashlight (the Poring Over the Picture photo in Chapter 8 is an example of painting with light).

To select the Bulb setting, simply place your camera in Manual mode and then rotate the Main Command dial to the left until the shutter speed displays Bulb on the rear LCD screen.

When you're using the Bulb setting, the shutter will stay open only for the duration that you are holding down the shutter button. You should also be using a sturdy tripod or shooting surface to eliminate any self-induced vibration.

BULB

If you are new to the world of photography, you might be wondering where in the world the *Bulb* shutter function got its name. After all, wouldn't it make more sense to call it the Manual Shutter setting? It probably would, but this is one of those terms that harkens back to the origins of photography. Way back when, the shutter was actually opened through the use of a bulb-shaped device that forced air through a tube, which, in turn, pushed a plunger down, activating the camera shutter. When the bulb was released, it pulled the plunger back, letting the shutter close and ending the exposure.

I want to point out that using your finger on the shutter button for a Bulb exposure will definitely increase the chances of getting some camera shake in your images. To get the most benefit from the Bulb setting, I suggest using the Nikon MC-DC2 remote cord (see Chapter 11 for more details). You'll also want to turn on the Long Exposure Noise Reduction feature.

Note that the D600 also has infrared receivers on the front and back that allow it to work with the ML-L3 wireless remote (more about that in Chapter 11 too). To use the ML-L3, the Release Mode dial needs to be set to Remote Control. In that setting, you will see – – (the icon for Time) rather than Bulb in the control panel. The difference with Time mode is that the shutter can only remain open for up to 30 minutes. I love the ML-L3 and use it all the time.

SHOOTING LIGHTNING

If you are going to photograph lightning strikes in a thunderstorm, please exercise extreme caution. Standing in the open with a tripod is like standing over a lightning rod. Work from indoors if at all possible.

AVOIDING LENS FLARE

Lens flare is one of the problems you will encounter when shooting in the bright sun. Lens flare will show itself as bright circles on the image (**Figure 9.4**). Often you will see multiple circles in a line leading from a very bright light source such as the sun. The flare is a result of the sun bouncing off the multiple pieces of optical glass in the lens and then reflecting back onto the sensor. You can avoid the problem using one of these methods:

- Try to shoot with the sun coming from over your shoulder, not in front of you or in your scene.
- Use a lens shade to block the unwanted light from striking the lens. You don't have to have the sun in your viewfinder for lens flare to be an issue. All it has to do is strike the front glass of the lens to make it happen.
- If you don't have a lens shade, just try using your hand or some other element to block the light.

USING THE SUN CREATIVELY

Have you ever seen photographs where the sun is peeking through a small hole and it creates a very cool starburst effect? There is actually a little trick to pulling it off, and it's fairly easy. The real key is to be shooting at f/22 (or whatever your smallest aperture is). Then you need to have just a small bit of the sunlight in your frame, either peeking over an edge or through a small hole. The other thing you need to do is make sure you are properly exposing for the rest of your scene, not for the bright bit of sunlight that you are allowing in. With a little practice, you can really make some very cool shots (**Figure 9.5**).

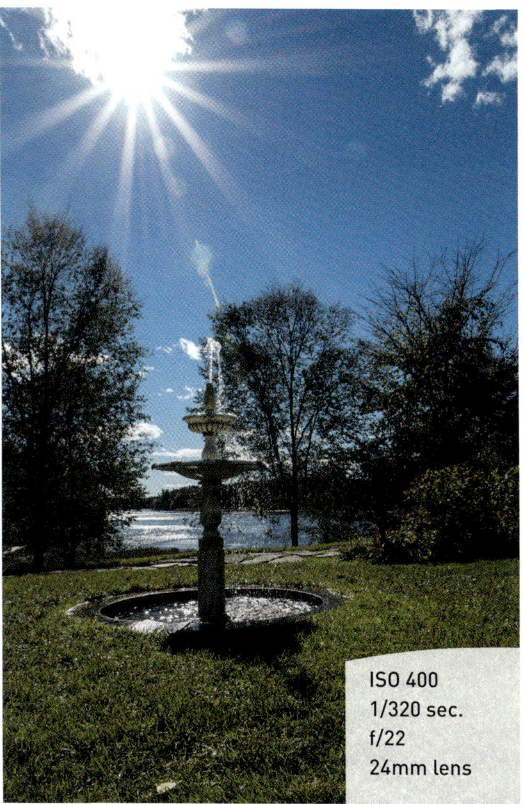

ISO 400
1/320 sec.
f/22
24mm lens

FIGURE 9.4
The bright sun has created flare spots that are visible as colored circles radiating down the image.

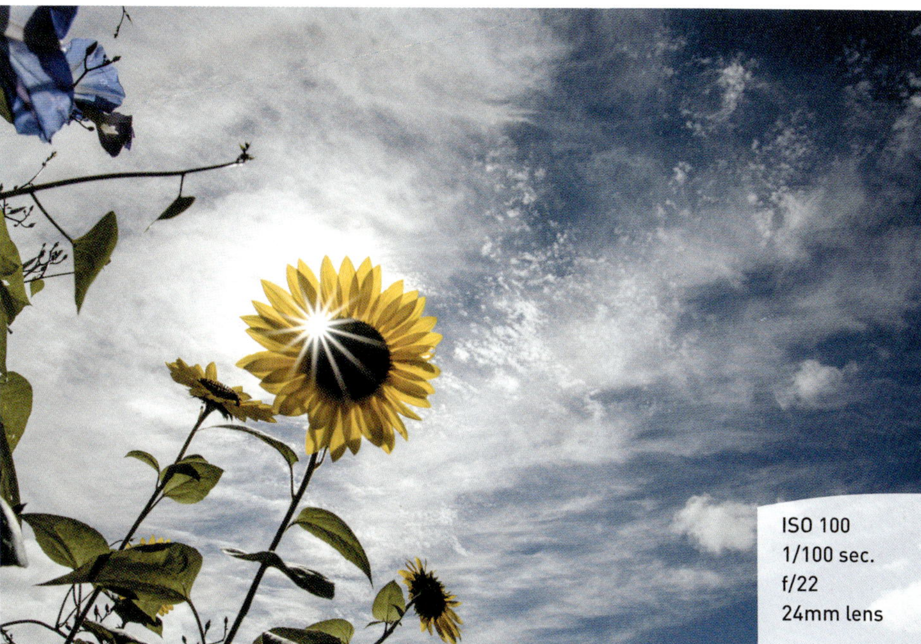

ISO 100
1/100 sec.
f/22
24mm lens

FIGURE 9.5
By letting the sun peek into my shot and using f/22, I was able to capture this starburst effect.

BRACKETING EXPOSURES

So what if you are doing everything right in terms of metering and mode selection, yet your images still sometimes come out too light or too dark? There is a technique called bracketing that will help you find the best exposure value for your scene by taking a normal exposure as well as one that is overexposed and one that is underexposed. Having these differing exposure values will most often present you with one frame that just looks better than the others. If I am in a tricky situation where I have to get the exposure right, such as an outdoor wedding, then I'll use bracketing. I start by spacing my exposures apart by one to two stops and taking three images: one normal exposure, one underexposure, and one overexposure.

As you are viewing the control panel and holding the exposure button, you can decide how much variation you want between bracketed exposures. You can choose from one-third of a stop all the way up to three full stops of exposure difference between each bracketed exposure. In a particularly difficult setting, I typically bracket in two-stop increments to help zero in on that perfect exposure, and then I just delete the ones that didn't make the grade. Remember, your lighting will dictate how many stops you want between exposures.

SETTING AUTO-EXPOSURE BRACKETING

4. You can quickly set your bracketing by holding the BKT button (on the front of your camera, directly below the flash button) while rotating the Main Command dial to 3F (three exposures) (**Figure 9.6**).
5. Continue holding the BKT button down, and rotate the Sub-command dial to the desired exposure increment setting (how many stops between each exposure).
6. If you are in Single Frame shooting mode, you will have to press the shutter button three times, once for each exposure. If you are in continuous shooting mode, press and hold the shutter button and the camera will take all three exposures. For more information on bracketing, review pages 153–155 of your manual.

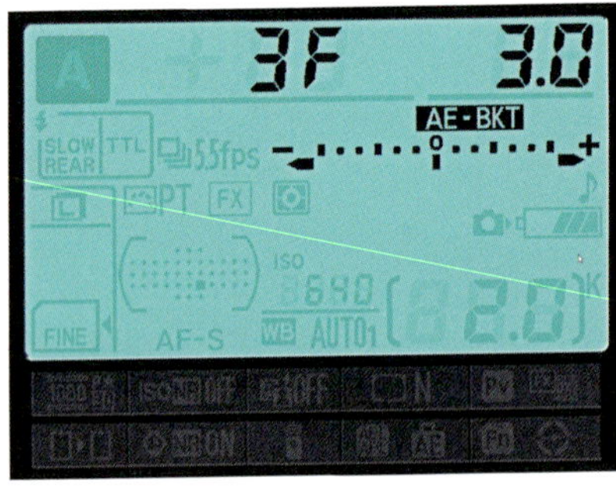

FIGURE 9.6
The information panel shows you how much bracketing is being applied on an over/under scale in the upper-right corner of the screen. The number and letter to the left tells you how many frames you're shooting; here, it's three frames, shown as 3F.

When I am shooting in the RAW file format, I typically shoot with my camera set to an exposure compensation of –1/3 stop to protect my highlights. If I am dealing with a subject that has a lot of different tonal ranges from bright to dark, I will often bracket by one stop over and one stop under my already compensated exposure. That means I will have exposures of –1 1/3, –1/3, and +2/3.

Another thing to remember is that auto-exposure bracketing will use the current mode for making exposure changes. This means that if you are in Aperture Priority mode, the camera will make adjustments to your shutter speed. Likewise, if you are in Shutter Priority, the changes will be made to your aperture value. This is important to keep in mind since it could affect certain aspects of your image, such as depth of field or camera shake. You also need to know that AE bracketing will remain in effect until you set it back to zero, even if you turn the camera off and then on again.

HIGH DYNAMIC RANGE (HDR) PHOTOGRAPHY

Another use for exposure bracketing is when you want to use special software to merge the bracketed exposures into a single high dynamic range (HDR) image. HDR can create stunning images by using the full tonal range of an image. Depending on your preference, they can look quite real or very surreal. I have found that people either love or hate HDR, but whichever side of the fence you are on, it is a wonderful way to understand the effects of exposure on an image.

HDR is often used in landscape, cityscape, and—believe it or not—interior design images. When you photograph a scene that has a wide range of tones from shadows to highlights, you have to make a decision regarding which tonal values you are going to emphasize, and then adjust your exposure accordingly. This is because your camera has a limited dynamic range, at least as compared to the human eye. HDR photography allows you to capture multiple exposures for the highlights, shadows, and midtones and then combine them into a single image using software (**Figures 9.7–9.10**).

A number of software applications allow you to combine the images and then perform a process called "tonemapping," whereby the complete range of exposures is represented in a single image. I will not be covering the software applications, but I will explore the process of shooting a scene to help you render properly captured images for the HDR process. Note that using a tripod is absolutely necessary for this technique, since you need to have perfect alignment of the images when they are combined.

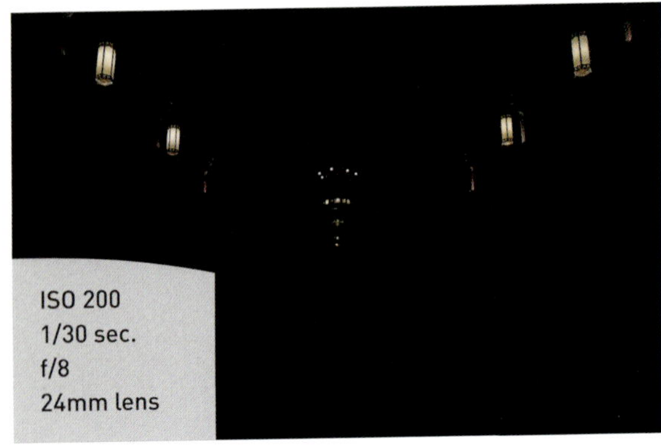

FIGURE 9.7
Three stops of exposure below normal, preserving the detail in the highlights.

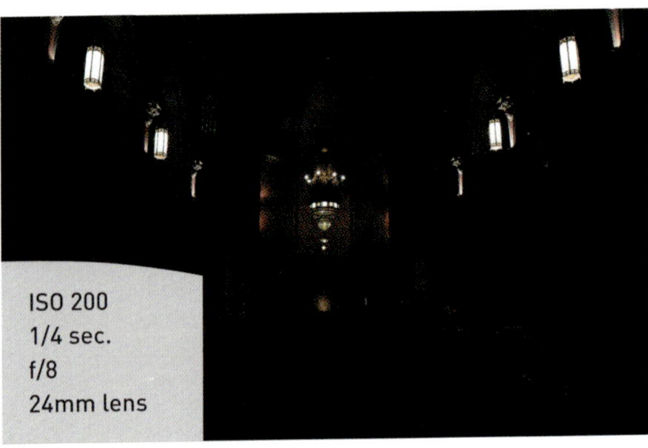

FIGURE 9.8
Normal exposure.

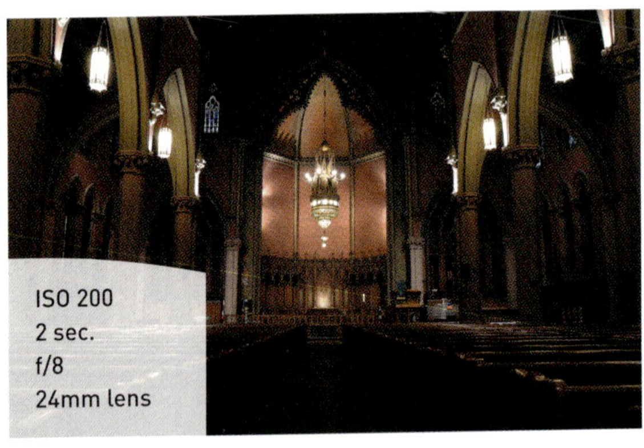

FIGURE 9.9
Three stops of exposure above normal, revealing the detail in the shadows.

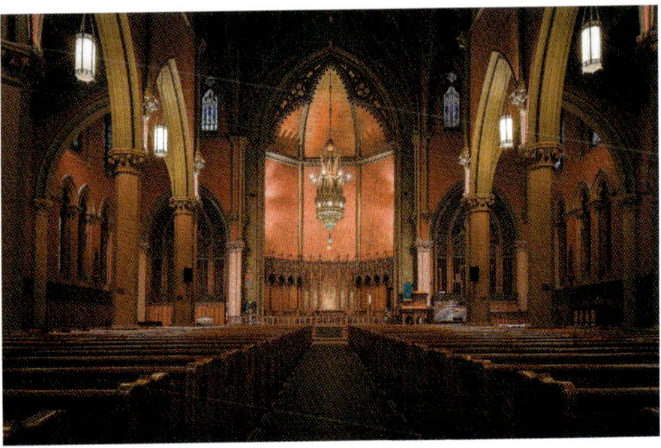

FIGURE 9.10
This tonemapped HDR image combines all three exposures into one.

SETTING UP FOR SHOOTING AN HDR IMAGE

1. Set your ISO to 100 or 200 to ensure clean, noise-free images.
2. Set your program mode to Aperture Priority. During the shooting process, you will be taking three shots of the same scene, creating an overexposed image, an underexposed image, and a normal exposure. Since the camera is going to be adjusting the exposure, you want it to make changes to the shutter speed, not the aperture, so that your depth of field is consistent.
3. Set your camera file format to RAW. This is extremely important because the RAW format contains a much larger range of exposure values than a JPEG file, and the HDR software needs this information.

4. Change your shooting mode to continuous. This will allow you to capture your exposures quickly. Even though you will be using a tripod, there is always a chance that something within your scene will be moving (like clouds or leaves). Shooting in the continuous mode minimizes any subject movement between frames.
5. Adjust the Auto Bracketing (BKT) mode to shoot three exposures in two- or three-stop increments, depending on the range of contrast in the scene. To do this, you will need to press the BKT button while moving the Main Command dial to the right.
6. Now use the Sub-command dial to adjust the bracketing increment.
7. Focus the camera, set the focus mode to manual, compose your shot, secure the tripod, and hold down the shutter button until the camera has fired three times. The result will be one normal exposure, as well as one underexposed and one overexposed image.

A software program such as Adobe Photoshop, Photomatix Pro, or Nik Software's HDR Efex Pro can now process your exposure-bracketed images into a single HDR file. Remember to turn the BKT function back to Off when you are done or the camera will continue to shoot bracketed images.

USING THE IN-CAMERA HDR FUNCTION

If you aren't sure about combining bracketed photos in a software application but want the benefits of the HDR process, you can turn to the built-in HDR function. It's not as robust as the three-exposure method just discussed, but it can produce some great results, especially when you're working in high-contrast locations.

The HDR setting has a couple of limitations. First, unlike with traditional HDR imaging, which depends on using RAW images, you must have your camera's quality setting set on JPEG. Also, the process uses only two exposures, so the amount of dynamic range captured between shadow and highlight is more limited.

The benefit of using the in-camera HDR is that you can pretty much just shoot like you normally would without having to go through all the hoops of camera settings and tripods (although using a tripod is always a good thing when possible). Also, just because the HDR is happening in the camera doesn't mean you don't have some options for changing the look of your processed image. The menu options for HDR allow you to change the exposure variation between one and three stops and to change the amount of smoothing applied. Smoothing controls how the images are blended together and really controls the HDR look of your image (**Figure 9.11**).

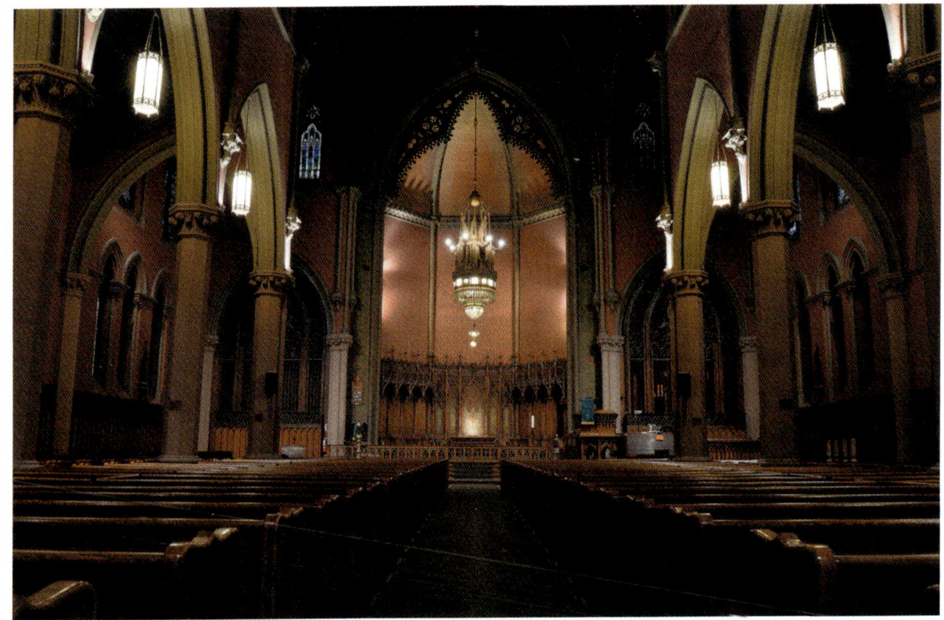

FIGURE 9.11 For comparison's sake, I shot the same scene with the in-camera HDR function. Not bad, but I prefer the quality and control I get from combining three RAW exposures in dedicated HDR software.

SETTING UP THE HDR FUNCTION

1. Set your camera to a quality setting of JPEG.
2. Press the Menu button, navigate to the shooting menu, highlight the HDR (high dynamic range) setting, and press OK (**A**).
3. Change the HDR mode from Off to either On (series) or On (single photo), and press OK. Series will continue to take HDR images until you turn the feature off, whereas the Single setting will allow you to take one HDR shot and then the feature will be turned off automatically (**B**).

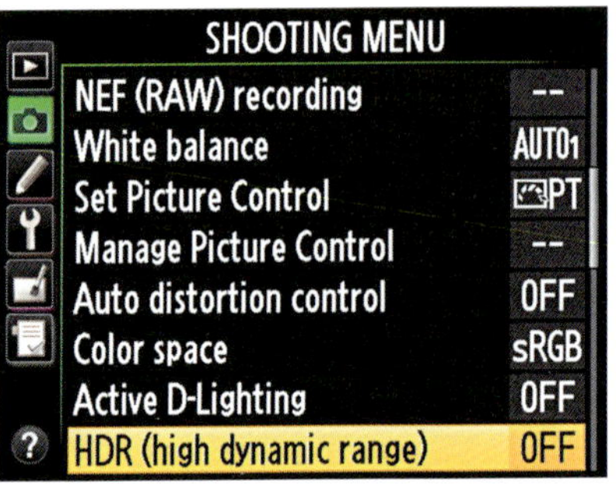

A

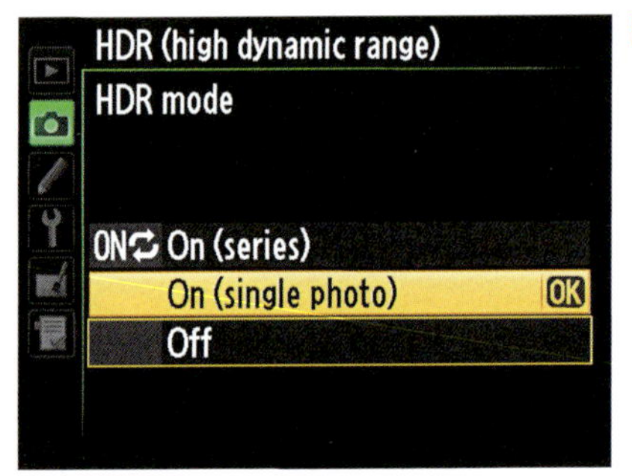

B

4. Select the amount of exposure differential. You can choose a setting from 1 EV (exposure value/stop) to 3 EV. The more contrast in the scene, the higher the value should be. The Auto setting will pick a setting based on what the Matrix meter determines appropriate (**C**).
5. The final option to set is the amount of smoothing. This is something you will need to experiment with to determine which effect you like the most. Just highlight Smoothing, pick the option you want, and press the OK button (**D**).

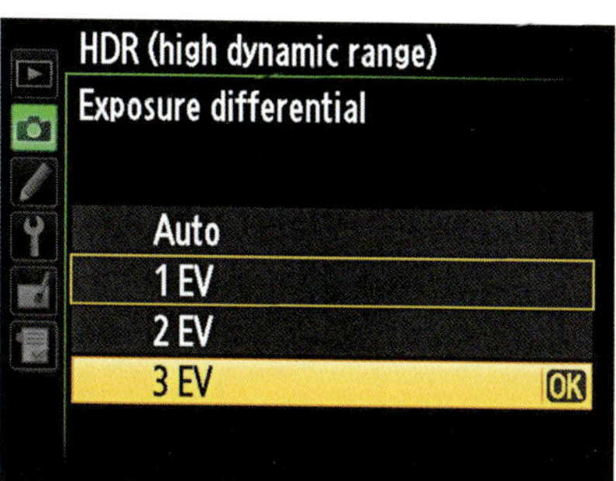

C

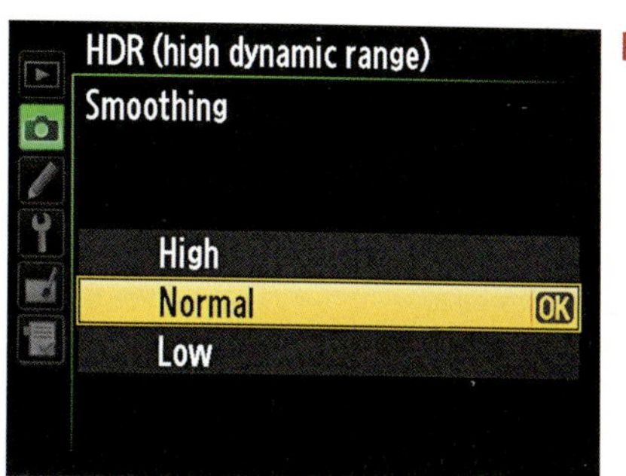

D

You can now exit the menu system, compose your shot, and take your HDR photo. You will not hear the camera shutter open and close twice like you normally would when taking two exposures. The camera will, however, take a little longer during the exposure process than you might be used to. Also, after the exposure is made, you will see the word "Job" and the HDR icon flashing in the control panel while the image is being processed. You won't be able to make any additional exposures until the camera has completed the HDR processing.

If your camera was set to Single, you will now be back in regular shooting mode. If you selected Series, you can continue shooting HDR images until the feature is turned off in the menu. If you can't remember which setting you picked, look for the HDR icon in the control panel. It will be displayed whenever the feature is active.

ACTIVE D-LIGHTING

The other option for taming contrast in scenes is Active D-Lighting (ADL). This feature operates in a similar fashion to HDR except that it uses a single frame and makes adjustments to the light and dark areas of the image at the time of exposure. The main goal of Active D-Lighting is to help you retain details in the shadows and highlights. It does this by lowering the exposure in the highlight areas and amplifying the shadows (**Figure 9.12**). **Figure 9.13** shows the same scene with Active D-Lighting turned off.

FIGURE 9.12 The Active D-Lighting feature can reduce the contrast and preserve details in shadows and highlights.

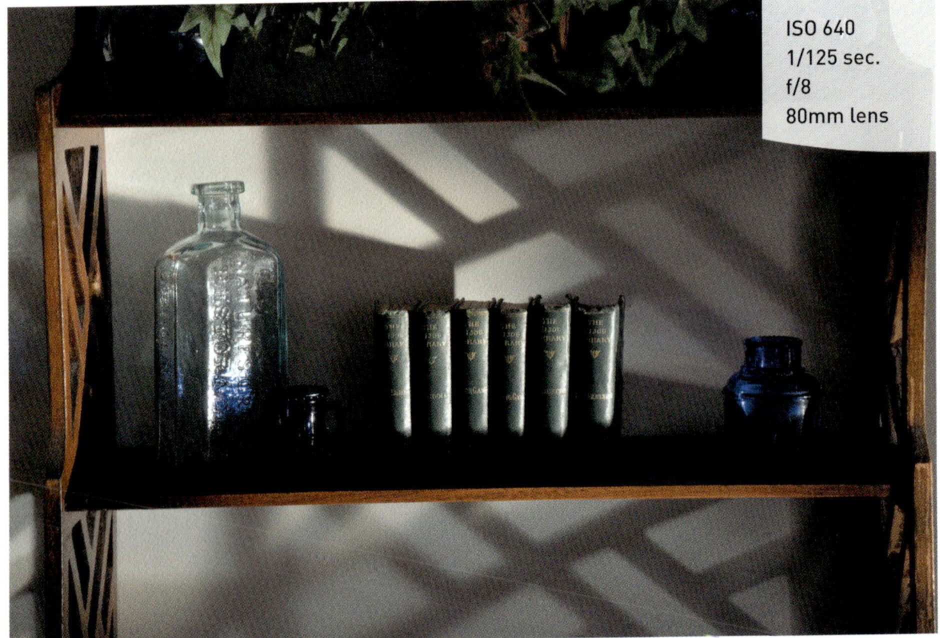

FIGURE 9.13 With Active D-Lighting turned off, the highlights are brighter and the shadows are darker.

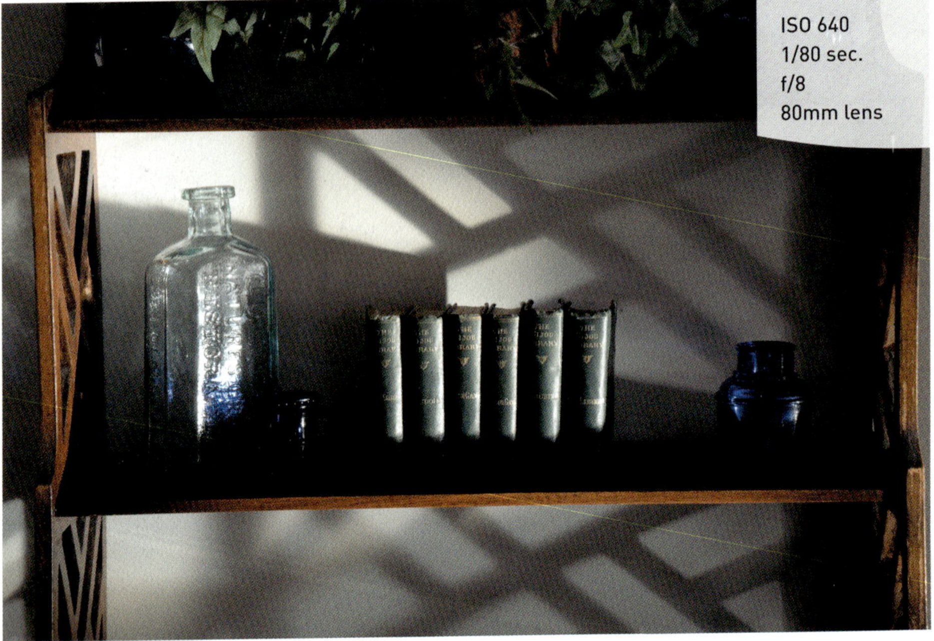

Active D-Lighting has five settings to choose from, ranging from Low to Extra High along with an Auto option. The key to using ADL is to make sure you are using the Matrix metering mode. Another thing to consider when shooting with ADL is the quality setting for the camera. If you are shooting in JPEG, the effect will be applied to the image in the camera as part of the standard processing. If you are shooting in RAW mode, the effect will appear to have been applied (when you look at your LCD monitor) but will not necessarily be displayed when you open the image in an image-processing program. That's because RAW files, by definition, have no processing applied to them. You can, however, reapply the ADL effect by opening your images in the Nikon ViewNX 2 software that came with your camera.

SETTING UP FOR ACTIVE D-LIGHTING

1. Press the Menu button and select Active D-Lighting in the shooting menu. Press OK (**A**).
2. Select the desired amount of ADL and press OK (**B**).

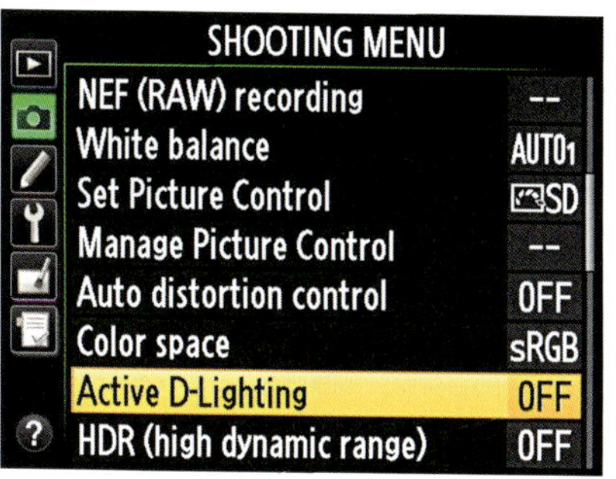

A

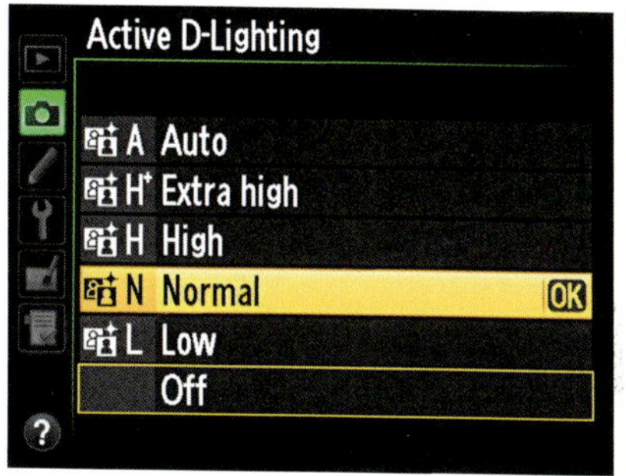

B

When ADL is selected in the menu, you should see the ADL icon in the control panel. ADL will stay active until you turn off Active D-Lighting in the shooting menu.

ADL BRACKETING

If you aren't sure which ADL setting is right for the subject you are photographing, you can set up your camera to bracket the ADL settings. Bracketing will switch between the settings automatically so that you don't need to go back to the menu each time you want to try a different setting. See page 158 of your manual to learn more.

SHOOTING PANORAMAS

If you have ever visited the Grand Canyon, you know just how large and wide open it truly is—so much so that it would be difficult to capture its splendor in just one frame. The same can be said for a mountain range, a cityscape, or any extremely wide vista.

THE MULTIPLE-IMAGE PANORAMA

To shoot a true panorama, you need to use either a special panorama camera (which shoots a very wide frame) or the following method, which requires the combining of multiple frames.

The multiple-image pano, as photographers often call a panoramic, has gained in popularity in the past few years; this is principally due to advances in image-processing software. Many software options are available now that will take multiple images, align them, and then "stitch" them into a single panoramic image. The real key to shooting a multiple-image pano is to overlap your shots by about 30 percent from one frame to the next (**Figure 9.14**). It is possible to handhold the camera while capturing your images, but the best method for capturing great panoramic images is to use a tripod.

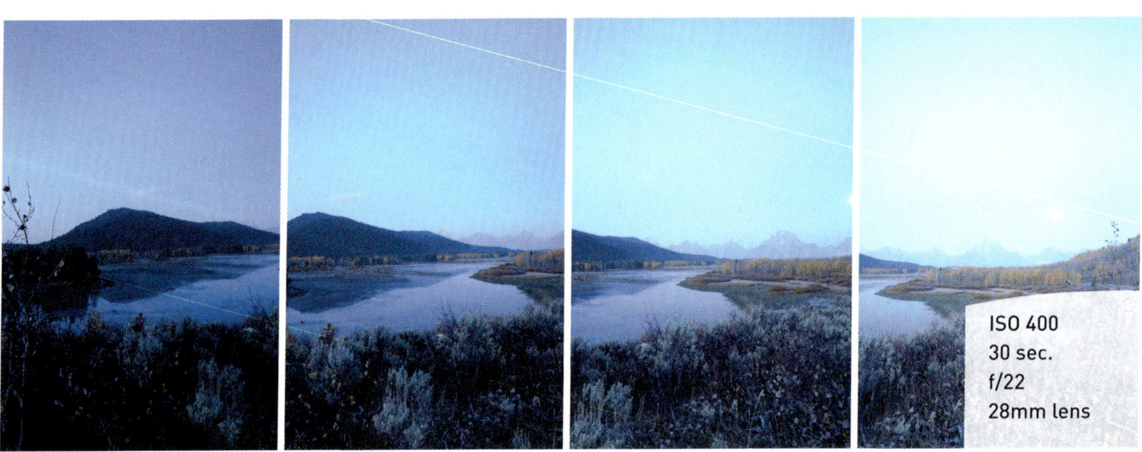

ISO 400
30 sec.
f/22
28mm lens

FIGURE 9.14
Here you see the makings of a panorama, with four shots overlapping by about 30 percent from frame to frame.

Now that you have your series of overlapping images, you can import them into your image-processing software to stitch them together and create a single panoramic image (**Figure 9.15**).

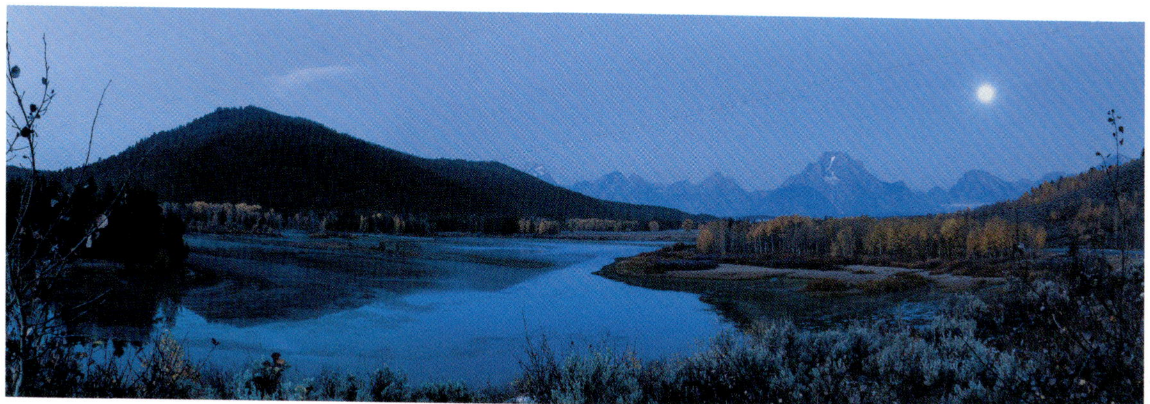

FIGURE 9.15
I used Adobe Photoshop to combine all of the exposures into one large panoramic image of the moon setting behind the mountains.

SORTING YOUR SHOTS FOR THE MULTI-IMAGE PANORAMA

If you shoot more than one series of shots for your panoramas, it can sometimes be difficult to know when one series of images ends and the other begins. Here is a quick tip for separating your images.

Set up your camera using the steps listed here. Now, before you take your first good exposure in the series, hold up one finger in front of the camera and take a shot. Move your hand away and begin taking your overlapping images. When you have taken your last shot, hold two fingers in front of the camera and take another shot.

When you review your images, use the series of shots that falls between the frames with one and two fingers in them. Then just repeat the process for your next panorama series.

SHOOTING PROPERLY FOR A MULTIPLE-IMAGE PANORAMA

1. Mount your camera on your tripod, and make sure it is level.
2. In Aperture Priority mode, use a very small aperture for the greatest depth of field. Take a meter reading of a bright part of the scene, and make note of it.
3. Now change your camera to Manual mode (M), and dial in the aperture and shutter speed that you obtained in the previous step.
4. Set your lens to manual focus, and then focus on the area of interest using the HFD method (covered in Chapter 7) of finding a point one-third of the way into the scene. (If you use the autofocus, you risk getting different points of focus from image to image, which will make the image stitching more difficult for the software.)
5. While carefully panning your camera, shoot your images to cover the entire area of the scene from one end to the other, leaving a 30 percent overlap from one frame to the next.

Then, use your favorite imaging software to combine the photographs into a single panoramic image.

CREATING A TIME-LAPSE MOVIE

We'll dive into the video features of the D600 in the next chapter, but if you want to try something completely different from standard video recording, you might want to explore time-lapse video, which allows you to take events that happen over long periods of time and speed them up so they can be watched in just a fraction of the time. This could be the blooming of a flower or maybe the setting of the sun on a colorful afternoon.

There are only two things you will need to capture time-lapse sequences. The first is a sturdy tripod. This is essential because the camera will be taking a lot of photos over a long period of time, and any movement in the camera will be distracting in the final video. The other thing you will need is something interesting to shoot. Some of my favorite subjects are clouds (**Figure 9.16**). I really like setting up my camera so that I can capture a nice landscape scene with clouds and then record several hundred frames over half an hour. The final videos are fairly short, but it's a lot of fun to watch the clouds quickly move across the sky.

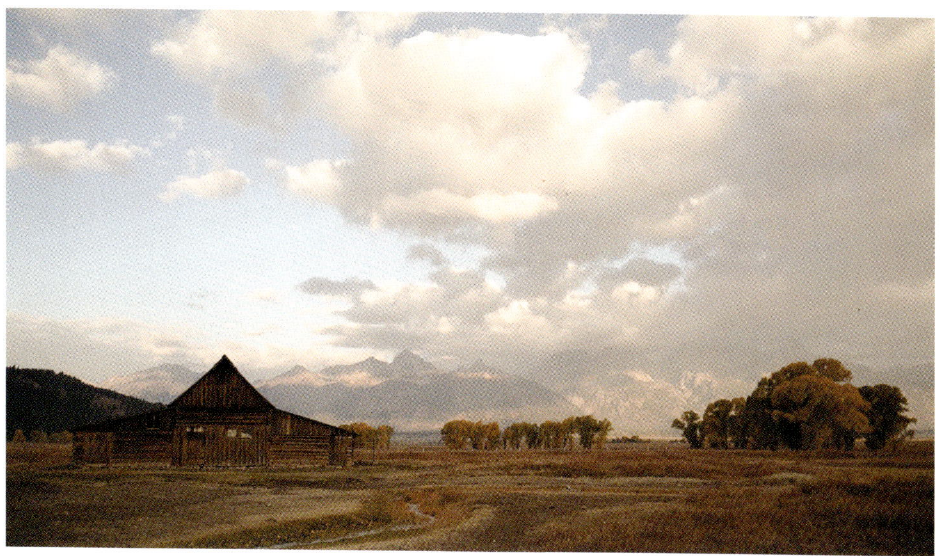

FIGURE 9.16
This is a frame from a time-lapse movie of moving clouds (check out the link to the video below).

You can check out a couple of short time-lapse movies I created with the D600 here:

- vimeo.com/53164268
- vimeo.com/53164269

SETTING UP THE TIME-LAPSE FEATURE

1. Set your exposure settings, activate the camera menu, select the Time-lapse photography option in the shooting menu, and press OK (**A**).
2. The feature will be set to Off, so press the right arrow on the Multi-selector to enter the next screen (**B**).

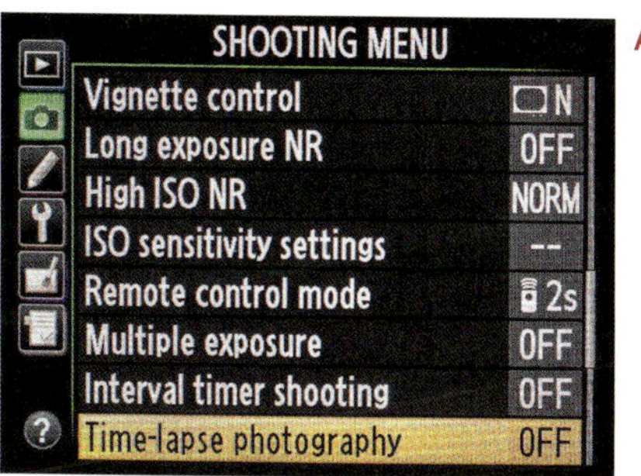

A

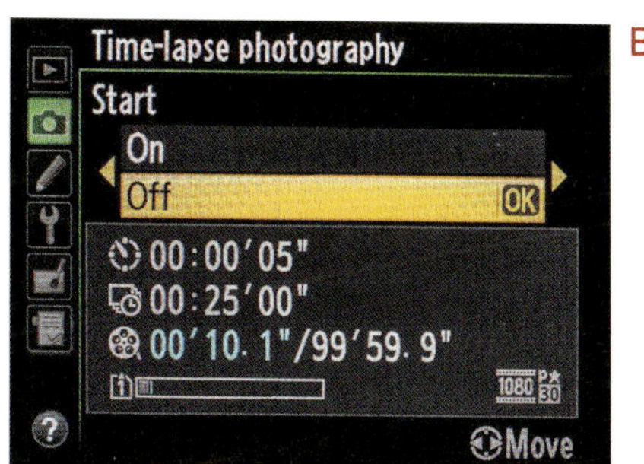

B

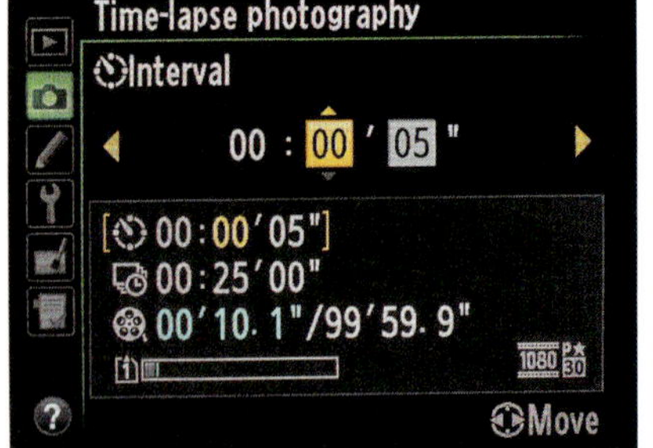

C

3. Set the interval for your shots. This is the amount of time you want between shots (**C**). You will need to experiment with this, but events that take place over a long period of time will have longer intervals. I set my cloud shots to about 30 seconds between shots.

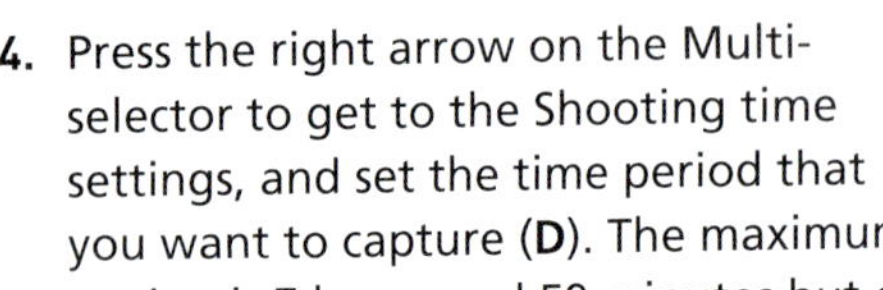

4. Press the right arrow on the Multi-selector to get to the Shooting time settings, and set the time period that you want to capture (**D**). The maximum setting is 7 hours and 59 minutes but could be less depending on the size of your memory card.
5. Press the right arrow on the Multi-selector again to return to the Start screen, highlight On, and press the OK button to begin the recording sequence (**E**).
6. The camera will begin shooting 3 seconds after you press the OK button. To end the sequence before the set time, push the OK button again. When the sequence is completed, you can press the Playback button to watch your video.

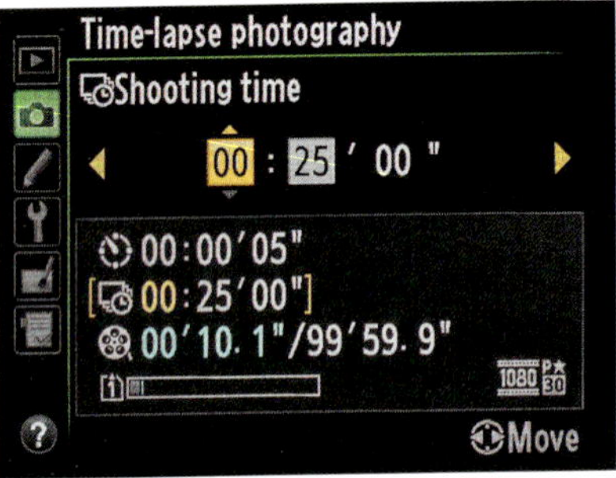

D

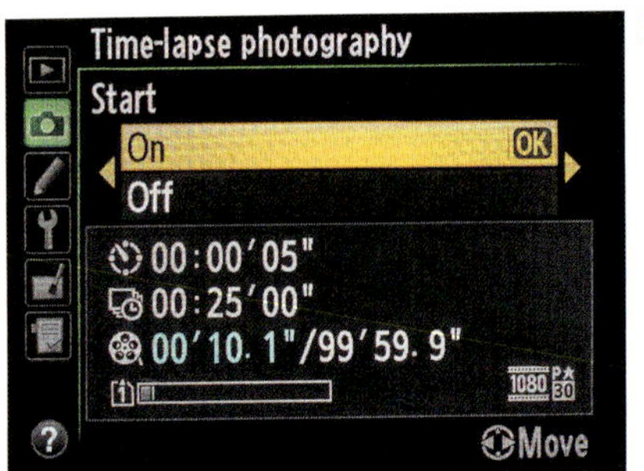

E

TIPS FOR TIME-LAPSE VIDEO

- Before activating the Time-lapse feature, set your camera up on the tripod and compose your scene.
- Take a few test shots before starting your sequence so you know your exposure is correct.
- Use manual focus so that the camera isn't trying to focus before each shot.
- Use a fully charged battery so you are sure to have enough juice for long sequences.

- Turn off the Auto-Image Review feature in the Display menu to save battery life.
- Use Manual mode if you are recording a sunset and want the scene to get darker as you go. A mode like Aperture Priority will always try to make the scene look normal.
- If you are shooting a night scene with long exposures, use an interval that is not only longer than your exposure time but also long enough to take the Long Exposure Noise Reduction into account.
- The Time-lapse feature uses the video-frame size to create the finished video sequence, so be sure to set this up in the Movie Settings menu before shooting your sequence.
- The length of your completed video will be displayed at the bottom of the main Time-lapse menu screen. If you want a video that is a specific length, keep an eye on this information and adjust your settings accordingly.

SHOOTING WITH THE INTERVAL TIMER

The only problem with the Time-lapse feature is that it creates the video but does not keep the individual frames, so you can't play with them later. If you would prefer to shoot a time-lapse sequence but create your own video file using a software solution, try using the Interval Timer Shooting feature. You can set similar options, such as interval time and number of total shots (up to 999 frames). Check out pages 164–167 in the user's manual for more info.

Another way I like to use interval timer shooting is when I want to photograph animals without physically being there to alter their behavior. For example, we've always had birdhouses stationed around our yard. I love to watch Eastern Bluebirds as they build their nest and raise their young (there's a shot of their eggs on the cover of this book). While they are very tolerant of human activity, they have their limits. To work around that, I put my camera on a tripod, got the exposure set just right in Manual mode, set the focus mode to manual, configured the interval timer to take a photo every 10 seconds over the span of about an hour, and walked away. I knew I wouldn't want all of those shots, but my hope was that I would get a couple that captured the birds at their best (**Figure 9.17**). And since the camera was locked down on a tripod, it was a snap to use Photoshop to combine them into one happy family portrait (**Figure 9.18**).

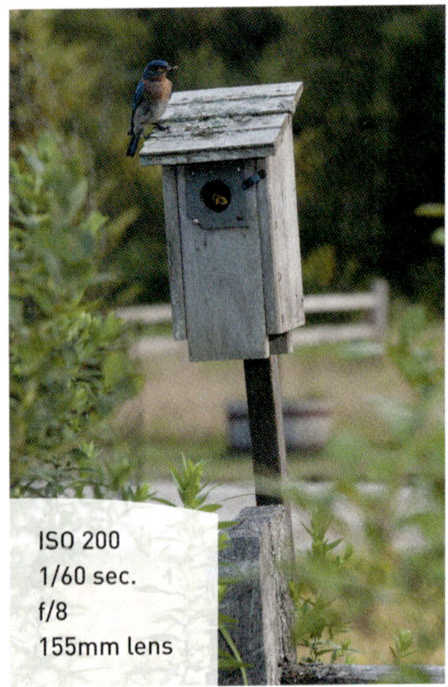
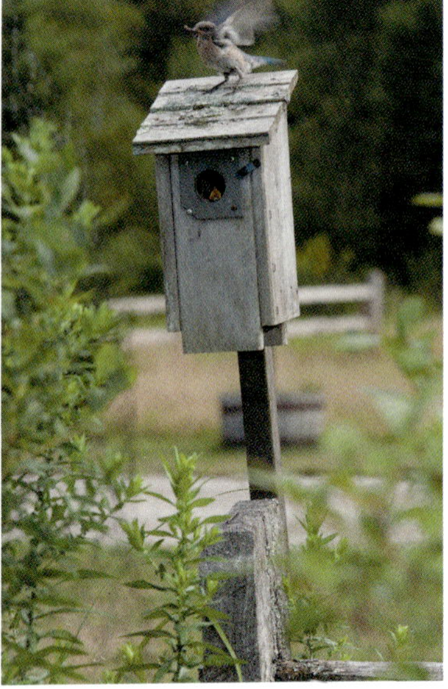

ISO 200
1/60 sec.
f/8
155mm lens

FIGURE 9.17
Out of about a hundred shots, I found two that I really liked.

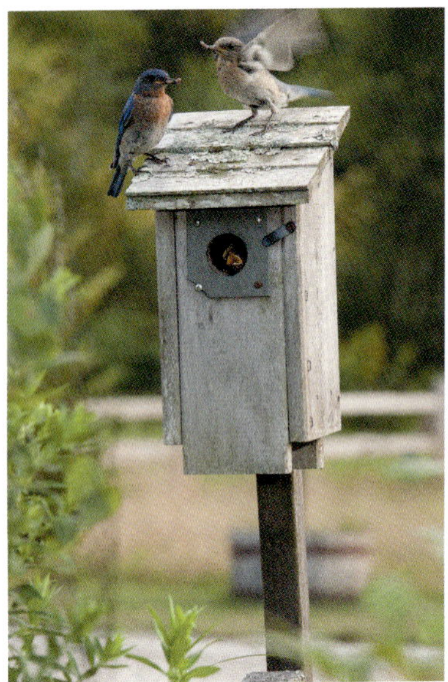

FIGURE 9.18
Interval timer shooting allowed me to create an image I would not otherwise have been able to capture—plus I wasn't even there!

Chapter 9 Assignments

Many of the techniques in this chapter are specific to shooting situations that may not come about very often. This is even more reason to practice them—when the situation does present itself, you will be ready.

Adding some drama to the end of the day

Because photographers don't meter correctly for them, most sunset photos don't reflect what the photographer saw. The next time you see a colorful sunset, take one shot metered from the sky and then one metered elsewhere and see what a difference it makes.

Making your exposure spot-on

Using the Spot metering mode can give accurate results, but only when pointed at something that has a middle tone. Try adding something gray to the scene and taking a reading off it. Now switch back to your regular metering mode and see if the exposure isn't slightly different.

Using the Bulb setting to capture the moment

This is definitely one of those settings that you won't use often, but it's pretty handy when you need it. If you have the opportunity to shoot a fireworks display or a distant storm, try setting the camera to Bulb and then playing with some long exposures to capture just the moments that you want.

Taming the contrast with Active D-Lighting

This is one of the easiest ways to capture a large dynamic range in a single click. I am often amazed at how well this setting can handle extremely contrasty scenes. But it can be overused in some scenarios, so it's important to know how the different levels of ADL work. The easiest way to do this is by bracketing your ADL shots. Take some brackets and compare the results in the LCD monitor.

Shooting HDR like a pro

If you really want to jump into the HDR pool, you will need to shoot multiple exposures and then download a program to process the photos. To start with, find an interesting subject, put your camera on a tripod, and frame your photo. Then set your ISO low, select an aperture setting in Aperture Priority mode, and then set your camera to a five-shot bracket sequence that goes from two stops under to two stops over. Next, download a trial program like HDRsoft's Photomatix Pro (www.hdrsoft.com) and start getting creative with your HDR photography.

Speeding up time

Even though it's not like real-time video making, I really enjoy making time-lapse sequences. The trick is to find a scene where something slowly changes over time. I mentioned that I like shooting cloudy-sky videos, but you could shoot an intersection, a sunset, or even slow boats moving in a harbor. Just pick a scene, set up on a sturdy tripod, and experiment. The only limit is your imagination.

Share your results with the book's Flickr group!

www.flickr.com/groups/d600fromsnapshotstogreatshots

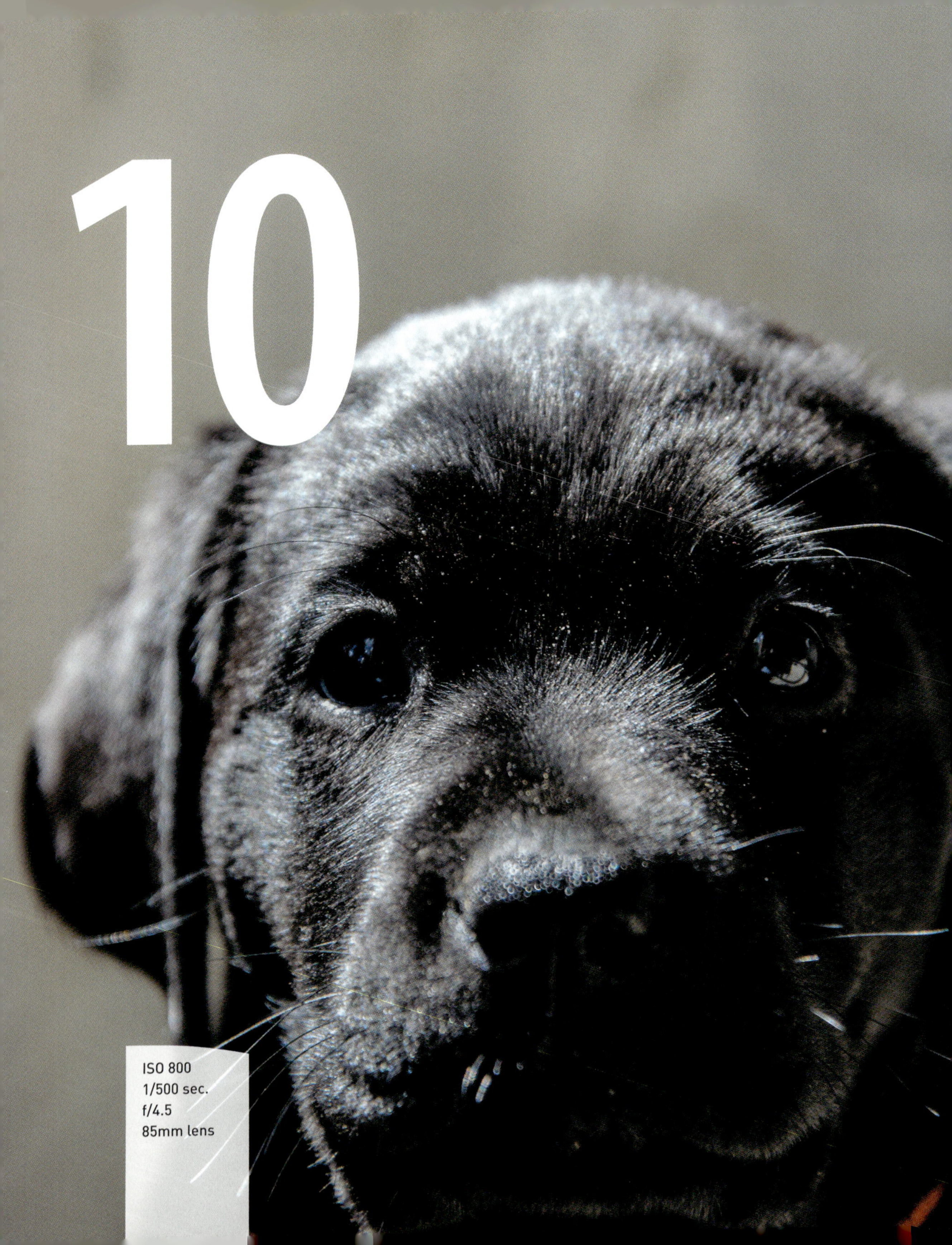
10
ISO 800
1/500 sec.
f/4.5
85mm lens

The Moving Picture

GETTING THE MOST OUT OF THE D600'S VIDEO CAPABILITIES

Probably one of the reasons you purchased the D600 over competing cameras is its ability to capture video—and not just regular video, but high-definition video. As I discussed in the book's introduction, the focus of this book is on the photography aspects of the camera, but that doesn't mean I am going to skip the video functions. The fact is that the line between photography and video is getting blurrier each day, especially since the inclusion of video capture in DSLR cameras. In this chapter, we will address some of the basics of video capture with the D600 and also take a look at some of the creative things you can do with your video. First, though, let's take a look at why the video capture feature is such a big deal in a DSLR.

IT'S ALL ABOUT THE LENSES

Video cameras have been around for a long time, so why is it such a big deal that you can now use your DSLR camera to record video? The answer is simple: it's all about the lenses. If you have any experience using a video camcorder, you know that it always seems like everything is in focus. While this isn't always a bad thing, it can also be pretty boring. Using DSLR video allows you to use faster lenses (larger apertures), which can give you more shallow depth of field in your videos. This shallow depth of field can add a sense of dimension and depth that is normally lacking in most standard video cameras. The truth is that many videographers are turning their attention from video cameras costing tens of thousands of dollars to the much more affordable DSLR video cameras to produce similar professional, high-definition results.

The D600 will not only allow you to capture video with a more shallow depth of field, it will also allow you the flexibility of using different lenses for different effects. While you may own only one lens right now, you have the ability to buy specialty lenses to enhance your video as well as your still capture. Any lens that you can use for still photography on your D600 can also be used for video, including an ultra-wide lens such as the AF Fisheye-Nikkor 16mm f/2.8 ED, the AF-S VR Zoom-Nikkor 70-300mm f/4.5-5.6G IF-ED, or even the AF Micro-Nikkor 105mm f/2.8D for getting extreme close-up videos.

RECORDING WITH LIVE VIEW

Video recording is a feature of the Live View capabilities of the camera, so you'll have to put it into active Live View mode to begin capturing video. This is done by rotating the Live View selector to the movie camera icon and then pressing the Lv button, which will activate Live View on the rear display (**Figure 10.1**).

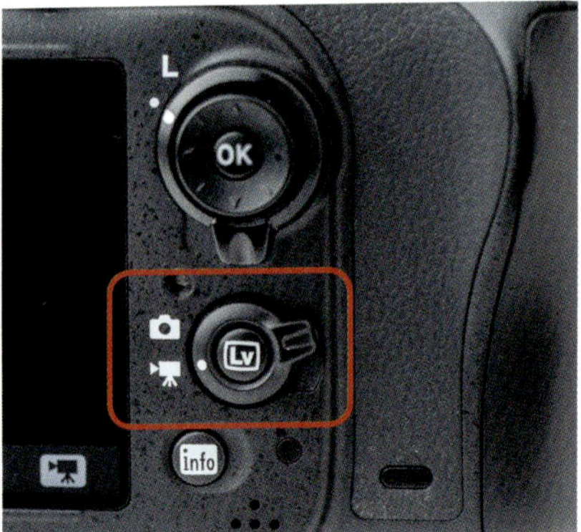

FIGURE 10.1
To activate Live View, rotate the Live View selector and press the Lv button.

Next, focus the camera by placing the red focus box on the subject and holding down the shutter button halfway until the focusing box turns green, indicating that your subject is in focus.

Once your subject is in focus, push the red Movie-record button, located on top of the camera near the shutter release button, to begin recording. As the camera begins to record, you will notice a few new icons on the LCD (**Figure 10.2**). At the upper left is a blinking red Record icon to let you know that the camera is in active recording mode. At the upper right, a timer counts down your remaining recording time. The recording time is directly related to the quality of video you have selected as well as to the capacity of your memory card. Lower-quality video and larger memory cards equal more recording time. To stop recording, simply press the Movie-record button a second time, which takes you back to Live View mode. To turn off Live View, press the Lv button or simply turn off the camera.

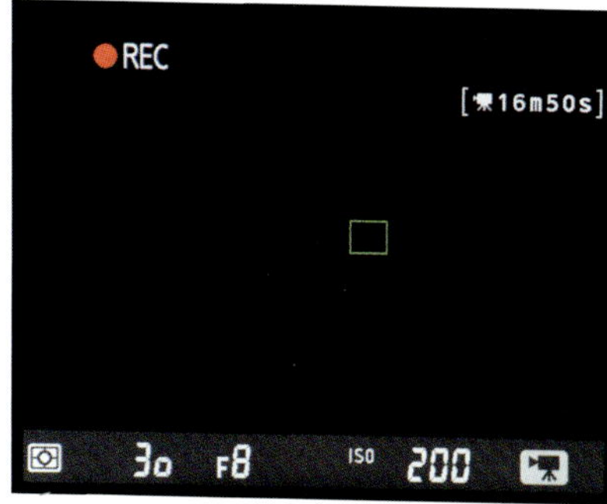

FIGURE 10.2
When recording is active, you will see a blinking red icon in the upper-left corner of the screen.

HOLD IT STEADY

I know a lot of people are just going to start shooting video right out of the box without adjusting the settings, so before I move on I have one word of advice: use a tripod. Have you ever watched a home video and felt like you'd just gotten off a roller coaster? Handheld video is rough to watch unless the person behind the camera knows what they're doing. Buy a tripod or tripod head that is constructed for video (I discuss video accessories later in this chapter). Typically, these tripods will have what are called "fluid," "smooth," or "shake-free" panning and tilt features. Trust me, a good investment in a nice tripod for your video will make the difference between professional-looking video and *The Blair Witch Project*.

VIDEO QUALITY

Now that we know the mechanics of recording a video, let's spend a little time looking at the settings you will use to dictate the quality of your video. First, we need to determine the size of the video that will be recorded. The best quality your D600 is capable of is high-definition video with a resolution of 1920x1080, aka 1080p. The *1080* represents the height of the video image in pixels, and the *p* stands for progressive, which is the method the camera uses to draw the video on the screen (more on this later).

The D600's other video resolution is 1280x720. For high-definition television and computer/media station viewing, you will be best served by using 1920x1080. If you plan on recording for the Internet or for portable media devices, first check the appropriate upload to that medium or device. Many social media sites, such as YouTube and Facebook, support HD video, as do the iPad, the iPod touch, and competing devices. But before you decide to render HD video, you should know the key benefit of using the lower resolutions: lower-resolution video requires less physical storage, because of its smaller pixel count. This means that more video will fit on your storage card, and it will take less time to upload the video to the Internet.

WHAT'S THE DIFFERENCE BETWEEN 1080P AND 1080I?

When it comes to video, two terms describe its quality and how it is captured and displayed on a monitor or screen: *progressive* and *interlaced*. Unlike a photo, a video frame is not displayed all at once but instead is drawn sequentially. Interlaced video first draws the odd-numbered lines and then the even-numbered lines. This odd-even drawing is what we sometimes call screen flicker. In progressive video, the type your D600 produces, the lines are drawn in sequence from top to bottom, usually resulting in better image quality and less screen flicker. For viewing purposes, progressive video is preferred, especially with higher-definition images.

Along with selecting a size for your video, you will also need to pick a frame rate. Video is, after all, a series of still image frames that are displayed in rapid fashion to make what looks like a moving picture. The standard for most video is 30 frames per second. The European standard is 25 frames per second. There is also a setting of 24 frames per second, which is the frame rate used for movies shot on film. There are also additional choices for the 1280x720 sizes, which include 60 (U.S.A.) and 50 (Europe) frames per second. These faster frame rates are great if you intend to do some slow-motion edits of your videos since they contain twice as many frames per second. This means they can be played at half-speed and still look nice and smooth.

SETTING MOVIE QUALITY

1. Press the Menu button, and use the Multi-selector to navigate to the shooting menu.
2. Using the Multi-selector, highlight Movie settings and press OK (**A**).
3. Highlight Frame size/frame rate and press OK, then choose your desired frame size/frame rate and press OK (**B**).
4. Select a movie quality and press OK (**C**).
5. Press the Menu button twice to exit Menu mode and return to shooting.

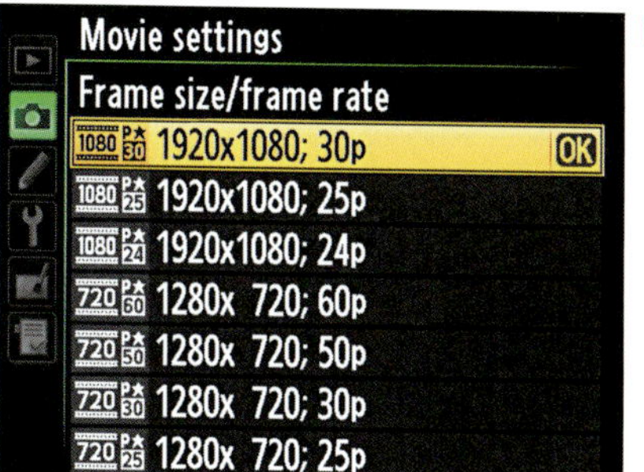

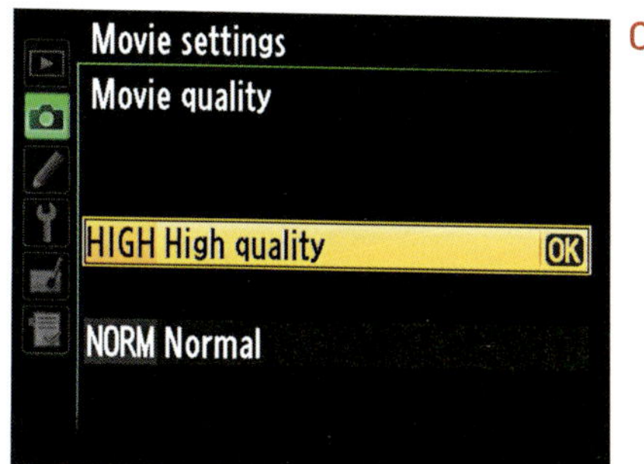

SOUND

The D600 can record audio to go along with your video, but there are a couple of things to keep in mind while using the built-in microphone (the two small holes right above the D600 nameplate). The first is to make sure you don't block the microphone with your finger and muffle any sounds you are trying to capture. The next thing you need to know about the sound is that it is mono, not stereo. This is lower-quality sound than you are used to hearing in movies and music.

To get stereo audio, you will need to use an external microphone, which can be connected via the port on the side (**Figure 10.3**). A nice step up from the built-in mic is the Nikon ME-1 external microphone, which records in stereo and, because it mounts atop the hot shoe, it picks up less noise from the AF motor. You can watch and listen to a thorough review of the ME-1, along with some comparisons to other external mic choices, at http://bit.ly/d5100Mic (it is used on a D5100 in the review, but the mic is the same).

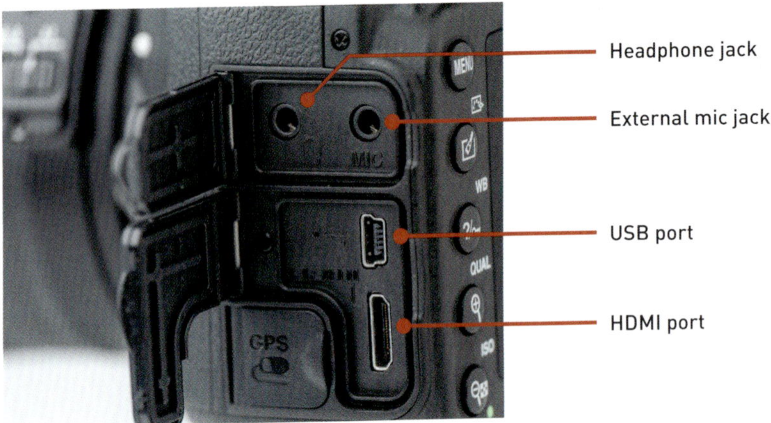

FIGURE 10.3 The headphone jack, external microphone jack, HDMI port, and USB port.

A welcome feature on the D600 is the addition of a headphone jack, which gives you the ability to monitor the sound being recorded by the mic. Using headphones that reduce or cancel ambient sound will improve your ability to monitor what is coming in through the mic.

TURNING OFF THE SOUND

Sometimes you may wish to turn the sound off altogether—maybe sound would be distracting or you plan to add your own soundtrack later.

CHANGING THE AUDIO SETTINGS

1. To make adjustments to the audio settings, go back into the Movie Settings menu, select Microphone, and press OK.
2. To enable the camera to automatically adjust the audio levels, select Auto sensitivity and press OK (**A**). If you want to adjust them yourself, highlight Manual sensitivity and press OK.
3. You can select an audio level from 1 to 20 by using the Multi-selector (**B**). Just be careful to watch your audiometers to make sure the audio level reaches zero only during the loudest moments.

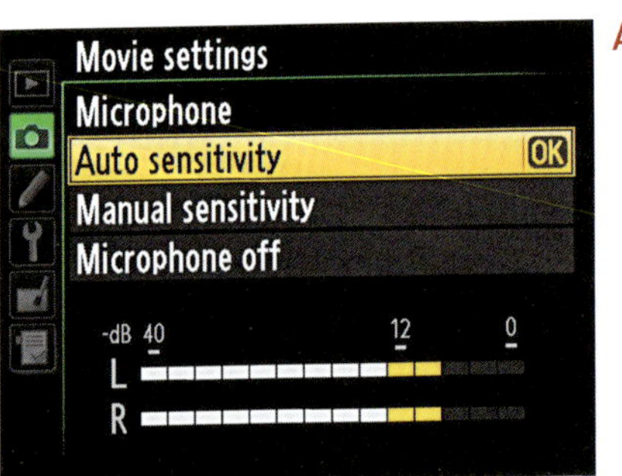

A

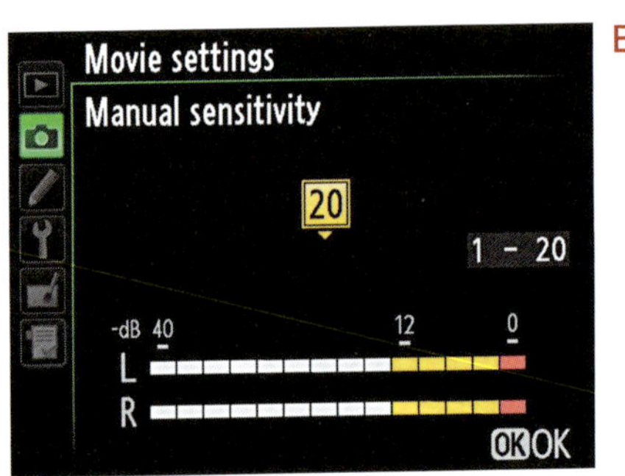

B

4. To turn off the microphone, highlight the Microphone off option in the menu and press OK (**C**).

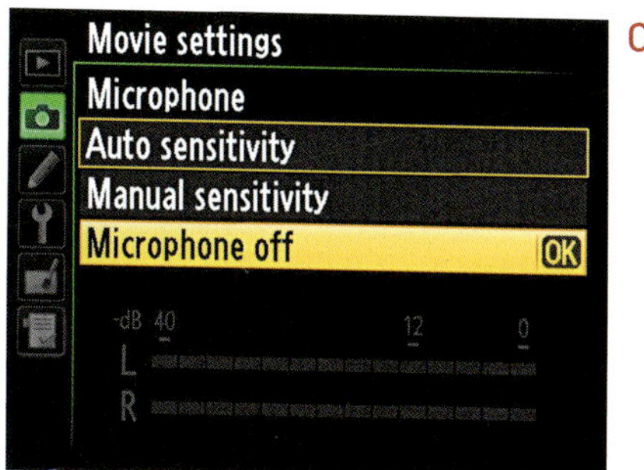

DEDICATING A SECOND CARD TO VIDEO

This is a nice option if you have a good reason for keeping your photos separated from your video files. For some people, it is just easier for importing purposes to have one card dedicated to photos and the other to video. Plus, it allows you to dedicate your fastest or highest-capacity SD card to video.

TO DEDICATE A VIDEO CARD

1. Press the Menu button, use the Multi-selector to highlight Movie settings in the shooting menu, and click OK (**A**).
2. Use the Multi-selector to highlight Destination, and click OK (**B**).
3. Select your desired SD card slot, and press OK (**C**).
4. Click the Menu button twice to return to shooting.

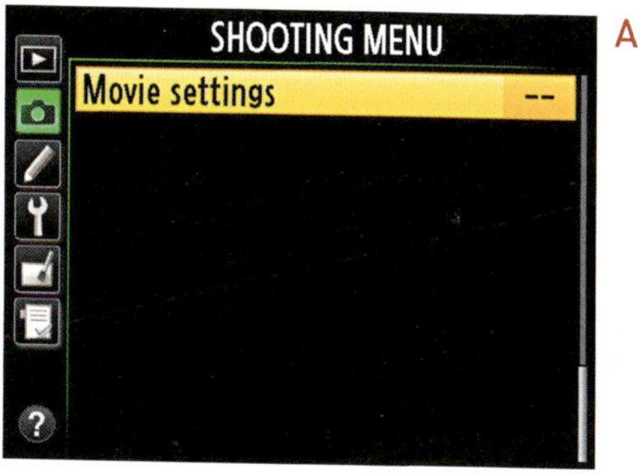

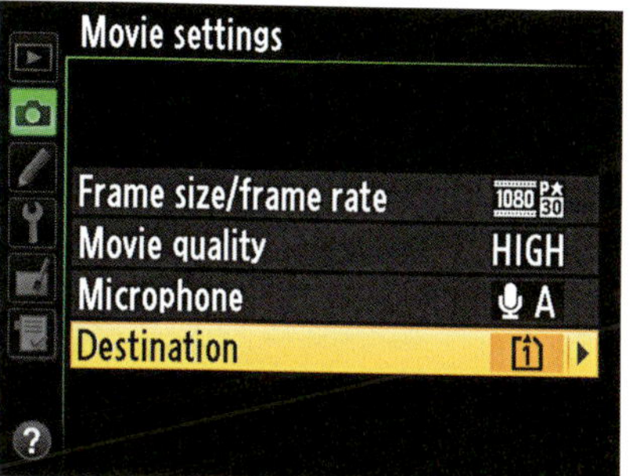

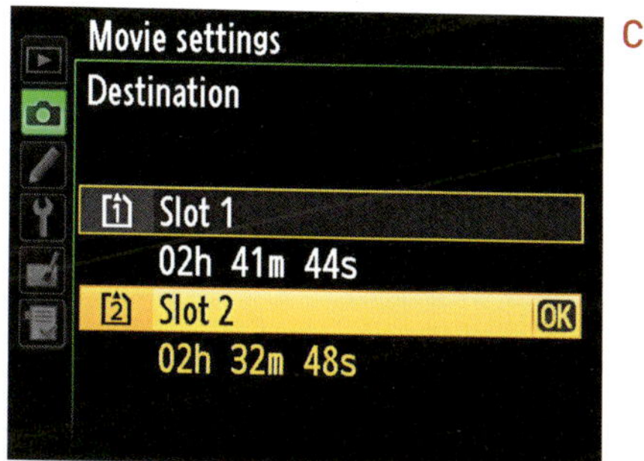

FOCUSING

Your D600 has several focusing options for Live View/Movie mode: Face Priority AF, Wide Area AF, Normal Area AF, and Subject Tracking AF. There are benefits to each focus-point option, and you will want to choose your focus mode depending on the subject of your video. See page 52 in your manual for more on the AF-area modes.

CHANGING THE AF-AREA MODE

Normal Area AF uses the small rectangular focus point to lock focus on a subject. The focus point can be manually moved around the frame by using the Multi-selector. You can also quickly bring the focus point back to the center of the frame by pressing the center button on the Multi-selector.

If you are going to be shooting landscapes or other scenes without people, you might want to consider using the Wide Area AF mode. This provides a larger focus area and makes it a little easier to get a quick focus lock on general subjects.

If you are going to be recording people, you can use the Face Priority mode. It automatically detects and focuses on your subject's face. If there is more than one person, the camera will focus on the closest one, but you can change from one face to another by using the Multi-selector.

For tracking a moving subject, use Subject Tracking AF. Place the focus point over your subject, and press the center button on the Multi-selector. The focus point will continue to track your subject until it leaves the frame or until you turn it off by pressing the center button again.

1. To change the AF-area, activate Live View mode by pressing the Lv button.
2. Press and hold the AF-mode button on the front of the camera.
3. Rotate the Sub-command dial until you see the icon for the desired AF-area mode in the top of the Live View display.

CHANGING THE FOCUS MODE

Of course, these modes will focus only if you are pressing the shutter release button (and that includes Subject Tracking AF). If you want your camera to actively focus while you are recording, you will need to change the mode from AF-S to AF-F (Full-time servo AF). When you activate AF-F, the camera will continuously focus using the focus mode you have selected.

1. To change the focus mode, activate Live View mode by pressing the Lv button.
2. Press and hold the AF-mode button on the front of the camera.
3. Rotate the Main Command dial until you see the icon for the desired focus mode in the top of the Live View display.

MANUALLY FOCUSING FOR MOVIES

While it's nice to use the autofocus for casual movie recording, if you really want to get serious you will probably want to manually focus your lens during recording. This is the way that the pros do it—and for good reason. The autofocus system in the camera is both slow and noisy. The noise comes from the internal focusing motors of the autofocus system. If you are using the built-in microphone, you will no doubt hear the autofocus system in your movies. This can be somewhat overcome by using an external mic (though your mileage may vary). Because of the mechanics of the system, the slowness of the autofocus system is something that can't be helped. Typically what you will see when using the autofocus is that your subject will move in and out of focus while the camera tries to lock in a sharp focus. To combat this problem, most professionals manually focus their cameras as they shoot. This requires a lot of practice and sometimes some special gear, but when done right it gives a more polished look to your video. To manually focus, just turn the AF-mode switch to M and use the focusing ring on your lens.

VIEW MODES

The Information On mode of Live View offers a lot of information for setting up your camera and lets you see things like the focus mode, the white balance, the frame size and rate, the selected picture control, and even the audiometer (**Figure 10.4**).

All of this is great stuff, but sometimes it can get in the way, which is why you have three other options available. For an uncluttered view, you can choose to turn off all information (**Figure 10.5**). The other two options are really helpful in composing your scene. The Framing Guides mode overlays a grid on the preview to help keep things squared up (**Figure 10.6**). The Virtual Horizon mode puts an active level indicator right on your screen; this lets you know whether you are holding the camera straight and whether the lens is tipped forward or backward (**Figure 10.7**).

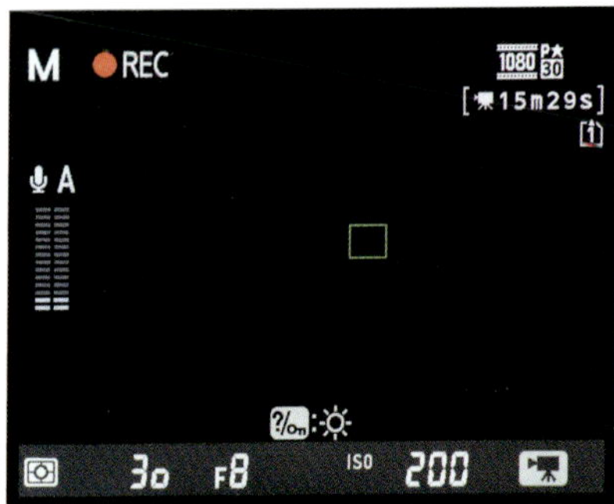

FIGURE 10.4
The Information On screen displays lots of video information.

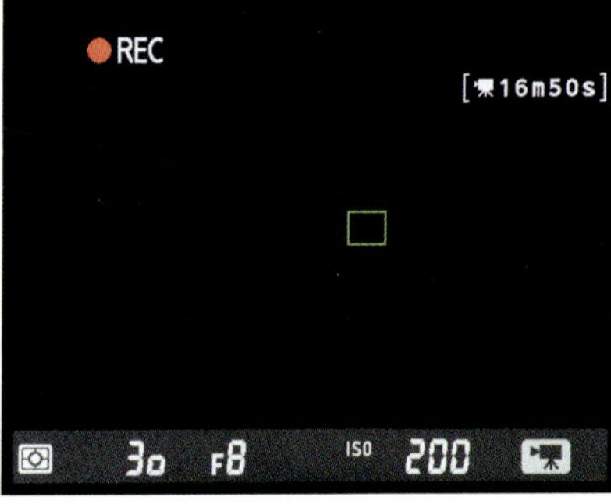

FIGURE 10.5
Use the Information Off mode for a clutter-free display.

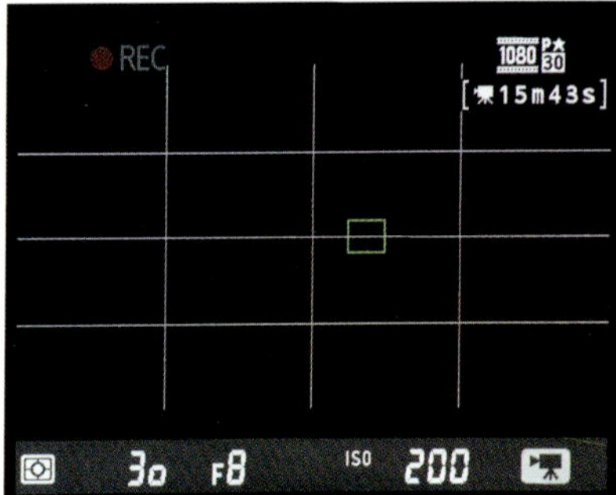

FIGURE 10.6
The Framing Guides mode helps with composition.

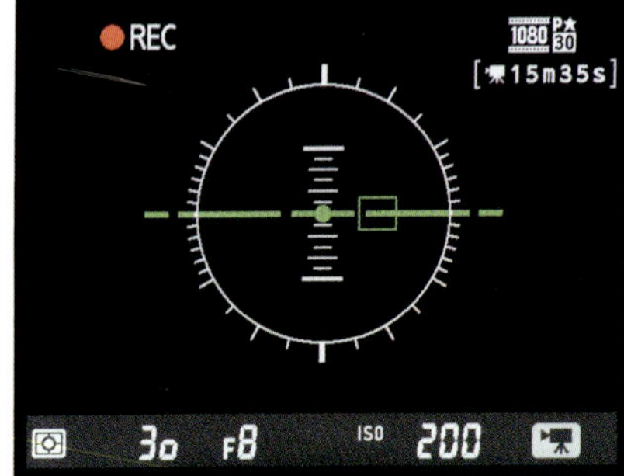

FIGURE 10.7
If your video always seems to be tilted, try using the Virtual Horizon mode.

ACCESSORIES FOR VIDEO

I've dedicated an entire chapter to accessories that will expand your photographic options, and many of those same accessories can also be used for motion capture, but there are a few video-specific accessories I want to mention here.

TRIPODS

The use of a tripod for video is not quite the same as for still-image applications. When you are shooting video, you want to present a nice, smooth video scene that is free of camera shake. One particular case for this is the pan shot. When you are following a subject from side to side, you want the viewer's attention to be focused on the subject, not on the shaky look of the video. To help in this effort, your preferred weapon of choice should be a tripod with a fluid head. A fluid head looks a little different than a standard tripod head, in that it usually has one long handle for controlled panning. To really make things smooth, the head uses a system of small fluid cartridges within the panning mechanisms so that your panning movements are nice and smooth. For around $130, you can get a fluid pan head that will mount on your existing tripod legs (if your existing tripod has a removable head). Another option to consider is a dedicated video monopod such as the Manfrotto Fluid Video Monopod (you can even get it with a panning head), which gives you the stability of a tripod but with a much smaller footprint.

CAMERA STABILIZERS

Aside from using a boom arm, there's really only one way to get jitter-free video on your camera while moving around: use a steady device. You have probably heard of SteadiCam rigs, but they can be cumbersome, expensive, and frankly a little bit of overkill for the normal video experience. But there are smaller, handheld rigs that provide the same benefit without the cost and bulk, like the ModoSteady from Manfrotto. One of the big advantages of this rig is that it has three different setups to choose from. The steady mode hangs a counterbalance under the camera to allow you to capture fluid-looking video movement. You can also move the balance arm to a different position and use it as a shoulder rig, much like the stock of a rifle. Finally, you can open the handle and turn it into a small tabletop tripod. That's a lot of functionality for under $100.

EASIER LCD VISION

I have one problem with shooting video on the D600 or any DSLR camera, and that is that I can't use the viewfinder as I record. Instead, I am forced to use the rear LCD screen, and while it is very large and sharp, my old eyes tend to make me hold the camera fairly far away from my body to see the screen. But there is another way, and it is perfect for old eyes like mine.

To really get a good look at what is happening in your LCD monitor, you should use a loupe like the Zacuto Z-Finder Pro 3X, which is made for 3.2" screens and attaches to the camera for hands-free operation. If you are going to be doing a lot of video recording, you will most certainly want to look into a device like this. Not only is it great for getting a better look at the LCD screen while recording, it also helps avoid glare on the screen while working outdoors.

GET YOURSELF A MINI-HDMI CABLE

When you are ready to play back your video, you can run the video directly from your camera to your TV. You'll need to use a TV capable of displaying high-definition video, which also means that you will want to use an HDMI cable to connect the camera to the TV. HDMI (High-Definition Multimedia Interface) cables will carry your uncompressed video to your HDTV in all its glory. The only problem is that your camera didn't include an HDMI cable in the box when you bought it. This means that you will have to purchase one to take advantage of HD playback. If you are thinking that you already own an HDMI cable for connecting your other media components to your TV, you might want to take another look. Your camera uses a mini-HDMI connection, so most standard cables designed for video components won't work. If you do decide to purchase one, make sure you get a mini-HDMI-to-HDMI cable. You can find them at most electronics stores where HD cameras and TVs are sold. (Here's a little hint for purchasing a mini-HDMI cable: search the Internet for the best prices. Most electronics stores have huge mark-ups on cables, and you can usually find a suitable one online for about a third of the price.)

GETTING A SHALLOW DEPTH OF FIELD

As I said earlier, getting the look of a production cinema camera means working with a shallow depth of field. The problem you might encounter when trying to get a large aperture in your video will be that the camera wants to use an auto-exposure mode to establish the correct camera settings for recording video. To get the benefit of a large aperture, you will need to work in either Aperture Priority or Manual mode.

If you are shooting in Aperture Priority mode, the camera will automatically adjust the shutter speed and ISO so that you can use your desired aperture setting. As the shutter slows to 1/30 of a second, the ISO will begin to rise to maintain an acceptable shutter speed. If you want to adjust the brightness or darkness of the scene, you can use the Exposure Compensation setting, which will fool the meter.

To really get control of your exposure, you will want to use the Manual mode setting. Manual will let you make the scene darker or lighter than will the other modes, which are striving for a perfectly metered scene. The problem is that sometimes you might want the scene to appear darker or lighter than it is, which is a great time to flip into Manual. There is no auto function in Manual, so you will need to adjust the aperture, ISO (try to keep it under 1600 for noise reasons), and shutter speed. Just as in Aperture Priority, you won't be able to set a shutter speed below 1/30 of a second. But since Manual mode has no auto adjustments, the Exposure Compensation feature will not render any difference in the exposure.

Note that you'll need to set your aperture before you engage Live View. Once you are in Live View (in either Aperture Priority or Manual mode), you will not be able to change the aperture. (See page 58 of the manual for a chart that shows what settings are adjustable in Live View movie mode.) So if you want a shallow depth of field in your video (**Figure 10.8**), choose a large aperture and then push the Lv button; if you want a wider depth of field (**Figure 10.9**), choose a smaller aperture first. You generally don't want to change exposure while recording video, so get your settings figured out before you start.

- Video at f/5.6: vimeo.com/53270933
- Video at f/18: vimeo.com/53270934

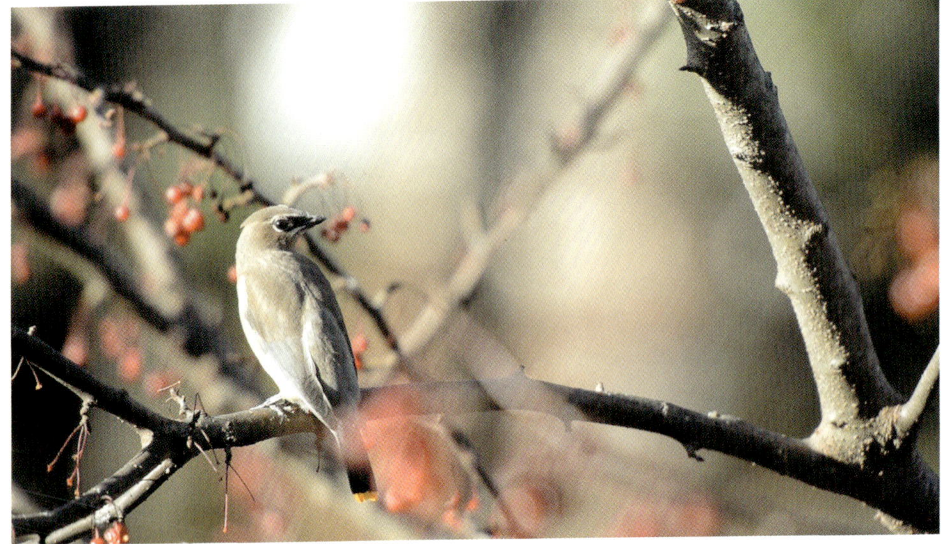

FIGURE 10.8
I selected an aperture of f/5.6 to get a shallow depth of field with this 400mm lens.

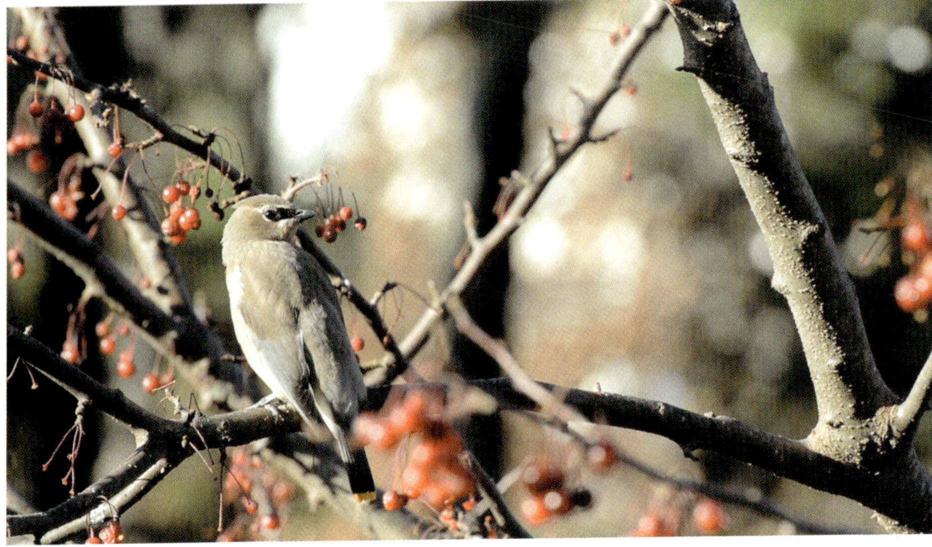

FIGURE 10.9
This cedar waxwing was kind enough to wait while I jumped out of Live View and changed the aperture to f/18 to increase the depth of field.

GIVING A DIFFERENT LOOK TO YOUR VIDEOS

USING PICTURE CONTROLS

Something that a lot of people don't realize is that you can use the picture controls to give your video a completely different look. Sure, you can use the Standard control for everyday video, but why not add some punch by using the Vivid setting? Nothing says HD like bright, vivid colors. Or maybe you want to shoot a landscape scene. Go ahead and set the picture control to the Landscape setting to improve the look of skies and vegetation. If you really want to get creative, try using the Monochrome setting and shoot in black and white. The great thing about using the picture controls is that you will see the effect right on your LCD monitor as you record so you will know exactly what your video is going to look like. Want to take things up a notch? Try customizing the picture controls and do things like shoot sepia-colored video. Check out the "Classic Black and White Portraits" section of Chapter 6 to see how to customize the look of the Monochrome picture control.

WHITE BALANCE

Another great way to change the look of your video is to select a white balance that matches your scene for accurate color rendition—or better yet, choose one that doesn't match to give a different feel to your video. You can completely change the mood of the video by selecting a white balance setting that is different from the actual light source that you are working in. Don't be afraid to be creative and try out different looks for you video.

TIPS FOR BETTER VIDEO

SHOOT SHORT SEQUENCES

Even though your camera can record fairly long video sequences, you should probably limit your shooting time to short clips and then edit them together. Here's the deal: most professional videos shot today are actually made up of very short video sequences that are edited together. If you don't believe me, watch any TV show and see how long you actually see a continuous sequence. I am guessing that you won't see any clip that is longer than about 10 seconds. You can thank music videos for helping to shorten our attention spans, but the reality is that your videos will look much more professional if you shoot in shorter clips and then edit them together.

TURN OFF THE SOUND

Earlier I told you how to turn off the audio option while recording your video. The truth is that the mono microphone does not produce audio that is up to the quality of the video. To make your videos stand out, try turning it off and then adding a music soundtrack. You will be amazed at how the right music can enhance a video. Of course you will need to do this on your computer, which will require special video-editing software (see the section "Editing Video," later in this chapter).

STAGE YOUR SHOTS

If you are trying to produce a good-looking video, take some time before you begin shooting to determine what you want to shoot and where you want to shoot it from. You can mark the floor with tape to give your "actors" a mark to hit. You can also use staging to figure out where your lens needs to be set for correct focus on these different scenes.

AVOID THE QUICK PAN

While recording video, your camera uses something called a rolling shutter, which, as the name implies, rolls from the top to the bottom of the frame. If you are panning quickly from one side to another, you will see your video start to jiggle like it is being shot through Jell-O. This is something that can't be overcome except by using a slower panning motion. If you are going to be shooting a fast subject, consider using a camera setting that utilizes a fast shutter speed. It won't eliminate the problem completely, but it should improve it a little.

USE A FAST MEMORY CARD

Your video will be recording at up to 60 frames per second, and as it is recording it's placing the video into a buffer, or temporary holding spot, while the camera writes the frames to your memory card. If you are using a slower memory card, it might not be able to keep up with the flow of video—with the result being dropped frames. The camera will actually not record some frames because the buffer will fill up before the images have time to be written. This will be seen as small skips in the video when you watch it later. You can prevent this from happening by using an SD card that has a speed rating of class 6 or higher. These cards have faster writing speeds and will keep the video moving smoothly from the camera to the card.

WATCHING AND EDITING YOUR VIDEO

WATCHING VIDEO

There are a couple of different ways for you to review your video once you have finished recording. The first is probably the easiest: press the Playback button to bring up the recorded image on the rear LCD screen, and then use the OK button to start playing the video. The Multi-selector acts as the video controller and allows you to rewind and fast-forward as well as stop the video altogether.

If you would like to get a larger look at things, you will need to either watch the video on your TV or move the video files to your computer. To watch video on your TV, you will need to purchase an HDMI cable (as discussed previously) and your TV needs to support at least 720p and have an HDMI port. Once you have the cable hooked up to your TV (tune your TV to the channel used for HDMI input), simply use the same camera controls that you used for watching the video on the LCD screen. See page 204 of the manual for more information on using the HDMI connection.

If you would like to watch your video on your computer, you will first need to download the files or access them using an SD card reader. For Apple owners, you can use Apple's QuickTime Player to watch the video. If it is too large for your screen, press Command-0 (zero) to make the video half-size, or Command-3 to fit the video to your screen. For Microsoft Windows users, it is possible to use the Windows Media Player, but you may need to download a special codec. Instead, try downloading the Apple QuickTime Player (www.apple.com/quicktime). The basic player is free and will allow you to view your movie files without any problems.

EDITING VIDEO

If you are a Mac owner, you can edit your HD video using the iMovie application. The latest version is chock-full of new video-editing features, including the ability to work with audio.

Windows XP users will have to purchase an editing program for editing HD video, since the Windows Movie Maker application doesn't do a very good job of handling HD video resolutions. If you are using Windows 7, Windows Live Movie Maker is a good basic video-editing application. There are also many other applications for Windows editing, such as Adobe Premiere Elements. You can find more information and download a trial version at www.adobe.com/products/premiereel. If you have Adobe Photoshop CS6, then you should definitely take advantage of the improved video-editing features that are now included in the Standard edition; this is currently my favorite option. Here's a short clip (**Figure 10.10**) edited entirely in Photoshop CS6: vimeo.com/user6708398/puppies (the password is snapshots).

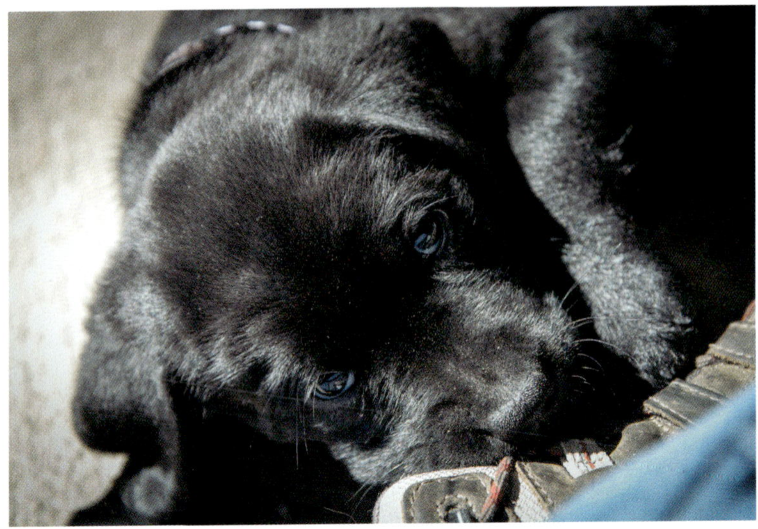

FIGURE 10.10
A frame from a D600 video edited in Photoshop CS6.

EXPANDING YOUR KNOWLEDGE

I have given you a couple of quick tips and suggestions in this chapter to get you started with your moviemaking, but if you really want to get serious there is a lot more you need to know. Videography can be a complex endeavor, and there is much to learn if you want to move beyond the simple video capture of the kids in the backyard or the trip to the amusement park. If you really want to explore all your camera has to offer in the way of video moviemaking, then I suggest you check out *Creating DSLR Video: From Snapshots to Great Shots* (**Figure 10.11**). It is packed solid with everything you need to know about taking your DSLR video making to the next level and beyond. Check out this sample chapter, "Exposure and Focus," and I think you'll agree: bit.ly/DSLRsnapshots4.

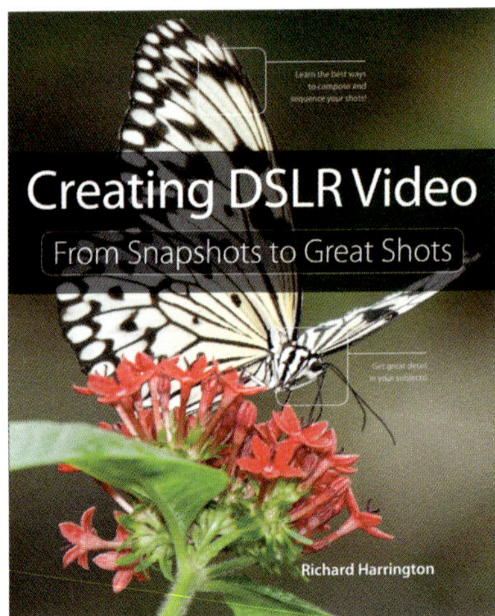

FIGURE 10.11
A great book for taking your video work to the next level.

Chapter 10 Assignments

Even if you don't think you will be shooting much video, it pays to know how to use it, because you just never know when it will come in handy. The truth is that I used to turn up my nose at the video functions in DSLR cameras, but over time I have come to appreciate the ability to create multimedia projects that offer expanded expression. Who knows, you just might be the next big indie director on the block.

Change your focus

There are several focus modes available for the Live View/Movie mode, and you should give all of them a try before deciding which method works best for you. Try setting AF-S mode and focusing prior to shooting, and then shoot a sequence with AF-F mode to see if you prefer to have the camera autofocus continuously while you shoot.

Abandon AF

Once you are comfortable with the autofocus methods, go ahead and turn it off and go manual. The hardest part is getting used to which way the focus ring needs to turn for closer and farther focus points. Try this: put a piece of tape on the lens barrel and write N and F (for near and far) on it so you know which way to go. Now try to capture a moving subject while adjusting focus.

Go shallow

Remember that one of the big deals in using your D600 for video is the shallow depth of field you can achieve. If you don't have a lens with a particularly large aperture, try using it wide open and getting close to your subject. The closer you are, the narrower the depth of field will look.

Change the look of your video

The picture controls are a great creative tool for making movies. Check out all the options to see if you can add some pizzazz to your video. Want to preview a picture control's effect? Activate Live View, press the Picture Control/Lock button, and then use the Multi-selector to preview the different picture controls.

Share your results with the book's Flickr group!

www.flickr.com/groups/d600fromsnapshotstogreatshots

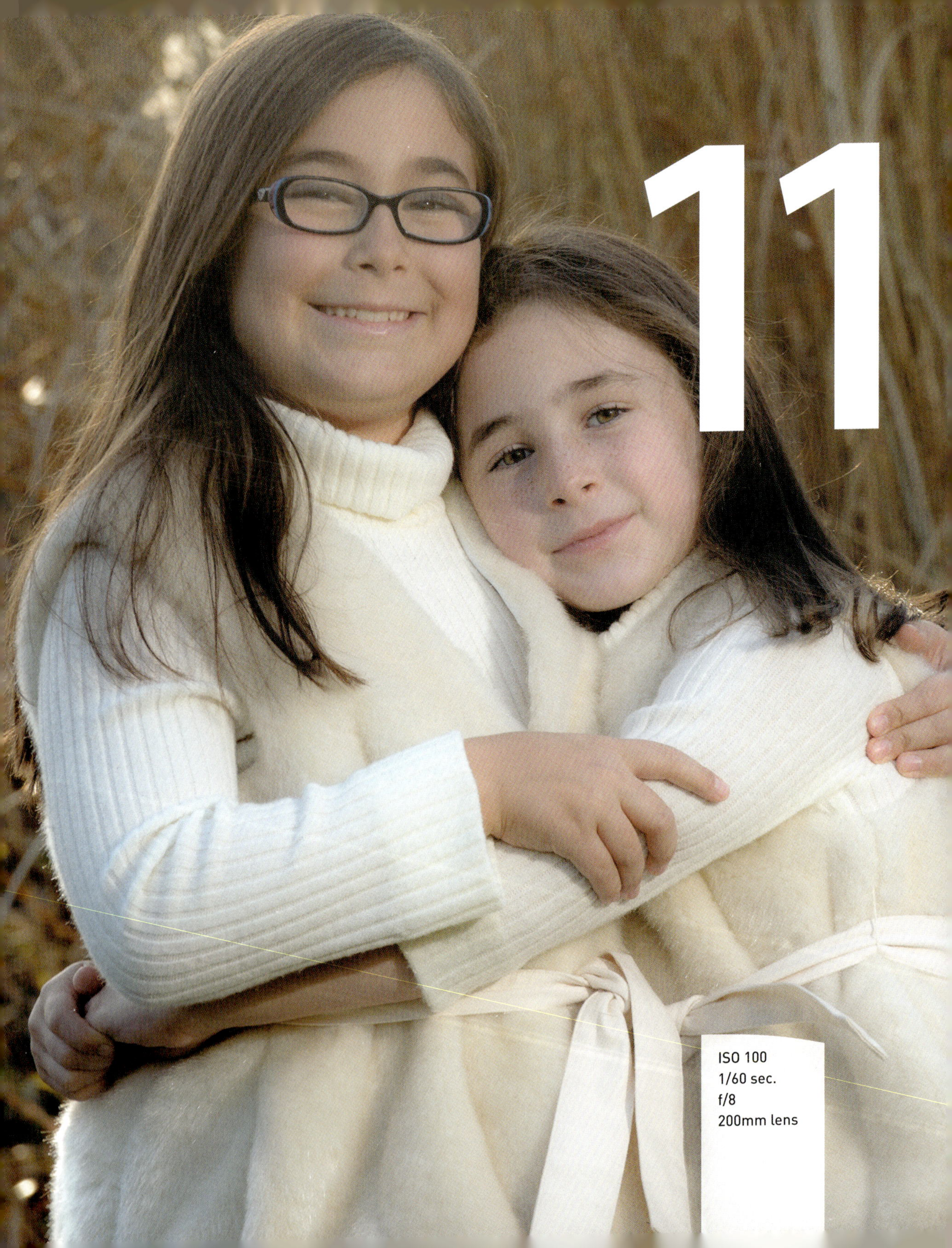
11
ISO 100
1/60 sec.
f/8
200mm lens

Accessorize

UPGRADES AND ACCESSORIES TO EXPAND YOUR CAMERA'S CREATIVE POTENTIAL

If you bought your camera with a lens, then you have everything you need to begin shooting with your D600. I took great care to ensure that almost all of the techniques covered in the book are not beyond your basic camera setup. That being said, there are some accessories that are essential for certain types of photography. Other accessories aren't necessarily essential, but they will improve the look of your images.

Let's take a look at some items that I believe are must-have accessories for your photography.

FILTERS

You should have several filters in your camera bag. Each one serves a unique purpose. Some say that digital-imaging programs such as Adobe Photoshop can duplicate the effects that the filters offer. This may be true, but I would rather screw on a filter than spend countless hours trying to replicate an effect on my computer. Here's another benefit to using a filter: lens protection.

SKYLIGHT

Probably the cheapest yet best investment you can make for your camera is buying a skylight filter. This filter is used more for its protective effects than for any visual boost. At one point in time, the skylight, UV, and haze filters were used to filter out UV light in order to add sharpness to distant subjects, correct a minute bluish color cast, and reduce the effects of haze in a film image. A digital camera offers the benefit of having filters that are built into the camera in front of the image sensor to eliminate the effects of haze and infrared light. Therefore, most of the visual benefits of using a skylight filter are not evident. So why, if there is no real visual difference, should you use a skylight filter? Because what they do offer is protection for your valuable lens for a relatively low price.

A 28–300mm Nikon VR lens will cost you about $970. A 77mm HOYA Skylight 1B filter costs around $35. As someone who often either forgets or loses lens caps, it's reassuring to me that a $35 filter protects the precious glass on the front of my lens without degrading the quality of my image. If it does get scratched, I just unscrew it and buy another. That beats the heck out of $970 or thereabouts to replace or repair a scratched front lens element.

POLARIZING

This one ranks right up there at the top of the list of must-own photography accessories. You won't find a self-respecting landscape photographer who doesn't have at least one polarizer in his or her camera bag (**Figure 11.1**).

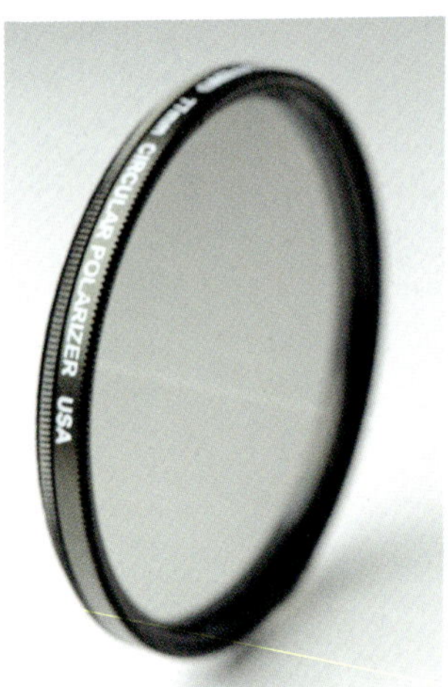

FIGURE 11.1
A Tiffen circular polarizing filter.

Light travels in straight lines, but the problem is that all those lines are moving in different directions. When they enter the camera lens, they are scattering about, creating color casts and other effects. The polarizer controls how light waves are allowed to enter the camera, letting only certain ones pass through. So what does that mean for you? With a polarizing filter, blue skies will appear darker, vegetation color will be more accurate, colors will look more saturated, haze will be reduced, and images can look sharper (**Figures 11.2** and **11.3**). Not bad for a little piece of glass.

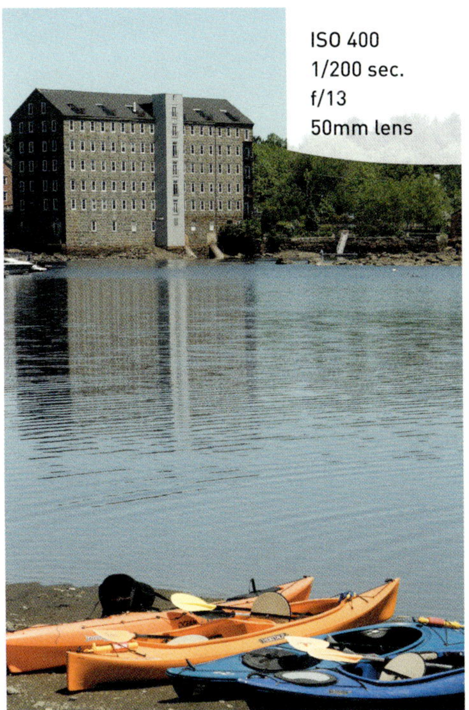

FIGURE 11.2
(left) Without using the polarizing filter, the scene looks a little low on contrast and has a blue color cast from the sky.

FIGURE 11.3
(right) After adding a polarizer, the colors are much more accurate and the color cast is now gone.

Most polarizers are circular and allow you to rotate the polarizing element to control the amount of polarization that you need. As the filter is rotated, different light waves will be allowed to pass through, such as a reflection on a body of water (**Figure 11.4**). Turn the filter a little and the light waves from the reflection are blocked, making the reflection disappear (**Figure 11.5**). Another benefit of the filter is that it is fairly dark, so when used in bright lighting conditions, it can act as a neutral density filter (you'll learn more in the next section), allowing you to use larger apertures or slower shutter speeds. The average polarizing filter requires an increase in exposure of about one and a half stops. This won't be an issue for you since you will be using the camera meter, which is already looking through the filter to calculate exposure settings. You should consider it, though, if your intention is to shoot with a fast shutter speed or use a small aperture for increased depth of field.

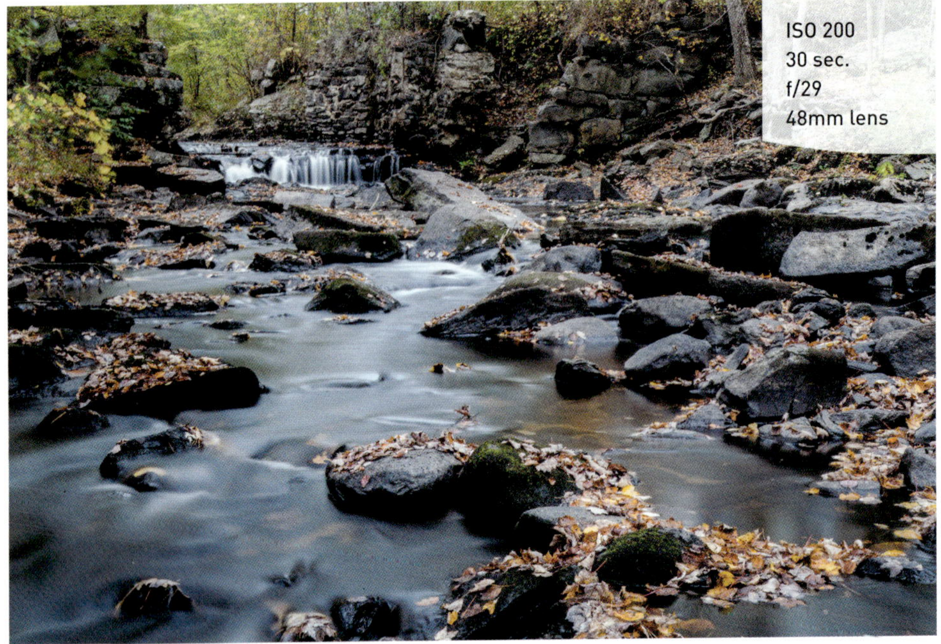

FIGURE 11.4
Before adding a polarizer, the light is reflected off the water.

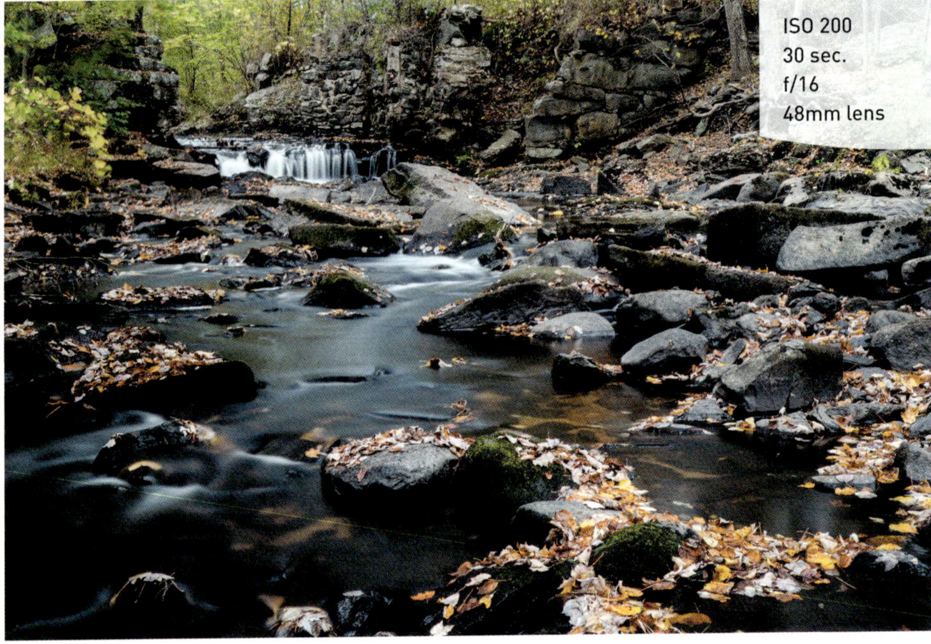

FIGURE 11.5
After adding a polarizer, you can see through the surface of the water.

NEUTRAL DENSITY (ND)

Sometimes there is just too much light falling on your scene to use the camera settings that you want. Most often this is the case when you want to use a slow shutter speed but your lens is already stopped down to its smallest aperture, leaving you with a shutter speed that's faster than you want.

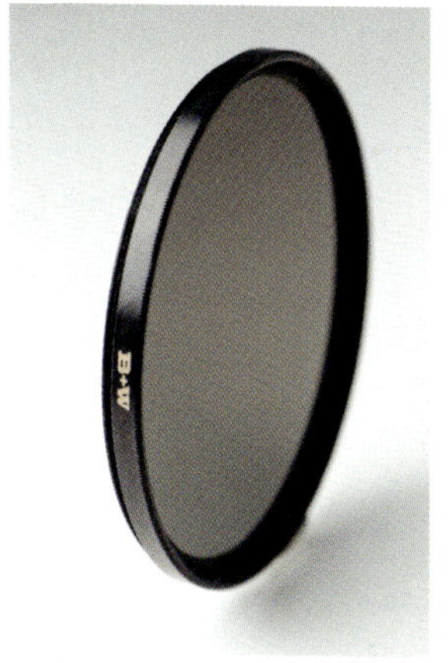

FIGURE 11.6
A B+W 77mm 0.9 ND filter.

A classic example of this is shooting a waterfall in bright sunlight. To get the silky look to the water, the shutter speed needs to be about 1/15 of a second or slower. The problem is that a proper exposure for bright sunlight is f/16 at 1/100 of a second with the camera set to ISO 100 (this comes from the Sunny 16 rule). If my lens has a minimum aperture of f/22, the slowest shutter speed I will be able to use is 1/50.

The way around this problem is to use a neutral density (ND) filter to make the outside world appear to be a little darker. Think of it as sunglasses for your camera. ND filters come in different strengths, which are labeled as .3, .6, and .9. They represent a one-stop difference in exposure per each .3 increment. If you need to turn daylight into dark, the .9 ND filter will give you an extra three stops of exposure (**Figure 11.6**). This means that, in my earlier example, I could get an exposure of f/16 at about 1/10 of a second. This would be an ideal exposure for getting silky smooth water in motion (**Figure 11.7**).

To see more B+W filters, check out www.schneideroptics.com.

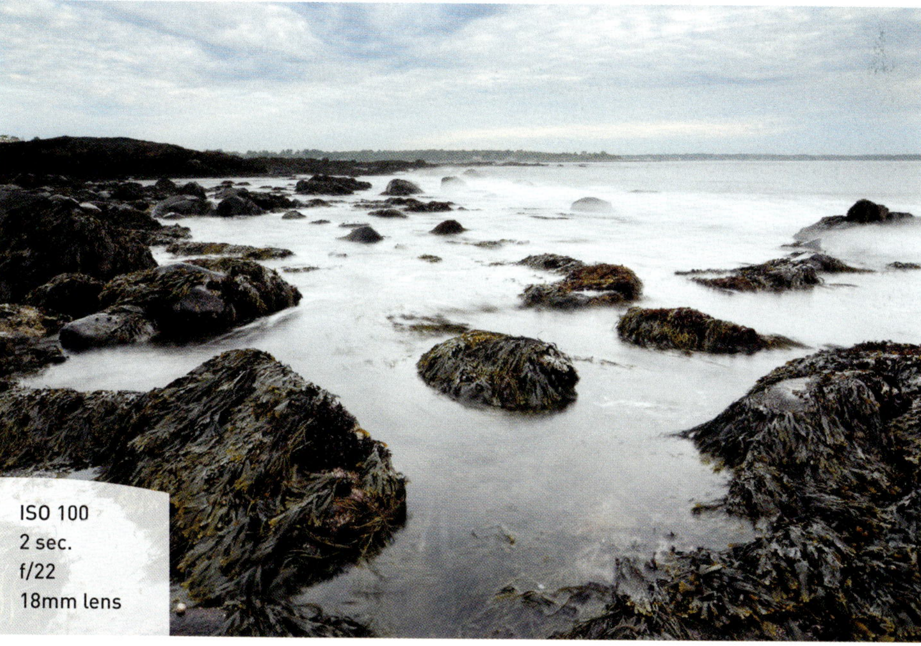

FIGURE 11.7
Using a .9 ND filter allowed me to use a long shutter speed in daylight to transform the waves into mist.

GRADUATED ND

Another favorite of the landscape photographer, the graduated ND has the benefit of the standard ND filter but graduates to a clear portion (**Figure 11.8**). This allows you to darken just the upper or lower portion of your scene while leaving the other part unaffected. This filter is most commonly used to darken skies that are too bright without affecting the ground area. If a regular ND is used, the entire area will get darker, so there is no visual change in the image as far as the brightness ratio between the sky and the ground is concerned.

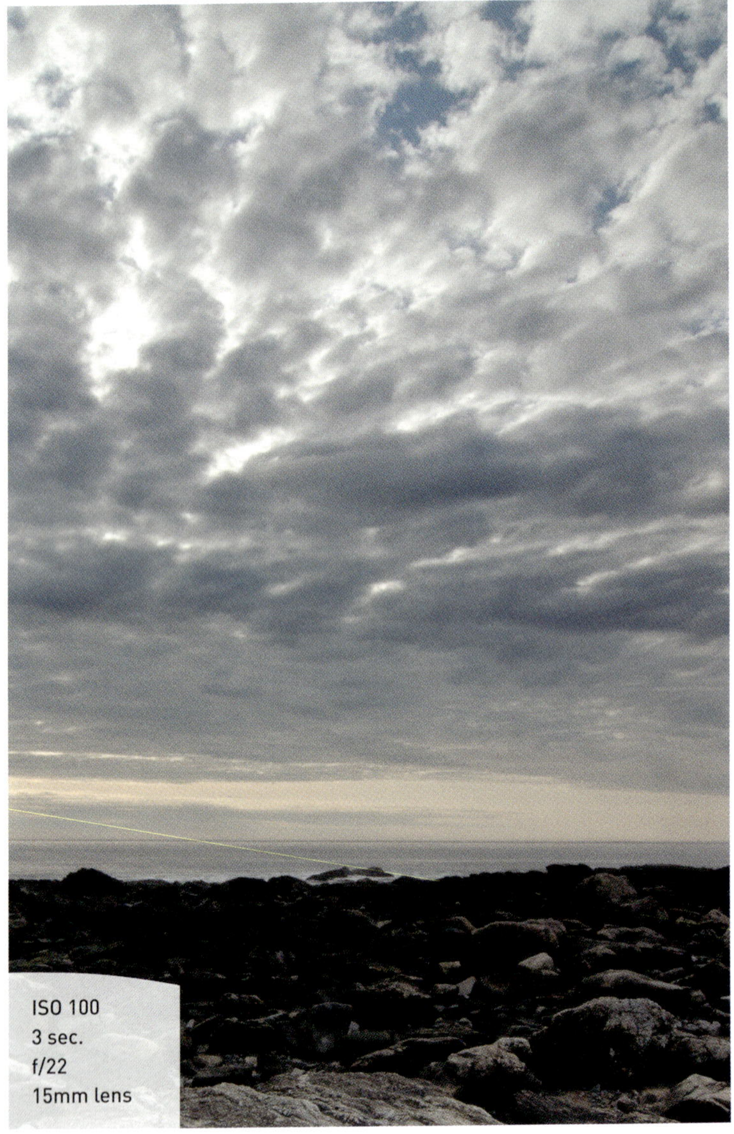

FIGURE 11.8
Graduated filters come in different strengths and transitions, from soft to hard, and allow you to expose for the darker areas (ground) without blowing out the brighter regions (sky).

You can purchase the graduated ND as a screw-on filter, but most photographers prefer to use the larger 4x6" version, which allows them to control exactly where the filter transitions from dark to transparent. There are many different options for graduated ND filters, such as the density factor (number of stops), as well as how gradual the transition is from dark to clear.

TRIPODS

If you buy only one accessory for your photography, do yourself a favor and make it a tripod. In general, any tripod is going to be better than no tripod at all. A tripod makes your photos sharper and lets you shoot in any lighting condition. There are more choices in tripods than there are in DSLRs. So how do you go about choosing the right one for you? The main considerations are weight, height, and head.

The weight of your tripod will probably determine whether or not you will actually carry it along with you farther than the parking lot. Many different types of materials are used in tripods today. The lightest is carbon fiber, which is probably the most expensive as well. More than likely, you should consider an aluminum tripod that is sturdy and that has a weight rating that is suitable for your camera as well as your lenses.

Make sure that the tripod extends to a height that is tall enough to allow you to shoot from a comfortable standing position. Nothing ruins a good shoot like a sore back. Taller tripods need to be sturdier to maintain a rigid base for your camera. You will also want to consider how low the tripod can go. If you want to do macro work of low-level subjects such as flowers, you will need to lower the tripod fairly close to the ground. Many new tripods have leg supports that allow you to spread the legs very wide and get the camera low to the ground.

The other determining factor when purchasing a tripod will be the type of head that it employs to secure the camera to the legs. There are two basic types of tripod heads: ball and pan. Ball heads use a simple ball joint that allows you to freely position the camera in any upright position and then clamp it down securely. This type of head is flexible and quick to use, but it can sometimes be difficult to switch between portrait and landscape orientations. They also tend to be slightly more expensive.

Pan heads employ a swivel and usually two hinged joints that allow the camera to pan left and right, move up and down, and adjust the position along the horizontal axis. Handles are typically employed to allow movement of the camera and lock down the position. The pan head is by and large the most popular tripod head style on the market. If you plan on shooting a lot of video with your D600, you might want to consider the pan-head style since it will deliver more functionality for your videography, specifically in panning from side to side.

If you really want to make your tripod shooting move faster, consider buying a tripod that utilizes a quick-release head. There are many styles of quick-release brackets; most use a small plate that screws into the bottom of the camera and then quickly locks into and releases from the tripod head.

The other thing to consider when purchasing a tripod is the leg locking system. Whether it is a lever-lock, locking rings, or some other system, make sure that you test it thoroughly to see how easy it is to lock and unlock the leg positions. Also check to see how smoothly the legs retract and extend. Avoid legs that stick, because they will probably only get stickier over time.

There are many different brands of tripod to choose from, but I suggest sticking to Gitzo (www.gitzo.com), Giotto's (www.giottos.com), Manfrotto (www.manfrotto.com), and Really Right Stuff (www.reallyrightstuff.com) for rock-solid tripods and tripod accessories.

WIRELESS OR CABLE RELEASES

When shooting long exposures, you can use the self-timer to activate the camera or you can get yourself a wireless or cable release. The wireless ML-L3 (**Figure 11.9**) uses an infrared beam (just like your TV remote) to fire the shutter from a distance of up to around 16 feet. The MC-DC2 remote release cord (**Figure 11.10**), which is an electronic release, attaches to the camera via the remote port and lets you trip the shutter.

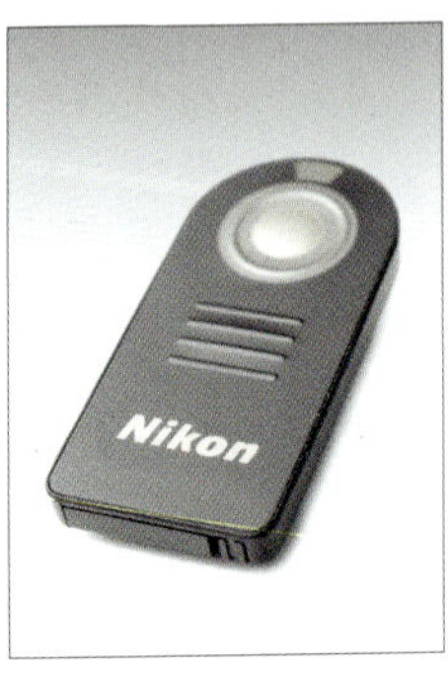

FIGURE 11.09
The Nikon ML-L3 wireless remote lets you activate the shutter without touching the camera.

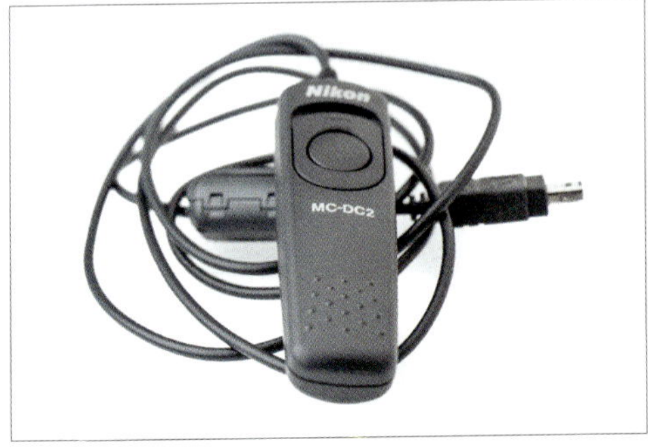

FIGURE 11.10
The Nikon MC-DC2 remote release cord is handy for really long exposures.

A remote release is the tool of choice when shooting with the camera set to Bulb (see Chapter 9). The idea of the release is that it allows shutter activation without having to place your hands on the camera. This is the best way to ensure that your images will not be influenced by self-induced camera shake. The ML-L3 sells for around $20, and the MC-DC2 sells for around $35, and both will work not only with the D600 but with several other Nikon DSLR models. A remote release also comes in handy for shooting macro work, where the tiniest vibration can affect the sharpness of your image.

A brand-new option for select smartphone and tablet users is the WU-1b wireless mobile adapter (check with Nikon for compatibility with your mobile device). The WU-1b plugs into the port on the side of the D600 (**Figure 11.11**) and allows you to wirelessly trigger the D600 from your smartphone (**Figure 11.12**), as well as to wirelessly transfer photos from the camera to your supported device (and then to the world via various social networking sites). The WU-1b could hide under a quarter, so when it's not in use be sure to keep it in the provided case, which attaches to your camera strap.

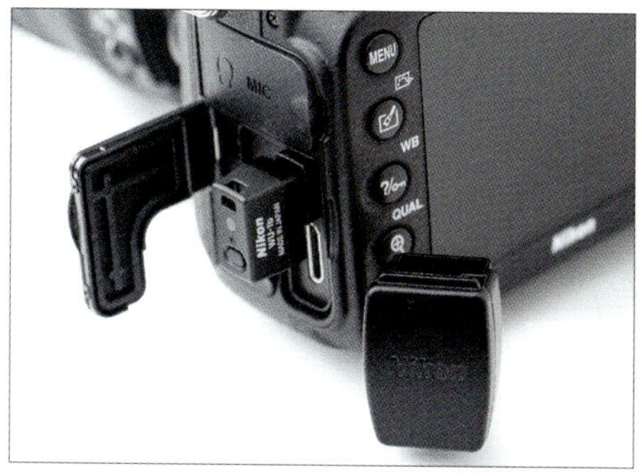

FIGURE 11.11
The Nikon WU-1b wireless mobile adapter plugged into my D600.

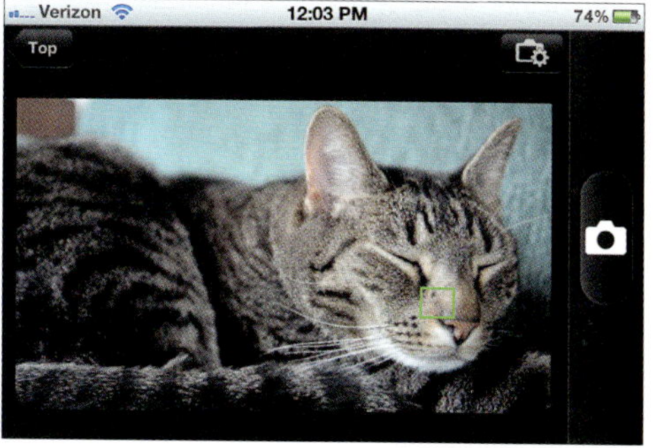

FIGURE 11.12
The Live View interface via the WMAU app on my iPhone 4S.

In the short time I've used the WU-1b, I've found it to be a fun accessory for accessing the Live View function without having to stand next to the camera, but I really don't like the way the adapter protrudes from the camera. The Wi-Fi signal created by the device is not very strong, so you can't go too far without losing the connection. For 99 percent of the times I'd need a remote release, my preference is the ML-L3 wireless remote, but it is nice to have options.

MACRO PHOTOGRAPHY ACCESSORIES

EXTENSION TUBES

Extension tubes are like spacers between your lens and your camera. The tubes are typically hollow, and their sole purpose is to move the rear of the lens farther away from the camera body.

A lens can only get so close to a subject and still be able to achieve a sharp focus. This is because as the subject gets closer, the focal point for the lens moves back to a point where it is behind the image sensor. Using an extension tube lets you move that focal point forward by placing the rear of the lens a little farther away from the camera sensor, thus letting you get the lens closer to the subject and enlarging it in your picture.

The tubes come in varying sizes, which are typically measured in millimeters. The more common sizes are 12mm, 20mm, and 36mm. The longer the tube, the greater the magnification factor (up to 1:1). The tubes are best used with lenses that are 35mm in focal length and longer. A wide-angle lens will have such a short focusing distance that you will be right on top of your subject. Nikon manufactures several extension tubes, or you can buy them from third-party manufacturers. Prices vary, but you will pay more for tubes that utilize optics in their design. You can also purchase sets of tubes with varying lengths that can be used individually or stacked together for greater magnification.

CLOSE-UP FILTERS

Another great way to jump into macro work is by purchasing a close-up filter (**Figures 11.13** and **11.14**). Close-up filters also come in varying magnifications but tend to be a little more expensive than extension tubes. This is because they are usually made of high-quality glass that works in concert with the lens. The filters and lenses can have some advantages over tubes, too. Because they screw onto the front of your lens, they don't interfere with any of the communication functions between the lens and camera body. They also result in less loss of light, so exposures can be slightly shorter than when you're using extension tubes. They do, however, work similarly to tubes in that they allow you to shorten

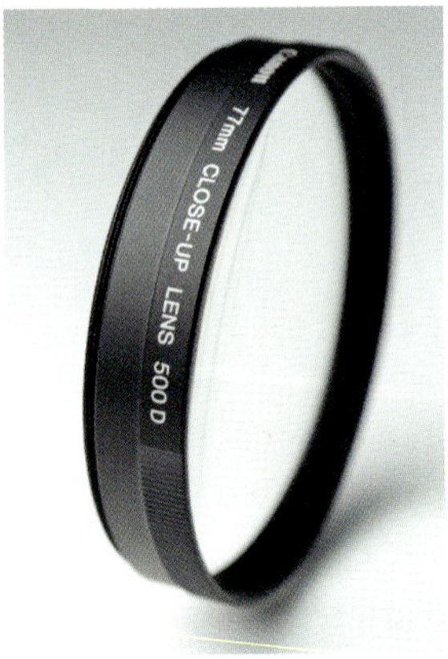

FIGURE 11.13
The Canon 500 D close-up filter. Yes, it's made by Canon, but since it is a screw-on filter it works with any camera model.

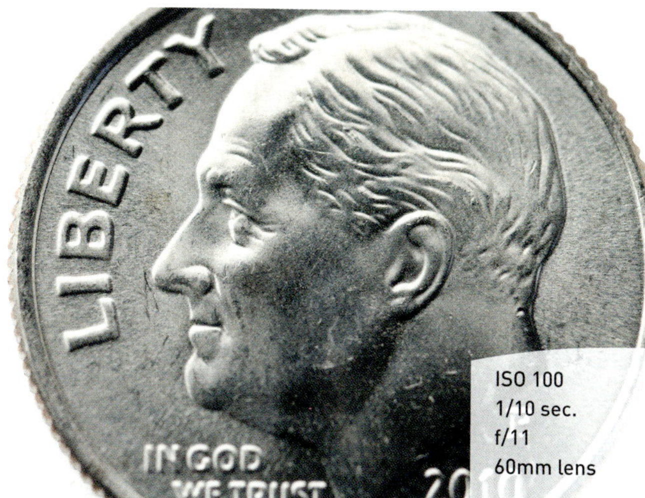

FIGURE 11.14
The Canon 500 D close-up filter on the Nikon 60mm 2.8 lens was used to help capture this dime.

the minimum focus distance of your lens so that you can move closer to your subject, thereby increasing the size of the subject on your sensor. Close-up lenses usually come in magnification factors like +1, +2, +3, +4, and +5. They can also be stacked, strongest to weakest, to increase the magnification factor.

The other difference is that they are usually screw-threaded onto your lens, which means that you have to purchase a specific thread diameter. So if your favorite lens has a 68mm filter thread, that is the size you would use for the close-up filter. The big downside is that if you want to use different lenses that have different thread sizes, you will have to buy multiple filters. This is why I prefer to work with a zoom lens—I can have a range of focal lengths to use with just one filter. Also, just as with most glass filters, the larger the diameter, the higher the price.

HOT-SHOE FLASHES

Earlier in the book I covered the built-in flash and what you can accomplish with it. Now that we have covered that, let me say that you really, really need to get yourself a hot-shoe mounted Speedlight flash if you want to take better flash images (**Figure 11.15**). For one thing, the external flash is going to be much more powerful than the pop-up version. Also, there is much more flexibility built into the Speedlight system of flashes than you could ever hope to get from the built-in version.

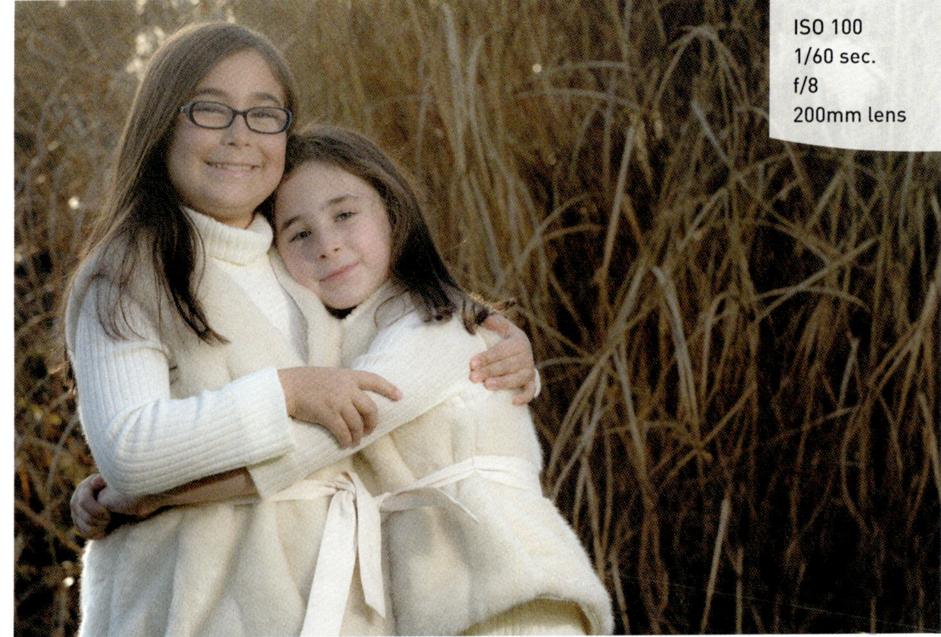

FIGURE 11.15 By moving my main flash off to the side of the subjects and firing through a diffusion panel, I was able to create a beautifully lit portrait.

Nikon currently has several Speedlight flashes for sale, but my recommendation is that you purchase the SB-700 or, better still, the SB-910 Speedlight. They will run somewhere in the neighborhood of $325 for the SB-700 and $545 for the SB-910, which can be a pretty hard pill to swallow at first. The pill will go down much easier once you have used one of these powerful and flexible flashes. Not only will your on-camera flash photography be much better, but you also gain the option of moving to a wireless, off-camera flash system that will give you much more flexibility. The great thing about the D600 is that the built-in flash can be used as a commander unit to control one of these more powerful flashes. Not only can you trigger the off-camera Speedlight, but you can also adjust the flash output right from the camera position. By using the menu in your camera, you can adjust exposure as well as communicate with multiple flash units. The possibilities are endless, and your flash photography will definitely move to the next level. See page 237 in the manual to learn more about using the built-in flash in Commander mode.

EXPOSURE COMPENSATION FOR FLASH

A cool new feature worth noting is that the D600 has the ability to separate exposure compensation from the flash level. That means you can shoot in Aperture Priority mode and just use the Exposure Compensation button to underexpose the background without affecting the amount of flash hitting your subject. Here's how to set it up:

1. Press the Menu button and navigate to the Custom Setting Menu.
2. Use the Multi-selector to highlight e Bracketing/flash (**A**) and press OK.
3. Highlight e4 Exposure comp. for flash (**B**) and press OK.
4. Highlight Background only (**C**) and press OK.

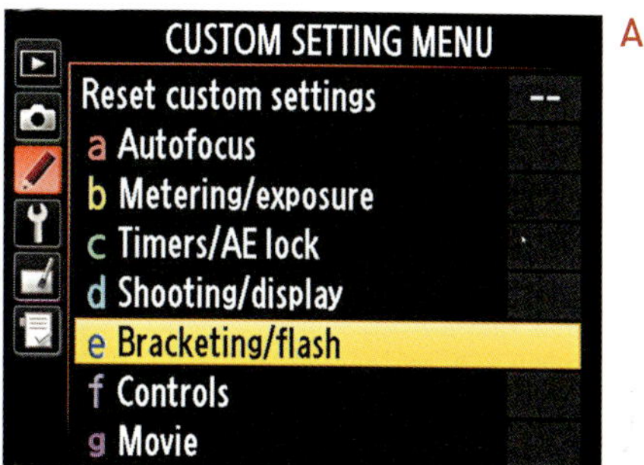

A

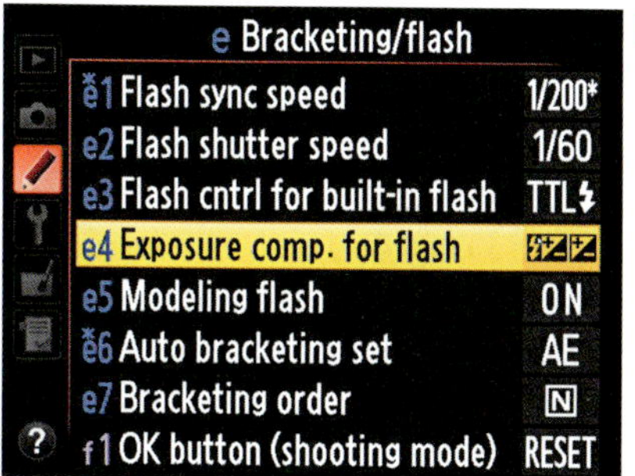

B

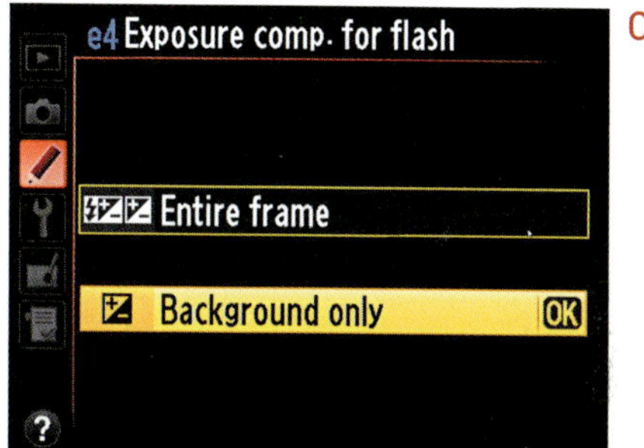

C

DIFFUSERS

While I am covering flashes, let's discuss a tool that lets you improve the light you are using in your portrait photography. A diffusion panel is a piece of semitransparent material, usually white, that you place between your light source and your subject. The fabric does as the name implies: it diffuses the light, spreading it out into a soft, low-contrast light source that makes any subject look better. You could make your own or buy one of the many commercially available versions. I prefer the 5-in-1 reflector kit made by Westcott. It not only has a very nice diffusion panel, but it also has reflective covers that slip over the diffusion panel so that you can bounce some fill light into your scene. Best of all, the entire system is collapsible, so it fits into a pretty small package for traveling. You'll find more information on Westcott diffusion panels at www.fjwestcott.com.

CAMERA BAGS

This topic is tricky because there is no one-size-fits all answer. How much gear you want to carry, how big you are, and your own style will all influence your bag purchasing decision.

I like to travel with my photo gear. Typically, my travel involves flying. This means that all of my camera equipment will be traveling in the cabin with me, not in the luggage compartment. I can't emphasize this enough: *Do not pack your camera in your checked luggage!* Thousands of cameras, lenses, and accessories are lost and stolen from checked luggage each year. The best way to ensure that it doesn't happen to you is to bring it on board and place it in the overhead storage. I like to bring my laptop as well, so I have found a couple of backpack camera storage systems that allow me to fit a camera body, several lenses, some accessories, my laptop, and even some snacks into one backpack-style bag that still fits under the seat in front of me or even in the overhead bin. I also prefer a backpack because I like the freedom of slinging the bag over my shoulder, leaving my hands free for other luggage. I am currently using a Think Tank Photo Airport Acceleration bag (www.thinktankphoto.com) for all of my travel needs.

The other bag that you should look into is a more traditional, shoulder-style bag. These bags are made to handle all sorts of camera bodies, lenses, and accessories, and they're usually completely configurable with moveable padded partitions so you can completely customize the bag for your own needs. My current bag of choice is the Boda Lens Bag (www.goboda.com). This small-looking bag easily holds a single camera body and two or three lenses, my iPad, extra batteries, multiple memory cards, and plenty more.

These two bags are the ones that I am using currently, but finding the perfect camera bag is truly the holy grail for photographers. The fact is that you can go through a lot of them searching for one that perfectly fits your every need and never find it. There are several bags presently taking up residence in my closet.

Another company that makes great bags is Lowepro. You can check out the full line of Lowepro camera gear at www.lowepro.com.

BITS AND PIECES

Since I just covered camera bags, let me share with you a couple of items that always travel in my bag.

The battle against dust is always a losing one, but that doesn't mean that you can't have your small victories. To help in the war against the dust speck, I carry three weapons of cleanliness.

LENS CLOTHS

A good microfiber lens cleaning cloth always comes in handy for getting rid of those little smudges and dust bunnies that seem to gravitate toward the front of my lens. I use one called a Spudz, which folds into its own pouch and has the added benefit of being gray. This means that I can use it as a gray card to get meter readings in Spot metering mode, or as a way to correct the white balance in my images when I bring them into my imaging software.

More information on Spudz cleaning cloths can be found at www.alpineproducts.com.

THE LENSPEN

For really stubborn smudges on my lens, I pull out my trusty LensPen (**Figure 11.16**). This nifty little device has a soft, retractable dust removal brush on one end and an amazing cleaning element on the other that uses carbon to clean and polish the lens element.

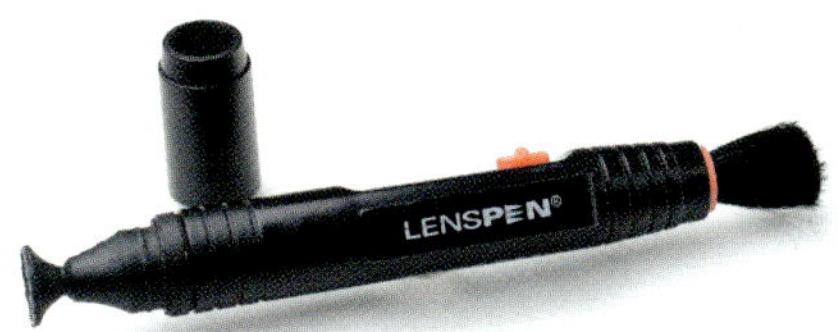

FIGURE 11.16
The LensPen lens cleaning tool.

More information on LensPen products can be found at www.lenspen.com.

AIR BLOWERS

Some folks prefer to use canned, compressed air to blow away dust, but the cans sometimes release fluid when they are tilted. For this reason, I always use my Rocket-Air blower from Giotto's (**Figure 11.17**). This funny-looking device is great for getting rid of tough dust, and it uses a clean air path so that the dust that you are blowing away doesn't get sucked into the ball and redeposited on your equipment the next time you use it.

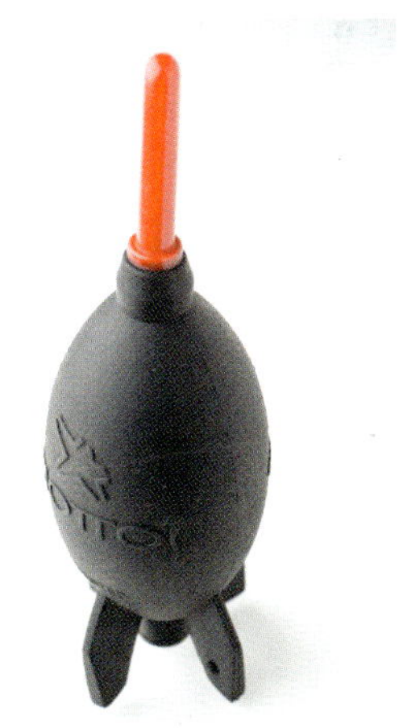

FIGURE 11.17
The Giotto's Rocket-Air dust blower.

BETTER LCD VISION

Having a large LCD screen is an amazing thing. The only problem is that it can be very hard to see in bright daylight conditions. I overcome this by using a Hoodman loupe. The loupe doesn't magnify your screen; it just provides a light-tight little tent for you to get a better look at your rear LCD. It has a handy lanyard so you can just let it hang around your neck and keep it within easy reach for checking out those great shots you just took. If you are going to work out in the bright sun, you will definitely want to keep one of these in your camera bag.

To check out all of the Hoodman accessories, head to www.hoodmanusa.com.

A WORD ABOUT LENSES

As you venture forward with your D600, the choices you make about which lenses to purchase will have a big impact on your photography (and your wallet). It is very likely that your lenses will outlive your camera body, so if you see yourself committed to photography for the long haul, I would encourage you to consider investing in professional-quality glass to get the most from your new full-frame camera (or FX, as Nikon refers to it). The good news about the D600 is that it is compatible with a wide range of lenses. Check out pages 285–291 of the manual for a list of compatible lenses.

Just because the D600 is a full-frame camera doesn't mean you should rule out your old crop-sensor (referred to by Nikon as DX) lenses right away. The lens you have is better than the one you don't have. If you have DX lenses, you can go under the Shooting Menu to Image area and set Auto DX crop to On (**Figure 11.18**) so that the D600 will automatically switch to using just the center of the sensor when a DX lens is attached (and recognized). This mimics the same 1.5 crop factor of DX camera bodies and reduces the effective pixel count to around 10.3 megapixels. See pages 89–90 in the manual to learn more about choosing the image area.

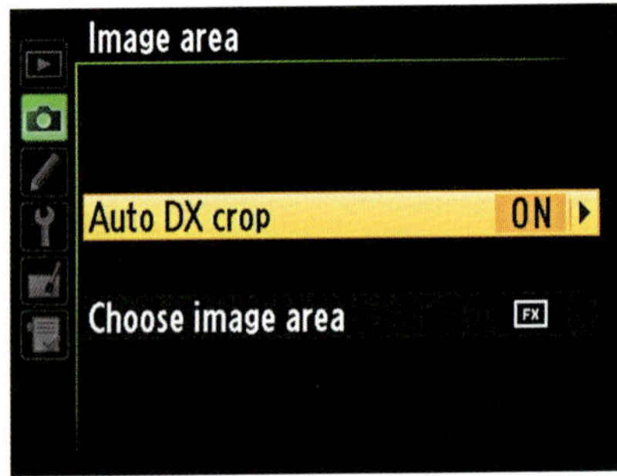

FIGURE 11.18
Setting Auto DX crop to On ensures that the D600 will use the center of the sensor when DX lenses are recognized.

A good way to try out a lens before you buy is to rent it for a weekend and put it through its paces. If you don't have a local camera store, photo studio, or friend to offer this service, there are a growing number of online rental agencies to check out. Two that I have used are www.borrowlenses.com and www.lensprotogo.com.

CONCLUSION

You can spend a lot of time worrying about having the right gadget, filter, or accessory to make your photography better. It can become an obsession to always have the latest thing out there. But you already have almost everything you need to take great pictures: an awesome camera and the knowledge necessary to use it. Everything else is just icing on the cake. So, while I have introduced a few items in this chapter that I do think will make your photographic life easier and even improve your images, don't get caught up in the technology and gadgetry.

Use your knowledge of basic photography to explore everything your camera has to offer. Explore the limits of your camera. Don't be afraid to take bad pictures. Don't be too quick to delete them from your memory card, either. Take some time to really look at them and see where things went wrong. Look at your camera settings and see if perhaps there was a change you could have made to make things better. Be your toughest critic and learn from your mistakes. With practice and reflection, you will soon find your photography getting better and better. Not only that, but your instincts will improve to the point that you will come upon a scene and know exactly how you want to shoot it before your camera even gets out of the bag.

Share your results with the book's Flickr group!

www.flickr.com/groups/d600fromsnapshotstogreatshots

INDEX

B

C

D

G

H

I

J

K

L

M

N

O

P

Q

R

S

T

U

V

W

Z

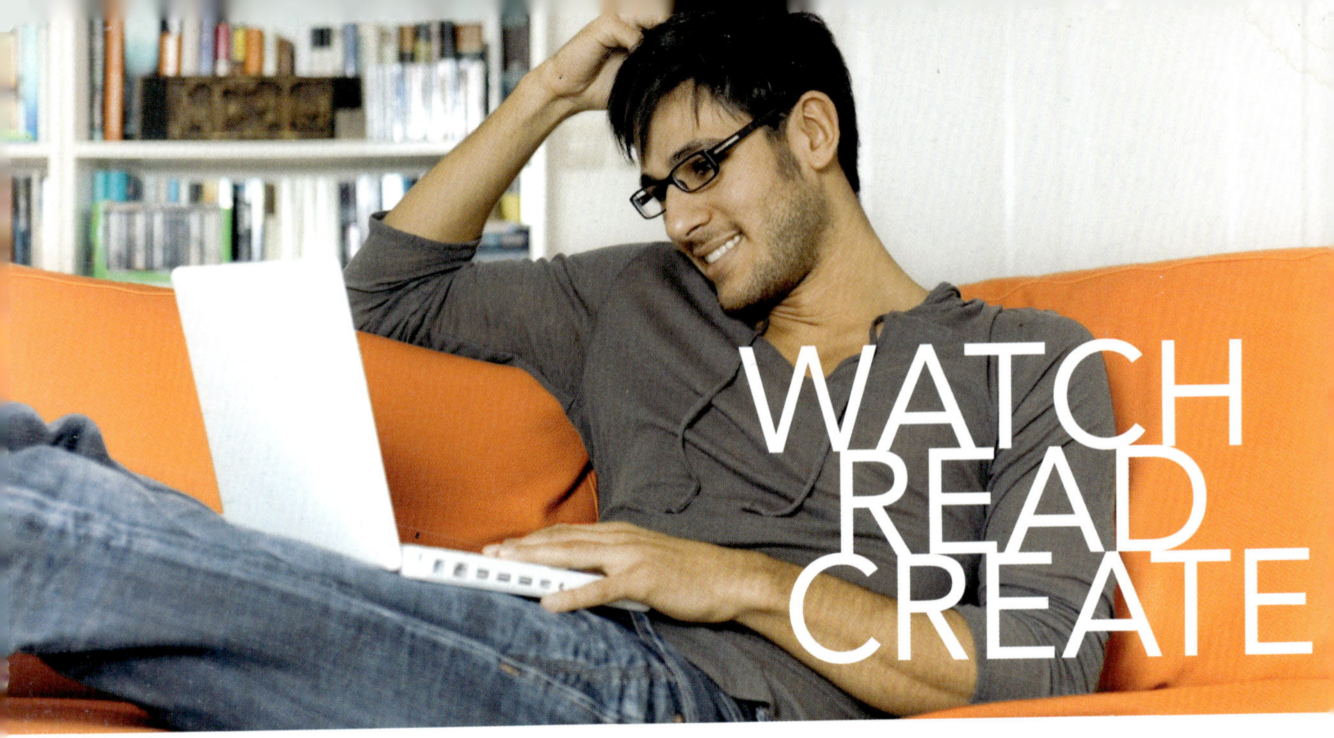